ADMINISTRATIVE LAW:
LEGAL CHALLENGES TO OFFICIAL ACTION

AUSTRALIA
LBC Information Services Ltd
Sydney

CANADA and USA
Carswell
Toronto

NEW ZEALAND
Brooker's
Auckland

SINGAPORE and MALAYSIA
Sweet & Maxwell Asia
Singapore and Kuala Lumpur

ADMINISTRATIVE LAW:
LEGAL CHALLENGES TO OFFICIAL ACTION

Sweet & Maxwell's Textbook Series

CARL EMERY M.A., LL.B. (Cantab.)
Hon. Fellow, Durham University Law Department
formerly Fellow of Emmanuel College, Cambridge

LONDON
SWEET & MAXWELL
1999

Published in 1999 by
Sweet & Maxwell Limited of
100 Avenue Road, London NW3 3PF
(http://www.smlawpub.co.uk)
Typeset by Dataword Services Limited, Chilcompton
Printed in Great Britain by
Bookcraft (Bath) Ltd

No natural forests were destroyed to make this product;
only farmed timber was used and replanted.

A CIP catalogue
record for this book
is available from
the British Library

ISBN 0 421 620005 X

To my teachers, colleagues and friends in the law.

PREFACE

The rules and principles of English law governing legal challenge to official action are complex and subject to frequent and rapid change. This students' textbook attempts to structure the subject accessibly, without either trivialising or understating its complexity. It provides a wide range of further reading references tied to specific points dealt with in the text. And, as explained below, it offers some assistance in keeping readers up-to-date, via the Internet, with legal developments following the date of the book's publication.

It may help readers to note the following features of the book:

- **Footnotes** With very few exceptions, footnotes are used only for references, or to suggest further reading.

- **Bibliographical references** In footnotes, **books** are cited by reference to author name(s) + abbreviated title: *e.g.* "de Smith. *JRAA*". In the Bibliography this short reference is followed by the full title: S.A. de Smith, *Judicial Review of Administrative Action* (1995, 5th ed., Woolf & Jowell). **Articles** are cited in footnotes by reference to author name(s) + date: *e.g.* "Arrowsmith (1990)". Again, in the Bibliography the short reference is followed by a full citation: Sue Arrowsmith, "Judicial Review and the Contractual Powers of Public Authorities" (1990) 106 L.Q.R. 275.

- **Case references** All England Law Reports are cited where possible, as being the reports to which students are likely most often to have access.

- **Unreported cases** may sometimes be found on an Internet web site, *e.g.* new House of Lords decisions are posted within hours on the Stationery Office web site (http://www.parliament.the-stationery-office.co.uk); a useful free service providing some Court of Appeal and High Court judgments is Smith Bernal's "Casebase" (http://www.smithbernal.com/casebase).

- **Boxed Text** is used on occasions in the book to isolate material which is outside, but related to, the main flow of discussion.

- **Flow charts and diagrams** are used to summarise complex areas dealt with in the text.

- **Electronic updating of text via Sweet & Maxwell's web site** (http://www.smlawpub.co.uk). Developments in the law subsequent to the publication of this book will appear on the Sweet & Maxwell web site as amendments and additions to the published text. The first web site up-date will appear simultaneously with the book's publication. The site will be updated regularly thereafter.

- **European Law** English administrative law contains rules and principles of both European Community law and Human Rights law. In this book, the European legal dimension is dealt with as a part of the topics on which it specially impacts. For reference, the European law sections of the book are listed below.

The European Communities Act 1972 — general account	Chapter 1, *section A 2*
The Human Rights Act 1998 — general account	Chapter 1, *section A 3*

The book deals with materials to hand as of July 1, 1999 but some further references have been added at proof stage.

I have endeavoured to thank personally each of the many people without whose help and encouragement this book would not have seen the light of day.

Carl Emery
July 6, 1999

TABLE OF CONTENTS

Table of Cases

Table of Statutes

Table of Statutory Instruments

Table of Rules of the Supreme Court

Table of European Treaties

Table of European Directives

Chapter 1

Introduction: Challenging Official Action

The prime focus of this book is upon the nature, operation and interaction of the various avenues of challenge to official action provided by English law. "Official action" means action by a person or body of persons in an official, or public, capacity.[1] "Action" includes failing to act where legally obliged to act. Official action includes legislative, executive and judicial acts and decisions: "official" is used in this book to encapsulate this wide spectrum of action which extends beyond the strictly "administrative".

A Official Action Subject to Legal Challenge

1 Lack of constitutional guarantees in English law

A cardinal feature of the written constitutions of western democracies is that they contain fundamental principles or guarantees which constitute criteria of legality for all official action within the state in question. Commonplace examples are an individual's rights to life and liberty, to fair treatment under the law, to freedom of conscience, expression and assembly, and to privacy. If an official act or decision (whether legislative, executive or judicial) contravenes any such rights, an individual will normally be able to challenge its legality and, where appropriate, obtain redress.

The absence of a written constitution in the United Kingdom has not, of course, meant that such rights are without legal protection. Both common law and statute have provided substantial protections, albeit at varying levels of adequacy at different times and in changing social and political contexts. Acts of (and proceedings in) Parliament[2] apart, official actions of all types of public authority have been, since the seventeenth century, in principle subject to legal challenge under English law. "In principle" because, as will be seen, the nature and extent of legal challenge is different in different cases, and in certain circumstances has been restricted or removed completely by Act of Parliament. As for challenging the lawfulness of Acts of Parliament themselves, the English legal doctrine of the sovereignty of Parliament has been an important

---

[1] The elusive criteria by which action may be characterised as "official" or "public" are considered in Chap. 3.

[2] *i.e.* the U.K. Parliament at Westminster. The Scottish Parliament established by the Scotland Act 1998 falls outwith the scope of this book. For the National Assembly for Wales established by the Government of Wales Act 1998, see Chap. 3, *section B 1 a*; Chap. 4, *section F*; Chap. 6, *section G*.

barrier to the development of guaranteed principles of constitutional legality. For until recently, it has been the case that, under this doctrine, all Acts of Parliament (statutes) are entirely immune from challenge in United Kingdom legal proceedings. Parliamentary sovereignty has meant that "it is not for [a] court to say that a parliamentary enactment, the highest law in this country, is illegal".[3] Thus where Parliament has enacted a statute restricting or removing individual legal protections in particular contexts, such legislation has been immune from legal challenge in United Kingdom courts and tribunals. In these circumstances, since a government with a comfortable majority in the House of Commons has virtual control of Parliament, legal rights and protections have been vulnerable to the prevailing political philosophy of the leading members of the governing Party.

This picture has been profoundly altered by two events: the accession of the United Kingdom to membership of the European Community in 1972; and the incorporation into United Kingdom domestic law of the European Convention on Human Rights in 1998.

2 THE EUROPEAN COMMUNITIES ACT 1972

European Community law provides to individual citizens of Member States a wide range of economic and other rights, *e.g.* freedom to import and export goods, to offer services, and to take up employment within the Community area. According to the Community law doctrine of "direct effect" these are "individual rights which national courts must protect".[4] Moreover, the Community law doctrine of the supremacy of Community law over the national (*i.e.* domestic) law of Member States[5] entails that if any official action in the United Kingdom (whether legislative, executive or judicial) contravenes directly effective Community law, United Kingdom courts and tribunals must give effect in proceedings before them to the Community provision and "disapply" conflicting national rules, including those contained in Acts of Parliament. This doctrine was incorporated into United Kingdom domestic law by section 2 of the European Communities Act 1972.

Under section 2(1) of the 1972 Act[6] "all such rights [etc.] arising by or under the Treaties . . . as in accordance with the Treaties are without further enactment to be given legal effect [*i.e., all directly effective provisions of Community law*] . . . in the United Kingdom shall be recognised and available in law, and be enforced, allowed and followed accordingly . . .". And section 2(4) makes it quite clear that statutes, whether enacted before or after the 1972 Act, are to be subject to directly effective Community law: ". . . any [other] enactment passed or to be passed . . . shall be construed and have effect subject to the foregoing provisions of this section".

The operation of these provisions is well illustrated by the notorious *Factortame* litigation. The Merchant Shipping Act 1988 contained provisions designed by the United Kingdom government to stop the practice of "quota-hopping" by Spanish fishing-vessel owners who were registering their boats in the United Kingdom so that their catches would be counted against the United Kingdom's E.C. fish quota, the Spanish quota having been exhausted. The legality of these provisions was challenged in the English courts by the Spanish owners who sought judicial review, arguing that the 1988 Act infringed their E.C. individual rights to trade freely within the Community area.[7] In *Factortame Ltd v. Transport Secretary (No. 3)*[8] the European Court of Justice

---

[3] *Cheney v. Conn* [1968] 1 All E.R. 779 at 782, Ungoed-Thomas J.

[4] *Van Gend en Loos* [1963] E.C.R. 1 at 13, ECJ; *Costa v. ENEL* [1964] E.C.R. 585 at 596, ECJ. On the doctrine of direct effect, see generally Hartley, *Foundns*, Chap. 7.

[5] Hartley, *ibid.*, pp. 218–220.

[6] Rudden & Wyatt, *BCL*, p. 693. Rudden & Wyatt is a good sourcebook for the text of Community law provisions. On E.C. Law in the U.K., see generally, Collins, *E.C.–U.K.*

[7] *Factortame Ltd v. Transport Secretary* [1989] 2 All E.R. 692 and subsequent cases (below).

[8] [1991] 3 All E.R. 769.

(ECJ), to whom the case had been referred[9] by the English court, ruled in favour of the Spanish owners and held that the impugned provisions of the 1988 Act should be disapplied.

The disapplication of these statutory provisions illustrates the operation of section 2(4) of the European Communities Act 1972 in making the 1988 Act[10] "subject to" the provision in section 2(1) of the 1972 Act that directly effective E.C. individual rights can be enforced in United Kingdom courts. At an earlier stage in the *Factortame* litigation[11] the Spanish owners had obtained a suspension of the operation of the impugned 1988 provisions pending the final resolution of the matter. In the course of the House of Lords' reference[12] of this aspect of the case to the ECJ Lord Bridge explained[13] that section 2(4) of the European Communities Act 1972 in effect requires United Kingdom courts and tribunals to proceed on the basis that **all previous and subsequent statutes are to be read as incorporating a statement that their provisions are to operate without prejudice to directly effective E.C. individual rights.** While this analysis appears to accommodate the English legal doctrine of the sovereignty of Parliament, it seems unlikely to satisfy the Community law doctrine of the supremacy of Community law. For it implies that if a post-1972 statute were to state expressly that its provisions were intended to override E.C. individual rights, a United Kingdom court or tribunal would be bound to apply this. The conundrum[14] is largely academic, since it would pale into insignificance by comparison with the political crisis which such legislation would precipitate regarding the future of the United Kingdom's membership of the E.C.

3 THE HUMAN RIGHTS ACT 1998

As has just been seen, the effect of section 2 of the European Communities Act 1972 is that the validity of a United Kingdom statute (as well as of any other official action) can be challenged in a United Kingdom court or tribunal on the basis that it transgresses E.C. individual rights. The legal protection given by the Human Rights Act 1998 to the rights and fundamental freedoms contained in the European Convention on Human Rights is less radical but still of great practical significance.

The Convention was ratified by the United Kingdom in 1951, binding the United Kingdom in international law. But only after its incorporation by statute into domestic law in 1998 can its provisions be invoked directly in United Kingdom courts and tribunals. The Act is to come into effect on October 2, 2000. Before examining the provisions of the 1998 Act it will be convenient to look briefly at the Convention itself.

(a) The Convention rights and their limitations

Article 1 of the Convention obliges the states who are parties to the Convention to "secure to everyone within their jurisdiction the rights and freedoms defined in [the Convention]." The rights and freedoms are essentially as follows: that one's right to life be protected by law[15]; the right not to be subjected to torture or inhuman or degrading treatment or punishment[16]; or to slavery or forced labour[17]; the right to liberty and security of the person subject to lawful arrest or

---

[9] On such references, see *section B 3 a*, below.
[10] As (in 1972) an "enactment . . . [yet] to be passed".
[11] *Factortame Ltd v. Transport Secretary (No. 2)* [1991] 1 All E.R. 70: see Chap. 5, *section B 2 b*.
[12] *Factortame Ltd v. Transport Secretary* [1989] 2 All E.R. 692.
[13] *ibid.*, pp. 700–701.
[14] See further Chap. 7 *Restrictions on Legal Challenge, section A 8*.
[15] Art. 2.
[16] Art. 3; see also 6th Protocol to the Convention, Arts 1 & 2: abolition of death penalty.
[17] Art. 4.

imprisonment[18]; the right to a fair trial[19]; the right not to be subjected to retrospective criminal legislation[20]; the right to respect for private and family life, home and correspondence[21]; the right to freedom of thought, conscience and religion[22]; the right to freedom of expression[23]; the right to freedom of peaceful assembly and association[24]; the right to marry and found a family[25]; the right to peaceful enjoyment of property[26]; the right to education[27]; the requirement that there be free elections at reasonable intervals by secret ballot[28]; and the right to enjoy the above rights and freedoms without discrimination on any ground.[29]

The rights are qualified both by express provision in the Convention and by the case law developed by the Strasbourg authorities responsible for administering and enforcing the Convention:

(i) *Express provision*

The rights under Articles 8-11 (family life, freedom of conscience, free speech, freedom of association[30]) are all stated in paragraph 2 of the articles to be subject to such restrictions as may be imposed by law as being necessary in a democratic society in pursuit of certain specified public interests such as national security; public safety, health or morals; the protection of the rights and freedoms of others. There are other similar provisions.[31] And there is a broad power to derogate from (*i.e.* to act inconsistently with) Convention rights in time of war or other public emergency.[32] Also, of course, there is some scope for judgment as to the appropriate level of protection to be afforded by any given state legal system in the context of Convention rights, *e.g.* with regard to abortion legislation and the right to life; or with regard to what constitutes lawful arrest or imprisonment for the purposes of Article 5.

(ii) *Case Law*

The Strasbourg authorities have accepted that the primary judgment as to whether permitted restrictions are necessary in particular circumstances is for the relevant national authority. But in making that judgment the authority must be satisfied that the specific public interest (purpose or objective) which is relied upon as necessitating the restriction is proportionate to, and therefore sufficient in the circumstances to override, the individual's interest in maintaining his rights: *i.e.*, essentially, public benefit must be judged to outweigh individual or private detriment. If an individual mounts a legal challenge it is ultimately for the Strasbourg authorities to rule on the issue of "proportionality"[33] but "in assessing the proportionality of the state's acts, a certain degree of deference is given to the judgment of national authorities when they weigh competing public and individual interests in view of their special knowledge and overall responsibility under domestic law."[34] This is referred to as the doctrine of "a margin of appreciation".

---

[18] Art. 5.
[19] Art. 6.
[20] Art. 7.
[21] Art. 8.
[22] Art. 9.
[23] Art. 10.
[24] Art. 11; see also 4th Protocol, Art. 2: freedom of movement and choice of residence.
[25] Art. 12.
[26] 1st Protocol, Art. 1.
[27] *ibid.*, Art. 2.
[28] *ibid.*, Art. 3.
[29] Convention Art. 14.
[30] Likewise freedom of movement under 4th Protocol, above.
[31] *e.g.* Arts 16–18; 1st Protocol Art. 1, para. 2.
[32] Art. 15.
[33] Harris, O'Boyle and Warbrick, *ECHR*, p. 11.
[34] *ibid.*, p. 13.

(b) Legal protection of Convention rights under the 1998 Act

The duty imposed on national authorities by Article 1 of the Convention to secure protection to individuals is in effect a duty to ensure that the state's legal system affords such protection, in particular by imposing on state (*i.e.* "public") authorities an obligation to act in conformity with the requirements of the Convention in the discharge of their public (*i.e.* legislative, executive or judicial) functions. The 1998 Act substantially achieves this. The key provision is section 6(1): "It is unlawful for a public authority to act in a way which is incompatible with a Convention right." Under section 1 "Convention rights" mean the rights as described and qualified in *subsection a* above.[35] Section 2 incorporates the Strasbourg case law.

- Since "public authority" includes a court or tribunal,[36] it follows that in so far as the outcome of cases is determined by judge-made (common) law, that law is now required by section 6(1) to be compatible with Convention rights. The implications of this for English administrative law will be considered later.[37]

- "Public authority" also includes statutory administrative authorities and, by express provision, other persons exercising public functions.[38] All official actions of such authorities must now be compatible with Convention rights.

- However, "public authority" does not include Parliament,[39] so that incompatibility between an Act of Parliament (or other "primary" legislation[40]) and a Convention right "does not affect the [Act's] validity, continuing operation or enforcement."[41] Subordinate legislation is similarly unaffected to the extent that it is protected by primary legislation.[42] Moreover, section 6(1) does not apply where a public authority has unavoidably acted incompatibly with a Convention right in giving effect to primary legislation which is itself incompatible with Convention rights[43]; or to subordinate legislation made under such primary legislation.[44]

Although, therefore, Parliament has not sought to impose upon itself a legal prohibition from acting incompatibly with Convention rights, three provisions of the 1998 Act do address the issue of such incompatibility:

- Section 3(1) provides that "So far as it is possible to do so, primary legislation and subordinate legislation must be read and given effect in a way which is compatible with the Convention rights". It remains to be seen whether this provision goes beyond the rule already adopted by English courts that "in construing any provision in domestic legislation which is ambiguous in the sense that it is capable of a meaning which either conforms to or conflicts with the convention, the courts will presume that Parliament intended to legislate in conformity with the convention . . .".[45]

---

[35] And as subject to U.K. "designated derogations and reservations" dealt with in ss.14 and 15. Ss.12 and 13 deal further with the Convention rights to, respectively, freedom of expression; and freedom of thought, conscience and religion for religious organisations.

[36] s.6(3)(a).

[37] Chap. 4, *section D 2 c.*

[38] s.6(3)(b), (5).

[39] s.6(3).

[40] Defined in s.21(1).

[41] s.3(2)(b).

[42] s.3(2)(c).

[43] s.6(2).

[44] s.6(2)(b).

[45] Lord Bridge in *Brind v. Home Secretary* [1991] 1 All E.R. 720 at 722j.

- Where this is not possible, section 4 provides that in any proceedings[46] in which the High Court, Court of Appeal or House of Lords[47] "is satisfied that [any statutory] provision is incompatible with a Convention right, it may make a declaration of that incompatibility."[48] Such declaration "does not affect the [provision's] validity, continuing operation or enforcement . . .; and is not binding on the parties to the proceedings in which it is made."[49] The effect of a declaration would thus be felt immediately in the political rather than the legal arena; but the government would be likely to correct a declared incompatibility rather than wait for the matter to be confirmed by proceedings in the European Court of Human Rights (ECHR) in Strasbourg. Section 10 and Schedule 2 contain provisions under which a government minister may, "if he considers that there are compelling reasons",[50] amend offending legislation swiftly by order[51] rather than through the slower process of statutory amendment.

- Finally, section 19 requires a minister who is piloting a Bill through Parliament to state (before the Bill's second reading) either that it is or that it is not compatible with Convention rights. This provision too is designed to expose the government to political pressure to ensure that its legislative programme complies with the Convention.

4 ACTIONS OF ALL TYPES OF PUBLIC AUTHORITY NOW SUBJECT TO LEGAL CHALLENGE UNDER ENGLISH LAW?

As already stated, Acts of (and proceedings in) Parliament apart, official actions of all types of public authority have been, since the seventeenth century, in principle subject to legal challenge under English law. Now, under the provisions of the European Communities Act 1972 and the Human Rights Act 1998, in certain circumstances challenges may be mounted in English courts and tribunals to the lawfulness of Acts of Parliament. It may thus be said that the actions of all types of public authority are now subject to legal challenge under English law.

Before surveying in *section B* the range of available avenues of legal challenge, it may be useful to summarise the parameters of challenge to the lawfulness of statutes under the two Acts just mentioned.

- Under the 1972 Act, all statutory provisions must be treated as "subject to" directly effective Community law. *i.e.*, to the extent that any statutory provision (whether previous or subsequent to the 1972 Act) is incompatible with directly effective Community law it must be treated as unlawful, and "disapplied" in English legal proceedings.

- Under the 1998 Act, in proceedings at High Court level or above the court may declare that a statutory provision is incompatible with a Convention right if satisfied that that is the case.

- While a declaration of incompatibility under the 1998 Act has no binding effect, incompatibility between statute and directly effective Community law under the 1972 Act results in the statute being disapplied. In that sense, the vulnerability of statute to

---

[46] See *section B 3 b* below.
[47] s.4(5).
[48] s.4(2).
[49] s.4(6).
[50] s.10(2).
[51] See Schedule 2 to the Act.

legal challenge may be said to be greater under the 1972 than under the 1998 Act. On the other hand, the scope of the 1998 Act is potentially far broader: it applies to any statutory provision whatever, not simply statutory provisions in the area of Community law. Both statutes give legal effect in the United Kingdom to supra-national legal regimes which regard themselves as superior to the domestic regimes of the nation states who adopt them. The question of whether either Community law or Convention rights may thus be regarded as "entrenched" (*i.e.* enjoying legal protection, irremovable by statute, against contrary provision in any previous or subsequent statute) in English law will be considered in a later chapter.[52]

B Avenues of Legal Challenge

1 The basic question: which avenue to choose?

Everyone knows that many official decisions can be appealed to a tribunal or other body. Everyone has heard of damages awards against the government and other public authorities. Most people these days have heard media accounts of successful "judicial review" challenges to the legality of official acts and decisions. And "ombudsmen" too figure from time to time in media reports. But where someone has a complaint about a particular exercise of public power and feels that the time has come to consider some form of legal challenge, what is the best course to take? The following questions may be considered.

Is there a right of appeal to some tribunal in this particular case? If so, what redress may be obtained? What grounds must be shown and what procedural hurdles crossed to obtain that redress? Where a complainant seeks not only reversal of but also compensation for an adverse decision, can this be obtained from an appeal tribunal or must one sue for damages in a civil court? Where there is no right of appeal how can you hope to get a decision overturned? Should you complain to an ombudsman, and, if so, which? When might it be sensible to consider seeking judicial review — who can apply, how, on what grounds, subject to what procedural constraints and with the hope of what remedies? What is the position if you are faced with what you believe is an unlawful official order or directive? May you safely ignore it and rely on its illegality by way of "collateral" defence to any enforcement proceedings which may be brought against you; or must you obey it unless willing to initiate your own legal challenge?

The aim of this book is to develop the student's ability to answer these questions in particular cases. Frequent reference will be made to actual and hypothetical fact situations. Examples of the latter are used in *section C* of this introductory chapter to demonstrate the need to grasp the legal rules and principles governing the operation and interaction of each of the five chief avenues by which legal challenge to official action may be mounted. These are:

- statutory appeal;
- application for judicial review;
- ordinary civil claim;
- criminal or civil collateral defence;
- complaint to an ombudsman.

---

[52] Chap. 7, *Restrictions on Legal Challenge*, section A 8.

In addition to these chief avenues of challenge, statute does often provide, on an ad hoc basis, complaints procedures of various types. Examples of these will be encountered from time to time in later chapters[53] where their relationship with other avenues of challenge will be considered.

2 THE FIVE AVENUES

(a) Statutory Appeal

Parliament has provided rights of appeal against very many types of official decision. There is of course the long-established system of appeals within the ordinary court structure.[54] Beyond this, in areas such as town and country planning, income tax, social security, immigration, employment, many local authority licensing regimes — and in many other areas — the appropriate avenue of challenge will be by way of an appeal:

Chapter 2 Appeals — Tribunals, Inquiries and Courts; Error of Law. As will appear, if one is seeking to challenge an official decision made in reliance upon some statutory power one will have a right of appeal only if this is expressly conferred by or under statutory provision. The rule is, then: no express statutory provision, no appeal.

However, as a general rule,[55] *if there is a statutory avenue of appeal* which is capable of yielding a remedy one seeks, *one should use it*. Accordingly, this is the first avenue of challenge to be examined in this book.

(b) Application for Judicial Review

Since the constitutional settlement of the seventeenth century the High Court[56] has asserted — and, within limits, has been allowed by Parliament to assert — a general common law (non-statutory) jurisdiction to "review" the legality of official action: *i.e.* to decide, in properly constituted legal proceedings, whether or not a particular exercise of official power is authorised by law. Today that jurisdiction can be directly invoked by bringing an application for judicial review (AJR).

Because of the wide availability of statutory appeal, it is correct to think of judicial review as a "residual jurisdiction".[57] Broadly, one should *resort to AJR only if no appeal mechanism is available* — as, for example, if a pressure group or individual seeks to challenge the legality of a newly-announced central or local government policy or general decision on resource allocation, or some subordinate legislation such as a statutory instrument or byelaw. Also by no means all official decisions on individual claims or applications for benefits or permissions are subject to statutory rights of appeal: here too AJR will be the appropriate avenue of challenge. Furthermore, as will be explained in Chapter 3, judicial review may be the only avenue by which to challenge decisions of persons and bodies exercising non-statutory official power. The residual character of judicial review points to its constitutional importance. As just stated, appeals exist only where specifically provided; but judicial review is always in principle available to challenge the legality of an exercise of official power unless it has been removed or restricted by statute. Statutory restriction of avenues of legal challenge will be considered in:

---

[53] *e.g.* Chap. 3, *section B 2 b* (consumer complaints to Director Generals of public utilities); Chap. 4, *section E 1* (statutory procedure for complaining to a minister); Chap. 8, *section B 3 c* (criminal summons; complaint to a minister or to a local court).

[54] Chap. 2, *sections B 1 a and C 1*.

[55] Chap. 2, *section E*.

[56] See Chap. 3, *section A 3* for the basis of this jurisdiction.

[57] LCR 226 (1994), para. 2.5.

Chapter 7 Restrictions on Legal Challenge. A question of particular importance in this connection is whether Parliament has the legal power to restrict or remove avenues of legal challenge which would otherwise be available to challenge official action allegedly transgressing Community law or Convention rights.[58]

In seeking to understand the residual role of AJR, one may find it instructive when considering a reported AJR — denoted by the title "*R* [*i.e.* "Regina" — the Crown — as in criminal prosecutions symbolising the public interest nature of the proceedings] *v. D* [the name of the defendant ("respondent") authority whose action is challenged], *ex p. C* [the name of the complainant ("applicant")]"[59] — to ask why the challenge in question has been brought by AJR rather than any other avenue of challenge.

The law on applications for judicial review will be dealt with as follows:

Chapter 3 Judicial Review — Public Law Jurisdiction considers what actions of what bodies or persons are subject to judicial review. Judicial review is a "public law" regime imposed in the public interest on bodies and persons exercising public (or official) power: where is the boundary to be drawn between the fields of public and private law?

Chapter 4 Judicial Review — Grounds deals with grounds for judicial review — the legal defects in an official act or decision which make it susceptible to judicial review. Those exercising public power are bound by a number of substantive and procedural legal constraints which are not imposed on private individuals and organisations. Public power is conferred for public purposes. Any exercise of such power for extraneous purposes or in an unfair manner or otherwise beyond the limits of the power conferred may be susceptible to judicial review.

Chapter 5 Applications for Judicial Review — Permission, Standing, Remedies and Choice of Procedure describes the machinery of AJR and focuses on the requirements of **permission** (permission of the court must be promptly sought before proceeding) and **standing** (who may apply); and on **remedies**. The chapter deals also with the so-called **"procedural exclusivity"** rule laid down by the House of Lords in *O'Reilly v. Mackman*[60] that *AJR rather than ordinary civil proceedings ("ordinary civil claim" — below) must be used to mount pure judicial review or public law challenges*: if one is simply invoking public law principles to seek public law remedies for infringement of rights derived from public law ("public" or "public law" rights) one must use the form of procedure specially designed for that purpose. Suppose, *e.g.*, that one seeks to challenge the legality of some aspect of a government department's use of its statutory powers of resource allocation. In the absence of some statutory appeal mechanism, AJR would be the appropriate avenue by which to challenge this alleged "public law wrong". Ordinary civil proceedings (used to bring both contractual and non-contractual, *e.g.* personal injury and other "tort", claims for damages or compensation in respect of "private law wrongs") would be inappropriate.

(c) Ordinary civil claim

Such ordinary civil proceedings may however be brought against public authorities in a wide variety of situations. Such proceedings, unlike AJR, may be commenced without obtaining prior permission from the High Court and within far more generous time limits than for AJR. Under the Civil Procedure Rules 1998,[61] ordinary civil proceedings take the form of what in this book is referred to as an "ordinary" civil claim to distinguish it from special types of civil claim, of which AJR is one.[62]

---

[58] Chap. 7, *section A 8*.

[59] For further explanation of this form of case title, see Chap. 5 (opening section).

[60] [1982] 3 All E.R. 1124.

[61] S.I. 1998 No. 3132 (L.17), r.7.2.

[62] *ibid.*, Sched. 1 to the RSC (Rules of the Supreme Court) Rules, Ord. 53, r.5(2A). See further: Chap. 5, *section C 1*.

A particular complaint or challenge may, as just observed, raise only issues of public law — in which case AJR — with its short time-limits and focus upon public law rights and remedies — rather than ordinary civil proceedings is the correct procedure to use. Conversely, there are many complaints against public authorities which will be regarded in law as raising only issues of private law, *e.g.* a straightforward contract claim arising out of an everyday supply of goods or services to a central or local government department; or a personal injury damages action by a member of the public knocked down in the public highway by the careless driving of a public authority vehicle. In cases of this sort the claimant will be invoking private law principles to seek private law remedies (principally damages) for infringement of rights derived from private law ("private" or "private law" rights). Such *pure private law claims may be brought only by ordinary civil proceedings* — with their longer time limits and focus upon individual rights and remedies — not by AJR. An ordinary civil claim is denoted by the title "*C* [the name of the claimant] *v. D* [the name of the defendant (*e.g.* public authority) against whom the claim is made]".

As will be seen in *section C* of the present chapter, the characterisation of a particular claim as involving "public" rather than "private" rights and remedies (or vice versa) is often problematic. The characterisation is, however, a matter of importance, for upon it will depend the extent and nature of the parties' rights and remedies. In particular, a person whose private rights have been infringed is entitled to damages, whereas damages are commonly not available to remedy loss flowing from unlawful official decisions which can be challenged on appeal or by AJR.

In what circumstances are damages available in respect of loss sustained through the exercise by a public authority of its public functions?

Chapter 8 deals with *Official Tort Liability* and examines the extent to which damage unlawfully inflicted by those exercising public functions gives rise to a liability to compensate those damaged.

Chapter 9 deals with *Official Contractual and Restitutionary Liability*.

Both these chapters will focus constantly upon a key question: what in any particular fact situation giving rise to a tort or contract claim is or should be the legal relevance of the fact that one party to the dispute is a public authority? *e.g.*, if a person sustains damage as a consequence of careless official decision-making or other official action, how far are or ought his or her chances of claiming compensation to be affected by the fact that the wrongdoer is acting in some official, or "public", capacity? Or to what extent do or should the public law principles of procedural fairness and proper purpose govern official contracting?

As these questions indicate, not all legal challenges to official action can be regarded as falling neatly within either the "public" or the "private" category. Many legal relationships involving public authorities (*e.g.* public authority employment and other contracts) seem to have both public and private elements. Some issues arising from such relationships may best be regarded as hybrid rather than as exclusively public or private — with the consequence that the law will have to balance private and public interests in the crafting of rights and remedies. To date, however, the English courts have tended to classify distinct issues as either "public" or "private". Under this approach, a case may be regarded as raising issues both of public law and of private law, *e.g.* suppose that a local authority demolishes a house under what they claim is their statutory power to do so. The house owner may have a private law trespass claim but he must first establish the public law claim that the authority had no power in the circumstances to demolish the house. In these "mixed" public law/private law cases questions as to court competence and best procedure arise in deciding by what procedure — AJR or ordinary civil proceedings — the case should be brought. These questions are considered in **Chapter 5** and further in:

Chapter 6 Collateral Challenge — Judicial Review Other Than by AJR.

Broadly *the rule in mixed cases is that the claimant may choose the procedure which suits him best.* He may attack the alleged public law wrong "directly" by AJR, adding his private law trespass claim "collaterally" within the same proceedings; or, contrariwise, he may seek to vindicate his private law claim directly by ordinary civil proceedings, mounting his public law attack collaterally within the same proceedings.

(d) Criminal or civil collateral defence

The "mixed case" question arises not only for persons who seek to initiate a legal challenge against a public authority but also for persons against whom proceedings (civil or criminal) are brought and who may wish to defend those proceedings by invoking judicial review principles, *e.g.*, a statute may authorise the making of certain regulations and may provide that breach of the regulations is a criminal offence. A person against whom criminal proceedings have been brought may wish to raise the defence that the regulations themselves are unlawful, eg because made for a purpose extraneous to the statute or in an unfair manner or otherwise beyond the limits of the rule-making power. Will the defendant be permitted to raise this defence for adjudication by the criminal trial court? Or, since the defence seeks to invoke judicial review principles, should the argument be able to be raised only by AJR? — in which case the defendant would need to seek an adjournment of the criminal proceedings to enable him to initiate separate judicial review proceedings. As will appear in Chapter 6, *English law on collateral defences is complex and uncertain*. Questions as to the availability to defendants of judicial review other than by "direct" challenge by AJR, *i.e.* collaterally or "indirectly", are considered there.

(e) Complaint to an ombudsman

In the United Kingdom ombudsmen are creations of a number of statutes enacted since the late 1960s. They are empowered to investigate complaints of "maladministration":

Chapter 10 Ombudsmen

Mostly, the remedies provided by ombudsmen rely on the cooperation rather than the compulsion of the public authority concerned. It is thus usually the case that if one is looking to force a public authority to remedy its unlawful official action, one will be looking ultimately either to appeal or to judicial review or to the imposition by a court of civil liability and a remedy of damages and/or injunction and/or declaration.[63]

3 RAISING COMMUNITY LAW OR HUMAN RIGHTS ISSUES AGAINST PUBLIC AUTHORITIES IN ENGLISH PROCEEDINGS

(a) Community law

(i) *Avenues of challenge*

If in England and Wales one seeks to challenge an official act or decision on the basis that it infringes directly effective E.C. individual rights, the most appropriate avenue of challenge may very well be by way of a statutory appeal procedure, *e.g.* in such fields as employment, social security or immigration. A well-known example is *Marshall v. Southampton and South-West Hampshire Area Health Authority*[64] where a woman dietician employed by the authority claimed successfully that the provision for different retirement ages for men and women employed in the public sector was contrary to E.C. law. M's claim was commenced in an industrial tribunal and was

---

[63] For this reason the examples discussed in *section C* below ignore the possibility of complaint to an ombudsman.
[64] [1986] 2 All E.R. 584.

referred to the ECJ by the Court of Appeal hearing M's appeal from the Employment Appeal Tribunal.

A quite different form of challenge will often be appropriate where a person is charged with a criminal offence and seeks to argue by way of defence that the legislation creating the offence infringes directly effective E.C. individual rights. A notorious example was the unsuccessful series of challenges[65] mounted by retailers to the validity of the (now repealed) Sunday Trading legislation. As will be explained in Chapter 6, *section F*, challenge by way of collateral defence is available without restriction in cases where Community law is relied upon.

Where neither of these avenues of challenge is appropriate, one may be considering either AJR or an ordinary civil claim. The choice between these two avenues of challenge will depend on whether or not the alleged infringement constitutes a public law or, on the contrary, a private law wrong. As will be explained in Chapter 8, *section E*, it will be comparatively rarely that an infringement will be "sufficiently serious"[66] for the authority in question to be liable to pay damages on the basis that the infringement constitutes a tort or other private law wrong. The important point here is that (as in the context of proceedings with no E.C. law dimension) the public law/private law classification will determine the appropriate avenue by which to mount a legal challenge alleging an infringement. As stated in *sub-section 2* above, in the absence of a statutory right of appeal, pure public law claims must be asserted by AJR; pure private law claims by ordinary civil proceedings; "mixed" cases may usually be brought either way, at the claimant's choice.

(ii) *Referring questions to the ECJ*

There is one important special procedural provision which may be resorted to in any type of proceedings where a question of "interpretation" of Community law arises. Article 234(2) (ex Art. 177(2)) of the E.C. Treaty[67] provides:

> "Where such a question is raised before any court or tribunal of a Member State, that court or tribunal may, if it considers that a decision on the question is necessary to enable it to give judgment, request the Court of Justice to give a ruling thereon."

The operation of this "preliminary reference procedure"[68] in English courts and tribunals will be discussed in Chapter 6 *section F*. As will then be explained, in a legal system where issues may properly be raised in courts or tribunals which are not best-equipped to decide them, it makes sense to facilitate the reference of such issues to the forum which is so equipped. As will appear, it may well be that English administrative law could be improved by the creation of a procedure (perhaps modelled on the E.C. preliminary reference procedure) whereby public law issues in mixed cases could be referred by lower courts and tribunals to the High Court.

(b) Convention issues — Human Rights Act 1998

It is necessary to deal separately with [1] claims that official action is unlawful under section 6(1) of the 1998 Act because incompatible with a Convention right; and [2] proceedings under section 4 for a declaration of incompatibility between a statutory provision and a Convention right.

---

[65] Culminating in *Stoke-on-Trent CC v. B&Q plc* [1993] 1 All E.R. 481, ECJ. See Chap. 4, *section D 2 b.*

[66] *Factortame Ltd v. Transport Secretary (No. 4)* [1996] All E.R. (E.C.) 301, ECJ.

[67] Art. 234 under the re-numbering of Treaty Articles by the Treaty of Amsterdam (which came into force on May 1, 1999). Hereafter, articles of the E.C. Treaty are cited by their Treaty of Amsterdam number followed by their previous number as in the text to this note. But, for ease of reference, the old numbering is used in treatments of pre-May 1999 reported cases, with the Amsterdam number following thus: "Article 59 [**Amst 49**]".

[68] Hartley, *Foundns*, Chap. 9; Anderson, *Ref. Note:* The reference is "preliminary" (see Art. 234(1) (ex Art. 177(1))) to the judgment of the referring court or tribunal.

(i) *Section 6 incompatibility claims*

Section 7(1) of the 1998 Act provides:

"A person who claims that a public authority has acted (or proposes to act) in a way which is made unlawful by section 6(1) may —

(a) bring proceedings against the authority under this Act in the appropriate court or tribunal, or

(b) rely on the Convention right or rights concerned in any legal proceedings, but only if he is (or would be) a victim of the unlawful act."

Under section 7(7) "victim" has the same meaning as in the Convention[69] which, as interpreted by the ECHR, requires that a claimant must be "directly affected in some way by the matter complained of".[70] Section 7(5) provides that section 7(1)(a) proceedings must be brought within one year of the date on which the act complained of took place or within such longer period as the court or tribunal considers equitable having regard to all the circumstances. But this is "subject to any rule imposing a stricter time limit in relation to the procedure in question": this provision will be considered later.[71]

Section 7(1)(a): where a victim "brings proceedings" Under section 7(2) a victim may proceed under section 7(1)(a) in whatever forum is "appropriate" by reference to procedural rules.[72]

As with infringements of E.C. individual rights, so with official action which is unlawful because incompatible with a Convention right, the most appropriate avenue of challenge may very well be by way of a statutory appeal procedure, *e.g.* a person with no right of abode in the United Kingdom may seek to challenge the immigration authorities' refusal of leave (permission) to remain on the basis of the incompatibility of the refusal with Convention rights. It seems likely that the section 7(2) procedural rules will prescribe that such challenge should be mounted through the ordinary immigration appeal system.[73]

In the absence of any appeal provision, a victim contemplating bringing proceedings will need to choose between AJR and ordinary civil claim. AJR will usually be the appropriate choice for the following reasons.

The choice between AJR and ordinary civil claim seems likely to depend on whether or not the alleged infringement of Convention rights (as with E.C. individual rights) constitutes a public law or, on the contrary, a private law wrong: here too it seems probable that pure public law claims will have to be asserted by AJR, and pure private law claims by ordinary civil proceedings; "mixed" cases will no doubt be able to be brought either way, at the claimant's choice. Section 8 of the 1998 Act gives guidance as to when damages may be awarded to remedy infringements of Convention rights: in particular, in determining whether to award damages (and, if so, the amount) an English court must take into account the principles applied by the ECHR in relation to the award of compensation under Article 41 of the Convention.[74] As will be explained in *section E* of Chapter 8, it is unclear whether there will be many circumstances in which a victim of an unlawful act under section 6 could obtain damages under section 8 where he could not,

---

[69] Art. 34.

[70] Harris, O'Boyle & Warbrick, *ECHR*, p. 632; on "indirect victims" see *ibid.* p. 637. See further Chap. 5, *section A 3 c.*

[71] Chap. 5, *section A 2.*

[72] (s.9 makes special provision with regard to proceedings where the allegedly unlawful official action is a "judicial act": see below.).

[73] See Chap. 2, *section B 2 d.*

[74] s.8(4).

irrespective of the Convention right point, obtain damages under the English domestic law of tort. On that basis, where a person's complaint is solely that his Convention rights have been infringed, AJR rather than ordinary civil proceedings will be the appropriate avenue of challenge — as, *e.g.*, in a challenge by journalists as victims of a government restriction on media coverage of the activities of a particular terrorist group.[75]

Section 7(1)(b) "reliance"   Section 7(1)(b) deals with cases where a victim is a party to proceedings brought by someone else — commonly against the victim himself — and seeks to "rely on Convention rights", particularly by way of defence.

As with E.C. cases, challenge by way of collateral defence is available without restriction. Thus, eg, a person prosecuted for a criminal offence may rely on a Convention right by way of defence. Suppose that a person, D, is prosecuted for practising osteopathy while not registered under the Osteopaths Act 1993.[76] Suppose also that D had been registered but that his name had been removed from the register by the Professional Conduct Committee following his conviction for soliciting as a male prostitute. D argues that his de-registration was unlawful as being incompatible with his Convention rights under Articles 8 and 14. His defence to the charge of unregistered practice is thus that he remained a registered osteopath and has thus not committed the offence charged. It would seem that section 7(1)(b) of the 1998 Act will permit D to raise his Convention arguments by way of defence in the criminal proceedings.

Section 9: proceedings in respect of "judicial acts"   As noted above, section 9 makes special provision where a victim brings proceedings under section 7(1)(a) claiming that a "judicial act" is incompatible with his Convention rights. "Judicial act" appears to include not only decisions of courts and tribunals but also any rulings by, or acts done on the instructions of, judges, magistrates, tribunal members and other judicial officers acting as such.[77] As will be explained later, the usual way to seek to overturn a judicial decision or ruling is by appeal where one is provided.[78] Where no appeal is provided, decisions and rulings of "inferior" courts (courts below High Court level) and tribunals may be challenged by way of AJR.[79] Accordingly, section 9(1) of the Human Rights Act provides that section 7(1)(a) proceedings may be brought "in respect of a judicial act" only by way of appeal or AJR (except where special provision is made by rules). But no such limitation applies as regards section 7(1)(b) — so that, *e.g.*, a defendant in contempt of court proceedings could challenge a judicial act on the basis that it was incompatible with his Convention rights. And in the limited circumstances in which judicial officers may be liable in tort,[80] it seems that a claimant seeking damages for infringement of a Convention right by a judicial act may bring ordinary civil proceedings in tort and, under section 7(1)(b), "rely on the Convention right concerned" in those proceedings.

(ii) *Section 4 declarations of incompatibility*

As previously stated,[81] under section 4(2) of the 1998 Act, in any proceedings in which the High Court, Court of Appeal or House of Lords "is satisfied that [a statutory] provision is incompatible with a Convention right, it may make a declaration of that incompatibility." The Act thus places no limit on the type of "proceedings" within which it may be argued before the above courts that a statutory provision is incompatible with a Convention right. It would seem, however, implicit in section 4(2) that the proceedings in question — whether appeal, AJR, civil or criminal

---

[75] *Cf. Brind v. Home Secretary* [1991] 1 All E.R. 720.
[76] s.32 creates the offence.
[77] s.9(5).
[78] Chap. 2, *section B 1.*
[79] Chap. 3, *section B 1 d.*
[80] Chap. 8, *section A 1 a* refers.
[81] *Sub-section A 3 b* above.

proceedings — must be properly constituted according to the principles outlined in *subsection 2*, above. A declaration of incompatibility may be sought within any such proceedings in the above courts.

C TACKLING ADMINISTRATIVE LAW PROBLEMS: CHOOSING THE BEST AVENUE OF CHALLENGE

Readers are likely to have obtained from the previous section only the haziest and most sketchy idea of the nature, operation and interaction of the various avenues of legal challenge to official action. It may be helpful at this stage to attempt to flesh out the bare descriptions of challenge mechanisms by reference to a couple of specific (hypothetical) fact situations. These example problems will show how choices of challenge mechanism arise in particular cases and what types of question need to be addressed in order to proceed satisfactorily.

1 GENERAL CONSIDERATIONS

The two examples to be taken are of a kind which a student could be expected to be able to tackle at the end rather than the beginning of an administrative law course. Indeed, readers may wish to return to these problems at a later stage as a means of checking progress made. But the aim at this point is not so much to solve the problems as to see what questions need to be asked and answered in order to solve them; and to give some preliminary idea of the approach to be taken in tackling administrative law problems generally. For example, many public authority decisions, like those in the examples, relate to the allocation of scarce resources or other state benefits in cash or kind. Such decisions generate many legal challenges. While each challenge will depend on all the particular circumstances of the case, there are recurring patterns of issue and argument. Some of the main lines which will become familiar as the book progresses are highlighted by the facts of the examples.

In tackling any particular problem one needs to consider three broad questions:

(a) What grounds are there for challenge?

The question here is in essence "What are you complaining about?" Are you saying that a particular decision was wrong or unfair? If so, why? Does your complaint amount to an assertion that the decision maker applied the wrong tests or applied the right tests wrongly? Or the complaint may seem to be focused on some action or omission rather than a decision — damage done to person or property in the course of operations by a public authority; or loss caused by a failure to carry out a contract.

(b) Who can rely on those grounds? . . .

A challenge may be mounted by the individual victim of a damage-causing act or by the individual subject of a decision. But by no means all official decisions are directed to a particular individual or individuals. A person may wish to challenge a decision to legislate in certain terms or to adopt a certain general policy for dealing with a large number of particular cases. Has the would-be complainant a sufficient interest or stake in the subject-matter of the complaint in order to be permitted to make the complaint?

(c) . . . by what procedure, and seeking what remedy?

As will be seen, initial examination of both the substance of the complaint and the person seeking to make it will give at least a provisional indication as to possible avenues of challenge and possible redress available.

Before showing how this approach may be applied to the solution of the two examples to be studied, it is worth noting at the outset that in solving problems a grasp of underlying legal policy considerations is critically important. The range of circumstances in which legal challenges to public power may possibly be mounted is vast. Many new fact situations will be without precedent. Individual case outcomes will turn on effective choice of procedure and case presentation. These in turn will depend on an awareness of the competing public interests at stake, in particular how to uphold the rule of law while balancing the interest of individual litigants in obtaining a remedy for their grievances against the need for efficiency, speed and certainty in the administrative decision-making process.

2 TWO EXAMPLES

EXAMPLE 1

(a) Legal background

Suppose that a National Lottery Funds Act was passed some years ago following a period of public disquiet regarding the allocation of public funds raised via the national lottery.

- The Act created a U.K. Business Enterprise Support Fund financed from lottery receipts and empowered to make "Business Enterprise" grants on a renewable basis to organisations or individuals who can satisfy the Fund of their "business need" for such support.

- The Act provides that any person aggrieved by a decision of the Fund on a grant application may appeal to the Fund's Appeal Committee whose decision is final.

- It is an offence under the Act for any person or organisation falsely to represent that they are in receipt of financial support from the U.K. Business Enterprise Support Fund.

The Fund's published policy on Business Enterprise grants is that "once an individual grant has been made, it will normally be renewed on an annual basis until such time as the Fund decides that the business need in respect of which the grant was made has been satisfied."

(b) Consider the following case:

Jeff, who runs a computer-assembly factory has been in receipt of a Business Enterprise grant for two years, but was recently informed by the Fund that it has decided that the business need in respect of which the grant was made has been satisfied, and that, accordingly, the grant will not be renewed. Jeff wishes to challenge the Fund's decision. He maintains that the Fund's financial advisers have radically overestimated the commercial strength of his business which, he says, will be placed in jeopardy by the discontinuance of the grant. Further, Jeff is concerned that if the discontinuance is publicised, certain persons will withdraw their financial support for his business. For this reason he wishes to continue to use business stationery bearing the legend: "Sponsored by the U.K. Business Enterprise Support Fund".

(c) Putting the questions

(i) *What grounds are there for challenge?*

[1] Both the Act and the Fund's policy require the Fund to decide whether there is still a business need for the grant. Jeff maintains that the decision that there is not is erroneous because the Fund's financial advisers have overestimated the commercial strength of his business.

[2] Jeff refers to "radical" overestimation by the financial advisers. Is there a suggestion of negligence or even conscious impropriety here?

(ii) *Who can rely on those grounds?* . . .

It seems from the facts given that only Jeff is likely to wish to challenge the Fund's decision not to renew his grant. Jeff can seek to rely on the above grounds under the circumstances now to be considered.

(iii) . . . *By what procedure, and seeking what remedy?*

Appeal   The Act provides that any person aggrieved by a decision of the Fund on a grant application may appeal to the Fund's Appeal Committee whose decision is final. As will be explained in Chapter 2,[82] such provision empowers the Committee to correct any error it perceives and, where appropriate, to reverse the decision. So the most obvious course is for Jeff to appeal.

If the appeal fails, two further avenues of challenge to be considered are AJR and ordinary civil claim:

AJR — *Error of law?*   The Appeal Committee's decision is final, but as will be seen in Chapter 7,[83] a statutory provision in these terms does not remove the courts' judicial review jurisdiction to rule that a public authority has gone wrong in law. As will be explained in Chapter 2,[84] the Fund would have erred in law, *e.g.*, if no reasonable person could have concluded that Jeff's business need had been satisfied or if its decision was in fact based wholly or partly on considerations other than the satisfaction of that need, *e.g.* the strength of competing applications or a shortage of funds. The Appeal Committee would have erred in law if on appeal it failed to correct any error of law by the Fund.

Remedies on AJR   On AJR the court can issue either a mandatory order requiring the question to be decided lawfully or a declaration indicating the correct legal position. If, in addition, Jeff can establish any civil (private law) claim (see next) damages may be awarded on AJR.

Ordinary civil claim   From what has just been said, it would appear that AJR could afford any remedy to which Jeff might conceivably aspire. So why consider an ordinary civil claim as an alternative?

---

[82] *Section B 1.*
[83] *Section A 1.*
[84] *Section D 6 a.*

- AJR is subject to a three month time limit,[85] A civil claim in tort, contract etc may be commenced within (usually) a six-year limitation period.

- AJR requires permission of the court[86]; an ordinary civil claim can be brought as of right by anyone with a "cause of action" (*i.e.* a sound legal basis for mounting a claim).

- The public law remedies of AJR are discretionary[87]; civil damages are available as of right.

- AJR is an exclusively High Court procedure, while an ordinary civil claim below a certain value may be commenced in a local county court.

A civil claim may therefore be much cheaper and more convenient for a complainant than AJR. Has Jeff any possible civil cause of action? It seems unlikely that the relationship between Jeff and the Fund is contractual, for no bargain has been struck between the parties. Any obligation which the Fund may have to renew Jeff's grant will have been generated by the statutory framework within which the grant was made and not by any *quid pro quo* provided by Jeff. Three possible tort claims may be considered: misfeasance in a public office; breach of statutory duty; negligence.

Misfeasance[88] would require Jeff to prove knowledge or recklessness on the part of the Fund that its decision was unlawful and likely to damage him. Perhaps the financial advisers' "radical overestimation" of the strength of Jeff's business is evidence of some level of conscious impropriety here.

Failing this, can Jeff base a civil debt action simply on the assertion that the Fund has *breached its statutory duty*[89] to pay him the grant? The argument might proceed as follows:

[1] When the Fund has exercised its grant-making power by deciding that a particular individual shall have a grant, the statute must be taken to impose a duty on the Fund to execute its decision and to pay the grant.

[2] Taking the statutory reference to making grants on a renewable basis together with the Fund's renewal policy, the duty to pay continues until a lawful decision is taken not to renew a particular grant.

[3] In Jeff's case the decision not to renew is unlawful (AJR above), so the Fund's duty to pay continues and Jeff may sue for its breach.

This argument is problematic, *e.g.* in that it could be retorted that the grant is renewable on an annual basis, and that no decision has yet been made to renew: until such time as the Fund decides to renew the grant for the current year, it may be argued that Jeff has a "public law right" to the benefit of a lawful decision rather than a "private law right" to claim the grant. On this reasoning, while Jeff might be able to obtain judicial review of the unlawful decision not to renew, his remedy would be simply a ruling on AJR that a correct decision must be taken.

A correct analysis of Jeff's legal position thus turns on the elusive distinction between "public" and "private" law rights and remedies referred to in *section B* of this chapter.

A further complication stemming from the same source is that even if Jeff can show that he has a private law right, to do so he must establish the unlawfulness of the Fund's decision not to

---

[85] Chap. 5, *section A 2.*
[86] *ibid., section A 1.*
[87] *ibid., section B 4.*
[88] Chap. 8, *section D.*
[89] *ibid., section B.*

renew the grant: [3] above. This requires him to resort to judicial review principles. Can those principles be invoked in the course of civil proceedings or must Jeff proceed by AJR? As will be shown in Chapter 5,[90] it appears that "mixed" public law/private law cases may be brought at the complainant's option either by ordinary civil proceedings or by AJR, at any rate unless the court regards the public law aspect of the case as so dominant that AJR is the only appropriate procedure.

A *negligence* action[91] is similarly fraught with difficulty. In the *Bedford/Dorset* case[92] in 1995 the House of Lords confirmed that formidable hurdles must be cleared by a complainant who seeks to establish that a public authority owed him a duty of care in the exercise of its public decision-making powers. Even if Jeff could establish

[1] that the decision not to renew his grant was unlawful;

[2] that the Fund should have realised this;

[3] that the Fund had no basis for not renewing so that its unlawful refusal will cause Jeff loss,

it is unlikely that Jeff would have a negligence claim if for no other reason than that the availability of appeal and review mechanisms in such contexts are commonly held by the courts to negative any "private law" duty of care.

The conclusion is that Jeff may succeed on appeal or AJR, but, unless he can establish misfeasance or make good his "private law right" argument, he is unlikely to have any debt or damages claim and so should not contemplate an ordinary civil claim.

Collateral defence to criminal proceedings   Jeff is said to be concerned that if the discontinuance of his grant is publicised, certain persons will withdraw their financial support for his business. For this reason he wishes to continue to use business stationery bearing the legend: "Sponsored by the U.K. Business Enterprise Support Fund". His difficulty is that it is an offence under the Act for any person or organisation falsely to represent that they are in receipt of financial support from the U.K. Business Enterprise Support Fund.

Two questions arise:

[1] If, pending the outcome of any direct challenge to the Fund's decision, Jeff does continue to use the stationery and is prosecuted, can he base a defence to the charge on the argument that he has been awarded what is in reality a continuing grant which has been unlawfully withdrawn, *i.e.*, that, in effect (since the withdrawal — the Fund's decision not to renew — is unlawful) he is still "in receipt of a grant"?

This argument, of course, essentially replicates the "private law right" argument suggested above in support of a tort claim for breach of statutory duty. However, as already explained, the success of the argument will depend in part on Jeff's ability to invoke judicial review principles to demonstrate that the Fund's decision is unlawful. This raises the second question:

[2] Even if Jeff has a good defence, can he mount that defence in the criminal trial court, or must he seek an adjournment of the trial in order that he may make an AJR?

---

[90] *Section C 1 c.*
[91] Chap. 8, *section C.*
[92] *X v. Bedfordshire C.C., E v. Dorset C.C. and other appeals* [1995] 3 All E.R. 353. See Chap. 8 *ibid.*

If (as was said above) a complainant bringing a "mixed" case to recover damages can normally choose between AJR and ordinary civil proceedings, one might suppose that a defendant to a criminal charge would be permitted to seek within the criminal proceedings the determination of a public law defence. But as will be explained in Chapter 6,[93] English law takes an unsatisfactorily restrictive approach to this form of collateral judicial review challenge. Jeff might well be unable to mount his defence except by separate AJR proceedings commenced by himself.

EXAMPLE 2

Example 2, like Example 1, relates to decisions of the fictitious United Kingdom Business Enterprise Support Fund

(a) Additional legal background (the legal background supplied for Example 1 is presupposed)

Suppose that in the light of pressure for funding of other permitted purposes, the Fund last week published a revised policy on Business Enterprise grants as follows: "once an individual grant has been made, it may be renewed on an annual basis until such time as the Fund decides that the business need in respect of which the grant was made has been satisfied, but the Fund reserves the right to discontinue grants following periodic reviews of its budgetary strategy."

(b) Consider the following case:

Two years ago Kate was awarded a Business Enterprise grant to assist her in establishing "Translation Unlimited", which offers language translation and interpreting services to firms in the North East of England. She has received the grant for two years and the business is becoming established. Suppose that yesterday she was informed by the Fund that following a review of its budgetary strategy, the grant is to be discontinued. Kate fears that as a consequence the business may collapse.

(c) Putting the questions

(i) *What grounds are there for challenge?*

Challenging the policy   Is the revised policy lawful in respect both of its substance and of the manner in which it was adopted?

With regard to substance, it might be argued that in apparently permitting immediate (no warning) and summary (no consultation) withdrawal of a grant, the policy is unlawful in so far as it fails to take account of the relevant consideration that such withdrawals could have catastrophic effect on the recipients of grants and in effect negative the beneficial effect of the grant, *i.e.*, it will cause public money to be wasted.

With regard to procedure, would it be lawful to revise the policy (if in fact the Fund has done so) having heard only representations from supporters of "other permitted purposes" and not from current recipients of grants?

Challenging its implementation   If lawful, can the revised policy lawfully be applied to existing grant-holders so as to frustrate their legitimate expectations? Kate may argue that in promulgating its original policy the Fund has created the expectation (upon which she has relied) that she

---

[93] *Section D.*

will continue to receive the grant until her business need is satisfied. This argument raises important questions (discussed in Chapter 4[94]) as to the balance to be struck by the law between the principle that a public authority should be able (on proper grounds) to change its policy; and the principle that individuals who have relied to their detriment on the "legitimate expectation" of a continuance of a particular policy should be able to enforce that expectation or at least be compensated if they are damaged by its withdrawal.

(ii) *Who can rely on those grounds? . . .*

[1] If the policy itself or, indeed, the general manner of its implementation by the Fund, is unlawful, some representative group such as the National Federation for Small Businesses may contemplate mounting a challenge as considered below ("the pressure group challenge").

[2] Kate's concern is to secure renewal of her grant. She may seek to attack the Fund's decision on her application. As just seen, this may or may not require her to impugn the lawfulness of the policy itself.

(iii) *. . . By what procedure, and seeking what remedy?*

The pressure group challenge   Since any pressure group ("associational"[95]) challenge would be concerned with the policy or its general application rather than any specific decision, the **appeal** procedure would not be appropriate, even assuming that the pressure group was "a person aggrieved". The only avenue of challenge would be **AJR**, raising issues of standing and capable of yielding a public law discretionary remedy designed to secure a correction in any unlawful aspect of the policy or its application. A substantive point of difficulty would be whether the policy "in vacuo" is a reviewable act, distinct from any individual applications of it such as in Kate's case (see Chapter 3[96]). If not, the AJR may need to be by Kate (albeit, as it may be, financially supported by the pressure group).

Kate   Plainly, like Jeff above, she can **appeal** — although it would be a question whether a statutory appeal tribunal such as the Appeal Committee has jurisdiction to question the lawfulness of the Fund's policy or to consider the legitimate expectation argument even though one or both of these issues would underpin Kate's challenge to the decision not to renew. As will be explained in Chapter 6,[97] it may well be that these "public law" issues can be determined only on AJR.

These doubts as to the appeal tribunal's jurisdiction may suggest that Kate's better course is at once to seek **AJR**.

Ordinary civil claim?   Kate, like Jeff in *Example 1* was awarded her grant under the original policy. Her prospects of a successful civil claim to force continued payment of the grant turn largely upon the same considerations as his. But even if Kate appears to have strong prospects of making out one of the private law claims considered in Jeff's case (breach of statutory duty seems the most likely), problems of choice between AJR and ordinary civil proceedings may bulk larger for her than for him. If she seeks to attack the lawfulness of the Fund's revised policy, the result will affect not only her own individual case but the Fund's general discharge of its public functions for the future. On that basis a court might rule that the public law aspect of the case is so dominant that AJR is the appropriate procedure.

[94] *Section E 2 b.*
[95] Chap. 5, *section A 3 c.*
[96] *Section C 1 a.*
[97] *Section E.*

D ADMINISTRATIVE LAW — PREVENTION OR CURE?

This book deals with the English version of what the French call "le contentieux administratif", *i.e.*, "litigation between a citizen and some organ of the state in an administrative context".[98] It is a book about cure rather than prevention. But the point is often made that "good administration is more to be desired than remedies for bad administration",[99] so that it is inadequate for undergraduate administrative law courses to dwell exclusively, as they tend to,[1] on public law rights and remedies. It is accepted that someone needs to pick up the pieces in individual cases, but is said to be of greater importance to work towards a reform of administrative law and practice which will reduce the likelihood of there being pieces to pick up. It may be that systematic structuring of administrative institutions and a balance between rules and discretion by reference to purpose can help to prevent the appearance of many of the pathological symptoms with which remedy-focused administrative law tends exclusively to deal.[2] Baldwin and McCrudden[3] discuss what steps can be taken to increase the "legitimacy" of regulatory agencies (be they government ministers, "QUANGOs", or other official or quasi-official bodies) — in particular looking at administrative rule-making as "a means of clarifying mandates and increasing openness, participation, control and accountability". On a practical level, "Implementation of mechanisms for lawful and transparent decision-making can be of far greater benefit to people from disadvantaged sectors of society than going to court or complaining to an ombudsman after the damage is done".[4]

Accepting that prevention is better than cure, it remains the case that problems of official illegality do and will continue to arise and to need solving. The existence of effective and accessible avenues of challenge is an important stimulus to improved administration. Disadvantaged people would be very much more disadvantaged if these avenues were not available to them. Both the protection of the individual and the efficient use of state resources require solutions to be principled and as far as possible predictable. As will appear in the course of the book, English administrative law is often deficient in these respects: analysis of specific areas of the law will include some consideration of current proposals for reform.

The machine of legal challenge to state power is large and complex. At the end of their administrative law course students will expect, and be expected, to have some real grasp of the workings of this machine. The test of this may be as follows. At first glance, examination problems such as those discussed in *section C* of this chapter commonly generate an impenetrable fog. As the course progresses, students should be able increasingly to see the outlines of legal rights and remedies emerging from this fog. If this book assists them in this it will have served its purpose.

[98] Brown and Bell, *Fr AL*, p. 5.
[99] Justice/A-S, p. 7.
[1] A survey in February/March 1996 indicated that, like this book, over 80 per cent of undergraduate courses or modules in administrative law in U.K. universities focus exclusively upon judicial review and other forms of legal challenge to official action.
[2] Craig, *AL*, pp. 21 *et seq.*, *cf. ibid.*, 1st ed., Chap. 6.
[3] Baldwin and McCrudden, *RPL*, Chap. 3; see also Baldwin (1994) in Richardson and Genn, *ALGA*, Chap. 7.
[4] PLP (1994), p. 4.

Chapter 2

APPEALS — TRIBUNALS, INQUIRIES AND COURTS; ERROR OF LAW

The first avenue of challenge to be examined is appeal. *Section A* looks at some basic features of what is usually the first line of appeal from administrative decisions — statutory tribunals — and contrasts tribunals with both statutory inquiries and courts. *Section B* gives a broad-brush sketch of the whole appeal network (tribunals, inquiries and courts) and examines a number of particular examples of appeal provision. *Section C* focuses on the role of the courts in the network. It will be seen that the role of the courts in administrative appeals is, broadly, confined to the correction of errors of law. This leads on to consideration in *section D* of that central notion in administrative law.

A ADMINISTRATIVE APPEALS: SOME BASIC FEATURES[1]

1 INDEPENDENT STATUTORY TRIBUNALS

There will be many situations in which what a complainant wants is simply (or at any rate principally) to have an official decision reversed or varied. There is in England and Wales a complex, but not comprehensive, network of statutory rights of appeal against administrative decisions, chiefly to independent statutory tribunals such as local social security appeal tribunals, income tax "commissioners" or education appeal committees. There is great variation in the composition and jurisdiction of different types of tribunal — reflecting successive governments' political judgments as to what in particular contexts is the appropriate and affordable level of appeal provision. The number and variety of tribunals reflects also the haphazard and unsystematic way in which the administrative appeal network has developed.[2] The network is too lacking in design to be called a system although, as will be seen in *section B*, certain main features recur.

Statutory appeal tribunals can be said to be "independent" (*i.e.* of the central or local government authorities against whose decisions they hear appeals) essentially because the tribunal members themselves are independent. They are not government employees. They are often part-time or unpaid individuals with their own professional expertise. Many categories of tribunal have full-time legally qualified chairmen whose independence reflects their professional standing.

---

[1] Wade and Forsyth, *AL*, Chaps 23 and 24; Craig, *AL*, Chap. 9; de Smith, *JRAA*, pp. 33–36; Justice/A-S, Chaps 9 and 10.
[2] For criticism of this haphazard structure and proposals for reform, see Woolf (1992), pp. 228–229.

2 WHAT TYPES OF DECISION ARE APPEALABLE?

Broadly speaking, statute provides for appeals only (but not always) against those official decisions which have an **immediate and direct impact on individuals**. Such decisions entail the application of rules or policies rather than their making or adoption. Take for example the rejection by a local social security benefit agency of an individual's claim to social security benefit. This will entail the application of detailed statutory rules to the particular circumstances of the claimant and is subject to appeal to an appeal tribunal.[3] By contrast, the rules themselves and the decisions involved in the rule-making process are not appealable but may be subject to judicial review.[4]

A person seeking to challenge a particular official decision made in reliance upon some statutory power will have a right of appeal only if this is expressly conferred by or under statutory provision. As stated in Chapter 1, the rule is: **no statutory provision, no appeal**. Because of the haphazard way in which the English appeal network has developed there remain a number of types of official decision which clearly have an immediate and direct impact on individuals but against which, by political happenstance, no appeal has been provided. Until 1997,[5] for example there was no appeal against decisions of local authorities under the homeless persons legislation. This not only denied homeless persons the sort of appeal which state benefit claimants generally have but also produced many *"faute de mieux"* attempts to fill the gap by AJR.[6] Because, as will be explained, AJR is limited to correcting errors of law, these attempts were often unavailing and tended simply to clog the system. As recommended by the Law Commission,[7] the Housing Act 1996, s.204[8] provides an appeal (limited to point of law) to a county court after an internal review procedure. This may alleviate the clogging problem but, as will appear, will provide only a limited scope for challenge by aggrieved individuals.

3 TRIBUNALS, COURTS AND STATUTORY INQUIRIES

The basic reasons for routing appeals through **tribunals** rather than courts are tribunals' relative cheapness and informality and the special expertise of their members in the particular field of the tribunal's jurisdiction.[9] However, as will be seen, the **courts** are usually brought in at the top of the appeal tree with ultimate jurisdiction to correct errors of law.

The statutory Council on Tribunals[10] (set up following the Franks Committee Report on *"Administrative Tribunals and Enquiries"*[11]) keeps under review the constitution and working of certain specified tribunals[12] but lacks "a clear general power to act as an advisory body over the whole area of administrative adjudication and the general pattern and organisation of tribunal structure", [13] Following government rejection of the Council's own recommendation that it should have such a role, the Justice-All Souls Committee recommended the creation of an Australian-style Administrative Review Commission.[14] The recommendation has not been implemented. The

---

[3] See *section B 2 c* below.
[4] See Chaps 3, 4, *section F*. For whether a person appealing against, *e.g.*, a withdrawal of benefit under new or changed rules can attack the validity of the rules in the appeal proceedings, see Chap. 6, *section E*.
[5] Housing Act 1996, Pt VII (below), replacing Housing Act 1985, Pt III.
[6] Woolf (1992), p. 226.
[7] LCR 226 (1994) paras 2.26, 2.27.
[8] *Ali v. Westminster C.C.* [1999] 1 All E.R. 450.
[9] Franks (below), paras 38, 105. *Section B* below contains details of the composition of some types of tribunal.
[10] See now Tribunals and Inquiries Act (TIA) 1992, ss.1–4.
[11] Cmnd. 218 (1957).
[12] TIA 1992, Sched. 1.
[13] C T Report (1980), p. 22.
[14] JUSTICE/All Souls Committee Report: *Administrative Justice: Some Necessary Reforms* (1988) (Justice/A-S), Chap. 4. On Tribunals generally and the Council, see *ibid.*, Chap. 9.

need for some effective and independent engine of reform is, however, clear, *e.g.*, empirical research[15] suggests that the general[16] non-availability of legal aid for tribunal proceedings seriously detracts from the effectiveness of tribunals as a check on administrative decision making. Without legal representation, and despite the efforts of many tribunal chairmen to identify parties' best points, the relevant law is usually highly complex and the scales are tipped against unrepresented persons.[17]

Some appeal situations involve the application in particular cases of more or less flexible policies rather than of more rigidly formulated rules. Here Parliament has used the mechanism of the **statutory inquiry** rather than a tribunal. "The statutory inquiry is the standard device for giving a fair hearing to objectors before the final decision is made on some question of government policy affecting citizens' rights or interests."[18] Examples are inquiries into proposals to build a motorway or power station or, more routinely, into periodic revisions of "structure" and "local" plans. In these situations inquiries are held before a decision is made; but, as stated above, there are situations in which an inquiry is part of an appeal process, *e.g.*[19] where a local planning authority has refused (or granted subject to unacceptable conditions) an application for permission for a proposed development. Here the applicant may appeal to the Secretary of State for the Environment and may require a public inquiry to be held locally by the inspector appointed by the minister to determine the appeal.[20]

B APPEAL PROVISION: GENERAL STRUCTURE AND PARTICULAR EXAMPLES[21]

1 GENERAL STRUCTURE

TABLE 1 illustrates the general structure of statutory appeal provision in England and Wales. It contrasts situations where an official decision is taken initially by an administrative authority — where the usual first line of appeal is to a statutory tribunal; and those where the initial decision is that of a court — when, usually, there is an appeal to a higher court.

- Appeal **"on the merits"** allows the person who is appealing (the "appellant") to invite the appeal tribunal or court to reconsider *all aspects* of the decision being appealed against: findings of fact and of law; inferences drawn from facts found; exercises of judgment in applying law to facts; exercises of discretion. Merits appeals are said to be "by way of rehearing"[22]: "The purpose of such appeals is to confer on the appellate court [or tribunal] the power to reverse the decision of the lower court [or other authority], if it considers that it was wrong"[23] — although sometimes considerations of expertise will mean that a case will be remitted (sent back for decision) to the initial decision maker.[24]

---

[15] Genn (1994), focusing on social security and immigration appeals.

[16] For exceptions see *ibid,*. p. 251, n.13.

[17] *ibid.*, pp. 272–284.

[18] Wade and Forsyth, *AL*, p. 964.

[19] For other examples, see Wade and Forsyth, *AL*, p. 911.

[20] On the "independence" of inspectors, see further Chap. 4, *section E 2 C (i)*.

[21] Wade and Forsyth, *AL*, pp. 915–920; Garner, *AL*, Chap. 11.

[22] See, *e.g.* RSC, Ord. 55, r.3(1), applying generally to statutory appeals to the High Court: *ibid*, r.1(1).

[23] Law Commission Consultation Paper (LCCP) No. 126, *Administrative Law: Judicial Review and Statutory Appeals* (1993) paras 18.5–18.6. [Parentheses added.].

[24] See, *e.g.*, *John Dee Ltd v. Commissioners of Customs & Excise*, The Times, July 20, 1995, CA.

- Appeal **"on** [point of] **law"**, by contrast, restricts the appellant to challenging *errors of law*. Conclusions on matters of fact and judgment (or "degree") and lawful exercises of discretion are sacrosanct where an appeal is confined to law. The distinction between errors of law and other errors (sometimes referred to compendiously as errors of fact) is discussed in *section D* below.

(a) **Appeals from decisions of courts** (right-hand side of *TABLE 1*)

The appeal structure from decisions of courts is long established, comprehensive and fairly well known (see further *section C1* below). Note the general principle of a single appeal on the merits, any further appeal being confined to law.

(b) **Appeals from decisions of administrative authorities** (left-hand side of *TABLE 1*)

The appeal structure from decisions of administrative authorities is of more recent origin, less systematised and less comprehensive. Broadly speaking too, as the Table shows, the same "merits/law" pattern can be discerned as in the case of appeals from decisions taken initially by courts; but the pattern is more haphazard and variable.

(c) **Three points of general application on statutory provision of rights of appeal**

(i) Where a statute simply provides for an "appeal", that means an appeal on the merits; if an appeal is to be limited to point of law, the statute will say so in terms. *As mentioned above, "merits" includes law as well as fact, judgment and discretion; "law" = law only.*

EXAMPLE — MERITS OR LAW? **contrast** Taxes Management Act (TMA) 1970, s.31(1): "An appeal may be brought against an assessment to tax . . . " *(appeal on the merits)*

with Tribunals and Inquiries Act (TIA) 1992, s.11(1): ". . . if any party to proceedings before *[a specified tribunal]* is dissatisfied in point of law with a decision of the tribunal he may appeal . . . " *(appeal on law only)*

(ii) Always be aware of the need to look carefully at every particular statutory appeal provision to see precisely what aspects of what decisions are covered, who may appeal, etc.

EXAMPLE — APPEALABLE MATTERS **contrast** Town and Country Planning Act (TCPA) 1990, s.78(1): "Where a local planning authority . . . refuse an application for planning permission . . . the applicant may by notice appeal . . . " *This gives a right to appeal against any aspect of a planning refusal.*

with *ibid.* s.174(1)–(2) "A person having an interest in the land to which an enforcement notice relates . . . may appeal . . . on any of the following grounds — *[Act specifies grounds]*". *This gives a right of appeal against an enforcement notice limited to specific grounds set out in the section.*

TABLE 1
(Chapter 2, section B1, p. 26)

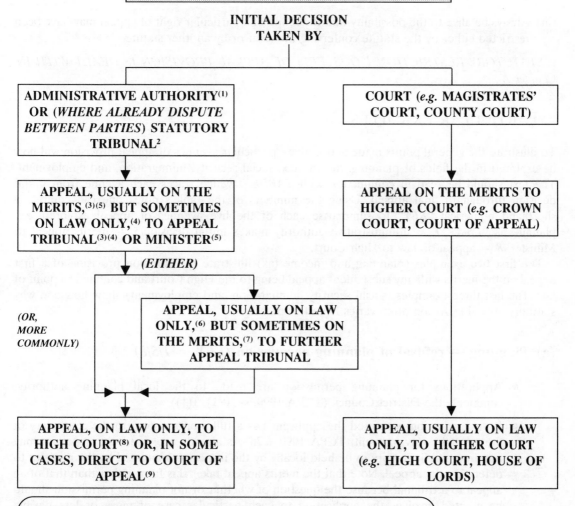

GENERAL STRUCTURE OF APPEAL PROVISION WITH EXAMPLES

INITIAL DECISION TAKEN BY

ADMINISTRATIVE AUTHORITY[1] OR (*WHERE ALREADY DISPUTE BETWEEN PARTIES*) STATUTORY TRIBUNAL[2]

COURT (*e.g.* MAGISTRATES' COURT, COUNTY COURT)

APPEAL, USUALLY ON THE MERITS,[3][5] BUT SOMETIMES ON LAW ONLY,[4] TO APPEAL TRIBUNAL[3][4] OR MINISTER[5]

APPEAL ON THE MERITS TO HIGHER COURT (*e.g.* CROWN COURT, COURT OF APPEAL)

(EITHER)

(OR, MORE COMMONLY)

APPEAL, USUALLY ON LAW ONLY,[6] BUT SOMETIMES ON THE MERITS,[7] TO FURTHER APPEAL TRIBUNAL

APPEAL, ON LAW ONLY, TO HIGH COURT[8] OR, IN SOME CASES, DIRECT TO COURT OF APPEAL[9]

APPEAL, USUALLY ON LAW ONLY, TO HIGHER COURT (*e.g.* HIGH COURT, HOUSE OF LORDS)

EXAMPLES (for details see Chap. 2, part B2)

[1] *e.g. Planning, Income Tax, Social Security, Immigration*
[2] *e.g. Employment — Industrial Tribunals*
[3] *e.g. Income Tax, Social Security, Immigration*
[4] *e.g. Employment — Employment Appeal Tribunal (EAT)*
[5] *e.g. Planning*
[6] *e.g. Social Security Commissioners*
[7] *e.g. Immigration Appeal Tribunal*
[8] *e.g. Planning, Income Tax*
[9] *e.g. Employment (from EAT)/Social Security (from Commissioners)/ Immigration (from IAT)*

EXAMPLE — WHO MAY APPEAL   contrast the commonly-found[25] "any person aggrieved", *e.g.* TCPA 1990, s.288 (*sub-section 2 a* below)

with more restrictive formulations such as "any party to proceedings before any [specified] tribunal", TIA 1992, s.11(1) (above); "the applicant", TCPA 1990, s.78 (above); "the claimant and such other person as may be prescribed", Social Security Act 1998, s.12(2)(b).[26]

(iii) Always be alive to the possibility that the scope of a particular right of appeal may have been restricted either by the statute conferring the right or by another statute.

STATUTORY RESTRICTION ("OUSTER") OF APPEAL PROVISION IS DEALT WITH IN Chapter 7.

2 PARTICULAR EXAMPLES

To illustrate the general points made above, five[27] particular avenues of appeal provision will now be explored in the fields of planning, income tax, social security, immigration, and employment. The text should be read in conjunction with *TABLE 1* which traces each avenue from initial decision through to final appeal. Using the numbers of the table's notes one can compile a shorthand numerical "*KEY*" to summarise each of the five avenues of appeal explored, *e.g.* planning is "*1/5/8*": *1* = administrative authority makes initial decision/*5* = merits appeal to Minister /*8* = appeal on law to High Court.

The first two examples (planning and income tax) illustrate the common provision of a first appeal on the merits with any subsequent appeal being to the High Court and confined to point of law. The last three examples (social security, immigration, and employment) show how and why statutory appeal provision often varies from this paradigm.

(a) Planning — refusal of planning permission *(KEY = 1/5/8)*

- Applications for planning permission are made to the local planning authority, commonly the District Council (TCPA 1990, ss.70(1), 1(1)).

- If an application is refused the applicant has a full merits appeal to the eSecretary of State for the Environment: TCPA 1990, s.78. As already explained, the appellant may require a public inquiry to be held locally by the inspector appointed by the minister to determine the appeal. Note that the merits appeal takes this form rather than that of an appeal to a tribunal because the question of whether or not planning permission should be granted involves the application to each particular case of more or less flexible planning policies rather than the type of rigid rules applicable in such fields as tax and social security (see next examples).

- The effect of TCPA 1990, s.288 is that "any person aggrieved" may appeal on point of law to the High Court against a decision on a section 78 appeal. As will be explained in Chapter 7, this "law" appeal is crafted so as to oust any other form of legal challenge (including judicial review) and thus is made available to any person aggrieved and not just to the applicant or the authority.

[25] LCCP 126 (1993), paras 19.9 *et seq.*
[26] For more examples see LCCP 126 (1993), Annex 3.
[27] For a useful Table summarising appeal provision in many more fields see Wade and Forsyth, *AL*, pp. 956–963.

(b) Income tax — disputed tax assessment *(KEY = 1/3/8)*

- Decisions that income tax must be paid ("assessments" to tax) are made by local tax inspectors (TMA 1970, s.29).

- A taxpayer who disputes an assessment may appeal on the merits to a tribunal of Commissioners (either "General" or "Special", at the appellant's option) of Income Tax (*ibid.*, section 31). Complex cases tend to go to Special Commissioners who are qualified lawyers; less complex cases to General Commissioners, non-lawyers who are experienced in fact finding (*e.g.* local magistrates). Here, in contrast to planning appeals, statute provides a tribunal for the merits appeal because what is in issue is the application of precise rules rather than flexible policies.

- Either the appellant taxpayer **or the inspector** may appeal on point of law from Commissioners to the High Court by a special form of procedure known as "case stated" (*ibid.*, section 56). The procedure requires the tribunal to set out its findings of fact and decision in a form designed to facilitate the identification of errors of law on appeal[28] Case stated was at one time quite commonly prescribed by statute for appeals from tribunals and courts (*e.g.* magistrates' courts) whose membership included non-lawyers but its advantages may today be regarded as outweighed by the laboriousness of the procedure, slowing the speed of case disposal.[29]

(c) Social security — Refusal of benefit claim *(KEY = 1/3/6/9)*

- Decisions on most benefit claims are made by local Department of Social Security (DSS) officers or by computers, in either case on behalf of the Secretary of State, (Social Security Act (SSA) 1998, ss.1, 2).

- Under SSA 1998, s.12(2) a dissatisfied claimant (and in sick or maternity pay cases the employer concerned) has a right to appeal on the merits to a ["unified"] appeal tribunal (UAT).[30] UATs are composed of a legally qualified chairman sitting with 2 lay members with relevant experience from "employer" and "employee" perspectives respectively.

- The appellant(s), the Secretary of State or the claimant's trade union may appeal on point of law against the UAT decision to a Social Security Commissioner, but only with leave (permission) of the UAT chairman or the Commissioner (SSA 1998, s.14). Commissioners are full-time, independent lawyers experienced in the field and appointed by the Lord Chancellor.

- There is a further law appeal to the Court of Appeal with leave of the Commissioner or the court: SSA, section 15.

Social security appeal provision thus varies in two respects from the paradigm under which a single merits appeal is followed by a law appeal to the High Court:

(i) The "pre-court" appeal on law to the Commissioner. By providing this second tribunal appeal Parliament was attempting to achieve consistency of decision making within the

---

[28] Emery and Smythe, *JR*, p. 42.
[29] LCR 226 (1994), paras 12.6–12.10.
[30] Replacing Social Security Appeal Tribunals and other tribunals: SSA 1998, s.4.

social security system. The appeal is "law only" so as to restrict the number of appeals going to the Commissioners (the further constraint of leave was introduced by the 1998 Act) and so as not to defeat the object and duplicate the work of UATs. But, as will be seen in *section D* below, this can jeopardise the achievement of consistency.

(ii) Provision of appeal from the Commissioners to the Court of Appeal rather than to the High Court acknowledges the status and expertise of the Commissioners.

(d) Immigration — refusal of entry or deportation *(KEY: 1/3/7/9)*

- Under the Immigration Act (IA) 1971, s.3, persons with no right of abode[31] in the United Kingdom require leave to enter from an immigration officer (section 4) at the point of entry.

- Different levels of appeal provision (or none) exist for persons refused entry, granted limited or conditional leave, or ordered to be deported for breach of limit or condition or for "the public good",[32] The most extensive level of provision exists in cases of refusal of entry and of deportation order for breach of condition.

- A merits appeal to an immigration adjudicator (one of a panel of independent officers appointed by the Lord Chancellor) is available to a person ordered to be deported for breach of condition (IA 1971, s.15) and (subject to exceptions[33]) to a person refused leave to enter (*ibid.*, section 13). In the latter case, however, a person with neither current entry clearance nor a work permit must return to his country of origin and mount the appeal from there (section 13(3)).

- Under IA 1971, s.20 any party to an appeal to an adjudicator has a further merits appeal (with leave[34]) to the Immigration Appeal Tribunal (IAT) consisting of a legally qualified chairman and two other members all appointed by the Lord Chancellor.

- Since 1993 (Asylum and Immigration Appeals Act, section 9) any party to the IAT appeal may appeal (with leave) to the Court of Appeal against a "final determination" of the IAT "on any question of law material to that determination." The previous absence of any appeal from the IAT was thought to have engendered a disproportionate number of AJRs against IAT rulings.[35]

These provisions differ from the paradigm as follows:

(i) Two merits appeals rather than a single one reflects not only the importance of the subject matter but also the need to achieve consistency of decision. The requirement of leave for IAT appeals is designed to prevent overload.

(ii) The law appeal to the Court of Appeal rather than to the High Court again acknowledges the status of the IAT which, however, may need further enhancement if confidence in the quality of its adjudication is to be reflected in a reduction of AJRs against its rulings.[36]

---

[31] Defined in, s.2.

[32] ss.15(5), 17(1).

[33] There is no appeal for persons unsuccessfully claiming a right of abode based on residence or parentage or for visitors or prospective students without places: Asylum and Immigration Appeals Act 1993, s.10.

[34] S.I. 1984 No. 2041, s.14.

[35] LCR 226 (1994), paras 2.16, 2.23; Bamforth (1995). But *cf.* below.

[36] *Cf.* Blake and Sunkin (1998).

(e) Employment — unfair dismissal, racial or sex discrimination in employment *(KEY: 2/4/9)*

- An employee alleging unfair dismissal,[37] or a person alleging discrimination in the employment field on grounds of race[38] or sex[39] may complain to an employment tribunal[40] (ET).[41] ETs are composed of a legally qualified chairman sitting with two lay members with relevant experience from management and trade union perspectives respectively.

- The Employment Tribunals Act[42] (ETA) 1996,[43] section 21 provides for an appeal on a question of law to the Employment Appeal Tribunal (EAT) from ET decisions in (*inter alia*) these cases. The EAT is composed of a High Court judge sitting with two employment relations experts appointed by the Lord Chancellor.

- There is a further law appeal to the Court of Appeal with leave of the EAT or the court: ETA, section 37.

These provisions differ from the paradigm as follows:

(i) The initial official decision (since there is already a dispute between parties) is that of a statutory tribunal rather than, as in the other examples, an administrative authority. Here, then, the ET is not an appeal tribunal but the initial decision-making body.

(ii) There is no merits appeal. This is unsatisfactory not only in terms of general principle but also, as will be explained, because inconsistencies between decisions of different ETs can often not be resolved by the EAT whose jurisdiction is confined to correction of error of law. As will be seen, the EAT has found itself somewhat constrained by this.

3 SUMMARY

Where statute provides an avenue of appeal against an official decision (whether of an administrative authority, a tribunal or a court) the most common level of provision is **a single appeal on the merits** to an appeal tribunal or court whose expertise relates to the matter at issue, with **any further provision** commonly restricted to an appeal **on point of law only** to the High Court or Court of Appeal (and thence, with leave, to the House of Lords in cases raising important points of law). Examples *a* and *b* above (Planning and Income Tax) illustrate this paradigm.

Examples *c, d and e* show that for administrative appeals this structure is often varied, perhaps by inserting a "pre-court" appeal on law (*e.g.* to Social Security Commissioners or to the EAT); or by giving no merits appeal (*e.g.* from ETs to the EAT); or by making a merits appeal subject to leave (*e.g.* from an immigration adjudicator to the IAT). These variations reflect the legislators' views in specific contexts on the optimum "division of labour" or boundaries of competence — with reference to expertise, cost and speed of adjudication — between courts on the one hand and tribunals or inquiries on the other.

---

[37] Employment Rights Act (ERA) 1996, Pt X.

[38] Race Relations Act (RRA) 1976, Pt II.

[39] Sex Discrimination Act (SDA) 1975, Pt II.

[40] "Industrial tribunal" until re-named by Employment Rights (Dispute Resolution) Act 1998, s.1(1).

[41] Respectively: ERA, s.111; SDA, s.63; RRA, s.54.

[42] Enacted as the Industrial Tribunals Act 1996; re-named by the Employment Rights (Dispute Resolution) Act 1998, s.1(2).

[43] Under, s.1 of which ETs are now established.

C THE APPELLATE JURISDICTION OF COURTS[44]

Having surveyed the general structure of appeal provision it will be useful now to focus more sharply on the appellate jurisdiction of courts and to explain more fully what appeal role Parliament has conferred on them.

1 APPEALS TO COURTS FROM OTHER COURTS

When courts are given statutory jurisdiction to hear **merits** appeals from decisions of other courts, those appeals are in areas (private law and criminal law) where courts are regarded as having special expertise and consequently have original ("first instance") as well as appellate jurisdiction.

In both civil and criminal appeals there is broadly the same "one appeal on the merits, then law only" structure as in the case of administrative appeals (see *TABLE 1*).

In civil matters an unsuccessful party is commonly able (in almost all cases now subject to leave[45]) to appeal on the merits ("by way of rehearing") from the court of first instance (county court or High Court) to the Court of Appeal (Civil Division). The rehearing is normally "on the documents", *i.e.* the Court of Appeal does not rehear witnesses but proceeds on the basis of transcripts or notes of their evidence. Consequently, on such appeals, the court will rarely differ from the first instance judge's assessment of the credibility and reliability of witnesses. On the other hand, the Court of Appeal is in as good a position as the trial judge to draw inferences of fact from witnesses' testimony and will also substitute its own rulings on questions of law when it finds that the lower court has erred.[46] A party may appeal from the Court of Appeal to the House of Lords with the leave of either court. Leave is commonly given only where a case raises a point of law of some doubt or difficulty.

Turning to criminal matters, a person convicted in a magistrates' court is entitled to a complete witness rehearing in the Crown Court from which he or the prosecution may appeal by case stated on point of law to the High Court and thence to the House of Lords (with leave of either court) on a point of law of general public importance. Either prosecutor or defendant may appeal directly from a magistrates' court to the High Court on point of law. For trials on indictment in the Crown Court, there is no appeal against an acquittal by a jury. But a convicted person may appeal to the Court of Appeal (Criminal Division) as of right on point of law and otherwise with leave of that court. Either prosecutor or defendant may appeal from the Court of Appeal to the House of Lords if the Court of Appeal certifies that a point of law of general public importance is involved and, in addition, either court gives leave.

2 APPEALS TO COURTS FROM STATUTORY TRIBUNALS

As regards matters within the remit of statutory tribunals: here, by contrast, courts do not have special expertise; do not have first instance jurisdiction; and where they have appeal jurisdiction it is **almost always confined to correcting error of law**. In these circumstances "an appeal to the courts on matters of fact would not . . . be desirable since it would constitute an appeal from a body expert in the subject to a relatively inexpert body".[47] On the other hand, during the last 30

---

[44] Bailey and Gunn, *ELS*, Chap. 17.
[45] Practice Direction [1999] 2 All E.R. 490, para. 2.1.2: expressly authorised under Access to Justice Act 1999, s.54.
[46] Practice Direction [1999] 2 All E.R. 490, para. 2.10.
[47] Franks, para. 105.

years governments have legislated ever more frequently to provide for rights of appeal on point of law from statutory tribunals to the High Court or (in the case of tribunals of particular eminence such as the Social Security Commissioners or the EAT) directly to the Court of Appeal. The Tribunals and Inquiries Act 1958 (now replaced by the Tribunals and Inquiries Act 1992) was a landmark. It provided, as section 11 of the 1992 Act[48] now provides, for appeal on point of law from specified[49] tribunals to the High Court (from which, under the ordinary court appellate structure, appeal lies to the Court of Appeal and, ultimately, the House of Lords). There had been similar isolated provisions in earlier statutes, but since 1958 such statutory provisions have become commonplace and now far outnumber the TIA coverage.

Among High Court "law" appeals derived from the TIA are those regarding many types of residential home licences, some education issues, some health and safety at work, and some national health issues. However many statutes conferring decision-making powers on public authorities will make their own special provision for appeals to a court on point of law (*e.g. examples a–e* in *section B 2* above).

A valuable rule of thumb is:

- WHEN IN DOUBT AS TO THE EXISTENCE OF AN APPEAL ON LAW FROM A STATUTORY TRIBUNAL TO THE HIGH COURT, ALWAYS CHECK TIA, S.11 AND SCHEDULE 1.

3 APPEALS TO COURTS FROM OTHER PUBLIC AUTHORITIES

Appeals to courts from public authorities other than courts or statutory tribunals are **commonly restricted to point of law**. The reason is the same as for tribunal appeals: the courts are regarded as competent to review answers given by administrative authorities to questions of law but not to questions of fact or judgment ("degree").

So, *e.g.*, there is provision for law appeals in many planning matters from the Secretary of State (himself often acting as an appellate tribunal from a local authority — see *example a* in *section B2* above) to the High Court on point of law.[50] And prior to the simplification of the social security appeals process by the Social Security Act 1998, on some social security questions (*e.g.*, whether certain contribution conditions are satisfied[51]) one could appeal on point of law from the Secretary of State to the High Court rather than to a UAT.

There is a significant category of exceptions to the general rule that appeals to courts in the administrative law context are restricted to point of law. Many[52] administrative functions of a sort discharged in the past by justices of the peace are today conferred by statute upon local authorities. Examples are the licensing of public entertainments,[53] of street trading[54] and of a variety of trades or occupations, *e.g.* sale of certain foods[55] and child minding, [56] No doubt because of local courts' experience in discharging such functions, and albeit that their discharge involves considerable elements of discretion, Parliament commonly provides for an appeal on the merits[57]

---

[48] *Section B 1 c* above.
[49] TIA 1992, s.11 and Sched. 1.
[50] TCPA 1990, ss.288–290.
[51] See the legislation at issue in *Social Security Secretary v. Scully* [1992] 4 All E.R. 1.
[52] But not all, *e.g.* liquor licensing: Licensing Act 1964.
[53] Local Government (Miscellaneous Provisions) Act 1982, s.1 and Sched. 1.
[54] *ibid.*, s.3 and Sched. 4.
[55] Food Safety Act 1990, s.19 and regulations made thereunder.
[56] Children Act 1989, s.71.
[57] *Sutton LBC v. Davis* [1995] 1 All E.R. 53 citing a number of examples of such appeals.

from the local authority to a magistrates' court and thence to the Crown Court on the merits or direct to the High Court on point of law.[58] Appeals on some matters, *e.g.* taxi licensing, are to the Crown Court direct.[59] Further appeal (commonly to a Queen's Bench Divisional Court) is, however, invariably restricted to point of law.

Note finally an important case in which Parliament has provided a merits appeal from an administrative authority with local jurisdiction directly to the civil courts. A district auditor may certify that a loss or deficiency in local authority accounts has been "caused by the wilful misconduct of any person" who must make recompense, as *e.g.* in May 1996 in the Westminster City Council "homes for votes" gerrymandering scandal. The surcharged individual has a full merits appeal to the county court or High Court (according to the amount in question).[60] From these courts there is the usual appeal to the Court of Appeal, which in April 1999 overturned the auditor's finding in the Westminster case.[61] In the absence of wilful misconduct, surcharges for unlawful items of account may be imposed only by the High Court on an application by the auditor for a declaration.[62]

4 SUMMARY ON APPELLATE REVIEW JURISDICTION OF COURTS

Parliament allocates appellate jurisdiction by reference to the competence of the particular court or tribunal concerned. In the context of administrative appeals, Parliament almost always allocates merits appeals to specialist tribunals but subjects those tribunals to law appeals to the High Court or Court of Appeal. As already stated, "merits" includes every aspect of a decision: findings of fact and of law; inferences drawn from facts found; exercises of judgment in applying law to facts; exercises of discretion. "Law" is plainly a far narrower concept. The question which now must be considered is: what is an error of law, and how are such errors to be distinguished from errors of other kinds?

D   WHAT COUNTS AS ERROR OF LAW?

1 IMPORTANCE OF THE QUESTION

As will now be clear, it is vital to understand the distinction between official errors of law and other errors. For the jurisdiction of courts to review administrative action is a jurisdiction confined, very largely, to the correction of errors of law. This is true not only of the courts' statutory appellate review jurisdiction, described above, but also of their common law (non-statutory) judicial review jurisdiction described in later chapters. Accordingly the reported cases referred to in this section to illustrate the notion of error of law are drawn from not only the statutory but also the common law review jurisdiction.

As will be explained, courts have this error of law jurisdiction over the administrative process because courts are regarded as being specially competent to correct legal error. Other aspects of administrative decision making are outside their special competence.

Put most simply, an error of law is an error by a deciding authority as to what the relevant law is or means: an error as to the statement or understanding of an applicable legal rule. An official

---

[58] Magistrates' Courts Act 1980, s.111 (case stated — *section B 2 b* above).
[59] See *Kelly v. Wirral MBC, The Times*, May 13, 1996.
[60] Local Government Finance Act 1982, s.20: see *Lloyd v. McMahon* [1987] 1 All E.R. 1118.
[61] *Porter v. Magill, The Times*, May 6, 1999.
[62] Under *ibid.*, s.19: see, *e.g. Hazell v. Hammersmith and Fulham L.B.C.* [1991] 1 All E.R. 545.

decision which is based on or reflects such error may be said to be wrong, or erroneous, in law. At what points in a decision-making process may an authority err in law; and how may errors of law be detected?

2 DECIDING AN ISSUE: THREE STAGES

Where a question is essentially whether or not a particular set of facts falls within a general category or concept, one may identify three stages in the resolution of the issue. The decision maker will have to [1] determine the relevant facts; [2] ascertain the relevant legal rules defining the category in question; and then [3] apply them to determine whether the facts fall within the category. Examples of such "category questions" which will be met below are whether a particular individual, X, is or is not an "employee" of Y or a "member of the family" of Z. Or whether a particular business transaction is for tax purposes a "trade".

As will now be shown, error of law may appear or occur at any of the three stages in answering a category question. Notice first, however, that many questions are not of the sort "Does a particular X fall within a general category Y?" Rather, they are questions of policy or discretion: which of a number of possible courses should be chosen? As will be explained later in this chapter, a modified version of the "three stage" analysis can be used to explain the notion of error of law in resolving such questions.

3 ERROR OF LAW IN FINDING FACTS

An authority errs in law if in the course of establishing the facts upon which it must proceed it breaches any evidential or other legal rule governing its fact-finding process, *e.g.*, in *Jeyaretnam v. Singapore Law Society*[63] the sole opposition MP to the Lee Kuan Yeu regime in Singapore had been convicted of accounting offences. The Privy Council held that the conviction was vitiated by error of law: the court had erred in law in finding certain facts on the basis of simple affidavit evidence whereas a solemn form of oath was prescribed for witnesses.

It is also an error of law to find facts on the basis of no evidence at all.[64] In *R. v. E Midlands Legal Aid Committee, ex p. McKenna*[65] an application for legal aid in civil proceedings was rejected by the Committee because it found as a fact that the applicant (the claimant in the civil proceedings) had rejected a settlement offer of £2000 from the defendant. On AJR the court quashed the Committee's decision for error of law because the Committee had received no evidence to support its finding. In fact the defendant had made a provisional offer which merely averaged £2000 among many claimants.

4 MISSTATING THE LAW

If a decision maker chooses to incorporate in his decision an express statement of what he regards as the relevant legal rules, he will err in law if he misstates those rules.

(a) Erroneous statement

Plainly a misstatement of what is the current statutory provision or case law on a matter is an error of law, *e.g.*, suppose that a local DSS adjudication officer rejects a claim by reference to a statutory

---

[63] [1989] 2 All E.R. 193.
[64] Practice Direction [1999] 2 All E.R. 490, para. 2.9.
[65] *The Times*, December 20, 1989.

provision which, he has not realised, has recently undergone a crucial amendment. Or that a local authority rejects an application under the homeless persons legislation in ignorance of a recent House of Lords decision on the correct meaning of "intentionally homeless" in that legislation.

(b) Erroneous elucidation

Equally, if a decision is based on an express interpretation by the decision-maker of a rule or an element of a rule, and a review court regards the interpretation as erroneous, the error is an error of law,[66] *i.e.* an error in stating the relevant legal rules. So, in *Dyson Holdings Ltd v. Fox*[67] a county court judge had held that for the purposes of the Rent Act 1968 the defendant was not a "member of the family" of the man with whom she had lived as if she were his wife for 40 years. It followed that the defendant was not entitled to Rent Act protection as a statutory tenant by succession when the man died. On appeal by the defendant on point of law the Court of Appeal reversed the county court. The judge had erred in law in treating the word "family" in the statute as a technical legal term whose meaning was fixed by a Court of Appeal decision in 1950. On the contrary, the word "family" bore its ordinary meaning. That meaning might change from time to time, and at any given time was to be established by judicial notice of how (at that time) the word was commonly used. The common usage of the word family had changed since 1950 so as to include a person such as the defendant even though she had no legal relationship to the deceased.

5 Error of law in applying law to facts

(a) Decision discloses error of law

Very commonly a decision-making authority will reach a decision without expressly *either* stating *or* setting out its understanding of the relevant law. But even where a decision contains no statement (and therefore no misstatement) of the decision maker's view of the applicable law, he must have a view. For the decision is nothing other than an application of law to facts. Sometimes it will be possible to show that in reaching a particular decision on certain facts the decision maker must have misunderstood the law. In these circumstances one may say that the error of law manifests itself at the stage of application of law to facts. How may this occur?

In *Edwards v. Bairstow*[68] a taxpayer had bought land for the purpose (later fulfilled) of re-selling it at a profit. He was assessed to tax on the basis that the profit was a profit of "trade". The General Commissioners allowed his appeal, but on appeal on point of law by the revenue, the House of Lords (reversing the High Court and Court of Appeal) held that the Commissioners had erred in law. A transaction whose sole purpose was resale for profit was the very paradigm of "trade". So, in deciding that the transaction in question was not trade, the Commissioners must have misunderstood the meaning of trade. (Although the Commissioners had not said expressly how they understood the statutory concept of trade, the indications from the case stated were that they thought the fact that the transaction was a "one-off" rather than the taxpayer's ordinary trade deprived it of the nature of trade.[69])

(b) The problem of "open texture"

It is crucial to realise that here the House of Lords was not "second-guessing" the Commissioners, *i.e.* the authority empowered by statute finally to determine the merits of the case. The House stressed the "open texturedness" of many rules and legal categories. As Lord Radcliffe said[70]:

[66] *Shah v. Barnet LBC* [1983] 1 All E.R. 226 at 233e (Lord Scarman); Emery and Smythe, *JR*, p. 105.
[67] [1975] 3 All E.R. 1030.
[68] [1955] 3 All E.R. 48.
[69] *ibid.*, p. 52E.
[70] *ibid.*, pp. 55–56.

"[T]he law does not supply a precise definition of the word 'trade' . . . In effect it lays down the limits within which it would be permissible to say that a 'trade' . . . does or does not exist. But the field so marked out is a wide one and there are many combinations of circumstances in which it could not be said to be wrong to arrive at a conclusion one way or the other. If the facts of any particular case are fairly capable of being so described, it seems to me that it necessarily follows that the determination . . . that a trade does or does not exist is not 'erroneous in point of law' . . .

All these cases in which the facts warrant a determination either way can be described as questions of degree and therefore as questions of fact."

These observations on the word "trade" apply equally to a vast range of legal categories of which the following are but random further examples[71]: "family", "employment", "ordinarily resident", "intentionally homeless", "park [land]", "[industrial] plant", "[building] alteration".

The matter may be put simply as follows. If one takes any general category it will be possible to envisage three types of particular situation: those which clearly do fit within the category; those which clearly do not; and those which arguably do but arguably do not.[72] For brevity these types will be referred to as "clearly yes", "clearly no" and "maybe". *Edwards v. Bairstow* says that if a decision maker classifies a "clearly yes" case as "no" or a "clearly no" case as "yes", he errs in law, for the classification shows that the decision maker has incorrectly understood the legal limits or parameters of the category.[73] In both "clearly yes" and "clearly no" cases "the law requires a particular answer"[74] (*i.e.*, "yes" or "no", as the case may be). Not so in "maybe" cases, for to classify a "maybe" case either way is not to err in law — either answer is within the parameters of the category. This merely reflects the open-texturedness, the relative imprecision, of verbal categories and acknowledges the inability of the law to supply highly precise definitions to fit all imaginable cases.

In *Edwards v. Bairstow* the Commissioners erred in law in deciding that a transaction which fell clearly within the category "trade" was outside the category. Consider by contrast the following "maybe" case. Suppose that X is working for Y. Certain statutory protections (*e.g.* against unfair dismissal) are available only to an employee (a person with a "contract of service") and not to a self-employed person hiring out his services to another (under a "contract for services"). Thus the question may arise whether X is or is not an employee of Y.

In *O'Kelly v. Trusthouse Forte plc*[75] an employment tribunal had decided that certain waiters hired by Forte on a weekly basis were not employees. It appeared[76] that the tribunal had treated the following features of the contract as "**pro-employment**": [1] the high degree of Forte control over the waiters' work activities; [2] their representation in the staff/company consultation process; [3] provision of clothing and equipment by Forte; [4] payment weekly in arrear with deduction of tax and national insurance. On the other hand the tribunal treated the following as **counter-indications**: [5] no regular wage: payment depended on work done from week to week; [6] no sick pay, pension rights or other fringe benefits enjoyed by permanent staff; [7] no mutuality of obligation to provide or accept work.

Allowing the waiters' appeal, the Employment Appeal Tribunal (EAT) held that the employment tribunal had erred in law because both the legal meaning of "employment" and the correct

[71] Taken from cases discussed in Emery and Smythe, *JR*, Chap. 3.
[72] Emery and Smythe, *JR*, p. 108.
[73] *ibid.*, pp. 115–116.
[74] Endicott (1998), p. 317.
[75] [1983] 3 All E.R. 456.
[76] *ibid.*, p. 464.

application of the concept to particular cases were questions of law. In the EAT's view the tribunal had applied the test incorrectly, so had erred in law.

But the Court of Appeal allowed Forte's appeal on law against the EAT's ruling. The EAT were wrong in holding that any "incorrect" application of the legal concept of employment, *i.e.* any application with which it disagreed — was an error of law. The employment tribunal had correctly identified all the relevant features of the contract. Since these pointed both ways, the case was in effect of the "maybe" type. The tribunal had not erred in law in deciding that the waiters were not employees; nor would it have done had it decided the other way. Only had there been a merits appeal could the EAT have properly reversed the tribunal's decision.

The same analysis would no doubt have applied if, *e.g.*, the taxpayer in *Edwards v. Bairstow* had purchased the land with a number of possible courses in mind, including its use as business premises or its resale for profit.

As already explained, in *Edwards v. Bairstow* itself the Commissioners erred in law by answering a "clearly yes" question in the negative. Obversely, in *Davies v. Presbyterian Church of Wales*[77] an employment tribunal erred in law by answering a "clearly no" question in the affirmative.[78] The tribunal had held that a Welsh presbyterian minister was an employee of his Church. The House of Lords confirmed the view of the EAT and Court of Appeal that the tribunal decision showed a misunderstanding of the legal concept of employment in failing to take account of the absence from the relationship of what is an essential feature of any contract: an intention to create legal relations.

(c) The Edwards v. Bairstow doctrine: rationale and objections[79]

(i) *Rationale*

All legal definitions (whether statutory or case law, or both, and however detailed) are more or less open-textured, *i.e.* they contain terms which are to some extent imprecise — so that it is always possible to cite particular cases which arguably do and arguably do not fall within those terms.

The *Edwards v. Bairstow* doctrine is simply that although a reviewing authority (tribunal or court) might legitimately disagree with a particular classification, one way or the other, within this open-textured area, it may not express its disagreement by categorising the classification as "wrong in law". For a decision either way in the open-textured area cannot be said to indicate that the decision maker has misunderstood the law, merely that he has gone one way rather than another within an area not precisely covered by the terms of the legal definition.

This means that if the reviewing authority has "merits" jurisdiction it may reverse the decision but if it has only "law" jurisdiction it may not.

(ii) *Objections*

Wade[80] **and Mureinik**[81]   argue that the *Edwards v. Bairstow* doctrine is illogical because as a matter of logic any error in rule application is an error of law. For an official decision is a statement of "what the law is" in the case in question. If in the opinion of a review court or tribunal the decision is wrong it is by definition wrong in law.

This objection fails to recognise that the process of defining what counts as error of law in the administrative law context (as in any other) is not a matter of *a priori* logic but, rather of shaping a

---

[77] [1986] 1 All E.R. 705. See also *Carmichael v. National Power plc* [1998] I.R.L.R. 301.

[78] See also *Kirkham v. Williams* [1991] 4 All E.R. 240: a mirror image of *Edwards v. Bairstow*.

[79] Emery and Smythe, *JR*, pp. 121–126; de Smith, *JRAA*, pp. 277–289.

[80] Wade and Forsyth, *AL*, pp. 946 *et seq.*

[81] (1982) 98 L.Q.R. 587.

concept to a purpose: the purpose of defining the sphere of competence of those bodies with jurisdiction over "law" as against that of those with jurisdiction over "merits". The doctrine grew up as a means of defining courts' "error of law" jurisdiction in administrative appeals. Since, as will be seen, the common law judicial review jurisdiction is now essentially a jurisdiction to correct errors of law, the doctrine defines that jurisdiction too. It is a way of acknowledging that in the administrative law context, matters of judgment are best left to the experts in a particular field. It is a way also of asserting that the ordinary courts are the most appropriate authorities to be charged with the definition of the limits of meaning of statutory language in the administrative law context, as in other contexts. This is no doubt debatable, but can be defended by reference to the superior[82] courts' breadth of experience in the field of statutory interpretation and their familiarity with developments in legislative techniques.[83]

One may note in passing that the House of Lords in *Edwards v. Bairstow* accepted that, as Denning L.J. pointed out in *British Launderers' Research Association v. Hendon Rating Authority*[84] some decisions (some applications of rules of law to fact situations) raise legal points of such difficulty and technicality (*e.g.* obscure points of property or trusts law) that only trained lawyers can resolve them. Here, the application of law to facts is in itself a matter of law, so that if an appeal court with jurisdiction to correct errors of law simply disagrees with the lower court's decision it can regard that court as having erred in law. The *Edwards v. Bairstow* doctrine is inapplicable in such cases, but in administrative law the standard case is not of this type. The composition of any particular authority reflects the legislature's judgment that persons with the specified qualifications and experience are best equipped to apply the law in the context in question. In administrative law the legislature routinely allocates to authorities consisting of or including non-lawyers the task of applying law to facts. Self-evidently the legislature regards the task as capable of being done by non-lawyers. It follows, as the *Edwards v. Bairstow* doctrine acknowledges, that such an authority does not err in law when applying law to facts simply because a court would have reached a different result, but only where the decision indicates that the decision maker has incorrectly understood the legal limits or parameters of the category in question.

Beatson[85] suggests that the doctrine is too imprecise to serve as an "organising principle"[86] enabling one to predict where the line between law and merits will be drawn in any particular case.

The force of this objection turns on whether, on studying the case law, one thinks that the courts commonly manipulate the "clearly yes" and "clearly no" boundaries of particular concepts so as to assert or decline review jurisdiction on an entirely pragmatic case by case basis. The cases discussed above and elsewhere[87] suggest the contrary and that administrative authorities and tribunals are able to operate on a day to day basis with a considerable measure of certainty over wide areas of their jurisdiction as to where the line will be drawn between law and judgment ("degree"). Two important caveats are however required:

   (i) As always, there will be cases where the highest courts will ignore doctrinal boundaries for pragmatic reasons in particular cases. *Smith v. Abbott*,[88] considered below, is a case in point.

---

[82] *i.e.*, High Court and above: see Chap. 3, *section B 1 d.*
[83] Emery and Smythe, *JR*, pp. 163–164; *cf.* Hare (1998), p. 131.
[84] [1949] 1 All E.R. 21.
[85] (1984) 4 O.J.L.S. 22.
[86] *ibid.*, p. 43.
[87] Emery and Smythe, *JR*, pp. 117–121.
[88] [1994] 1 All E.R. 673.

(ii) "[T]here is always a penumbra of uncertainty in the meaning of statutory words. But the very notion of penumbra implies the existence of areas which clearly are, and others which clearly are not, in shade. The precise extent of the penumbra, of the open-texture of statutory provision, can be established only by authoritative rulings in particular cases."[89]

Pitt[90] objects that the *Edwards v. Bairstow* doctrine fails to "take rights seriously". It is, she says, an abdication of a court's responsibility to dismiss an appeal (as in *O'Kelly v. Trusthouse Forte*) against a decision which it may believe to be wrong simply because it is a decision whose wrongness (or rightness) is a matter of judgment or "appreciation".

This objection may be answered as follows. The quintessential feature of the *Edwards v. Bairstow* doctrine is that it recognises that within their fields administrative authorities and tribunals have a competence and expertise on matters of fact and judgment which cannot be matched in the ordinary courts. Thus, in so far as the doctrine draws a "competence line" between the ordinary courts on the one hand and administrative authorities and tribunals on the other, far from not taking rights seriously, the doctrine takes them seriously enough to leave specialist judgments in specialist hands.

However, the objection does have force where, as in *O'Kelly*, the doctrine is applied so as to restrict the jurisdiction of a higher statutory tribunal to correct what it perceives to be the error of a lower tribunal. In areas such as social security, immigration and employment (see *examples c–e* in *section B 2* above) Parliament has sought to achieve consistency in the law applied by a very large number of local first instance tribunals by providing for appeal from such tribunals to a higher tribunal. One way to avoid congesting the higher tribunal with more appeals than it can handle is (as with the Social Security Commissioners and the Employment Appeal Tribunal) to restrict appeals to point of law. But if, as ruled by the Court of Appeal in *O'Kelly*, "error of law" in this context is interpreted according to *Edwards v. Bairstow*, the jurisdiction of the higher tribunal is unacceptably restricted. Large companies like Trusthouse Forte may well hire casual staff on identical terms all over the country. As Pitt explains,[91] the very question of judgment answered in one way by the London employment tribunal in *O'Kelly* might be answered in the opposite way by an employment tribunal in, say, Liverpool. If neither answer is wrong in law, neither may be corrected by the EAT. In the result, casual waiters in Croydon would have fewer employment rights than casual waiters in Crosby engaged on identical terms.

One way to avoid unjust anomalies of this kind would be for statute to confer "merits" rather than "law" jurisdiction on such tribunals as the EAT and Social Security Commissioners, avoiding congestion by subjecting appeals to a leave requirement as with the Immigration Appeal Tribunal. Another solution, not requiring statutory change, would be for the courts to reverse *O'Kelly* and to rule that within any particular hierarchy of specialist tribunals, "error of law" is to be interpreted according to the *British Launderers'* rather than the *Edwards v. Bairstow* doctrine: the latter would continue to apply in determining the "law" jurisdiction of the ordinary courts on appeals from the highest level of specialist appeal tribunals. The effect of this would be that senior specialist tribunals like the EAT and Social Security Commissioners would be able to correct any errors of application by lower tribunals, while the ordinary courts (with no special expertise in such fields as employment and social security law) would be restricted to the more "hands-off" *Edwards v. Bairstow* approach.

---

[89] Emery and Smythe, *JR*, p. 123; see also Endicott (1998) p. 317.
[90] (1985) 101 L.Q.R. 217.
[91] (1985) 101 L.Q.R. at pp. 231–232, citing *Nethermere Ltd v. Taverna* [1984] I.R.L.R. 240, discussed at *ibid.*, pp. 221–223.

AVOIDING AN ANOMALY

The "same terms, different rights" anomaly can of course arise not only where (as in the employment context) there is provision for appeal to a higher specialist tribunal from each of a large number of local appeal tribunals, but also where (as in the income tax context) the only appeal from a local tribunal is to the ordinary courts on point of law. In *Fitzpatrick v. IRC No. 2; Smith v. Abbott* [1994] 1 All E.R. 673, English and Scottish tax commissioners had reached opposite answers to the question whether journalists bought newspapers and periodicals in order to *prepare* themselves to carry out their journalistic duties or, on the contrary, as part of the *performance* of those duties. The English commissioners said the latter (relieving the journalists of liability to pay tax on that part of their income paid to them by their employers for the purpose of newspaper purchase); the Scottish commissioners took the opposite view with the opposite result. Lord Templeman in the House of Lords (hearing the separate law appeals together) said that the English and Scottish commissioners "cannot both be right. The facts of all the . . . cases were indistinguishable. . . . The deductibility of the expenses of purchasing newspapers by thousands of journalists cannot vary from journalist to journalist according to the composition or differing views of different commissioners" (*at p. 679). The House held (by 4:1) that the Scottish Commissioners were correct.*

Upon examination, *Smith v. Abbott* appears to be (as the English Court of Appeal, the Scottish Court of Session and Lord Browne-Wilkinson dissenting in the House of Lords (see especially *ibid.*, at pp. 692–693) held) a "maybe" case like *O'Kelly*. It may thus be regarded as a case in which a commonsense result was reached at the cost of the ordinary courts assuming a jurisdiction over issues of judgment for which they are equipped neither by the statutory terms of their appellate jurisdiction nor by the expertise of their members. It is difficult to see how a consistent and satisfactory body of law can develop in such areas without the statutory creation of a higher specialist tribunal between local tribunals and the ordinary courts.

6 OTHER TYPES OF ERROR OF LAW

(a) Error of law in exercising discretion

So far this section has focused on the identification of errors of law in deciding "category questions", *i.e.* questions as to whether or not a particular set of facts falls within a general category or concept. But, as was said above, many questions are not of this sort. Rather, they are questions of policy or "discretion": which of a number of available courses should be chosen?

Since this chapter deals with appeals, and since, as has been explained, statute tends to provide for appeals only against decisions which have an immediate and direct impact on individuals, it will be instructive to draw some examples of discretionary decisions from cases of this sort.

(i) *Examples of discretionary powers*

There is commonly a substantial element of discretion in official powers to grant or refuse various types of **licences** — and, if granting, to decide what if any conditions to impose. Examples already referred to in this chapter are the licensing of liquor sales, public entertainments, street trading, food sales, child minding, and taxis; also the "licensing" of land development by planning permissions.

Again, while many **state benefits** (whether in **cash** or in **kind**) are non-discretionary (*i.e.* can be claimed as of right by prescribed categories of person), many are available only at the discretion of the relevant authority, *e.g.* discretionary social security payments or education or property improvement grants. Also discretionary is the level at which to provide for established needs such as housing for homeless persons, special educational or welfare facilities or NHS medical treatment for those in need, and the protection of children judged to be in danger of abuse.

Examples could be multiplied, but the present concern is to show how in the course of exercising discretion a decision maker may err in law. First, what are the legal nature and limits of "discretion"?

(ii) *"Relevant" and "Irrelevant" considerations*

To say that a decision maker has discretion in taking a particular decision or answering a particular question is to say that the decision or answer is not, so to say, "dictated" by (albeit open-textured) legal rules. The decision maker is, within limits, free to fashion his decision by choosing the weight he will give to an often wide range of (sometimes conflicting) considerations, *e.g.*, planning decisions must be taken by reference not only to the architectural merits of the particular proposal but also to local planning policies, road safety factors and so on. Discretionary benefit allocation must take account of not only individual need but also fair distribution of available resource.[92] All such matters are **"relevant"** or **"proper"** considerations for the decision maker. On the other hand, to grant planning permission for a block of flats only on condition that the developer would make the flats available to persons who were on the local authority's housing waiting list,[93] or to revoke a street-trader's licence, cutting off his livelihood, because he had used abusive language to a council security officer who was reproving him for urinating in a side street when public conveniences were closed,[94] would be to exercise a discretionary power by reference to **"irrelevant"** or **"improper"** considerations, *i.e.*, to use the discretion for a purpose for which it was not granted.

As these examples show, what is relevant or irrelevant will always depend upon a correct appreciation of the **purpose** for which a particular discretion is conferred, a difficult and often controversial issue which will be discussed further in Chapter 4, *Grounds for Judicial Review*,[95] in which context the question most commonly arises. It suffices for present purposes, however, to grasp the broad idea of "relevant" and "irrelevant" considerations. In this connection it is important to note that there are two kinds of "relevant" consideration — mandatory and non-mandatory, *i.e.*, those which must and those which need not but may be taken into account.[96] For unless (which is rare) the statute conferring discretion gives an exhaustive list of relevant considerations, the authority will necessarily have some discretion in its choice, as well as in its balancing, of relevant considerations. Reverting to the examples just given, it would no doubt be permissible (but not mandatory) for a planning authority to take account of research on the social effects of certain types of housing, or for an authority allocating discretionary benefits to take account of research predicting an up-turn or down-turn in particular types of need.

(iii) *"Wrong considerations"* — *error of law in exercising discretion*

Subject to one qualification, error of law in the exercise of discretion means, as Lord Upjohn said in *Padfield v. Minister of Agriculture*,[97] "taking into account some wholly irrelevant or extraneous

---

[92] On the relevance of scarce resources in discretionary benefit allocation see Chap. 4, *section C 3 b.*
[93] *R v. Hillingdon L.B.C., ex p. Royco Ltd* [1974] 2 All E.R. 643.
[94] *R v. Barnsley M.B.C., ex p. Hook* [1976] 3 All E.R. 452.
[95] *Section C 2.*
[96] Irvine (1996 Wed.), p. 67.
[97] [1968] 1 All E.R. 694 at 717F.

consideration, or . . . wholly omitting to take into account a [mandatory][98] relevant consideration". The planning and street trading cases just cited exemplify error of law of the first-mentioned type: shortage of council housing and an isolated and trivial lack of decorum are, respectively, wholly beyond the purposes for which the discretionary powers in question were conferred. Conversely, a benefit-conferring authority would err in law by failing to take account of a relevant consideration if, *e.g.* , it exhausted its annual budget on a "first come, first served" basis without attempting to estimate the likely size of demand over the whole budget period.

Essentially such decisions are erroneous in law (*i.e.* showing erroneous understanding of an applicable legal rule) because, as Lord Reid said in *Padfield*,[99] citing the judgment of Lord Greene M.R. in *Associated Provincial Picture Houses Ltd v. Wednesbury Corporation*,[1] they are made without regard to "those matters which he is bound to consider" or with regard to "matters which are irrelevant to the matter that he has to consider". **For convenience, errors of law of this *Wednesbury/Padfield* type will be referred to as "wrong considerations".** In intervening only on a wrong considerations basis the courts are declining to review the balance struck by the decision-maker in weighing competing relevant considerations against each other or, within limits, the decision maker's choice of what relevant considerations to place in the scales. In the context of discretionary decisions this establishes a "competence line" between administrative authorities and courts similar to that established by the *Edwards v. Bairstow* doctrine[2] in a non-discretionary context.

The qualification mentioned above is that taking account of an irrelevant consideration does not count as an error of law if the decision-maker can show that the decision was based also on relevant considerations which would by themselves have justified the decision,[3] *e.g.* in the *Westminster Corporation* case[4] the corporation decided, taking account of proper considerations, to provide subterranean public conveniences at a particular location. This decision was held lawful even though the corporation had also taken account of the (legally irrelevant) fact that access to the lavatories would provide a pedestrian subway linking two sides of a busy street. The approach currently adopted by the courts is to uphold such a decision unless satisfied that it was "materially"[5] or "substantially"[6] influenced by the irrelevant consideration, as, *e.g.*, in *R. v. Lewisham L.B.C., ex p. Shell United Kingdom Ltd*[7] where the authority had decided to boycott Shell products because of the company's commercial links with the then apartheid regime in South Africa. The Divisional Court[8] held this decision unlawful because it was driven not merely by the council's proper concern to promote good race relations but also by its improper desire to punish the company for its commercial support for apartheid.

(iv) *"Second stage" and "third stage" errors*

It remains to point out that "wrong considerations" errors of law, like "category" errors, may be identifiable either (a) from what the decision maker has said about his understanding of the relevant law; or (b) by a process of inference where, given the facts of a particular case, the

---

[98] Parenthesis added: see previous paragraph.
[99] [1968] 1 All E.R. at 710.
[1] [1947] 2 All E.R. 680.
[2] [1955] 3 All E.R. 48: *subsections 5 b and c* above.
[3] See, *e.g. Westminster Corporation v. LNW Railway Co.* [1905] A.C. 426.
[4] *ibid.*
[5] *R. v. Inner London Education Authority, ex p. Westminster City Council* [1986] 1 All E.R. 19 at 36.
[6] *R. v. Rochdale M.B.C., ex p. Cromer Ltd* [1982] 3 All E.R. 761; *Lewisham* case (next note) at p. 951j.
[7] [1988] 1 All E.R. 938.
[8] *i.e.* a court of two or more judges of the High Court, in this case, of the Queen's Bench Division. Most AJRs are heard in the Queen's Bench Division ("Crown Office List"): see Chap. 5, *section A 1.*

decision reached is one which could not have been reached by an authority who properly understood the law:

e.g. (a) If in a decision letter or in background correspondence the decision maker, while enumerating a number of relevant considerations, consistently fails to mention another (mandatory) relevant consideration, or refers expressly to an irrelevant consideration, one may say that the law has been in effect misstated — the *Royco* and *Hook* cases (above) provide examples of errors of this type.

(b) But, as with category decisions falling within the *Edwards v. Bairstow* doctrine, there may be circumstances where one can point to nothing wrong in what a decision maker has actually said about his understanding of the legal limits of his discretion; but where, nevertheless, "the decision [is] so perverse that no reasonable body *properly directing itself* could have reached such a decision".[9] The words emphasised are critical, pointing out that there may be cases where it can be said by reference to the decision alone that it could not have been reached if the authority had confined itself to considerations relevant to the purpose for which the power was granted. An error of law is thus disclosed. Errors of law of this type are commonly termed "*Wednesbury* unreasonableness" by reference to the judgment of Lord Greene in the *Wednesbury* case[10] where he referred to "a conclusion so unreasonable that no reasonable authority could ever have come to it".[11] This, he observed, "is unreasonable in one sense. In another sense it is taking into consideration extraneous matters".[12]

Consider, *e.g. Williams v. Giddy*[13] where commissioners had discretion to award a civil servant a pension not exceeding one month's pay for each year of service. They awarded Giddy only one penny for each year of a certain period of his service. The reason for this award did not appear from any statement by the commissioners — they were in all probability trying to cover up an initial error in calculating the full period of his service. But as Lord Macnaghten said:[14]

"Whatever their motive may have been . . ., an illusory award such as this — an award intended to be unreal and unsubstantial — though made under guise of exercising discretion, is at best a colourable performance, and tantamount to a refusal by the Board to exercise the discretion entrusted to them by Parliament."

In these circumstances one can see from the decision itself that the decision maker must have applied the wrong test, *i.e.*, based his decision on wrong considerations.

Applying the "three stage" analysis used above,[15] (a) manifests itself as "second stage" error of law — a misstatement of the law; and (b) as "third stage" error — error in applying the law to the facts of a particular case. As with the issue of statutory purpose, the *Wednesbury* analysis will be discussed further in Chapter 4.

---

[9] Browne-Wilkinson L.J. in *Wheeler v. Leicester City Council* [1985] 2 All E.R. at 158 (emphasis added).
[10] See above.
[11] *ibid.*, at 685C.
[12] *ibid.*, at 683A.
[13] [1911] A.C. 381.
[14] *ibid.*, pp. 385–386.
[15] *Sub-section 2.*

(b) Procedural error of law

Statute often makes express provision for detailed rules of procedure to be followed by decision makers. In the absence of such express provision, there are many circumstances in which the courts have held that it is to be implied from the nature of a particular official power that the decision maker must observe basic rules of procedural fairness or "natural justice".

One type of procedural error of law has already been noted, *i.e.* "error of law in finding facts" — *sub-section 3* above where it was explained that an authority errs in law if in the course of establishing the facts upon which it must proceed it breaches any evidential or other legal rule governing its fact-finding process. Other types of procedural error will be dealt with in Chapter 4, *section E, Procedural Impropriety*, but for the sake of completeness it may simply be stated here that a decision maker errs in law by any serious breach of an important express procedural requirement or any breach of the rules of natural justice, or duty to act fairly, where applicable.

7 SUMMARY

Three broad types of error of law have been identified in the above discussion:

[1] "serious procedural errors" — including not only breach of evidential or other rules governing a fact-finding process, but also any serious breach of an important express procedural requirement or any breach of the rules of natural justice, or duty to act fairly, where applicable;

[2] "category errors" — errors in formulating the correct test to apply in answering "category questions";

[3] "wrong considerations" — taking account of legally irrelevant (or failing to take account of legally relevant) considerations in exercising discretionary powers.

It has been explained that errors of types [2] and [3] may appear either:

(a) from what the decision maker has said about his understanding of the relevant law; or

(b) by a process of inference where, given the facts of a particular case, the decision reached is one which could not have been reached by an authority who properly understood the law. In these circumstances one can see from the decision itself that the decision maker must have applied the wrong test or, as the case may be, based his decision on wrong considerations.

TABLE 2 suggests a sequence of questions which if answered in any particular case will establish whether or not an official decision is vitiated by error of law, *i.e.* by an error as to the statement or understanding of an applicable legal rule. The table starts with procedural impropriety because this often conceals errors of substance in a decision: errors of substance may become apparent once procedural irregularities (particularly failures properly to explain a decision) are corrected and the decision-making process becomes transparent.

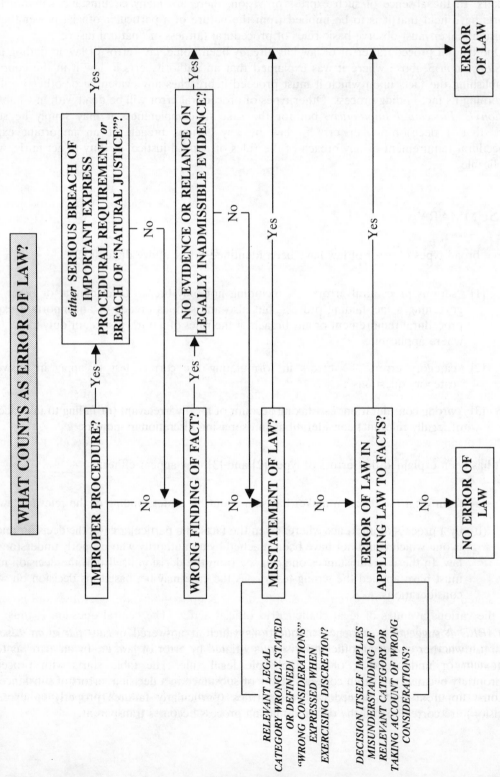

TABLE 2

NOTE: EFFECT OF CORRECTING AN ERROR OF LAW

The point to be made here is that the correction of an error of law may or may not, according to circumstances, settle the issue between the parties.

Suppose that a court or tribunal with jurisdiction to correct only error of law has identified such error in a particular decision. Of course it must correct the error, but does that necessarily dispose of the issue between the parties? Clearly not, *e.g.*, suppose that on facts similar to those of *O'Kelly v. Trusthouse Forte plc* [1983] 3 All E.R. 456 (*sub-section 5 b* above), an employment tribunal were to take account of an extraneous factor or omit to consider a salient one. Correction of this error of law would establish the correct basis for deciding the contract of service/contract for services issue. But it would not decide the issue. Who should decide it? Surely the authority most competent to do so. The principle is, thus, that where after an appeal on law an issue of fact or judgment remains to be decided, the issue should be remitted to the authority with merits jurisdiction (see Emery (1987), p. 271), in this case the employment tribunal. This principle is of course subject to contrary statutory provision which, controversially, has been held to give not only the EAT but also the Court of Appeal jurisdiction to dispose of a case such as that in the above example. See *Shepherd Ltd v. Jerrom* [1986] 3 All E.R. 589; Emery (1987), p. 269.

Contrast a case like *Edwards v. Bairstow* (*sub-section 5 b* above) or *Davies v. Presbyterian Church of Wales (ibid.)* Here, the correction of the error of law "decides the case": once the error has been identified, there is no issue left. In *Edwards* the answer is that the venture is trade; in *Davies*, that the relationship is not employment. So in these cases, there is nothing to remit, and it is proper for the review court to rule to that effect. (See LCR 226 (1994), para. 8.16 recommending the formal recognition of this principle for judicial review as well as appeals.)

The position is similar where the corrected error of law is of the "wrong considerations" rather than the "category" type (see *Emery and Smythe, JR*, pp. 201–205), *e.g.*, in *ex p. Hook*, following the stall-holder's successful AJR, the local authority would be unable to remove his licence on the basis of his abusive retort to the council officer. Contrastingly, in *ex p. Royco*, following the developer's successful AJR of the council's decision to grant permission subject to the housing waiting list condition, the council would remain free to re-decide the planning application and to impose whatever lawful conditions it thought fit.

E CONCLUSION: APPEALS AS A WAY OF CHALLENGING OFFICIAL DECISIONS

As stated in Chapter 1, the prime focus of this book is upon the nature, operation and interaction of the various avenues of legal challenge to official action. The central question is thus: *Where someone has a complaint about a particular action by a person or body of persons in an official, or public, capacity and feels that the time has come to consider some form of legal challenge, what is the best course?*

What can be said on this now that the network of appeal provision has been studied?

In terms of a systematic approach to problem-solving, *i.e.*, when advising a complainant in a particular case, one should always at the outset consider two questions:

[1] Is there an avenue of appeal available against the decision in question? If yes,

[2] Is the appeal on the merits or confined to point of law?

These questions are of prime importance in deciding in all cases what form of legal challenge to pursue because, quite simply, if an appeal is available it is likely to be the only available avenue of challenge. Why is this the case?

- It may be that the complainant is seeking to challenge an official finding of fact or exercise of judgment or discretion in areas where reasonable people may differ. If so, the only chance of mounting a successful legal challenge (complaint to an ombudsman apart) is by "merits" appeal: appeal *not* restricted to point of law.

- Even if the complaint, on analysis, turns out to be that an error of law has been made, the general rule laid down by the courts (as will be explained later[16]) has been that direct[17] challenges must be mounted by way of appeal (where there is one) rather than by AJR. It follows that, generally speaking, only where a challenge, if made out, would entitle the complainant to "private law" (*e.g.*, tort or contract) damages, can he sensibly contemplate raising an appealable error of law collaterally in ordinary civil proceedings rather than directly on appeal. As will be explained in due course[18] malice apart, *e.g.* malicious refusal of a licence or planning permission, it will be rarely[19] that an erroneous decision which is appealable will also give rise to a damages claim.

The conclusion is that, broadly speaking, if there is a statutory avenue of appeal which is capable of yielding a remedy one seeks, one should use it.

[16] Chap. 5, *section C 2.*
[17] For "direct" and "collateral" challenge, see Chap. 1, *section B 2 C.*
[18] Chap. 8, *Official Tort Liability.*
[19] As, *e.g.* in *Hutchings v. Islington L.B.C.* [1998] 3 All E.R. 445.

Chapter 3

JUDICIAL REVIEW — PUBLIC LAW JURISDICTION

Chapter 2 concluded by explaining that, broadly speaking, if there is a statutory avenue of appeal which is capable of yielding a remedy one seeks, one should use it. But what is the position if one seeks to challenge the legality of a particular official decision or other action from which there is no such appeal? This chapter and Chapters 4 and 5 consider in what circumstances recourse may be had to what was described in Chapter 1 as the "residual jurisdiction" of judicial review.

A INTRODUCTION — JUDICIAL REVIEW AND PUBLIC LAW

1 WHAT IS JUDICIAL REVIEW?

In Chapter 1 it was said that since the constitutional settlement of the seventeenth century the High Court[1] has asserted — and, within limits, has been allowed by Parliament to assert — a general common law (non-statutory) jurisdiction to "review" the legality of official action, *i.e.* to decide, in properly constituted legal proceedings, whether or not a particular exercise of official power is authorised by law.

This wide statement raises the following questions:

1. What constitutes an "exercise of official power"?

2. What is meant by "authorised by law"?

3. When will legal proceedings be "properly constituted"?

4. On what basis has the High Court asserted and been allowed by Parliament to assert this review jurisdiction?

This chapter will deal with question 1 by asking what actions of what authorities are subject to judicial review. Chapter 4 on *Grounds for Judicial Review* deals with question 2; Chapter 5 on *Applications for Judicial Review* and Chapter 6 on *Collateral Challenge* deal with question 3. Question 4 will be addressed later in this section.

---

[1] See *subsection 3* below.

2 BOUNDARIES OF JUDICIAL REVIEW UNCERTAIN

As will be shown, each of questions 1–3 can be answered in general terms which give useful guidance in many cases. But none of these questions can be answered with a particularity which provides an acid test in every conceivable case. A number of reasons for this may be considered:

(a) Flexibility of case law definitions of scope of review

The answers to the questions are to be found principally in reported decided cases. The concepts of "exercise of official power" and of what exercises are and are not "authorised by law" cover an infinity of possible cases. In very many new cases there will be scope for argument about the extent to which the law has been settled by earlier decisions.

(b) Definitions themselves constantly being changed by the courts

More fundamentally, the courts are constantly re-fashioning the concepts themselves. It will be shown in this chapter and in Chapter 4 that since the mid-1960s the highest appellate courts, the Court of Appeal and the House of Lords, have very greatly expanded the ambit of judicial review. The re-fashioning has reflected a fundamental reappraisal by the judges of their constitutional role in controlling the exercise of public power. As long ago as 1981 Lord Diplock observed that "Any judicial statements on matters of public law if made before 1950 are likely to be a misleading guide to what the law is today".[2] This reappraisal has been to some extent "reactive" and to some extent "proactive", reflecting changing judicial views as to the proper scope of judicial review:

(i) *Courts' reaction to changes in location of power in the state*

The courts have reacted to important shifts in the distribution of legal power within the state — in particular and most recently to the 1979-1997 Conservative government's shift from a philosophy of state control to one of market forces — a shift hardly reversed by the present New Labour Government. As will be seen in this chapter, the courts' reaction has made more elusive the identification of what actions of what authorities are subject to judicial review.

(ii) *Courts' developing understanding of their constitutional role*

Most elusive of all, and most controversial, are the principles upon which the review courts operate in locating, and from time to time re-locating, the boundaries of their judicial review jurisdiction. The question "What are these principles, and what are their legal and constitutional bases?" will be addressed during the detailed study of judicial review in this and subsequent chapters. But before commencing this detailed study question 4 (above) will now be considered briefly.

3 ON WHAT BASIS HAS THE HIGH COURT ASSERTED, AND BEEN ALLOWED BY PARLIAMENT TO ASSERT, ITS JUDICIAL REVIEW JURISDICTION?

The historical basis of the judicial review jurisdiction of the High Court (and the courts exercising appellate jurisdiction over the High Court, the Court of Appeal and the House of Lords) is the

---

[2] *R. v. IRC, ex p. National Federation of Self-Employed and Small Businesses Ltd* [1981] 2 All E.R. 93 at 103f.

common law role of the Court of King's Bench as supervisor of the legality of the acts and proceedings of statutory public authorities. The King's Bench jurisdiction was transferred by the Judicature Act 1873 to the High Court which was created by that Act. But why should the courts have such jurisdiction?

(a) Official power needs a special "public law" regime

In the United Kingdom as elsewhere it has been accepted as a "constitutional fundamental"[3] (albeit in the United Kingdom unwritten) that public, or official, power needs special legal treatment. This reflects the "instrumental" nature of public authorities: they exist only for the public benefit. The rights and liberties of other legal persons (human, corporate, etc.) are regarded as worthy of legal protection for the sake of the private benefits thus conferred on the persons concerned. But the public interest requires that those exercising public power must, on the one hand, be subjected to **special controls** and, on the other, be granted **sufficient latitude** to fulfil their intended functions. Judicial review plays an important role in the promotion of this public interest. What, in brief, are the special "public law" features of judicial review?

(b) Special controls

(i) *Keeping authorities within the limits of their public purpose*

The judicial review jurisdiction of the High Court embodies the principle that the range of lawful official action should be limited by reference to:

- the substantive scope of the special powers and duties of public bodies[4];
- the purposes for which discretions are conferred on public bodies[5]; and
- the need for procedural fairness in official decision making.[6]

In short, public bodies should act only within the confines of the public purposes for which they exist. Private individuals, on the contrary, may act as they wish subject only to express legal restraints imposed in particular circumstances.

(ii) *Broad range of potential challengers*

The special High Court public law procedure of application for judicial review (AJR)[7] is available to any member of the public adjudged to have a "sufficient interest" in mounting the challenge. Unlike ordinary civil proceedings, AJR is not restricted to persons with an individual claim (or "cause of action"), *e.g.* in contract or tort.

(c) Sufficient latitude

The public interest would not be served by a judicial control of official action which was unduly restrictive or intrusive. Thus:

[3] Wade, *CF,* Chaps 4 and 5.
[4] Chap. 4, *section B.*
[5] Chap. 4, *sections C and D.*
[6] Chap. 4, *section E.*
[7] Chap. 1, section B 2; Chap. 5 *sections A and B.*

(i) *Judicial review is "supervisory"*

As said above, judicial review is a jurisdiction to decide whether or not a particular exercise of official power is authorised by law; it is not a jurisdiction to substitute the court's judgment for that of the administrator. In conferring discretionary and other decision-making powers on public authorities the law maps out a wide field within which, subject to any merits appeal, those authorities are the final arbiters. In this sense judicial review sets the field boundaries; it does not referee the game.

This is merely to reiterate the point made at length in Chapter 2 with regard to the "merits/law" divide in the context of appeals. As was said there, the jurisdiction of courts to review administrative action is a jurisdiction confined, essentially, to the correction of errors of law. Courts have this jurisdiction over the administrative process because the correction of legal error is what courts are regarded as specially competent to do. Other aspects of administrative decision making are outside their special competence.

This having been said, it is also true, that the location of the merits/law divide, particularly in the context of review of discretionary power, is often a matter of acute controversy and raises profound constitutional issues (this will be discussed in Chapter 4[8]).

(ii) *"Public authority protection features" of AJR*

Whilst being available to a wider category of complainant than ordinary civil proceedings, the AJR procedure also incorporates a number of special "public authority protection features": the requirement of **permission** from the court for proceedings to be brought; the flexibility of **"sufficient interest"** (it may be used to restrict as well as to amplify the availability of judicial review); a **very short time limit** (one must ordinarily commence an AJR within three months of the challenged action); and, perhaps most significantly, the fact that **remedies on AJR are available subject to the court's discretion** rather than (as with civil damages or debt claims) "as of right".

These procedural features of AJR[9] are designed to enable the court to balance (a) the public interest in subjecting public authorities to the rule of law and in enabling individual litigants to obtain a remedy for their grievances, against (b) the (sometimes conflicting) public interest in achieving speed and certainty in administrative decision making affecting the whole community or large sections of it.[10]

(d) ". . . within limits allowed by Parliament to assert": Parliament and the courts

Detailed consideration of the extent to which Parliament (or, more realistically, the Government, which effectively controls the parliamentary legislative process) has sought to restrict the courts' assertion of judicial review jurisdiction — and of the courts' response — must be postponed until Chapter 7, *Restrictions on Legal Challenge*. However, as already observed,[11] until recently, under the doctrine of the sovereignty of Parliament, all Acts of Parliament have been entirely immune from challenge in United Kingdom legal proceedings. Thus where Parliament has enacted a statute which, in a specific area, restricts or removes individual legal protections — in particular judicial review or other avenues of legal challenge to official action — such legislation has been immune from challenge in UK courts and tribunals. As outlined in Chapter 1, and as will be

---

[8] *Sections C and D.*
[9] Chap. 5, *sections A and B.*
[10] LCR 226 (1994), para. 2.1 *et seq.*
[11] Chap. 1, *section A.*

considered in more detail in Chapter 7, this picture has been profoundly altered by the accession of the United Kingdom to membership of the European Community in 1972; and the incorporation into U.K. domestic law of the European Convention on Human Rights in 1998.

4 JUDICIAL REVIEW AS PART OF PUBLIC LAW

It must be remembered that while judicial review is an important feature of the public law regime, it is only one feature. Indeed, as observed in Chapter 1, because of the wide availability of statutory avenues of appeal, it is correct to think of judicial review as a "residual jurisdiction".[12]

But judicial review is not even, by any means, the whole of the common law (judge-made) public law regime. In particular, as will be explained in Chapters 8 and 9, the courts have fashioned special rules governing official liability in tort and contract: rules designed to reflect the public interest considerations mentioned above regarding the need for a special public law regime. Here too, striking an acceptable balance between control and latitude has proved to be both controversial and intractable.

A prime difficulty in defining the limits of official liability in tort and contract lies in establishing clearly the proper scope of public law regulation. How far should the special regime of public law extend? Should it extend to all activities of all persons and bodies acting in an official capacity, or should a line be drawn between, say, exercises of official power and "ordinary" contractual or operational activities? Should the legal relationships of public authorities with their employees or contractors, for example, be subject to the same regime of judicial review as applies to decisions reached by those same authorities in the exercise of their statutory powers and duties in areas of licensing or state benefits?

The answers given by the courts to questions of this nature will determine, however imprecisely, the respective territories of "public law" and "private law" for purposes of legal challenge to official action in English law.[13] And they will also constitute the foundation for answering questions as to how, within the public law sphere, the "special control" and "sufficient latitude" referred to above should be balanced in the public interest, *e.g.* suppose that a pressure group seeks judicial review of a government decision to build a nuclear power station or to grant a tax amnesty or impose restrictions on media broadcasting or publication or to spend the overseas aid budget on a controversial project. Where, in the public interest, should the courts locate the boundary between "supervisory" review and "merits"? And how far should the special "public authority protection features" of AJR be applied so as to reject a challenge to what may be in substantive terms a demonstrably illegal official decision?[14]

Striking an acceptable balance between control and latitude has proved to be a most controversial and intractable issue in the judicial development of public law and in the relationship between the courts and the executive. Questions as to the proper reach and scope of public law for purposes of legal challenge to official action are questions which under present constitutional arrangements fall mainly (*i.e.* subject to express statutory provision) to be answered on a case by case basis by courts exercising judicial review and other jurisdiction in litigation involving public authorities. Whether to date the answers have been satisfactory is, of course, much debated.[15] The study of those answers which follows in this and succeeding chapters may

---

[12] LCR 226 (1994), para. 2.5.
[13] For an excellent introduction to the notion of "public" law and its distinction from "private" law for these purposes, see Cane, *Intr. AL,* Chap. 2. See also de Smith, *JRAA,* pp. 155–167. Allison, *Dist.* provides an extended account in a historical and comparative perspective.
[14] Cane (1994).
[15] Le Sueur (1995).

provide a foundation for exploration of the perennial and kaleidoscopic issue of how law can and should limit state power.[16] The sometimes uneasy accommodation which has been reached between the judicial and the executive power ultimately reflects the judgment of successive governments as to the political/electoral desirability of continuing to accept legal constraints upon their exercise of power — constraints imposed by the courts in the exercise of their assumed constitutional role of subjecting government to the rule of law.

As already stated, the remainder of this chapter will consider what constitutes an "exercise of official power": what actions of what authorities are subject to judicial review?

B REVIEWABLE AUTHORITIES

A major feature of the courts' recent expansion of the ambit of judicial review (*section A 2 b* above) has been a re-orientation of their approach to the question "what authorities are subject to judicial review?"

Since the mid-1980s the courts have answered this question by reference to substantive rather than, as previously, to formal criteria: by reference to the true nature, rather than to the formal source, of official power.[17] Judicial review had previously been largely confined to authorities exercising statutory powers. But in applying judicial review only to statutory authorities the courts had largely failed to recognise what they have now begun more consistently to recognise, that much of what may be regarded as official power does not derive from statutory authorisation.

Accordingly, the following survey of reviewable authorities will deal first with authorities exercising statutory power, then with persons and bodies exercising non-statutory official power.

1 AUTHORITIES EXERCISING STATUTORY POWER[18]

(a) Central government; the Welsh Assembley

Much official power in England and Wales is wielded by central government departments under statutory authority. Most government powers are statutory — conferred on "the Minister" or "the Secretary of State".[19] Many examples of government statutory powers have already been encountered in the discussion of appeals in Chapter 2 and many more will be encountered in this and succeeding chapters.

Government ministers and departments, like other authorities, are subject to judicial review in the exercise of their statutory powers. The reviewability of the government in its exercise of non-statutory power is considered in *sub-section 2* below.

Devolution of central government powers to the Welsh Assembly

The Government of Wales Act 1998 (GWA) provides for the devolution to the Welsh Assembly[20] of functions previously exercised by any minister of the Crown in relation to Wales.[21] These are

---

[16] See Taggart (1997) and Allison (1997) in Taggart, *Prov.* More generally, see Harlow and Rawlings, L&A, especially Chaps 1–5, 17.

[17] See generally Oliver (1987).

[18] Wade and Forsyth, *AL*, Chaps 3 and 4; Craig, *AL*, Chaps 3, 4, 6, 7.

[19] See Wade and Forsyth, *AL*, pp. 53–54.

[20] Chap. 1, *section A 1* above.

[21] GWA, s.22(1).

mostly statutory and range over a very wide field including agriculture and industry, planning, housing, health, social services, highways and heritage.[22] The Act contains provisions[23] prohibiting the Assembly from acting contrary to Community law, human rights and United Kingdom international obligations. Schedule 8 provides for the resolution of "devolution issues,"[24] *i.e.* legal challenges to the validity of Assembly action in the exercise or purported exercise of these devolved powers. The provisions on devolution issues are considered later.[25]

(b) Agencies

(i) *Statutory agencies*

It has long been a practice of governments to procure the creation of statutory agencies funded and empowered to carry out particular types of public function. These statutory agencies operate somewhat at arm's length from the Government itself and are commonly referred to as "QUANGOs" — quasi-autonomous non-governmental organisations. Familiar examples include the Civil Aviation Authority, the Monopolies and Mergers Commission (now the Competition Commission), the Police Complaints Authority, Regional Health Authorities and NHS trusts. In their discharge of statutory duties or exercise of statutory powers all such statutory agencies are clearly reviewable authorities.

(ii) *"Next steps" agencies*

Since 1989 the Government has chosen to hive-off to non-statutory agencies many statutory functions previously discharged directly through government departments. This "Next Steps" policy[26] stemmed from Mrs Thatcher's "Efficiency Unit" and reflects the view that "service delivery" can be more effectively and economically achieved by "operational" agencies separate from the government departments whose policies they are created to implement. A key feature of the separation is the fostering of a more entrepreneurial attitude within agencies via strict "budget-centre" accountability and the encouragement of self-generated funding. Now familiar Next Steps agencies are the Driver and Vehicle Licensing Agency (DVLA), the Highways Agency, the Land Registry, the Passport Agency and, more politically sensitive, the Prison Service, the Employment Service, and the Social Security Benefits, Contributions and Child Support Agencies.

The extent of this initiative is shown by the fact that at the end of 1998 there were 142 Next Steps Agencies[27] employing some 79 per cent of all civil servants. It is well-established by the so-called "*Carltona* principle"[28] that Parliament will be presumed by the courts to have authorised delegation by a minister to his departmental staff at an appropriate level. However, doubt has been expressed as to the lawfulness of the Next Steps type of delegation of statutory power. The argument[29] is that the *Carltona* principle presupposes a unity of purpose, control and account-ability within the department or authority concerned. Next Steps Agencies are designed precisely to separate political from financial accountability and so depart radically from this paradigm. But this argument may give insufficient weight to the Civil Service (Management Functions) Act 1992,

[22] See GWA, Sched. 2.
[23] Ss.106–108.
[24] Sched. 8, para. 1(1).
[25] Chap. 4, *section F.*
[26] "Improving Management in Government: the Next Steps" (1988) HMSO; Craig, *AL,* pp. 91–95, 106–109.
[27] N.S. Report (1998), p. 326.
[28] *Carltona Ltd v. Commissioners of Works* [1943] 2 All E.R. 560.
[29] Freedland (1996).

s.1 which gives wide power to ministers to delegate their functions "to any other servant of the Crown" which would include the chief executive of a Next Steps agency.

Assuming that statutory functions are lawfully delegated to Next Steps Agencies, are the agencies subject to judicial review in respect of their exercise of those functions? The agencies themselves are creations not of statute but of governmental civil service reorganisation, so (unlike statutory agencies) probably cannot themselves be the subject of legal proceedings challenging the exercise of a delegated function. Probably, therefore, such proceedings should be brought against the delegating department.

NEXT STEPS AGENCIES AND THE "CONTRACT STATE"

The creation of *Next Steps Agencies* was one feature of the general policy thrust of the 1979-1997 Conservative government which led to the creation of what is colloquially referred to as "the contract State" (See, *e.g.* Fredman and Morris (1994), p.69; see generally Harden, *CS*; Austin (1997)). Other now-familiar features of the contract State are:

- *"Privatisation"* of, *e.g.* water, gas and electricity;

- *Competitive Tendering and "Contracting-out" of Public Services*

This privatising of the public sector can be seen as one side of a coin whose obverse is the process of *"Corporatism"* — described by Cane (Cane, *Intr. AL*, pp. 21–22) as "involv[ing] co-operative arrangements between government and non-governmental groups or institutions under which the latter, either in return for some benefit or in order to avoid some disadvantage, agree to act on a way which will further government policy". Examples of such arrangements are the many "self-regulating organisations" (SROs) in such diverse fields as City commercial practice, Press complaints, and advertising standards.

On the matter of legal control a key question is how far if at all the public law regime of judicial review does or should govern each of these diverse types of arrangement. For self-regulation and privatisation see *sub-section 2 b below*; for competitive tendering see *section C 2 a*; for "contracting-out" (*i.e.* public authorities make contracts with private businesses under which the businesses provide the public with services which statute requires or empowers the authorities to provide or cause to be provided) see Chapter 9.

(c) Local government and police

Examples of statutory functions of local authorities — in such fields as town and country planning, housing homeless persons and the licensing of trades and occupations — have already been encountered in the discussion of appeals in Chapter 2. Many more (*e.g.* local taxation (rating), education, social services and highway maintenance) will be encountered in due course. Local authorities are of course subject to judicial review in the exercise of their statutory functions.

Turning to the police, only the London Metropolitan Police are under direct central government (the Home Secretary's) control. The other 40 or so forces are based broadly on local government county areas and are administered by statutory police authorities composed of local councillors, members appointed by the Home Secretary, and magistrates. The day-to-day disposition of the police, however, falls to the Chief Constable of the force concerned. He is appointed by the police authority subject to the Home Secretary's approval. Moreover, the Home

Secretary has wide statutory powers under the Police Act 1996 as to general police organisation. The powers of the police are also mainly statutory (the 1996 Act) but important among their non-statutory powers is the discretion whether or not to prosecute, a discretion which has been on occasion the subject of judicial review proceedings.[30]

(d) Courts and tribunals

The prime distinction here is between "superior" courts on the one hand and "inferior" courts and statutory tribunals on the other. Inferior courts and tribunals are subject to judicial review. Superior courts are not.

(i) Superior Courts

The principal superior courts are the High Court, Court of Appeal and House of Lords. Since common law supervisory judicial review is a jurisdiction *of* the High Court, it cannot be exercised *over* that court: High Court judges have never, for obvious reasons, sought jurisdiction to review the decisions of other High Court judges.[31]

There are certain other courts which are not subject to supervisory review — either because they are by statute denominated "superior" courts, e.g. the Courts-Martial Appeal Court[32] and the Restrictive Practices Court[33]; or because their "constitution, jurisdiction and powers and . . . relationship with the High Court"[34] are such as to have led the High Court to disclaim supervisory jurisdiction over them, e.g. the Central Criminal Court.[35] The Crown Court also is a superior court[36] but is subject by statute[37] to supervisory review except for "matters relating to trial on indictment".[38]

(ii) Inferior courts and tribunals

County courts are for most purposes inferior courts and therefore, like magistrates' courts, subject to the supervisory review jurisdiction.[39] As explained in Chapter 2, the normal mode of challenge to a decision of a court or statutory tribunal will be appeal (where provided by statute) rather than AJR. But where there is no, or no adequate, appeal provision — or where the jurisdiction of a court to entertain a particular case is challenged, as e.g. in the notorious *Pinochet*[40] extradition proceedings — AJR may be used.[41]

[30] See, *e.g.* the *Blackburn* case: *section C 1 a* below.
[31] *Re Racal Communications Ltd* [1980] 2 All E.R. 634. Confirmed in the context of human rights litigation by Human Rights Act 1998, s.9(2).
[32] Courts-Martial (Appeals) Act 1968, s.1(2).
[33] Restrictive Practices Court Act 1976, s.1(1).
[34] Goff L.J. in *R. v. Cripps, ex p. Muldoon* [1983] 3 All E.R. 72.
[35] *R. v. Central Criminal Court Justices, ex p. L.C.C.* [1925] All E.R. Rep 429.
[36] Supreme Court Act (SCA) 1981, s.45(1).
[37] SCA, s.29(3).
[38] A problematic phrase: *Smalley v. Warwick Crown Court* [1985] 1 All E.R. 769 and subsequent cases.
[39] See County Courts Act 1984, ss.83, 84.
[40] *R. v. Bow Street Metropolitan Stipendiary Magistrate, ex p. Pinochet Ugarte (No. 1)* [1998] 4 All E.R. 897; *(No. 2)* [1999] 1 All E.R. 577; *(No. 3)* [1999] 2 All E.R. 97.
[41] For choosing between appeal and AJR as modes of challenge when both are in principle available, see Chap. 5, *section C 2.*

2 PERSONS AND BODIES EXERCISING NON-STATUTORY OFFICIAL POWER

(a) The Crown: the "royal prerogative" and judicial review[42]

(i) *"Prerogative power"*

In medieval times the Crown's "prerogative" power (*i.e.* the special power legally inherent in the office held by the reigning monarch) was wide-ranging. Since the constitutional settlement of the seventeenth century that power has been largely superseded by statutory powers conferred on ministers. What little remains is almost all under government control because the Crown — the monarch as a legal entity — acts politically only as advised by its ministers. Where government ministers act in reliance on prerogative powers, are their acts and decisions subject to judicial review?

A broad distinction may be drawn between "prerogatives of state" and "prerogatives of government". The prerogatives of state include such constitutional functions as summoning and dissolving Parliament, making treaties and declaring war. Such powers are so broad and undefined as to make it impossible to apply legal criteria to determine the lawfulness of their exercise which, in consequence, is said to be "non-justiciable". Ordinarily, then, there is no question of judicial review of the exercise of such powers. However, in *R. v. Foreign Secretary, ex p. Rees-Mogg*[43] Lord Rees-Mogg applied for judicial review of the government's ratification of the Maastricht Treaty on European Union. One basis for the AJR was that the ratification was in breach of section 6 of the European Assembly Elections Act 1978 which provides that no treaty extending the powers of the E.C. Parliament shall be ratified without approval by Act of the United Kingdom Parliament. Although the argument was rejected on the merits, the High Court did accept that it had jurisdiction to review the exercise of the treaty-making prerogative as here qualified by statute in a manner which was amenable to judicial scrutiny.

The prerogatives of government include the prerogatives of pardon and mercy, the conferring of honours and titles, and also some legislative power, *e.g.* re. civil servants' terms of service. These powers are not by nature obviously non-justiciable. Also in *Council for Civil Service Unions (CCSU) v. Minister for Civil Service*[44] the House of Lords reversed the previously prevailing judicial approach by holding that in principle supervisory review can be invoked to challenge not merely an assertion by the government that a particular prerogative power exists, but also the manner in which such prerogative powers as do exist are exercised by the Government.

In the *CCSU* case, the House held that the Prime Minister, Mrs Thatcher, had acted unfairly in withdrawing Government Communication Headquarters (GCHQ) civil servants' right of trade union membership without consultation. However, the Government successfully invoked "national security" considerations (the need to avoid possibly damaging industrial action by GCHQ members) as justifying the unfairness. Their Lordships did hold that in order to rely on this ground the Government must produce evidence that the decision was in fact based on security considerations. But it seems unlikely that the courts will go further than to require a minister to establish that he did, as a matter of fact, characterise as "security considerations" the grounds on which he acted. The question of the propriety of this characterisation is regarded for domestic law purposes (but not under E.C.[45] or Convention[46] law) as "par excellence a non-justiciable question".[47]

---

[42] Wade & Forsyth, *AL*, pp. 382–386; Craig, *AL*, pp. 538–539; de Smith, *JRAA*, pp. 316–322.
[43] [1994] 1 All E.R. 457. Rawlings (1994).
[44] [1984] 3 All E.R. 935. Wade (1985), pp. 190–197.
[45] *R. v. Home Secretary, ex p. McQuillan* [1995] 4 All E.R. 400.
[46] Harris, O'Boyle and Warbrick, *ECHR*, pp. 394–396; *cf.* pp. 430–432 (Commission dismissed *CCSU* case).
[47] [1984] 3 All E.R. at 952, Lord Diplock. See also *R. v. Home Secretary, ex p. Cheblak* [1991] 2 All E.R. 319.

In *R. v. Home Secretary, ex p. Bentley*[48] the *CCSU* principle that the courts can review the exercise of justiciable prerogative powers was successfully invoked against the government's refusal to exercise the prerogative of pardon. On AJR by the sister of Derek Bentley (executed in 1953 for complicity in the murder of a policeman), the Divisional Court held that while the Home Secretary's policy of not recommending a free pardon unless the convicted person appeared morally as well as technically innocent was probably not justiciable, the minister had acted unlawfully in failing to consider granting a conditional (as distinct from a free) pardon which would have acknowledged that Bentley should not have been hanged. The court observed that "the question was simply whether the nature and subject-matter of the decision was amenable to the judicial process". But in *Reckley v. Minister of Public Safety*[49] the Privy Council in a Bahamas death sentence case held that a government minister's exercise of the prerogative of mercy was not justiciable. Distinguishing *Bentley* as an "exceptional case"[50] Lord Goff endorsed an earlier dictum of Lord Diplock that "mercy is not the subject of legal rights. It begins where legal rights end."[51] It followed, the Privy Council held, that the condemned man could not challenge either the minister's refusal to exercise clemency or the failure to give him the right to address a constitutional committee which advised the minister on any plea for mercy. One may concede that the exercise of such prerogatives as those of pardon and mercy carry a very wide discretion; but it is not at all clear why a decision should be immune from review if, say, bias or animosity could be shown.

(ii) *Prerogative power and legal capacity*[52]

Legally, the Crown is a common law "corporation sole" — a non-statutory legal entity whose capacity to act (unlike that of a statutory authority) is in general no more circumscribed than that of a private individual. The *CCSU* case[53] indicated that the availability of judicial review against Crown action will not depend on what Lord Diplock described[54] as "esoteric" distinctions between prerogative power strictly so-called and the Crown's legal capacity: any non statute-based official action of the Crown, if justiciable, may be regarded as a "prerogative" act. The Government can thus no longer regard itself as immune from judicial review simply because it is acting through the Crown's common law capacity rather than exercising either prerogative or statutory powers. Recent cases suggest that the criterion of reviewability is whether the Crown action (*i.e.* action of a minister of the Crown acting as such) in question constitutes "de facto"[55] an exercise of public power.

Take, for example, the grant or refusal of a passport. In law a passport is simply a statement by the Crown as to the status of the individual concerned. De facto, of course, it is a document of vital importance to the passport holder. In *R. v. Foreign Secretary, ex p. Everett*[56] the Court of Appeal held that an official refusal to grant or renew a passport is reviewable. A very different example of the courts' new willingness to review government action which de facto, though not strictly in law, constitutes an exercise of official power is *R. v. Environment Secretary, ex p. Greenwich L.B.C.*[57] where the Divisional Court held that a decision by the Department of the Environment to issue an information leaflet about the highly unpopular local "poll" tax (since

---

[48] [1993] 4 All E.R. 442.
[49] [1996] 1 All E.R. 562.
[50] p. 572f.
[51] *de Freitas v. Benny* [1976] 3 W.L.R. 388 at 394.
[52] See Harris (1992).
[53] *Council for Civil Service Unions (CCSU) v. Minister for Civil Service* [1984] 3 All E.R. 935 (above).
[54] ibid. at 950.
[55] See *subsection b* below for judicial use of this phrase.
[56] [1989] 1 All E.R. 655.
[57] *The Times*, May 17, 1989.

replaced) would be reviewable if the applicant could demonstrate (which in the event it could not) that the leaflet was so inaccurate as to be mere government propaganda.

This expansion of judicial review jurisdiction is, of course, likely to place some strain on the constitutional relationship between the courts and the Government — as is illustrated by a recent case arising from government policy on state compensation to victims of injuries criminally inflicted. An early indication of the courts' developing willingness to define their review jurisdiction by reference to substantive rather than, as previously, to formal criteria had come in 1967 when the Divisional Court held that the decisions of the Criminal Injuries Compensation Board were reviewable.[58] The Board was set up not by the exercise of prerogative power strictly so-called but by the Crown in the exercise of "its ordinary powers as a natural person".[59] The Board was placed on a statutory basis by the Criminal Justice Act 1988. The statutory scheme (like the original) provided for compensation on a tort damages basis. Section 171 provided that the scheme was to be implemented "on such day as the Secretary of State may . . . appoint". By 1993 no day had been appointed but the Home Secretary then announced in a government White Paper that the statutory scheme would be repealed unimplemented and that the Government would implement instead a new "prerogative" scheme based on a flat-rate tariff which would on average halve the compensation payable. In R. v. Home Secretary, ex p. Fire Brigades Union[60] a number of public sector unions whose members were more than usually exposed to crimes of violence applied for judicial review and ultimately obtained from the House of Lords (by 3:2) a declaration that section 171, while it remained unrepealed, required the Home Secretary to keep under review the possibility of implementing the statutory scheme. Thus he acted unlawfully in not doing this and in announcing a new prerogative scheme while the statutory scheme remained unrepealed.

At one level the case is an uncontroversial illustration of the proposition that prerogative power exists only in so far as statute has not limited it. On a different view it might be said that the House of Lords unwarrantedly restricted the Government's freedom to make and announce new policy. But it is quite clear that the Government could at any time introduce legislation (as it did)[61] to repeal the statutory scheme: the court's intervention can be defended not only as a correct interpretation of existing statute law but also on the constitutional basis that the government may not repeal a statute (albeit unimplemented) by "prerogative action".[62]

(b) Bodies with "de facto" official power[63]

(i) The "Datafin" Principle

In the CCSU case[64] in 1984 the House of Lords tackled the question of the susceptibility of the Government to judicial review in its exercise of Crown prerogative power by reference to substance rather than to legal form. The House took what might be described as a realistic rather than a legalistic approach. The thrust of the reported cases considered above is as follows: when the Government (relying on the unlimited legal capacity of the Crown) sets up a compensation fund for those suffering criminal injuries or grants or refuses passports or organises a nation-wide

[58] R. v. Criminal Injuries Compensation Board, ex p. Lain [1967] 2 All E.R. 770.
[59] Wade, CF, pp. 47–48.
[60] [1995] 2 All E.R. 244.
[61] [1995] P.L. 464.
[62] Barendt (1995).
[63] Wade and Forsyth, AL, pp. 659–667; Craig, AL, pp. 769–783; de Smith, JRAA, pp. 167–191.
[64] Council for Civil Service Unions (CCSU) v. Minister for Civil Service [1984] 3 All E.R. 935: subsection a above.

"mail shot" to promote its policies, it is *de facto* exercising official muscle. Within the limits of justiciability such action should be judicially reviewable because it is in reality a manifestation of official power and should therefore be subject to the special regime of public law control.

In the *Datafin* case,[65] two years after the *CCSU* case, the Court of Appeal adopted the same approach in determining that public law rules should apply (via judicial review) to bodies which, while not being public authorities or exercising statutory powers, nevertheless could be regarded as *de facto* exercising public functions. In the case, Datafin plc sought judicial review of what it alleged was a procedurally unfair decision of the Panel on Take-overs and Mergers in rejecting the company's complaint that a competitor in a takeover battle had breached City rules on the matter. The Panel argued that it was not subject to judicial review — that it was a body set up not by statute or by government but by City institutions as part of City "self-regulation"; and that it therefore fell beyond the reach of public law control. But the court held that the Panel *"de facto"*[66] was exercising "public law functions"[67] and in so doing was subject to judicial review. The Government had refrained from legislative regulation of City affairs precisely because it regarded the non-statutory arrangements (in which the Panel played a central role) as adequate.

In brief, then, the *Datafin* principle is that any body ("outwith Parliament"[68]) is subject to judicial review in respect of any public function which he, she or it performs — a principle since applied by Parliament in defining "public authority" for the purposes of section 6 of the Human Rights Act 1998.[69]

(ii) *The "surrogacy" and "consensual" criteria*

The judgments in *Datafin* indicate that prima facie a function will be classified as a "public law" function if (applying what may be termed the "surrogacy criterion") it can be shown to be a function which — like that discharged by the Panel[70] — the Government would have had to perform had the body in question not been performing it. However, even where the surrogacy criterion might be regarded as satisfied, a body will not be subject to public law regulation where its "sole source of power is a consensual submission to its jurisdiction"[71] — for public power is by definition imposed upon, rather than assented to by, individuals. This exclusionary criterion will be termed the "consensual criterion".

As will now be shown, reference to the case law following *Datafin* demonstrates both that these two criteria provide only the vaguest guidance to classifying particular functions as public or private[72] and that the criteria themselves are in many respects unsatisfactory.

(iii) *Post*-Datafin *case law — the "surrogacy criterion"*

The non-statutory bodies which have been held reviewable applying the *Datafin* surrogacy criterion include many self-regulating organisations (SROs)[73] in such fields as marketing and

---

[65] *R. v. Panel on Take-overs and Mergers, ex p. Datafin plc* [1987] 1 All E.R. 564. Beatson (1987), p. 50; Wade (1987).
[66] [1987] 1 All E.R. at 567e, Donaldson M.R.
[67] ibid., p. 583f, Lloyd L.J.
[68] Lord Woolf M.R. in *R. v. Parliamentary Commissioner for Standards, ex p. Al Fayed* [1998] 1 All E.R. 93 at 97c: Commissioner, like others "engaged within Parliament" not subject to judicial review but to House Committees of Standards and Privileges (*ibid.*, p. 97–d). But *cf. section A 3 d* above and Chap. 7, section A 7.
[69] s.6(3)(b), (5).
[70] In the spirit of "corporatism" referred to in *sub-section 1 b* above.
[71] [1987] 1 All E.R. at p. 577a, Donaldson M.R.
[72] Craig, *AL*, pp. 770–1.
[73] *Sub-section 1 b* above.

advertising,[74] insurance,[75] and investment.[76] Also within the criterion are certain service-providing bodies in such diverse fields of public concern as public health[77] and livestock breeding control.[78]

The cases say that the bodies in question are subject to judicial review in the exercise of their public functions. This indicates that those functions are of sufficient public impact and concern for the law to provide machinery whereby the bodies, in performing them, can be required to act fairly within the legal constraints imposed on public authorities in their exercise of official power. On that basis it is difficult to understand why a decision of the Jockey Club in the exercise of its "quasi-licensing power"[79] to decide whether or not to allocate race meetings to a particular race course or of the Football League in deciding whether or not to admit a new club[80] do not fulfil the *Datafin* surrogacy criterion. Contrary to the courts' view in, respectively, *R. v. Disciplinary Committee of the Jockey Club, ex p. Aga Khan*[81] and *R. v. Football Association Ltd, ex p. Football League Ltd*[82] that the functions of such bodies are not governmental, one might have thought that activities of such national public concern as horse-racing and football would have to be regulated by the Government if they were not satisfactorily "self-regulated". Moreover, if one is focusing on the "reality" of power, the decisions in the examples just given had as profound an effect on the complainants as the decisions of the bodies mentioned in the previous paragraph had upon the complainants there. And it is not clear that the complainants in the situations referred to in this or the previous paragraph would have had a contractual or any other legal remedy. It is true that *Stevenage F.C. v. Football League Ltd*[83] shows that even in the absence of any contractual nexus there may be redress under the narrow restraint of trade doctrine. But *Datafin* could provide the basis for expanding that doctrine to produce a wider principle. As Carnwath J. observed in *Stevenage*:

> "As between Stevenage and the League, viewed as purely private bodies, there was no legal nexus . . . However, when one looked at the matter more generally different considerations arose. The League was not simply an independent body. It was an important part of the elaborate structure established for the control of professional football in the interests of the participants and the public generally."

Finally, the "need for regulation" point no doubt does not apply, although the "no other remedy" point may well do, to a decision of a religious disciplinary authority to expel a minister, depriving him of his living. It seems that such decisions are not reviewable.[84]

(iv) . . . *The "consensual criterion"*

Turning to the consensual criterion: here, as stated above, the notion is that the courts should not impose public law standards and grant public law remedies in respect of contracts freely entered into by private individuals.

---

[74] *R. v. Advertising Standards Authority Ltd, ex p. Insurance Service plc, The Times,* July 14, 1989; *R. v. Code of Practice Committee of British Pharmaceutical Industry, ex p. Professional Counselling Aids Ltd, The Times,* November 7, 1990.

[75] *R. v. LAUTRO, ex p. Ross* [1993] 1 All E.R. 545.

[76] *R. v. FIMBRA, ex p. Cochrane, The Times,* June 23, 1989; *R. v. Association of Futures Brokers and Dealers, ex p. Mordens Ltd, The Times,* September 6, 1990; *R. v. Investors' Compensation Scheme Ltd, ex p. Weyell* [1994] 1 All E.R. 601.

[77] *R. v. Ethical Committee St Mary's Hosp, ex p. Harriott* [1988] 1 F.L.R. 512.

[78] *R. v. Hereford Herd Book Society, ex p. O'Neill, The Times,* July 19, 1995.

[79] Simon Brown J. in *R. v. Jockey Club, ex p. RAM Racecourses Ltd* (1990) [1993] 2 All E.R. 225 at 248e.

[80] *e.g.* as in *Stevenage F.C. v. Football League Ltd, The Times,* August 1, 1996 (Carnwath J.); affirmed, CA; *The Times,* August 9, 1996. On this case see further below.

[81] [1993] 2 All E.R. 853.

[82] [1993] 2 All E.R. 853.

[83] Above.

[84] *R. v. Chief Rabbi, ex p. Wachmann (1991)* [1993] 2 All E.R. 249.

As will be explained in *section C* of this chapter it is not obvious why public authorities should not be under special obligations in at least some of their contractual activity. But, that aside, the consensual criterion surely should not apply in respect of contractual arrangements **not** freely entered into, as, *e.g.* with individuals' membership of sport or trade governing bodies where membership is a prerequisite of livelihood. In this respect also both the *Aga Khan* and the *Football League* cases (above) are unsatisfactory. In *Aga Khan*[85] the Court of Appeal applied not only the surrogacy but also the consensual criterion to hold that the Aga Khan could not challenge by AJR the jockey club's disqualification of his horse from the Oaks on suspicion of doping. The applicant's remedies were in contract only. And in the *Football League* case[86] Rose J. likewise used the consensual as well as the surrogacy criterion in ruling that the Football Association's decision to create a separate Premier League was not reviewable.

Submission to the jurisdiction of a trade or professional association is commonly not truly consensual. If the association were exercising statutory functions (such as those of the General Medical Council[87] and other statutory disciplinary bodies), public law standards would apply. Where a body satisfies the *Datafin* surrogacy criterion should it not be reviewable in respect of its action under a contract which the other party has in effect no choice but to enter?

Moreover, even where there is an element of true consent in submitting to the jurisdiction of, say an SRO, why should this be determinative of reviewability where the body is plainly carrying out a public function? An unsatisfactory case in this connection is *R. v. Insurance Ombudsman Bureau, ex p. Aegon Life*.[88] The Insurance Ombudsman is one of an increasing number of non-statutory ombudsmen[89] created by industries and professions as part of self-regulatory regimes. Other familiar examples are the Legal Services and Financial Services ombudsmen. In the *Aegon Life* case, Rose L.J. in the Divisional Court held that the Bureau was not reviewable because insurance companies could choose whether to belong to it or, on the contrary, to leave complainants to whatever court remedies they might have. The Bureau was created by the insurance industry on a voluntary basis to deal with complaints by the public against its members. The fact that a particular company may have chosen freely to submit to the Bureau's jurisdiction surely does not mean that the Bureau is not performing a public function once that submission has been made.

(v) *Are privatised utilities "Datafin-reviewable" authorities?*[90]

During the 1980s and early 1990s the public telecommunications, gas, electricity and water services (utilities) were floated on the stock market and sold by the government to private shareholders.[91] Privatisation of these public services was, of course, one facet of the Conservative Government's drive towards replacing state control in many areas with control achieved via the mechanisms of commercial competition: "market regulation". The *Datafin* case law (above) represents the courts' response to another facet of this policy: government preference in appropriate fields for self-regulation rather than statutory control. Has the *Datafin* case law any relevance in the context of privatised utilities? Are there any circumstances in which actions or decisions of those operating privatised public services such as telecommunications, gas, electricity and water may be subject to judicial review?

To answer this question one needs some idea of the legal structure of the privatised utilities: see below.

---

[85] *R. v. Disciplinary Committee of the Jockey Club, ex p. Aga Khan* [1993] 2 All E.R. 853.
[86] *R. v. Football Association Ltd, ex p. Football League Ltd* [1993] 2 All E.R. 833.
[87] See, *e.g. R. v. General Medical Council, ex p. Gee* [1987] 1 All E.R. 1204, QBD and CA; 2 All E.R. 193, HL.
[88] [1994] C.O.D. 426.
[89] Statutory ombudsmen are dealt with in Chap. 10.
[90] Borrie (1989); Craig, *AL*, pp. 349–360.
[91] Telecommunications Act 1984; Gas Act 1986; Electricity Act 1989; Water Industry Act 1991.

LEGAL STRUCTURE OF PRIVATISED UTILITIES

Sections from the Gas Act 1986 are cited for example below. Following the enactment of the Competition and Service (Utilities) Act 1992 which was aimed at levelling-up quality control for all utilities, the regulatory regimes for telecommunications, electricity and water are broadly similar.

In broad terms the legal regime under which all the utilities operate is that statute provides for government authorisation or licensing of suppliers of the service in question, *e.g.* Gas Act 1986, s.7. Regulation is thereafter achieved by a statutory "Director General" (DG) (*ibid.,* section 1) enforcing statutory standards as to, *e.g.* supply, (*ibid.* section 10) fixing of tariffs, (*ibid.* section 14) standards of quality (*ibid.* section 16) and standards of performance (Competition and Service (Utilities) Act 1992, s.11).

Compensation is payable to customers in respect of individual failures to meet prescribed standards of performance (1986 Act, s.33A(5), inserted by 1992 Act, s.11). The DG can resolve disputes and make "final" orders having the effect of a county court judgment (1986 Act, s.33A(9)). Moreover, if a supply company fails on a more widespread basis to meet standards such as those referred to in the previous paragraph the DG can, subject to detailed statutory requirements of procedural fairness (*ibid.* section 29), make such final or provisional order "as is requisite for the purpose of securing compliance" (*ibid.* sections 28(1),(2)); a breach of such order causing loss or damage to individuals may give rise to damages liability (*ibid.* sections 30(6)).

Standing back from this welter of detail one may address the question put in the text: are there any circumstances in which actions or decisions of those operating the privatised utilities may be subject to judicial review?

It is true that the legitimate purposes of a PLC and its legal capacity to pursue them for the private profit of its shareholders are very different from those of a classical statutory public authority. But it seems most unlikely that the commercial aspect of utility PLCs would induce the courts to rule categorically that none of their acts and decisions are amenable to judicial review. In so far as the operation remains so heavily underpinned by statute, it appears that in principle not only decisions of the DG but also shortcomings of suppliers' performance fall within the scope of public law regulation. Even where compensation is payable to individuals (who might therefore be thought to have private law rather than public law rights) public law principles may be kept in play by the provision that "the making of compensation . . . shall not prejudice any other remedy which may be available".[92]

In *Datafin* terms, privatised utilities seem plainly to fulfil the "surrogacy" criterion: there seems little doubt that, as state monopolies, publicly owned utilities would be regarded as exercising public powers. Consider, *e.g. Foster v. British Gas plc,*[93] — an E.C. case where the House of Lords applied a ruling by the ECJ that *pre*-privatisation British Gas was an arm of the state for purposes of direct effect of Community directives.[94] Mere change of ownership does not make these basic services any the less something which the state would have to provide if private enterprise did not. And the consensual criterion should not necessarily exclude public law jurisdiction in these cases. Even if there is a contract between supplier and consumer, the consumer may have (in the absence of effective consumer-level competition, *e.g.* as at present in the water industry) no real choice whether or not to contract with a particular undertaking. Moreover it is not clear that the

---

[92] 1988 Act, s.33A(5).
[93] [1991] 2 All E.R. 705.
[94] On direct effect of directives, see Chap. 8, *section E 1.*

relationship between supplier and consumer is contractual: in *Norweb plc v. Dixon*[95] Norweb mistakenly billed D for electricity which he had not in fact used and secretly adjusted his meter to collect the charge. Norweb were acquitted of the offence of harassing with demands for the payment of a "debt due under a contract" on the basis that the relationship between a public electricity supplier and a customer was statutory rather than contractual.

However, even if in principle privatised utilities are *"Datafin*-reviewable" authorities, in practice there is likely to be little scope for judicial review except, perhaps, by suppliers challenging decisions of the DG — and even some of those are at least partially immunised from judicial review by express statutory provision.[96] As far as consumers are concerned, very many of the types of complaint which they may wish to raise seem now to be catered for by the statutory regime of standards and remedies sketched above. Consistently with the idea of judicial review as a residual jurisdiction, it is not normally available where other specially-provided remedies are adequate.[97] However, should circumstances arise where a supply company acts in a manner which appears to contravene public law principles but this does not induce the DG to act, it may very well be that individuals on their own behalf as consumers, or perhaps as representing the public interest, might seek a judicial review ruling on the true extent of the company's public functions or, perhaps, the DG's statutory duties.

(vi) *Conclusion* — Datafin *and the boundaries of public law*[98]

It is easy both to over-state and to under-state the importance of the *Datafin* extension of the categories of reviewable authority.

On the one hand, high expectations were generated by the courts' expressed willingness in such cases as *CCSU* and *Datafin* to define the scope of judicial review jurisdiction by reference to the true nature, rather than to the formal source, of official power. It must be conceded that these expectations have been to some extent disappointed. As the case law demonstrates, the "surrogacy" criterion has yielded no great clarity in the definition of "public function".[99] And the "consensual" criterion has been used to exclude from review jurisdiction bodies which, both on the surrogacy criterion and on what many people would regard as a commonsense view of what counts as public power, should be included.

On the other hand, much of what prior to the 1980s was plainly "government power" has now been diffused among many different varieties of non-statutory and non-government-controlled bodies. This demonstrates both the need for and value of the courts' development of the *Datafin* principle. If by reference to the public interest considerations sketched in *section A* of this chapter it is accepted that official power needs a special "public law" regime, it follows that a legal regime which failed even to attempt to define the scope of official power by reference to current and changing government philosophy and practice would be radically deficient.

As their use of the consensual criterion shows, the courts have been particularly concerned to prevent the intrusion of public law principles into legal relationships which are essentially matters of private rather than public law. While different views may be held on the balance between public and private interest in, say, the regulation of the activities of privatised utilities or trade or professional associations, it is difficult to see why the existence of a contractual relationship or contractual remedies should automatically label a matter as one of private law only. So multi-faceted a question as the proper scope of public law regulation is unlikely to be resolved by the application of any single litmus test. As will appear, the problematic issue of the relation between

---

[95] [1995] 3 All E.R. 952.
[96] See *e.g.* Gas Act 1986, s.30(1)–(3): a time-limited (42 days) ouster clause: see Chap. 7, *section A 6.*
[97] See Chap. 5, *section C 2.*
[98] Hunt (1997) in Taggart, *Prov. cf.* Aronson (1997), *ibid.*
[99] Pannick (1988), (1992).

contract and public law has also hindered progress towards a satisfactory answer to the question to be tackled in *section C* following, *i.e.* what actions of reviewable authorities are reviewable? More generally, the demarcation of the proper domains of public law and private law was hindered rather than helped by the evolution in the 1980s of rules of procedural exclusivity requiring public law cases to be brought by judicial review and private law cases by ordinary civil proceedings. Problems and possible solutions in this area will be considered in Chapter 5. As regards the development of a satisfactory judicial demarcation of the public-private law boundary, it may be possible in broad terms to say no more than that "an issue is subject to public law if (a) it is one about which the public has a legitimate concern as to its outcome and (b) it is not an issue which is already satisfactorily protected by private law".[1] Beyond that, one may hope for the development of case law which delivers more than it has to date of what was promised when *Datafin* was decided and which currently is making "exceptionally heavy weather"[2] of the process of establishing the boundaries of public law regulation.

C REVIEWABLE ACTION

Judicial review jurisdiction was characterised at the start of this chapter as a jurisdiction to decide whether or not a particular exercise of official power is authorised by law. *Section B* above considered the question of what bodies are to be regarded as performing "official" functions and as, on that basis, subject to judicial review in the performance (or non-performance) of those functions. But not all official actions of reviewable authorities are reviewable — only those actions which count as "exercises of official power". This section explores that notion.

- **Action not reviewable because power not actually "exercised"**
  An official action of a reviewable authority may not be reviewable because it is not an actual "exercise" of power. The action in question is, rather, a statement of intention or policy, perhaps even a threat, regarding such exercise (a flexing of official muscle); or it may be simply an official statement as to the legal position on a particular matter which gains force or credence from the status of the maker of the statement. There are however some circumstances in which action within these categories will be treated by the courts as an "exercise" of power, and so reviewable. *Sub-section 1* below deals with these.

- **Action not reviewable because what is exercised is not "power"**
  An official action of a reviewable authority may not be reviewable because it is not an exercise of "power" but, rather of contractual or other legal freedom or capacity. *Sub-section 2* considers the extent to which judicial review jurisdiction may be invoked to take public law control into such areas: in particular into the sphere of public authority contracting.

On these issues, as on the definition of reviewable authority, the case law displays a shift of emphasis from form to substance, from *"de jure"* to *"de facto"* — particularly in cases where the courts perceive either unfairness or abuse of discretion by reviewable authorities. One may observe here also a "toe in the water" unwillingness to carry too far too quickly a jurisdiction newly-asserted.

---

[1] Woolf (1995) p. 64; *cf.* Craig, *AL,* p.777.
[2] Harlow (1997), p. 257.

1 EXERCISING LEGAL POWER OR MERELY FLEXING OFFICIAL MUSCLE?

Until the mid-1980s both judges and commentators emphasised that actions of public authorities did not count as "exercises" of power, and so were not reviewable, unless they changed the legal balance sheet in some way, *e.g.* the refusal or withdrawal of licences or benefits, whether under statutory or prerogative or de facto (*Datafin*) power. So, in the *CCSU* case[3] Lord Diplock said that "To qualify as a subject for judicial review [a] decision must have consequences which affect some person . . . either (a) by altering rights or obligations of that person . . . or (b) by depriving him of some benefit or advantage which . . . he can legitimately expect . . .". Similarly, Professor Wade in 1988 wrote of "whether some issue is being determined to some person's prejudice in law".[4] On this basis one would have said that the types of action to be discussed under headings *a*, *b* and *c* below were not reviewable.

(a) Official statements of policy / general intention

In *R. v. Liverpool C.C., ex p. Employment Secretary*[5] a resolution by the (Labour) City Council that it would withdraw grant aid from any organisation which participated in a new (Conservative) Government training scheme was quashed on an AJR brought by the secretary of state. The resolution did not itself affect anyone's legal rights (it simply threatened to do so: the AJR alleged "threatened abuse of discretionary powers by imposition of sanctions"); but it could clearly be regarded as at least a flexing of official muscle.

Contrast *R. v. Halton B.C., ex p. Poynton*[6] where P, who wished to become a part-time licensed taxi-driver, failed to obtain judicial review of his local authority's adopted policy of granting licences only to "full-timers": [1] the court would not review policy "in vacuo"; and [2] judicial review in these circumstances would pre-empt the appeal procedure available to the applicant if he made an unsuccessful licence application. Similarly, in *R. v. City of Westminster, ex p. Tansey*[7] the court declined to review "in advance of any actual decision" a resolution by a local authority to discharge its homeless persons' duties by the use of hostels and hotels.

The *Liverpool* case shows that statements of intention to act unlawfully can in themselves be reviewable if they contain an element of abuse of discretion: public authorities should be restrained from using the weight of their position to threaten or pressurise people to refrain from exercising their legitimate freedom of action. But *Poynton* and *Tansey* suggest that in the absence of some abusive or punitive element in a statement of policy or intention, complainants will be told to postpone their challenge until they can point to a specific decision applying the allegedly unlawful policy: challenging the policy itself will be premature.

Note however that where a policy is not to act in a particular way but to refrain from so acting, the policy will be reviewable if it can be shown that by not acting the authority is actually in breach of its legal duties. In *R. v. Metropolitan Police Commissioner, ex p. Blackburn*[8] the Commissioner had adopted the policy of not prosecuting casinos for certain offences under the betting and gaming legislation unless there were complaints of cheating or a casino had become the haunt of

---

[3] [1984] 3 All E.R. 935 at 949.
[4] Wade's *Administrative Law* (6th ed.) p. 638; Wade and Forsyth, *AL* (7th ed., 1994), p. 634 omits "in law".
[5] [1989] C.O.D. 404.
[6] *The Times,* March 10, 1989.
[7] (1989) 21 H.L.R. 57.
[8] [1968] 1 All E.R. 763.

criminals. The Court of Appeal held that the policy was reviewable since it amounted to a breach by the Commissioner of his (non-statutory) public duty to enforce the law of the land.

(b) Official statements as to legal position

Just as (in a case such as the *Liverpool* grants case, above) a statement of intention may constitute a reviewable exercise of official power, so, sometimes, may a mere statement by a public authority of its understanding of the legal position on a particular matter. Although such statements in themselves can alter nobody's legal position, they can affect how people behave, precisely because of the status and apparent authority of the body concerned.

In *Gillick v. West Norfolk, etc. Health Authority and Department of Health and Social Security*[9] the DHSS had issued a departmental circular saying that parental consent was not invariably required in order for doctors to give contraceptive advice to girls under 16. Mrs G, as mother of such a girl, sought a declaration that the circular was wrong in law. Although she failed on the substantive point, the House of Lords accepted that there are circumstances where "if a government department . . . promulgates in a public document . . . advice which is erroneous in law"[10] the court has jurisdiction to review[11] and correct the error by an appropriate declaration.

Lord Bridge characterised this as "a significant extension of the court's power of judicial review"[12] which he said stemmed from the grant of a declaration by the House of Lords in an earlier case, *Royal College of Nursing v. Department of Health and Social Security.*[13] There the College sought a declaration that a DHSS circular was wrong in law to endorse the legality of a certain abortion procedure in which nurses were asked to participate. The DHSS successfully counterclaimed for a declaration that the view in the circular was correct in law. In earlier cases declarations had been granted in respect of erroneous official pronouncements as to an individual's liabilities (*e.g.* to be prosecuted for failure to provide information which had been unlawfully demanded by the revenue[14]) or rights (*e.g.* to carry out quarrying operations on one's land without planning permission wrongly said to be required).[15] But in the *Royal College* and *Gillick* cases what was reviewed was an abstract official statement on "a pure question of law"[16] not tied to a specific case.

The courts have made occasional but not extensive use of this "significant extension" of their review power. For example, in 1999 a government circular pressurising GPs (on grounds of cost) not to prescribe Viagra on the NHS was declared unlawful:[17] it was likely to cause GPs to breach their duty to provide whatever treatment they regarded as appropriate. In *Gillick* itself, though, Lord Bridge stressed that "In cases where any proposition of law implicit in a departmental advisory document is interwoven with questions of social and ethical controversy, the court should . . . avoid . . . proffering answers to hypothetical questions of law which do not strictly arise for decision."[18] Certainly in *R. v. Employment Secretary, ex p. Equal Opportunities Commission*[19] where the Government had made what proved to be an erroneous statement that the United Kingdom was not in breach of its equal pay obligations under E.C. law the House of Lords pointedly

---

[9] [1985] 3 All E.R. 402.
[10] Lord Bridge at p. 427e.
[11] *ibid.* See also Lords Fraser at 405d, Scarman at 416e, Templeman at 436h.
[12] [1985] 3 All E.R. at 427e.
[13] [1981] 1 All E.R. 545.
[14] *Dyson v. Att.-Gen.* [1912] 1 Ch. 158.
[15] *Pyx Granite Co. Ltd v. Ministry of Housing and Local Government* [1959] 3 All E.R. 1.
[16] Lord Bridge in *Gillick* [1985] 3 All E.R. at 427b. But *cf.* Wade (1986), pp. 174–176.
[17] *R. v. Health Secretary, ex p. Pfizer Ltd, The Times,* June 17, 1999.
[18] *ibid.,* p. 427f.
[19] [1994] 1 All E.R. 910.

granted judicial review (by way of a declaration) on a basis other than the *Gillick* erroneous advice principle — *i.e.* that United Kingdom law was inconsistent with E.C. law, not that the government's contrary statement amounted to a reviewable error.[20] The *Greenwich* poll tax leaflet case[21] may be an example of the invocation (albeit unsuccessful) of the *Gillick* principle. The *Greenwich* case, with its reference to "government propaganda", perhaps indicates that the jurisdiction to review statements of law (as with that to review statements of policy) will be most readily exercised in cases with overtones of abuse of power. Whether either jurisdiction will be much exercised in other types of case remains to be seen. "In the United States there is a doctrine of 'ripeness [for review]' the basic rationale of which 'is to prevent the courts, through avoidance of premature adjudication, from entangling themselves in abstract disagreements over administrative policies, and also to protect [administrative] agencies from judicial interference until an administrative decision has been formalized and its effects felt in a concrete way by the challenging parties'."[22] It has been suggested that "[w]ith the benefit of such a concept courts would have a better tool, to guide them in the exercise of the supervisory jurisdiction over advice and recommendations or by the use of advisory declarations and clearer guidance as to the circumstances and the type of issue in which such relief is appropriate."[23]

Note on the remedy of declaration

The remedy of declaration[24] plays an important part in public (as well as in private) law, see, *e.g.* the *Royal College* and *Equal Opportunities Commission* cases (above). Its role as a judicial review remedy is considered in Chapter 5.[25]

The following points may be noted here for future reference.

- Order 15, rule 16 of the Rules of the Supreme Court provides: "No claim or other proceeding shall be open to objection on the ground that a merely declaratory judgment or order is sought thereby, and the court may make binding declarations of right whether or not any consequential relief is or could be claimed."

- A declaration is "binding" in that it can be relied on in any subsequent proceedings alleging a breach of those rights but, unlike other remedies available for breach, *e.g.* various types of injunctions or damages, it is not mandatory, so that action inconsistent with a declaration is not a contempt of court.

- Official action taken under the protection of a declaration will lose that protection if, on appeal, the declaration is held to have been wrongly granted. In *St George's Healthcare NHS Trust v. S*[26] Hogg J. had granted a declaration dispensing with the consent of a pregnant woman, S, to a caesarian delivery of her baby. The Court of Appeal held that the declaration was wrongly granted and that the hospital would, accordingly, be liable in trespass for performing the operation.[27]

(c) Official lists and records

A good example of the shift of emphasis from form to substance in defining what counts as an "exercise" of power is provided by the willingness of the court to review decisions of local

---

[20] See [1994] 1 All E.R. at 919c; see also [1993] 1 All E.R. at 1048g, CA.
[21] *R. v. Environment Secretary, ex p. Greenwich L.B.C., The Times,* May 17, 1989: *section B 2 a* above.
[22] Beatson (1998), p. 222.
[23] *ibid.,* On advisory declarations see Chap. 5, *section B 2 c.*
[24] The leading work on the remedy is *Zamir & Woolf on the Declaratory Judgment* (2nd ed., 1993).
[25] *Section B 2 c.*
[26] [1998] 3 All E.R. 673.
[27] *ibid.,* p. 702a–d.

authorities to list suspected individuals in non-statutory "child abuse registers". In *R. v. Norfolk C.C., ex p. M,*[28] a decision subsequently approved by the Court of Appeal,[29] the Divisional Court quashed the decision of a social services case conference to place M's name on the register without giving him a hearing. The registers had no statutory authority but their form was prescribed by ministerial circular. In itself the listing did not change the suspect's legal position but plainly might lead to a variety of future legal consequences. On this basis[30] the listing was reviewable.

In *ex p. M* the court dismissed the council's argument that the listing was a "purely clerical or ministerial act, internal to the council's own administrative procedures". No doubt public authorities often have occasion to gather and record information which may relate to future decisions which clearly affect the legal position of individuals. The child abuse register cases show that there are circumstances in which judicial review can be invoked well before such effects are felt.

2 Public Law or Private Law?[31]

The discussion turns now to consider the question of what official action will be regarded as an exercise of "power" (and so subject to the public law regime of judicial review) rather than simply an exercise of contractual or other legal freedom or capacity (and so subject only to private law rules).

Here again until the mid-1980s it appeared to be part of English public law doctrine that in their choice of and dealings with contractual partners public authorities were governed by ordinary private law principles, except in so far as those were modified by or under statute in specific contexts. In their contractual dealings public authorities were not subject to judicial review because contract was a matter of private, not public, law. It has been seen in the discussion of the *Datafin* case law that a rigid doctrine that all contractual relationships are to be governed purely by ordinary private law rules of contract draws an artificial and unsatisfactory line between public and private law regulation. As will now appear, it is by no means obvious why as a matter of principle the same contractual freedoms which are accorded by the law to a private individual contracting on his own account should be accorded to a public authority contracting in pursuit of its public powers and duties. It will now be shown that, at any rate in the context of a public authority's choice of its contractual partners, the courts have taken significant steps towards recognising this.

(a) Public law standards in choice of contractual partner?

In *R. v. Lewisham L.B.C., ex p. Shell U.K. Ltd*[32] a decision by the Lewisham council to boycott Shell products because of the company's commercial links with the then apartheid regime in South Africa was quashed by the Divisional Court on AJR on the ground that a public authority must not use its power to pressurise persons into refraining from exercising their legitimate freedom of action. This was in effect the same basis for intervention as in the *Liverpool* grants case[33]; but what was remarkable about the *Lewisham* case was that the court found no difficulty in

---

[28] [1989] 2 All E.R. 359.
[29] *R. v. Harrow L.B.C., ex p. D* [1990] 3 All E.R. 12.
[30] [1989] 2 All E.R. at 365g.
[31] Craig, *AL*, pp. 144–146, 772, 778; Fredman and Morris (1994) pp. 76–80.
[32] [1988] 1 All E.R. 938.
[33] *R. v. Liverpool C.C., ex p. Employment Secretary* [1989] C.O.D. 404 (*subsection 1 a* above).

classifying as an exercise of public power what was in law simply a decision by the authority not to contract with Shell.

In *Lewisham* the court "applied" *Wheeler v. Leicester City Council*[34] in which the House of Lords granted judicial review of the council's refusal to renew Leicester Rugby Club's licence to use a municipal sports ground. Here too the AJR succeeded on the basis that the council's purpose was to "punish" the club for not pressing its members to refrain from touring South Africa. But in *Wheeler* the council was relying on statutory powers under the Open Spaces and Public Health Acts whereas in *Lewisham* the council relied simply on its freedom to contract with whomever it chose and by reference to whatever criteria or considerations it chose. The novelty of *Lewisham* was that the court appeared to take the view that because local authorities are creations of statute and "only [have] powers given to [them] by statute",[35] all their actions (including choice of contractual partner) may be subject to scrutiny under public law principles.

The novelty of this judicial approach was somewhat overtaken, at any rate as regards local authorities, less than four months after the *Lewisham* decision when sections 17-20 of the Local Government Act 1988 came into effect. Section 17 requires local and other specified[36] public authorities (not including central government departments) to disregard "non-commercial considerations" in their choice of contractor for "contracts for the supply of goods or materials, for the supply of services or for the execution of works". "Non-commercial considerations" include tendering companies' labour relations records (except, as provided by section 18, regarding race relations) and "any political industrial or sectarian affiliations or interests of tendering companies".[37] An authority will be deemed to be in breach of section 17 if in the course of a tendering process it asks questions or offers draft clauses relating to non-commercial matters.[38] As to enforcement, section 19[39] provides that where an authority has breached section 17, potential contractors not only have a sufficient interest for AJR but also may claim damages suffered in consequence of the breach, limited to expenditure reasonably incurred in making an unsuccessful tender. (Note that the "non-commercial considerations" provisions just described were underpinned by provisions in Part I of the Act designed to encourage "contracting-out" of local authority services such as refuse collection, cleaning, schools catering, and maintenance of grounds and vehicles.[40] This policy has been carried much further by the Deregulation and Contracting Out Act 1994 and will be considered later.)[41]

As mentioned, the 1988 Act does not apply to central government contracts. It is true that all public authorities including government departments and public utilities (whether or not privatised) are bound by E.C. rules on public procurement. In the protection of Community rights these rules cover broadly similar ground to the 1988 Act provisions considered above, although they take a less formalistic approach to the control they seek to achieve.[42] However, their impact somewhat is limited by the fact that they apply only to higher-value contracts, *e.g.* the Public Works Directive applies only to contracts worth more than €5 million.[43]

Statute and E.C. regulation apart, how far will the courts go after *Lewisham*[44] in applying judicial review principles to public authorities' decisions as to their choice of contractual partner? *Lewisham*, like *Liverpool*,[45] was a case with clear overtones of oppressive official behaviour, and in

---

[34] [1985] 2 All E.R. 1106.
[35] Neill L.J. [1988] 1 All E.R. at 949e.
[36] Sched. 2.
[37] s.17(5).
[38] s.19(10).
[39] Ss.(7), (8).
[40] 1988 Act s.2 and Sched. 1.
[41] Chap. 9, *section C.*
[42] See Craig, *AL,* pp. 156–159 for details.
[43] Public Works Contracts Directive 93/37, Art 6(1): Rudden and Wyatt, *BCL,* p. 440.
[44] *R. v. Lewisham L.B.C., ex p. Shell U.K. Ltd* [1988] 1 All E.R. 938.
[45] *R. v. Liverpool C.C., ex p. Employment Secretary* [1989] C.O.D. 404.

that sense, of abuse of power. In the absence of such features, to what extent will these decisions be regarded as subject to judicial review — say for unfair procedure or because based on non-commercial considerations? In the latter connection the use by central government of its contractual patronage to further its social and economic policies is well documented.[46]

Two reported AJRs alleging procedural unfairness show that different courts may adopt different perspectives in this area. In *R. v. Lord Chancellor, ex p. Hibbit (a firm)*[47] H, a firm of court shorthand writers, applied unsuccessfully for judicial review of a decision of the Lord Chancellor's Department to award a contract to another firm. The Divisional Court accepted that the department had dealt unfairly with H's tender but held that the action was not reviewable. Rose L.J. said it was not appropriate to equate tendering conditions adopted in the exercise of a common law ability to contract with a statement of policy or practice or with policy decisions in the spheres of inland revenue, immigration and the like, control of which were the special province of the state. The challenged decision lacked a sufficient public law element. But in *R. v. Legal Aid Board, ex p. Donn & Co.*[48] D, a firm of solicitors, obtained judicial review of the Board's award to other firms of a contract for legal aid representation of a "Gulf War syndrome" multi-party action. Taking the nature and purpose of the tendering/selection process together, Ognall J. held that the public dimensions of the matter made it justiciable in public law. On the facts, D's tender had not been fairly dealt with.

It seems unlikely that *Donn* and *Lewisham* can be distinguished from *Hibbit* on the basis that the former cases involved statutory authorities whereas the latter was a case of the Crown contracting under its common law capacity: in *Donn* the court based its ruling on reviewability not on the argument that the Board's functions were "statutorily underpinned"[49] but on an "overall impression"[50] that the matter fell in the domain of public rather than of private law. If the test of reviewability is to be the nature rather than the source of power, it may well be that the government's hitherto legally unfettered freedom to use contract as an instrument of policy is being brought to an end by the courts.[51]

While it is arguably in the public interest for the courts to police the fairness of tendering procedures for official contracts, it is easy to see that too intrusive an approach may encourage over-frequent challenges by disappointed tenderers. Again, it may be thought in the public interest for the courts to exercise some control over the use of official commercial patronage for non-commercial purposes; but in the absence of statutory guidance this is delicate ground. Moreover, literally interpreted, the provisions of the 1988 Act may prove too great a restriction on what many would regard as the legitimate uses of official contractual patronage.[52] The cases just considered show that different courts may take different views on where the public interest lies: views which future judicial review rulings will need to accommodate.

(b) Public law standards in treatment of contractual partner?

Here too, it appeared until recently to be established legal doctrine that the exercise by parties to a contract of their rights under the contract is a matter governed solely by the ordinary (*i.e.* private) law of contract. But if public law standards are to apply to the processes by which official contracts are concluded, will those standards also have some application to public authorities'

[46] Cane, *Intr. AL,* p. 256; Wade & Forsyth, *AL,* pp. 410, 802; Craig, *AL,* pp. 144–146.
[47] [1993] C.O.D. 326. Oliver (1993).
[48] [1996] 3 All E.R. 1.
[49] [1996] 3 All E.R. at 9a.
[50] *ibid.,* at 11h.
[51] See generally Arrowsmith (1990).
[52] Craig, *AL,* pp. 137–8.

exercise of their contractual rights once a contract has been made? To date, the cases do not suggest any general application of public law standards to determine the lawfulness of public authorities' exercise of their contractual rights.

In *R. v. Wear Valley D.C., ex p. Binks*[53] B had obtained a contractual licence from the local council to sell fast food from her van parked on the council's land. The council revoked the licence which under the terms of the contract they were entitled to do. On AJR by B, the court quashed the revocation on the ground of unfairness. It is true that here the court applied public law principles to the exercise of contractual rights; but the case is of limited significance since the council was simply using the mechanism of contract to discharge its public licensing function — which was plainly subject to public law regulation by judicial review.

In *Jones v. Swansea City Council*[54] J was the tenant of commercial premises owned by the council. The council as landlord refused to grant her permission to change the use of the premises. J alleged that the refusal was based on certain councillors' animosity towards her husband, himself a councillor who led a political group which had wrested control of the council from the Labour group which had regained control at a later election. J claimed damages for the tort of misfeasance in public office, an element of which, as will be seen[55] is an abuse of official power. The Court of Appeal rejected the council's argument that a public authority's exercise of its contractual right as landlord to refuse a change of use (which on ordinary private law principles would be lawful even though malicious) was a matter of private law only. Slade L.J. said that there was:

> "no reason why a decision taken by the holder of a public office, in his or its capacity as such holder, with intent to injure the party thereby affected or with knowledge that the decision is *ultra vires*[56] should be incapable of giving rise to a misfeasance action merely because the decision is taken in the exercise of a power conferred by a contract and in this sense has no public element."[57]

While Slade L.J. observed that the boundaries of judicial review and misfeasance are "by no means necessarily co-terminous",[58] the case does show that for some purposes at least a public authority's exercise of its contractual rights may constitute an abuse of power. It seems unlikely, however, that such exercise would at present attract judicial review without the element of malicious or intentional infliction of damage which is required for misfeasance liability.

D CONCLUSION

The court's view on whether a particular legal challenge raises issues of public law, whether the case concerns the exercise of a "public function" or of "public power", will determine whether or not the grounds[59] and remedies[60] of judicial review may be invoked by the person making the challenge: see *TABLE 3* for a summary of the effect of the case law discussed in *sections B and C* above.

[53] [1985] 2 All E.R. 699.
[54] [1989] 3 All E.R. 162, CA; [1990] 3 All E.R. 737, HL.
[55] Chap. 8 *section D*.
[56] Latin for "beyond [the authority's] powers": see Chap. 4 *section B 1*. (Footnote added.)
[57] [1989] 3 All E.R. at 174j; see also Nourse L.J. at 186g.
[58] *ibid.* at 174h.
[59] See Chap. 4.
[60] See Chap. 5.

TABLE 3

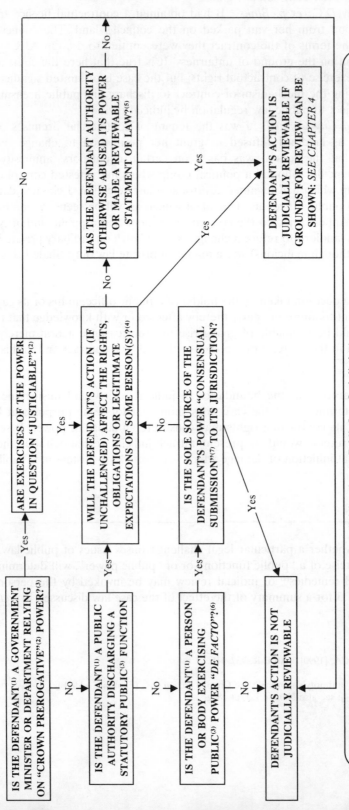

REVIEWABLE AUTHORITIES AND REVIEWABLE ACTION

IS THE DEFENDANT[1] A GOVERNMENT MINISTER OR DEPARTMENT RELYING ON "CROWN PREROGATIVE"[2] POWER?[3]

ARE EXERCISES OF THE POWER IN QUESTION "JUSTICIABLE"?[2]

HAS THE DEFENDANT AUTHORITY OTHERWISE ABUSED ITS POWER OR MADE A REVIEWABLE STATEMENT OF LAW?[5]

IS THE DEFENDANT[1] A PUBLIC AUTHORITY DISCHARGING A STATUTORY PUBLIC[3] FUNCTION

WILL THE DEFENDANT'S ACTION (IF UNCHALLENGED) AFFECT THE RIGHTS, OBLIGATIONS OR LEGITIMATE EXPECTATIONS OF SOME PERSON(S)?[4]

IS THE DEFENDANT[1] A PERSON OR BODY EXERCISING PUBLIC[3] POWER *DE FACTO*?[6]

IS THE SOLE SOURCE OF THE DEFENDANT'S POWER "CONSENSUAL SUBMISSION"[7] TO ITS JURISDICTION?

DEFENDANT'S ACTION IS NOT JUDICIALLY REVIEWABLE

DEFENDANT'S ACTION IS JUDICIALLY REVIEWABLE IF GROUNDS FOR REVIEW CAN BE SHOWN: *SEE CHAPTER 4*

NOTES (references are to sections of Chap. 3, Judicial review — Public Law Jurisdiction)

[1] "Defendant" is used to denote the party whose action is challenged, though the challenged party in an AJR is technically a "respondent"

[2] For Prerogative power and justiciability, see *section B 2 a*

[3] For whether reviewable authorities are discharging public functions or exercising public powers in their selection of and relationship with contractual partners, see *section C 2*

[4] See *section C 1*

[5] see *section C 1 a–c*

[6] For the *Datafin* "surrogacy" criterion, see *section B 2 b*

[7] For the *Datafin* "consensual" criterion, see *section B 2 b*

The problem of defining the reach of public law jurisdiction has arisen in contexts other than those considered above, including:

- **Whether decisions to appoint or dismiss public employees are subject to judicial review.**

- **Whether breaches by a public authority of its statutory duties are remediable by judicial review or, on the contrary, by tort damages.**

These questions have assumed particular prominence in the context of disputes as to whether a particular challenge has been mounted by the correct procedure, *i.e.* by AJR rather than ordinary civil proceedings or vice versa. This will be considered in Chapter 5 which will contain further discussion of the public law/private law divide and of how that distinction is, and should be, dealt with by English law.

Chapter 4

JUDICIAL REVIEW — GROUNDS

On what grounds may one seek judicial review of official action where such action is reviewable under the principles explained in Chapter 3?

A INTRODUCTION: "ERROR OF LAW" *VIS-À-VIS* "ILLEGALITY", "IRRATIONALITY" AND "PROCEDURAL IMPROPRIETY" AS GROUNDS FOR JUDICIAL REVIEW

1 "ERROR OF LAW"

In *Page v. Hull University Visitor*[1] the House of Lords made it clear that in general[2] "any error of law" made by a reviewable authority in reaching a decision will ground judicial review.[3]

"Error of law" was explained in Chapter 2 as an error as to the statement or understanding of an applicable legal rule. The types of error of law there identified[4] were:

(1) "serious procedural errors" — including not only breach of evidential or other rules governing a fact-finding process, but also any serious breach of an important express procedural requirement or any breach of the rules of natural justice, or duty to act fairly, where applicable.

(2) "category errors" — errors in formulating the correct test to apply in answering "category questions" (*i.e.* whether or not a particular set of facts falls within a general category or concept such as, *e.g.*, "employee", "member of [a particular] family", "trade")[5];

(3) "wrong considerations"[6] — taking account of legally irrelevant (improper), or failing to take account of legally relevant (proper) considerations in exercising discretionary powers.

---

[1] [1993] 1 All E.R. 97.
[2] For exceptions, see *section B 3 c* below.
[3] See Lords Browne-Wilkinson at 107h, Griffiths at 100a, Slynn at 111e; unanimously endorsed by the House in 1996 in *Williams v. Bedwellty Justices* [1996] 3 All E.R. 737 at 743.
[4] See summary and *TABLE 2* in Chap. 2, *section D 7*.
[5] Chap. 2, *section D 2*.
[6] Chap. 2, *section D 6 a*.

As also explained in Chapter 2, errors of types (2) and (3) may appear either:

(a) from what the decision maker has said about his understanding of the relevant law; or

(b) by a process of inference where, given the facts of a particular case, the decision reached is one which could not have been reached by an authority who properly understood the law. In these circumstances one can see from the decision itself that the decision maker must have applied the wrong test or, as the case may be, based his decision on wrong considerations.

2 "ILLEGALITY", "IRRATIONALITY", "PROCEDURAL IMPROPRIETY"

In 1984 in the *CCSU* case[7] Lord Diplock said that "one can conveniently classify under three heads the grounds upon which administrative action is subject to control by judicial review. The first ground I would call 'illegality', the second 'irrationality' and the third 'procedural impropriety'."[8]

Lord Diplock defined these terms as follows[9]:

- *Illegality:* the failure of a decision maker to "understand correctly the law that regulates his decision-making power and [to] give effect to it."

- *Irrationality:* "what can by now be succinctly referred to as '*Wednesbury* unreasonableness'.[10] It applies to a decision which is so outrageous in its defiance of logic or of accepted moral standards that no sensible person who had applied his mind to the question to be decided could have arrived at it."

- *Procedural Impropriety:* "[F]ailure to observe basic rules of natural justice or failure to act with procedural fairness towards the person who will be affected by the decision. . . . [A]lso failure by an administrative tribunal to observe procedural rules that are expressly laid down in the legislative instrument by which its jurisdiction is conferred, even where such failure does not involve any denial of natural justice."

How does this classification of reviewable error in terms of "illegality", "irrationality" and "procedural impropriety" relate to the classification in *section 1*, above, of error of law in terms of "serious procedural errors", "category errors" and "wrong considerations"?

"Illegality" defined as the failure of a decision maker correctly to understand or apply the relevant law plainly embraces both category errors and wrong considerations ((2) and (3) above) whether appearing from what the decision maker has said or by inference ((a) and (b) above). "Procedural impropriety" plainly embraces serious breach of an important express procedural requirement or breach of the rules of natural justice, or duty to act fairly, ((1) above). Breach of evidential or other rules governing the fact-finding process ((1) above) can be classified as either illegality or procedural impropriety. They are dealt with in this chapter under the former head.

This leaves "Irrationality" (or "*Wednesbury* unreasonableness") in so far as it extends beyond "Illegality" as just defined) which, Lord Diplock said, "by now can stand upon its own feet as an accepted ground on which a decision may be attacked by judicial review."

---

[7] *Council of Civil Service Unions v. Minister for the Civil Service* [1984] 3 All E.R. 935: see Chap. 3, *section B 2 a.*
[8] *ibid.*, p. 950h.
[9] *ibid.*, p. 951.
[10] *Associated Provincial Picture Houses Ltd v. Wednesbury Corporation* [1947] 2 All E.R. 680.

3 PLAN OF THIS CHAPTER

The extended notion of *Wednesbury* unreasonableness apart, it should now be clear that Lord Diplock's *CCSU* statement of grounds for judicial review essentially corresponds with Lord Browne-Wilkinson's briefer statement in *Page* that "any error of law" will ground judicial review. As explained in Chapter 2, courts are often given **statutory** jurisdiction to hear appeals against errors of law; but on what basis do the superior courts assert a **common law** jurisdiction to review such errors? This chapter examines the different types of error of law as grounds for the exercise of the common law review jurisdiction as follows:

- *Section B, Illegality (1) — Anisminic and the Extension of Ultra Vires* deals with judicial review of "category" and fact-finding errors of law.

- *Section C, Illegality (2) — Discretionary Power and the "Purpose Axiom"* deals with "wrong considerations" errors.

- *Section D, Free-Standing Grounds: Irrationality. Infringements of Community and Convention Rights. Proportionality* considers "irrationality" as a "free-standing" ground for judicial review. It then examines the extent to which the European Communities Act 1972 and the Human Rights Act 1998 have introduced further free-standing grounds for review, in particular the principle of "proportionality".

- *Section E, Procedural Impropriety* deals, as already stated, with breach of important express procedural requirements and of the rules of natural justice, or duty to act fairly.

- *Section F, Grounds for Judicial Review of Delegated Legislation* deals with certain special issues which arise in defining the grounds upon which the superior courts will review the legality of delegated legislation (*i.e.* official rules and regulations made in the exercise of legislative powers conferred by statute).

B ILLEGALITY (1) — *ANISMINIC* AND THE EXTENSION OF *ULTRA VIRES*[11]

1 "BOUNDARY" *ULTRA VIRES*

As will shortly be explained, it is only since the *Anisminic* case[12] in 1968 that it has become true that (as said above) in general any error of law will ground judicial review of an exercise of official power.

Before *Anisminic*, judicial review was available where a public authority acted outside territorial or functional or temporal or other (*e.g.* financial) boundaries set down by statute. In unlawfully crossing such boundaries, authorities were said (in a phrase imported into public law from company law in the nineteenth century) to act "*ultra vires*" (beyond [their] powers). *Ultra vires* action included both acting outside an authority's field of statutory **power** and failing to act in a particular field when under a statutory **duty** to do so.

---

[11] Wade and Forsyth, *AL*, Chap. 9; Craig, *AL*, Chap. 15; de Smith, *JRAA*, Chap. 5.
[12] *Anisminic Ltd v. Foreign Compensation Commission* [1969] 1 All E.R. 208.

(a) Statutory powers

In ruling on *vires* questions the courts established what may be termed "the express or implied authority doctrine". Under this doctrine statutory authorities are not limited to doing what statute expressly authorises them to do: additionally, "whatever may fairly be regarded as incidental to, or consequential upon, those things which the legislature has authorised ought not (unless expressly prohibited) to be held, by judicial construction, to be *ultra vires*"[13]

Thus, *e.g.*, in *Att.-Gen. v. Manchester Corporation*[14] a statutory power to run tramways for the purpose, *inter alia*, of carrying parcels was held to extend by implication to the provision of ancillary services including doorstep collection and delivery of parcels carried on tram routes. Contrast *London County Council v. Att.-Gen.*[15] where a statutory power to work tramways was held not to extend to the provision of a bus service linking tram termini across the River Thames but not confined to tramway passengers.

For local authorities the tolerance of the express or implied authority doctrine was further extended by section 111(1) of the Local Government Act 1972. Local authorities are empowered (subject to any contrary statutory provision) to do ". . . any thing . . . which is calculated to facilitate, or is conducive or incidental to, the discharge of any of their functions." The ambit of section 111 will be explored later.[16]

(b) Statutory duties

Examples of reviewable failures to act in a particular field when under a statutory duty to do so would be the police decision in *R. v. Metropolitan Police Commissioner, ex p. Blackburn*[17] not to prosecute casinos for offences under the betting and gaming legislation; or where, as in *R. v. West Yorks Coroner, ex p. Smith*[18] a coroner declines in breach of his statutory duty to hold an inquest on a body located within his area on the (legally wrong) ground that the death had occurred abroad.[19]

2 NOTE: PATENT ERROR ("ERROR ON THE FACE OF THE RECORD")[20]

Before seeing how the *Anisminic* case has enormously expanded the classical notion of *ultra vires*, it should be noted that the High Court has since the seventeenth century asserted also a quite different alternative basis for review, *i.e.*, that an error (almost always of law) appeared "on the face of the record" of the public authority decision in question.

This assertion of jurisdiction to, as it were, "keep the public record straight", *i.e.* free from patent error, led to the development of highly technical rules to determine whether or not an error was apparent — patent — on the face of the record. The "patent error" jurisdiction was nonetheless important in the pre-*Anisminic* era. But now that in general all errors of law are reviewable, whether patent or not, the doctrine has lost its importance. For, in "extend[ing] the doctrine of *ultra vires*" the *Anisminic* case "rendered obsolete the distinction between errors of law on the face of the record and other errors of law".[21]

On what basis, then, did the courts so extend the *ultra vires* doctrine?

---

[13] Lord Selborne in *Att.-Gen. v. Great Eastern Railway Co.* (1880) 5 App. Cas. 473 at 478.
[14] [1906] 1 Ch. 643.
[15] [1902] A.C. 165.
[16] Chap. 9, *section B 1.*
[17] [1968] 1 All E.R. 763: see Chap. 3, *section C 1 a.*
[18] [1982] 3 All E.R. 1098.
[19] For further examples see Emery and Smythe, *JR*, pp. 134–136.
[20] Wade and Forsyth, *AL*, pp. 306–311.
[21] Lord Browne-Wilkinson in *Page v. Hull University Visitor* [1993] 1 All E.R. 97 (above) at 107d.

3 ANY ERROR OF LAW NOW *ULTRA VIRES*: THE *ANISMINIC* PRESUMPTION

(a) The presumption and when it applies

(i) *The* Anisminic *case*

Until the House of Lords' decision in *Anisminic Ltd v. Foreign Compensation Commission*[22] the courts in interpreting public law statutes had adopted the presumption that category errors of law made by a statutory authority operating within its territorial, functional, temporal etc boundaries were not to be regarded as taking the authority *ultra vires*. This is not to say that such category errors were never treated as taking a statutory authority *ultra vires* or "outside jurisdiction" (a phrase of equivalent meaning commonly used instead of *"ultra vires"* when dealing with authorities of a judicial or quasi-judicial nature). On the contrary, there were many reported cases before *Anisminic* in which the presumption that a category error was not jurisdictional (*ultra vires*) was held to have been rebutted. But there were also many cases where the presumption was held to prevail. There was no clear test, and the whole area was an unpredictable forensic lottery.[23] In the *Anisminic* case the House of Lords abandoned the existing presumption and adopted its opposite, *i.e.* that, subject to contrary statutory indication, any error of law made by an authority in exercising its statutory functions will take the authority *ultra vires* and thus ground judicial review.

In the *Anisminic* case the (English) company was claiming compensation for loss of its Egyptian premises which had been sequestrated by the Egyptian government during the 1956 Suez crisis and sold on to an Egyptian government agency (TEDO). The Foreign Compensation Commission (FCC)[24] had a statutory duty to distribute to qualified claimants sums paid as reparations by the Egyptian Government to the United Kingdom Government. Under the relevant statutory instrument, FCC were directed to treat a claim as established if they were satisfied that, *inter alia*, both the claimant and any "successor in title" of the claimant were British nationals. FCC interpreted "successor in title" to mean "subsequent owner" or "assignee". On that basis TEDO was the claimant company's successor in title: it was not a British national, so the company's claim failed.

The company successfully sought judicial review of the FCC's ruling: a majority (3:2) of the House of Lords held that "successor in title" meant "person succeeding to property on death or (in the case of a company) liquidation". On that basis Anisminic Ltd had no successor in title, and TEDO's nationality was immaterial. FCC had, accordingly, erred in its construction of the statutory instrument. The majority of the House held that FCC's error of law in misinterpreting "successor in title" meant that it had asked itself a wrong question — a question it was not empowered to ask — and so had carried itself outside its jurisdiction (*ultra vires*). The reasoning of the majority indicated that, as a general rule, whenever an authority had "misconstrued the provisions giving it power to act"[25], *i.e.* perpetrated a category error of law, it was in future to be regarded as having acted *ultra vires* or outside jurisdiction in a new, "broad", sense to be contrasted with jurisdiction in the "narrow" sense referred to above as "boundary" *ultra vires*.[26]

---

[22] [1969] 1 All E.R. 208.
[23] For a brief discussion, see Emery and Smythe, *JR*, pp. 136–140. See also the first instance judgment of Browne J. in *Anisminic* [1969] 2 A.C. 223 at 237.
[24] Established by Foreign Compensation Act 1950, s.1.
[25] Lord Reid at [1969] 1 All E.R. 213I.
[26] See Lord Reid at 213–214, Lord Pearce at 233; *cf.* Lord Wilberforce at 243–245.

(ii) *From* Anisminic *(1968) to* Page *(1992)*

In later cases, notably *Re Racal Communications Ltd*,[27] *O'Reilly v. Mackman*[28] and *Page v. Hull University Visitor*,[29] the House of Lords has confirmed that the effect of *Anisminic* was to create a presumption that in general whenever a public authority exercising official (*i.e.* either statutory or non-statutory) power errs in law, it acts *ultra vires*. As Lord Browne-Wilkinson said in *Page*: "[after *Anisminic*] it was to be taken that Parliament had only conferred the decision-making power on the basis that it was to be exercised on the correct legal basis: a misdirection in law in making the decision therefore rendered the decision *ultra vires*."[30]

As just stated, it appears that the presumption applies generally to any exercise of official power, statutory or non-statutory. On this basis, category errors of law by "*Datafin*"[31] reviewable authorities or by a minister in the exercise of Crown prerogative power would ordinarily take the decision-maker *ultra vires*. That this is the case appears from the fact that in *Page* the issue was whether, and to what extent, the decisions of a university visitor as to the construction of the university's statutes are subject to judicial review. A university visitor's powers stem from common law, not statute. Although by a majority of 3:2 the House of Lords held that the *Anisminic* presumption did not apply, the basis for this ruling was not that the presumption applies only to statutory powers but that "the common law has for 300 years recognised that the visitor's decision on questions of fact and law are conclusive and are not to be reviewed by the courts".[32] It followed that the courts' power to review the decisions of a university visitor extended only to matters of "boundary *ultra vires*" (jurisdiction in the narrow sense), abuse of discretion or procedural impropriety.

(iii) *The presumption applied: case law examples*

Reverting briefly to the three types of error of law listed at the start of this chapter the following examples of the application of the *Anisminic* presumption may be noted:

Serious procedural errors   It will be explained in *section E* below that it was plain long before *Anisminic* that *breach of important express procedural requirements* and of the *rules of natural justice*, or *duty to act fairly* are errors of law carrying an authority *ultra vires*.

As regards *breach of evidential* or *other rules governing the fact-finding process*: "To convict or commit for trial without any admissible evidence of guilt is to fall into an error of law."[33] But that such error carries an authority *ultra vires* has become clear only recently. In 1996 in *Williams v. Bedwellty Justices*[34] the House of Lords quashed a committal on this basis, and confirmed that "by accepting the full and inevitable scope of the *Anisminic* principle"[35] it follows that such error is jurisdictional.. The *Bedwellty* case confirms also that the *Anisminic* presumption applies as much to inferior courts as to other reviewable authorities,[36] although, as will be explained later,[37] the presumption may in certain circumstances be held to be rebutted.

It should be noted that as a general rule, in the absence of any breach of evidential or other rules governing a fact-finding process, findings of fact, though erroneous, will be held to fall within an authority's jurisdiction. Such error will therefore be beyond the reach of judicial review.[38] But it

---

[27] [1980] 2 All E.R. 634 at 638–639.
[28] [1982] 3 All E.R. 1124 at 1129.
[29] [1993] 1 All E.R. 97.
[30] [1993] 1 All E.R. at 107d.
[31] *R. v. Panel on Take-overs and Mergers, ex p. Datafin plc* [1987] 1 All E.R. 564: Chap. 3, *section B 2 b.*
[32] *ibid.*, at 109b.
[33] Lord Cooke in *Williams v. Bedwellty Justices* [1996] 3 All E.R. 737 at 743d.
[34] *ibid.*
[35] *ibid.*, at 744f.
[36] See also *R. v. Greater Manchester Coroner, ex p. Tal* [1984] 3 All E.R. 240: Emery and Smythe, *JR*, p. 157.
[37] Chap. 7, *section A 3.*
[38] See Yeats (1994), pp. 142 *et seq.*

may sometimes be possible, particularly where statutory powers affect the liberty of the individual, to persuade a court that an authority's jurisdiction exists only if certain "precedent facts" are established and that, accordingly, it is for a review court to decide whether or not those facts exist. The House of Lords took this line in *Khawaja v. Home Secretary*[39] with regard to the statutory power to deport illegal entrants. But in *Bugdaycay v. Home Secretary*,[40] on the statutory power to grant or refuse asylum-seekers leave to enter the United Kingdom, the House affirmed and applied the general rule.

Errors in formulating the correct test to apply in answering a "category question"   *Anisminic* itself involved an error of this type which appeared from what the Commission said about its understanding of the relevant law. An example of review of a category error where, contrastingly, it can be seen from the decision itself (rather than from any express statement) that the decision maker has applied the wrong test is *Islam v. Hillingdon L.B.C.*[41] Islam had been evicted from one-room rented accommodation when he was joined in the United Kingdom by his wife and four children from Bangladesh. His application to the council for accommodation under the homeless persons legislation[42] was rejected on the basis that he had become homeless intentionally. Under the statutory provisions this entailed that Islam had ceased to occupy "accommodation which is available for occupation both by him and by any other person who might reasonably be expected to reside with him" (*i.e.* his wife and family). On Islam's AJR the House of Lords (applying the *Edwards v. Bairstow* doctrine[43]) observed that any authority coming to that conclusion had plainly misunderstood the statutory word "available" which connotes some capacity to do the job in question: a single room cannot be said to be "available" to accommodate six people. The authority's decision was thus *ultra vires*.[44]

The exercise of discretionary powers by reference to wrong considerations   As will be seen in *section C* below it was plain long before *Anisminic* that the exercise of discretionary power on wrong considerations is an error of law carrying an authority *ultra vires*.

(iv) *"Vires" (powers) or "power"?*

The phrase *"ultra vires"* more or less adequately described the basis for judicial review at a period when that process was concerned largely with preventing public authorities going beyond the boundaries of their statutory powers. As will now be apparent, judicial review today extends far beyond "boundary" statutory vires: it has been suggested that "judicial review has moved on from the *ultra vires* rule to a concern for the protection of individuals, and for the control of *power*, rather than *powers*, or *vires*".[45] This may be illustrated by reference to the development of the notion of reviewable action considered in Chapter 3 as well as to the modern expansion of the grounds for review discussed in this chapter. But the phrase *"ultra vires"* is still much-used in the cases to describe official action which, because based on error of law, constitutes an unlawful exercise of public power and is thus susceptible to judicial review. Moreover, recent judicial pronouncements of the highest authority indicate that it remains true that "the juristic basis of judicial review is the doctrine of *ultra vires*".[46]

---

[39] [1983] 1 All E.R. 765 — applied by the Privy Council in *Tan Te Lam v. Detention Centre Superintendent* [1996] 4 All E.R. 256 (whether Vietnamese boat people were detained "pending removal" was a precedent fact).

[40] [1987] 1 All E.R. 940.

[41] [1981] 3 All E.R. 901.

[42] Housing Act 1996, Pt VII, replacing Housing Act 1985, Pt III.

[43] See Chap. 2, *section D 5.*

[44] [1981] 3 All E.R. at 912b.

[45] Oliver (1987), p. 543.

[46] Lord Browne-Wilkinson in *Boddington v. British Transport Police* [1998] 2 All E.R. 203 at 218h; see also Lord Steyn at 225f. For the context of these remarks, see Chap. 6, *section D 2.*

As stated above, and as illustrated in this and subsequent chapters, the *ultra vires* doctrine has, since the nineteenth century, been treated by judges as the chief theoretical basis for judicial review. "The *ultra vires* principle is based on the assumption that judicial review is legitimated on the ground that the courts are applying the intention of the legislature."[47] Thus, "[u]nder our present constitution, judicial review does not challenge but fulfils the intention of Parliament. [The] ready acceptance of *ultra vires* [by] the judges . . . marks the maintenance of the proper balance of powers between the elected and non-elected parts of the constitution."[48] This orthodox doctrine embodies the notion that the common law jurisdiction of the courts to review official action is ultimately subject to any clearly expressed statutory restriction. In recent years some judges (writing extra-judicially) and some academics have argued[49] that the time is now ripe for the replacement of the orthodox doctrine by an assertion that judicial review, like any other part of the common law, can better be legitimated by reference to "the true policy considerations"[50] which in themselves should provide a "reasoned justification which is acceptable in normative terms for the controls which are being imposed".[51] The difficulty with this approach is that (despite protestations that there is no necessary link[52]) it does seem often to lead its proponents to challenge the orthodox proposition that judicial review is ultimately subject to any clearly expressed statutory restriction. For many, then, "to abandon *ultra vires* is to challenge the supremacy of Parliament."[53] Of course, an end to the supremacy of Parliament might very well be a good thing. But if the acts of the democratically-elected legislature are to be vulnerable to being struck down by judges, this power should be given to the judges by the people in some form of constitutional re-settlement; it should not be taken by the judges themselves.[54]

The "*vires* or power?" question thus raises issues of fundamental constitutional importance as to the situation of ultimate authority ("sovereignty") within the state. These issues, along with kindred issues arising from United Kingdom membership of the E.C. and incorporation of the European Convention on Human Rights will be further explored in Chapter 7, *Restrictions on Legal Challenge*.[55]

(b) The *Anisminic* presumption — legal background and constitutional basis

(i) *Legal background*

It was mentioned above that there were many pre-*Anisminic* cases in which the then existing presumption that a category error was not jurisdictional (*ultra vires*) was held to have been rebutted. In most of those cases the reason why the party seeking judicial review needed to show that the error he was alleging carried the authority *ultra vires* was that the statute under which the challenged decision was taken contained a standard-form provision forbidding judicial review of any "decision or order" of the kind being challenged. As will be more fully explained in Chapter 7,[56] "ouster" clauses of this type were from the early 1700s interpreted by the courts as precluding judicial review on the basis of patent error but not on the basis of *ultra vires*. Essentially the reasoning was that a decision or order which is *ultra vires* is not a "decision or order" at all but,

---

[47] Craig (1998), p. 64.
[48] Forsyth (1996), p. 137; Elliott (1999) elaborates and provides further references.
[49] Craig (1998) and references there cited. See further Chap. 7, *section A 7 b*.
[50] *ibid.*, p. 76.
[51] *ibid.*, p. 90.
[52] *ibid.*, p. 87.
[53] Forsyth (1996), p. 134.
[54] See *ibid.*, p. 140.
[55] *Sections A 7–8*.
[56] *Section A 2 a*.

rather, is a "nullity".[57] Thus a clause forbidding judicial review of a "decision or order" does not preclude judicial review where what is challenged is *ultra vires*.

In the *Anisminic* case itself the statute[58] provided that "The determination by the Commission of any application made to them . . . shall not be called in question in any court of law." One may say therefore that the company's lawyers began the proceedings believing that their task was to persuade the court not merely that the FCC's interpretation of "successor in title" was wrong in law but also (and primarily) that (contrary to the then existing presumption) the error was jurisdictional. On existing principles this would have secured victory in the case. What they actually achieved was, so to speak, "surplus to requirements": the effect of the House's adoption of the new presumption was in effect to make it unnecessary in the future for a person seeking review of an official error of law in the teeth of a "shall not be questioned" clause to establish that the error of law carried the authority *ultra vires*. The presumption now is that it does. It is for the authority to show that the case has special features which indicate that the presumption should not apply.

In the pre-*Anisminic* era, litigants needed to persuade the court that a challenged error of law carried the authority *ultra vires* in order to "side-step" an ouster clause. Put another way, by their rulings on the question of what errors of law counted as *ultra vires*, the courts were deciding what errors they would or would not review when faced by an ouster clause. In *Anisminic* (as subsequently interpreted) the House of Lords decided that as a general rule the courts could review all errors of law.

Anisminic greatly increased the number of decisions which could be judicially reviewed for error of law. The presumption that errors of law are jurisdictional means (1) that many erroneous decisions which might previously have been protected from review by an ouster clause are clearly not now protected.[59] It means also (2) that many errors of law which were previously not reviewable because neither jurisdictional nor patent are now reviewable.

(ii) *Constitutional basis for the* Anisminic *presumption*

While it is of course true that the interpretation of statutes is in United Kingdom constitutional law a matter for the courts, the judicial adoption of any new canon of interpretation which (albeit subject to contrary statutory provision[60]) shifts the existing allocation of legal control of power substantially towards the courts and away from the executive requires justification.[61] The following points may be made:

- Parliament's reaction to the *Anisminic* decision itself is instructive. In section 3(2) of the Foreign Compensation Act 1969 Parliament provided an appeal on point of law from the FCC to the Court of Appeal (but no further[62]). One may think that this hardly indicates a view that the House of Lords acted unconstitutionally in ruling in *Anisminic* that the courts had jurisdiction to review the FCC's errors of law.

- Far more broadly, essentially the same point can be made by reference to the very extensive allocation by Parliament to the courts of jurisdiction to correct a wide range of official errors of law by way of appeal on law (see Chapter 2). This surely indicates that Parliament regards "error of law" as not only a sufficiently clear but also a broadly

---

[57] Lord Reid in *Anisminic* [1969] 1 All E.R. at 213. On whether action which is a "nullity" (or "void") can have any legal effect prior to the recognition of its invalidity by a court see Chap. 6, *section D 4*.

[58] Foreign Compensation Act 1950, s.4(4).

[59] See *e.g. R. v. Home Secretary, ex p. Fayed* [1997] 1 All E.R. 228 at 235.

[60] See *sub-section a* above and *c* below.

[61] See Cooke (1997); Hare (1998).

[62] s.3(8).

satisfactory notion for demarcating the spheres of competence of the superior courts and of the authorities subject to their review jurisdiction.

● This point is, of course, a two-edged sword: it invites the rejoinder that it is for Parliament rather than the courts to decide when the courts should have jurisdiction to correct errors of law. On the other hand, on a "separation of powers" approach[63] it may be said that it is the function of Parliament to legislate and the courts to interpret and that therefore "Adjudication on law is ultimately for the courts".[64]

It must remain an open question whether the courts have been justified since *Anisminic* in taking to themselves an even broader jurisdiction to correct errors of law than Parliament has seen fit expressly to confer. The constitutional issues raised by the expansion of the courts' review jurisdiction have figured most prominently in the field of judicial review of discretionary power which will be considered in *sections C and D* below. But there are many striking examples of the political sensitivity of the courts having jurisdiction to interpret words and phrases used in broadly-drafted statutes and other instruments. A recent prominent example was the majority ruling by the House of Lords in *R. v. IAT, ex p. Shah (UN High Commissioner for Refugees intervening)*[65] that under the Geneva Convention on Refugee Status women may be regarded as "a particular social group" and as such entitled to refugee status if able to establish a well-founded fear of persecution in their home state.

(c) Rebutting the presumption

It has been shown above that the courts now adopt a presumption that any error of law in the exercise of official power grounds judicial review. To speak in terms of a "presumption" indicates that the courts acknowledge that in particular situations Parliament (or, as in *Page*,[66] the context in which non-statutory power is conferred) can make it clear that the presumption is not to apply. In such a situation the courts' *vires* review jurisdiction would be confined, as in *Page*, to matters of "boundary *ultra vires*", abuse of discretion or procedural impropriety.

In what situations will Parliament be taken to have indicated that the *Anisminic* presumption is not to apply? This question will be dealt with fully in Chapter 7 but some basic points may be made briefly here.

● A statutory provision that decisions, etc. "shall not be questioned in any court" obviously will *by itself* have no effect upon the *Anisminic* presumption. That presumption is relevant to what counts as a decision; not to the effect of such a clause upon the courts' jurisdiction to review what is in effect a "non-decision".

● There are circumstances in which the particular statutory context in which an ouster clause is used may lead to the conclusion either (1) that the *Anisminic* presumption is rebutted or, (2) that judicial review is more extensively restricted. An example of (1) is where a statutory provision removes in a particular class of case a right of appeal on point of law which would normally be available; and of (2) where a statute expressly permits challenge during a limited time period but precludes it thereafter. These examples will be examined in Chapter 7.

---

[63] Hare (1998), pp. 127 *et seq.*
[64] Cooke (1997), p. 79.
[65] [1999] 2 All E.R. 545.
[66] *Page v. Hull University Visitor* [1993] 1 All E.R. 97: *sub-section a(ii)* above.

- The terms in which an ouster clause is drafted may likewise make it clear either that the *Anisminic* presumption is rebutted or that judicial review is more extensively restricted. Again, this matter, together with such restraints as are imposed by Community law and by Convention[67] law on a state's power to restrict judicial review, will be dealt with in Chapter 7.

C ILLEGALITY (2) — DISCRETIONARY POWER AND THE "PURPOSE AXIOM"[68]

1 JUDICIAL REVIEW OF ERROR OF LAW IN THE EXERCISE OF DISCRETIONARY POWER

The notion of error of law in the context of the exercise of official discretion has already been explained and examples given in Chapter 2.[69] To summarise what was said there:

- Public discretionary power is power to choose one course of action rather than another by reference only to considerations relevant to the public purpose for which the discretion was conferred.

- Error of law in the exercise of discretion means "taking into account some wholly irrelevant or extraneous consideration, or . . . wholly omitting to take into account a relevant consideration"[70] — referred to in Chapter 2 as "wrong considerations" of the *Wednesbury/Padfield*[71] type.

- In reviewing only on the *Wednesbury/Padfield* "wrong considerations" basis the courts are drawing a "competence line" between administrative authorities and the courts themselves similar to that described by reference to *Edwards v. Bairstow*[72] and *O'Kelly v. Trusthouse Forte*[73] in a non-discretionary or "category" context.

As seen in the previous section of this chapter, only since the *Anisminic* case have the courts adopted this competence line to define their common law jurisdiction to review category errors of law. But "wrong considerations" errors in the exercise of discretionary power have long been regarded by the courts as taking an authority outside the functional boundaries of its power, *i.e.* *ultra vires*, and subject to judicial review on that basis. As observed in Chapter 2, however, a correct appreciation of the purpose for which a particular discretion is conferred is often a difficult and controversial issue.

2 ERROR OF LAW IN EXERCISING DISCRETION: FINDING THE STATUTORY PURPOSE

The purpose axiom   The courts treat it as axiomatic that "Parliament must have conferred . . . discretion with the intention that it should be used to promote the policy and objects of the Act;

---

[67] *i.e.* European Convention on Human Rights.

[68] Wade and Forsyth, *AL*, Chaps 11–12; Craig, *AL*, Chap. 17; de Smith, *JRAA*, Chap. 6, pp. 295–316; 330–375; Galligan, *Discr. Pwr*, Chaps 5–6.

[69] *Section D 6 a.*

[70] Lord Upjohn in *Padfield v. Minister of Agriculture* [1968] 1 All E.R. 694 at 717F.

[71] *Associated Provincial Picture Houses Ltd v. Wednesbury Corporation* [1947] 2 All E.R. 680; *Padfield v. Minister of Agriculture* previous note. See Chap. 2, *section D 6 a, "Wrong Considerations" — Error of Law in Exercising Discretion.*

[72] [1955] 3 All E.R. 48.

[73] [1983] 3 All E.R. 456.

[these] must be determined by construing the Act as a whole, and construction is always a matter of law for the court."[74]

Courts "discover" statutory purpose The above quotation clearly reveals the nature and scope of the latitude enjoyed by the courts themselves in reviewing discretionary power. The whole process depends on discovering the statutory purpose ("the policy and objects of the Act") and that is "always a matter of law for the court." Where, as is very frequently the case, the statute in question does not expressly articulate its purpose, the availability of judicial review in particular cases turns primarily on the court's willingness to "discover" (*i.e.* determine) the purpose — be it wide or narrow — and, of course, on the skill of advocates in arguing the case. In these circumstances, as will appear below, "discovering the statutory purpose" is a creative (a law-making) activity: "discovering the purpose" is a form of words to describe this process rather than a genuine search for and illumination of something which was in the collective "mind" of Parliament at the time it legislated.

"Hard-edged" or "soft-edged" judicial review?   In these circumstances, then, the courts have a wide latitude in determining the level or intensity of review.[75] For a court to "discover" limiting statutory purposes where none are expressed in the statute is to equip itself with a sharp (or "hard-edged") tool with which to probe the merits of the decision. Conversely, to decline to go down this road is to use judicial review as a blunt (or "soft-edged") tool, capable of cutting off only the most blatant excursions beyond the broad boundaries of statutory discretion — and encouraging governments to procure the conferment upon themselves of statutory discretionary powers in the broadest of terms. It will be seen that prediction of result in this area is often extremely difficult or impossible because the cases show different levels of intensity at different times, from different courts, and in different circumstances.

With regard to Parliamentary expression of statutory purpose, it should be recalled[76] that section 3(1) of the Human Rights Act 1998 provides that "So far as it is possible to do so, primary legislation and subordinate legislation must be read and given effect in a way which is compatible with the Convention rights". The effect of this legislation in the context of judicial review of the exercise of discretionary power will be considered in *section D* below.

For the present, reported cases exemplifying the purpose axiom can be considered under three heads:

(a) Purpose expressed in statute

An example of express provision as to purpose is where a statute provides that a licensing authority may impose conditions on a licence for certain specified purposes only, *e.g.* local authorities may grant public entertainments licences subject to conditions "imposed for all or any of [four specified] purposes, but no others."[77] The specified purposes include securing the safety of persons present at the entertainment and preventing persons in the neighbourhood being unreasonably disturbed by noise. A condition for any non-specified purpose would be *ultra vires*.

A statutory purpose may be expressed in more general terms such as that planning authorities in dealing with planning applications must have regard to "material" considerations,[78] *i.e.*, they must have regard to all, and to only, planning issues. A good example of breach of this express statutory purpose is *R. v. Hillingdon L.B.C., ex p. Royco*[79] where planning permission to erect a

---

[74] Lord Reid in *Padfield v. Minister of Agriculture* [1968] 1 All E.R. 694 at 699C.
[75] Woolf (1998), p. 590.
[76] See Chap. 1, *section A 3 b*.
[77] Local Government (Miscellaneous Provisions) Act 1982, Sched. 1, para. 4(4).
[78] Town and Country Planning Act 1990, s.70(2).
[79] [1974] 2 All E.R. 643. See also Chap. 2, *section D 6 a*.

block of flats had been granted subject to a condition that the developer would make the flats available to persons who were on the local authority's housing waiting list. The Divisional Court quashed the decision on the basis that the conditions were *ultra vires*: planning discretions are not conferred to enable local authorities to foist their housing duties onto private developers.

A further point of general importance regarding judicial review of statutory discretionary power may be made, in passing, by reference to the *Royco* case. The planning legislation uses the common statutory formula that the authority may impose such (material) conditions "as they think fit".[80] Other similar common formulas are "if the authority is satisfied" or "if it appears to the authority". The courts interpret subjective language of this sort as requiring not merely that the authority does actually think fit (etc.) but also that there are grounds on which it could properly (*i.e.* having regard to the purpose for which the power is conferred) think fit (etc.).[81]

Re-focusing on the specific question of express statutory indication of purpose, the courts have sometimes been accused of too hard-edged an approach, *i.e.* of interpreting such express indications in a manner which imposes unwarranted restrictions on the exercise of an authority's discretion. Thus in *Bromley L.B.C. v. Greater London Council*[82] where in order to finance a 25 per cent cut in London public transport fares the council (GLC) had exercised its statutory power[83] to make grants to the London Transport Executive (LTE). The statute provided that in making grants the GLC should have regard to LTE's duty to try to run its operation on a break-even basis. The statute also provided that GLC could make grants to LTE "for any purpose". The House of Lords took the view, in effect, that the broad general reference to "**any** purpose" was, on the proper construction of the statute, made subject to LTE's specific "break-even" duty. It followed that it would be *ultra vires* to make a grant designed to relieve LTE of that duty by financing an operational deficit stemming from the 25 per cent fares cut. The difficulty with this ruling is that the statute provided no clear guidance on whether the break-even duty was to be read as subject to any grants received or, on the contrary, as a duty to be pursued without regard to any such grants. In these circumstances it may be argued that the court should have given the GLC the benefit of the doubt.

(b) Purpose expressed outside statute

Where statutory words conferring discretionary power leave in doubt the purpose for which the discretion is conferred it is often, as in the *GLC* case just considered, vain to seek to illuminate this elusive purpose without reference to sources outside the statute itself. In particular cases light may be shed, *e.g.*, by any official reports on which the legislation may have been based, and also by Hansard reports of the parliamentary debates on the legislation during the course of its enactment. Nevertheless until relatively recently the courts took a very restrictive approach, largely refusing to refer to extra-statutory sources as aids to statutory construction. However, in 1992 in *Pepper v. Hart*[84] the House of Lords signalled a major change of approach.

In *Pepper v. Hart* and later cases[85] the courts have expressed a new willingness to consult a wide range of extra-statutory materials in seeking the purpose of a statute. In order to resolve ambiguity in a particular statutory provision a court will now refer to clear ministerial statements

---

[80] Town and Country Planning Act 1990, s.70(1)(a).
[81] See *Royco* at [1974] 2 All E.R. p. 649f; see too *Secretary of State for Education v. Tameside M.B.C.* [1976] 3 All E.R. 665 at 681j (Lord Wilberforce), 703c (Lord Russell); also *Roberts v. Hopwood* [1925] All E.R. Rep 24: *sub-section c* below, *Associated Provincial Picture Houses Ltd v. Wednesbury Corporation* [1947] 2 All E.R. 680: *ibid.*
[82] [1982] 1 All E.R. 129.
[83] Under the Transport (London) Act 1969, s.3(1).
[84] [1993] 1 All E.R. 42.
[85] See Cross, *SI*, pp. 152–164.

in Parliament (as recorded in Hansard) and also to relevant pre-parliamentary materials such as official reports. *Three Rivers D.C. v. Bank of England (No. 2)*[86] carries this further: such materials may also be referred to in order to elucidate in doubtful cases the *general purpose (or mischief) of a statute* rather than to construe a specific ambiguous provision — at any rate when seeking the purpose of a statute whose intention is said to be "to introduce into English law the provisions of an international convention or of a European directive". Here "the court's approach . . . may well be more flexible"[87] than usual.

Pepper v. Hart has engendered great controversy.[88] It is of course true that there will be circumstances in which a linguistic ambiguity in a statute can be resolved by reference to what was said in Parliament or in an official report whose recommendations Parliament plainly intended to implement. It appears,[89] *e.g.*, that under the *Pepper v. Hart* approach, the House of Lords would have reached the opposite result in the *GLC* case.[90] On the other hand, there will be many circumstances in which there is great scope for debate as to what ministerial, etc. statements are "clear" and as to what other material is "necessary in order to understand such statements".[91] In 1994 the then Attorney-General, Sir Nicholas Lyell, identified a question "on which I doubt if it is yet possible to form a considered view"[92]: "Lord Bridge[93] has welcomed the liberating effect of the decision and has forecast that the decision will in fact reduce the amount of litigation because cases will be settled by reference to Hansard when they might otherwise have proceeded to the courts for adjudication. The Lord Chancellor on the other hand [who dissented in *Pepper v. Hart*], expressed his concern that the decision might increase the cost of litigation."[94] Certainly, the availability to the courts of extra-statutory materials to assist them in discerning statutory purpose does not appear to have reduced the flow of administrative law cases in which that is the central issue.

(c) Purpose to be inferred from statutory context

Often the words in which a statute confers discretionary power will give no express indication of its purpose; and in such a case it may be that "*Pepper v. Hart*" researches yield no clear indication of the purpose which the statute has failed to express. In these circumstances it is left to the courts to infer — or conjecture — from the context in which the power is conferred what limits Parliament is to be taken to have imposed upon the purposes for which the power in question may properly be used.

It need hardly be said that so nebulous a process can produce controversial results.[95] But even in this area there are some clear and unexceptionable cases such as *R. v. Barnsley M.B.C., ex p. Hook*,[96] the case of the street-trader whose local authority licence had been revoked because he had used abusive language to a council security officer who was reproving him for urinating in a side street when public conveniences were closed. Few would suppose that the purpose for which Parliament had conferred licensing discretion upon the local authority should be taken to extend to depriving Mr Hook of his livelihood as a punishment for an isolated and trivial lack of

[86] [1996] 2 All E.R. 363.
[87] Clarke J., *ibid*, at 366e.
[88] See Lester (1994).
[89] See Cross, *SI*, p. 155, n.13.
[90] *Bromley L.B.C. v. Greater London Council* [1982] 1 All E.R. 129 (above).
[91] Lord Browne-Wilkinson in *Pepper v. Hart* [1993] 1 All E.R. at 69e.
[92] Lyell (1994), p. 8.
[93] [In *Pepper v. Hart* [1993] 1 All E.R. at 49.] Note added.
[94] *ibid*.
[95] For a critical assessment of the courts' record, see Beloff (1994).
[96] [1976] 3 All E.R. 452. See also Chap. 2, *section D 6 a.*

decorum. In *Padfield v. Minister of Agriculture*[97] the Minister was held to have acted *ultra vires* when he used his statutory discretion for self-serving political motives in refusing to refer a complaint by certain milk producers to a Milk Marketing Board committee. The purpose of the Minister's discretion was to enable him to consider whether a particular complaint was of a kind likely to be resolved via the statutory machinery. It was not to enable him to avoid political embarrassment.[98]

These are clear cases. There are, however, many reported cases where courts have reviewed exercises of official discretion by reference to limiting purposes inferred by the courts without any obviously sound basis. In the notorious 1920s case of *Roberts v. Hopwood*[99] the issue was whether the Labour-controlled Poplar Borough Council had acted *ultra vires* in increasing the minimum wage for its employees to a level which was both (a) substantially above the minimum wage level for equivalent work in other sectors, and (b) equal as between men and women. The relevant statute empowered the authority to pay such wages as it thought fit: the council said it thought fit to fix wages not according to usual criteria such as the going rate for the job, but according to some absolute principle of what it thought a "model employer" should pay. The House of Lords held the decision *ultra vires*: the council's discretion had not been exercised according to proper criteria.

On the one hand it may seem plausible to suppose that Parliament's purpose in conferring a discretion to fix wages was to give the authority only the same degree of latitude as was enjoyed by private employers de facto governed by usual wage-fixing criteria. On the other, it may be asked on what basis a court could infer (even in the 1920s) that Parliament intended local authorities to take no account of what they judged to be their social responsibilities in fixing wage levels. Is this not a question for electors when next at the ballot box rather than for judges in a court? Today (and irrespective of Human Rights Act points) review courts would be likely to regard moral or social considerations as matters which could lawfully be taken into account, but not as being able to be the sole basis of an exercise of discretion. Thus in *R. v. Somerset C.C., ex p. Fewings*[1] the Court of Appeal decided that the council had acted *ultra vires* in banning fox-hunting on its land on purely moral principles instead of, as the statute[2] required, attempting to form a balanced objective judgment on what would be "for the benefit, improvement or development of their area" as a whole. The court held (reversing Laws J.[3] on this point) that moral considerations were relevant and might properly be taken into account but that they had to be balanced with other considerations of land management.

Roberts v. Hopwood is a prominent example of what was referred to above as "hard-edged" judicial review of official discretion, *i.e.*, by discerning a limit to the statutory purpose which is not expressed in the statute and arguably ought not to be implied, a court equips itself with a sharp tool with which to probe the merits of a decision. Two more examples may be given. In *Wheeler v. Leicester City Council*,[4] as related in Chapter 3, the House of Lords granted judicial review of the council's refusal to renew Leicester Rugby Club's licence to use a municipal sports ground on the basis that the council's purpose was to "punish" the club for not pressing its members to refrain from touring South Africa. But it is hard to see the basis on which the House drew the (implied) purpose of the council's statutory powers of recreation ground management so narrowly as to make it unlawful for the council to base its revocation of the club's licence upon the council's general statutory duty[5] to carry out its functions with due regard to the promotion of good race relations.

---

[97] [1968] 1 All E.R. 694.
[98] Lord Reid, *ibid*, at 701C.
[99] [1925] All E.R. Rep. 24.
[1] [1995] 3 All E.R. 20.
[2] Local Government Act 1972, s.120(1)(b).
[3] [1995] 1 All E.R. 513.
[4] [1985] 2 All E.R. 1106.
[5] Race Relations Act 1976, s.71.

A more recent example of "hard-edged" review is *R. v. Coventry C.C., ex p. Phoenix Aviation*[6] in which livestock exporters obtained judicial review of decisions taken by a number of air- and sea-port authorities not to carry live veal calves in order to avoid the disruption being caused to port operations by animal rights protesters. The Divisional Court held that such discretion as port authorities have in deciding what freight to carry does not extend so far:

"... public authorities must beware of surrendering to the dictates of unlawful pressure groups. ... Of course, on occasion, a variation or even short-term suspension of services may be justified ... [but] this is not an area where [public authorities] can be permitted a wide measure of discretion. As when fundamental human rights are in play, the courts will adopt a more interventionist role.[7]

Here, then, the court invoked the necessity of upholding the rule of law as the basis for inferring limits on the purpose for which discretion was conferred. But *Phoenix* may be regarded as an extreme case: "The authorit[ies] had given in to unlawful threats. 'None of them, it appears, gave the least thought to the awesome implications for the rule of law of doing what they propose'".[8] In a subsequent case[9] the House of Lords unanimously rejected a *Wednesbury/Padfield* challenge to a police decision to limit the times during which live exports would be permitted in the face of disruptive behaviour by protestors. The decision struck a lawful balance between the protection of lawful commercial activity and the conservation of scarce police resources.[10]

Wednesbury/Padfield *"wrong considerations" review as "soft-edged"*

The distinction between hard-edged and soft-edged review reflects different degrees of judicial willingness to adopt presumptions of statutory interpretation of the type adopted in the *Phoenix* case: presumptions which (unless rebutted by clear statutory provision) will amount to substantive limitations on the purposes for which discretion may be exercised. In contrast with the cases just discussed, the decision in the *Wednesbury* case[11] is soft-edged, displaying as it does an unwillingness by the court to "read into" a statutory discretion limitations of purpose which are not expressed. In *Wednesbury* a cinema licensing authority empowered to grant licences subject to such conditions as it thought fit imposed the condition that no children under 15 should be admitted on Sundays. The purpose of the condition appears to have been the "well-being and the physical and moral health of children".[12] It was argued by the licensee that the purpose of the licensing power (and so of the power to impose conditions) was public safety, not moral guidance of the young, and that accordingly the condition was *ultra vires*. Although at least "tenable",[13] the argument and the licensee's challenge failed.

More generally, of course, the "wrong considerations" approach articulated in the *Wednesbury* and *Padfield*[14] cases is "soft-edged" in the sense explained in Chapter 2[15] that it confines a review court to the question whether, in exercising a discretion, the decision maker failed to place the requisite considerations in the scales of the balance. The court may not concern itself with

---

[6] [1995] 3 All E.R. 37.

[7] Simon Brown L.J. at 62e–g.

[8] *R. v. Sussex Chief Constable, ex p. ITF Ltd* [1999] 1 All E.R. 129 at 140f: Lord Slynn, citing Simon Brown L.J. in the *Phoenix* case.

[9] *Ex p. ITF Ltd* (previous note).

[10] *ibid.*, at 141f (Lord Slynn). On scarcity of resources as a relevant consideration in discretionary decision-making, see *sub-section 3 b* below.

[11] *Wednesbury Associated Provincial Picture Houses Ltd v. Wednesbury Corporation* [1947] 2 All E.R. 680.

[12] *ibid.*, at 683B.

[13] Sedley (1994), p. 277; see also, Carnwath (1996), pp. 246–248.

[14] *Padfield v. Minister of Agriculture* [1968] 1 All E.R. 694.

[15] *Section D 6 a.*

whether the balance was properly struck, *i.e.*, it may not inquire whether too much emphasis was placed on one relevant consideration or too little on another. *Wednesbury* has been applauded on this basis by judges who favour self-restraint in this area[16]; but it is regarded as unacceptably restrictive by those who favour a more interventionist approach.[17] More will be said in *section D* on the subject of hard- and soft-edged review, but cases have been cited above to show the difficulties and uncertainties which flow from the "purpose axiom" where, as is common, discretionary power is conferred without clear statutory indication of the purposes which an authority must have in view when exercising that power.

3 RECURRING ISSUES IN JUDICIAL REVIEW OF THE EXERCISE OF OFFICIAL DISCRETION

Given the multitude of different circumstances in which discretion is conferred on public authorities, it will be difficult or impossible to predict with certainty in any particular case not already covered by case law authority[18] how a review court will approach the matter of "discovering" the statutory purpose. However, there are certain types of issue relating to the lawfulness of the exercise of discretionary power which, by their nature, tend to recur again and again. Some broad principles do emerge from the reported cases in which such recurring issues arise.

(a) The relevance of pre-adopted policies to the exercise of discretion in particular cases

Fairness and consistency in the exercise of discretionary power will commonly demand that an authority formulates a policy — a set of guidelines — as the basis upon which individual decisions will be made. But the statutory purpose of conferring a discretion will be defeated if such a policy is treated by the authority as an unbreakable rule. A decision which mechanically applies the policy and leaves no room for the exercise of any discretion in the individual case will thus be *ultra vires*. The discretion is said to have been "fettered" by the policy. In *British Oxygen Co. Ltd v. Minister of Technology*[19] Lord Reid said: "What the authority must not do is to refuse to listen at all. But a Ministry or large authority may have had to deal already with a multitude of similar applications and then they will almost certainly have evolved a policy so precise that it could well be called a rule. There can be no objection to that, provided the authority is always willing to listen to anyone with something to say . . ."[20]

In the *British Oxygen* case, the Ministry (empowered to make grants towards capital expenditure on new industrial plant) had refused the Company a grant towards the £4 million it had spent on gas cylinders costing £20 each. The Ministry's policy was not to give grants for items costing singly less than £25. The House of Lords found, however, that the Ministry was still willing to hear any arguments from a particular applicant as to why the policy should not apply to his case. In *R. v. Harrow L.B.C., ex p. Carter*,[21] on the other hand, the authority had adopted a rigid policy that homeless persons who had a "local connection" in another authority's area must be referred to the other authority. Mrs C obtained judicial review of her automatic referral: "The council's

---

[16] See *e.g.* Irvine (1996 *Wed.*). See also Irvine (1996 Resp.).
[17] See *e.g.* Laws (1993), especially at p. 69. See also Laws (1995), Laws (1996).
[18] For a case already covered, see *e.g. R. v. Devon and Cornwall Chief Constable, ex p. Hay* [1996] 2 All E.R. 712.
[19] [1970] 3 All E.R. 165.
[20] *ibid.*, at 170–171.
[21] *The Times*, November 3, 1992.

discretion not to refer such persons was fettered. . . . The policy of the council did not recognise that in all cases there had to be room for exceptions . . ."

A policy adopted by an authority must, of course, be consistent with the policy and objects of the Act in question. Otherwise the policy becomes itself an irrelevant consideration, as *e.g.* in *Padfield*[22] or *Roberts v. Hopwood*[23] (above). Action based upon it will be unlawful for this reason and irrespective of any question of fettering.

Note: Other types of unlawful "fettering" or surrendering of discretion are dealt with in Chapter 9, *Official Contractual and Restitutionary Liability.*[24]

(b) The relevance of scarce resources

In what circumstances will it be lawful for an authority to take into account the scarcity of its resources when exercising statutory discretions? When (in the absence of any express statutory provision on the matter) will the courts infer that it falls within the ambit of the statutory purpose for the authority to shape its exercise of statutory powers by reference to the size of its budget?

The courts have made it clear that they recognise that when Parliament confers discretionary powers on public authorities it is fully aware that budgets are finite. Decisions whether, and if so how, to exercise such powers necessarily involve hard financial choices. It is for the authority, not the courts, to match limited resources to competing needs in the knowledge that many highly deserving calls will have to be rejected. In *R. v. Cambridge District Health Authority ex p. B*[25] the Court of Appeal (reversing Laws J.[26]) rejected an AJR of the health authority's decision not to fund treatment for a 10-year-old girl dying of leukaemia. The treatment would have cost £75,000 and was estimated by some expert medical opinion to have as much as a 10–20 per cent chance of success. On the question of the relevance of budgetary considerations Bingham M.R. said: "It is common knowledge that health authorities of all kinds are constantly pressed to make ends meet. . . . Difficult and agonising judgments have to be made as to how a limited budget is best allocated to the maximum advantage of the maximum number of patients. That is not a judgment which the court can make."[27] The House of Lords has since indicated that this approach applies to public authorities generally: ". . . the courts cannot enter upon the assessment of such 'policy' matters" as "the allocation of finite financial resources between the different calls made upon them."[28]

Of course, there are many situations where a public authority has no discretion whether or not to allocate resources to a particular purpose. Many statutes in many different fields impose unqualified duties upon public authorities to confer benefits upon individuals who can satisfy certain criteria. Common examples would be duties to pay non-discretionary social security benefits, to provide school places[29] or to house homeless persons. Where a person is entitled to a specific level of financial benefit prescribed by statute, an authority cannot decline to pay the prescribed sum on the basis of scarcity of resources. But in allocating non-financial benefits such as housing accommodation or provision for special educational needs, authorities will commonly have discretion as to the precise level (and therefore cost) of the provision to be made. Suppose that in one financial year provision has been made at a certain level but that in a subsequent financial year the authority wishes to reduce the level in response to new budget constraints.

[22] *Padfield v. Minister of Agriculture* [1968] 1 All E.R. 694.
[23] *Roberts v. Hopwood* [1925] All E.R. Rep. 24.
[24] *Section B 1 c, 2 b* (Unlawful fettering by contract); *Section C 1* (Unlawful fettering by delegation).
[25] [1995] 2 All E.R. 129.
[26] *The Times*, March 15, 1995.
[27] [1995] 2 All E.R. at 137e–f; cited with approval by Lord Slynn in *R. v. Sussex Chief Constable, ex p. ITF Ltd* [1999] 1 All E.R. 129 at 137d.
[28] *X v. Bedfordshire C.C., E v. Dorset C.C.* [1995] 3 All E.R. 353 at 370b.
[29] *ibid.*, at 397–399.

In *R. v. Gloucestershire C.C., ex p. Barry* the Court of Appeal[30] held that where there is a statutory duty to provide for a particular need the question of whether a particular individual has that need is a matter to be assessed independently of the availability of resources to meet it. On the other hand, an authority could revise the level at which it had previously met the need (just as it will have fixed that level initially) by reference to its currently prevailing financial circumstances. This power to reassess the level of provision would be subject to (a) any express statutory restrictions on local authorities' room for manoeuvre (*e.g.* the duty to act according to ministerial guidelines re the provision of educational services for disabled persons with learning difficulties[31]) and (b) the proviso that the level of provision was fixed by reference to the minimum amount necessary to make genuine provision for the need and not solely by reference to the need to achieve a certain financial target.[32]

The Court of Appeal decision in *Barry* attempted to strike a balance between public authorities' freedom to determine spending priorities and their duties to make genuine provision for individual needs in specific cases. But it was reversed by the House of Lords[33] by a 3:2 majority. The case concerned the duty of local authorities under section 2(1) of the Chronically Sick and Disabled Persons Act 1970 which provides: "Where a local authority . . . are satisfied . . . that it is necessary in order to meet the needs of [a] person [in a specified category] to make arrangements for [certain] matters . . . then . . . it shall be the duty of that authority to make those arrangements". In 1992 the Gloucestershire authority had decided that to meet the needs of B (a person in the specified category) it was necessary to provide home help twice a week and meals-on-wheels four times a week. The council in 1994 informed B that because of severe cuts in central government funding it would no longer be able to meet his "full needs as assessed".[34] The House of Lords restored a declaration granted by the Divisional Court that it was unlawful to reassess need (as the council had done in B's case) solely on resource grounds but (reversing the Court of Appeal) the majority held that the assessment of a person's "needs" required the authority to take account of its resources — rather, perhaps, as a parent takes account of his resources in deciding what are a child's needs: "a person's need for a particular type or level of service cannot be decided in a vacuum from which all considerations of cost have been expelled."[35] The minority endorsed the view of the Court of Appeal that "need" is a matter to be assessed independently of the availability of resources to meet it.[36] This seems strongly supported by reference to the legislative history of section 2 and to subsequent legislation and the government report on which it was based.[37]

The effect of the majority ruling in *Barry* appears nevertheless to be that where an entitlement is based upon an authority's assessment of a claimant's "need" (undefined) in certain areas of life, the authority's resources will be relevant to that assessment.[38] But once an authority accepts that such need exists, it must provide for that need: lack of resources is no excuse.[39] Moreover, a subsequent decision of the House of Lords, *R. v. East Sussex C.C., ex p. T (A Minor)*,[40] shows that an authority's resources are not relevant to the assessment of need where an entitlement is based

---

[30] [1996] 4 All E.R. 421.
[31] *R v. Islington L.B.C., ex p. Rixon*, The Times, April 17, 1996, Sedley J.
[32] *R. v. Hillingdon L.B.C., ex p. Queensmead School Governors*, The Times, January 9, 1997, Collins J.
[33] [1997] 2 All E.R. 1.
[34] *ibid.*, at 3g.
[35] *ibid.*, at 11e, Lord Nicholls.
[36] *ibid.*, at 5d-6f, Lord Lloyd.
[37] *ibid.*, at 7–8.
[38] *Cf. R. v. Birmingham City Council, ex p. Mohammed* [1998] 3 All E.R. 788 which, however, seems hardly distinguishable from *Barry*.
[39] *R. v. Sefton Metropolitan B.C., ex p. Help the Aged* [1997] 4 All E.R. 532 at 543e (Lord Woolf M.R.).
[40] [1998] 2 All E.R. 769.

solely upon certain specified statutory criteria such as those defining "suitable education",[41] Here only those criteria are relevant in deciding the suitability of provision: the authority thus acted unlawfully in deciding on resource grounds to reduce home tuition for a child suffering from ME from five to three hours per week. Lord Browne-Wilkinson observed[42]:

> "The argument is not one of insufficient resources to discharge the duty but of a preference for using the money for other purposes. To permit a local authority to avoid performing a statutory duty on the grounds that it prefers to spend the money in other ways is to downgrade a statutory duty to a discretionary power."

However "if there is more than one way of providing 'suitable education', the LEA would be entitled to have regard to its resources in choosing between different ways of providing suitable education."[43]

D "FREE-STANDING" GROUNDS[44]: IRRATIONALITY. INFRINGEMENTS OF COMMUNITY AND CONVENTION RIGHTS. PROPORTIONALITY

1 "*WEDNESBURY* UNREASONABLENESS": "ILLEGALITY" OR "IRRATIONALITY"?

(a) "*Wednesbury* unreasonableness" as "illegality"

In the *Wednesbury* case, Lord Greene M.R. defined "unreasonableness" as a ground for judicial review of administrative discretion by reference to the Poplar council's decision in *Roberts v. Hopwood*[45]: the decision was "'unreasonable' . . . in the sense . . . that in fixing the [wage level] they had fixed it by reference to something which they ought not to have entertained and to the exclusion of those elements which they ought to have taken into consideration."[46] "Unreasonableness" as thus understood is plainly a type of "illegality" in terms of Lord Diplock's *CCSU* classification in that, on the purpose axiom approach, it shows that the decision maker has failed to "understand correctly the law that regulates his decision-making power and [to] give effect to it".[47]

(b) "Unreasonableness" as a separate head of review: "irrationality"

In the *Wednesbury* case Lord Greene continued: "There is no authority to support the proposition that the court has got some sort of overriding power to decide what is reasonable and what is unreasonable."[48] But if the purpose axiom is correctly seen as in many cases masking what is in

---

[41] Education Act 1996, s.19(7).
[42] [1998] 2 All E.R. at 777b.
[43] *ibid.*, at 775d.
[44] Craig, *AL*, pp. 409–446; de Smith, *JRAA*, Chap. 13 ; Chap. 6, pp. 323–330.
[45] [1925] All E.R. Rep. 24 (*section C 2 c* above).
[46] Lord Greene in *Associated Provincial Picture Houses Ltd v. Wednesbury Corporation* [1947] 2 All E.R. at 684C. See also Chap. 2, *section D 6 a*.
[47] Lord Diplock in *Council of Civil Service Unions v. Minister for the Civil Service* (the *CCSU* case) [1984] 3 All E.R. 935 at 951: *section A 2* above.
[48] [1947] 2 All E.R. at 684C.

reality a process whereby the judges rather than Parliament set the bounds of administrative discretion,[49] there may be a virtue in acknowledging this reality. In the *CCSU* case Lord Diplock may seem to have done so when he said that "*Wednesbury* unreasonableness" "by now can stand upon its own feet as an accepted ground on which a decision may be attacked by judicial review".[50] He adopted the label "irrationality" and spoke in terms of "a decision which is so outrageous in its defiance of logic or of accepted moral standards that no sensible person who had applied his mind to the question to be decided could have arrived at it."[51] Moreover Lord Diplock said[52] that "further grounds" might emerge through subsequent case law. He referred particularly to "proportionality", a principle of the administrative law of the E.C. and some Member States as well as of the interpretation of the European Convention on Human Rights ("the Convention"). The principle is discussed below.[53]

(c) Irrationality and judicial interventionism

Lord Diplock's statement might be taken to signal either a more "hard-edged" or, on the contrary, a more "soft-edged" approach to judicial review of discretion. On the one hand, Lord Diplock's references to logic, accepted moral standards and proportionality have been said to "clear the way for the courts to develop general principles of substantive administrative law"[54] such as proportionality itself, the fulfilment of legitimate expectations and observance of fundamental human rights. On the other hand, reference to a decision "so outrageous . . . that no sensible person . . . could have arrived at it" suggests a very high threshold for judicial intervention. In the event the statement has been taken by the courts to signal each approach in different circumstances.

(i) *"Strong" and "weak" discretions*

Dismissing an AJR of a decision of the Lord Chancellor that a particular judge, after promotion to the Court of Appeal, should not be requested to continue to preside in the series of *Maxwell* fraud trials, Henry L.J. observed that "There are no statutory limits placed on the exercise of that discretion: it is a 'strong discretion'".[55]

Plainly, the broader the terms in which a statute confers a discretion, the less susceptible is the exercise of that discretion to judicial review by reference to limitations on statutory purpose as discussed in the previous section. But it is of course true, as also appears from that discussion, that what may appear at first sight to be "strong" discretions can sometimes be "weakened", *i.e.* made more susceptible to judicial review, by judicial willingness to adopt a creative stance in "discovering the statutory purpose".[56]

In the context of strong discretions, the courts have treated Lord Diplock's *CCSU* analysis as confirming the need for judicial restraint. As one would expect, governments tend to procure for themselves broad discretions to further their political aims by the making of rules and regulations (delegated legislation). As will be illustrated in *section F* of this chapter, the House of Lords during the 1980s took the approach that where "[a] statute has conferred a power on the Secretary of State which involves the formulation and the implementation of national economic

---

[49] *Section C 2 above.*
[50] [1984] 3 All E.R. 935 at 951: *section A 2 above.*
[51] *ibid.*
[52] [1984] 3 All E.R. at 950h.
[53] *Sub-section 2.*
[54] Jowell and Lester (1987), p. 370.
[55] *R. v. Lord Chancellor, ex p. Maxwell* [1996] 4 All E.R. 751 at 755e.
[56] See cases discussed in *section C 2 above.*

policy and which can only take effect with the approval of the House of Commons, it is not open to challenge on the grounds of irrationality short of the extremes of bad faith, improper motive or manifest absurdity."[57] In this context of strong discretions, as Henry L.J. said in the *Maxwell* case: "Decisions so unreasonable as to warrant interference jump off the page at you".[58] This judicial approach has been mirrored in many cases where unsuccessful attempts have been made to secure judicial review of the exercise of strong discretions, *e.g.* a government decision to ban the broadcasting of the voices of Irish terrorist organisations and their sympathisers;[59] or to ban homosexuals from the armed services;[60] resource-allocation decisions of public authorities;[61] decisions of the Parliamentary ombudsman not to investigate a complaint.[62]

(ii) *"Free-standing" grounds for judicial review?*

But in a number of other respects Lord Diplock's speech has underpinned a more interventionist judicial approach[63]:

(1) As explained in Chapter 3, much official power is now non-statutory. The notion that grounds for judicial review may be regarded as "free-standing", *i.e.* as existing independently of the "purpose axiom limits" of any given statutory discretion, is of importance here. It provides a conceptual basis for such arguments as that the Crown's choice of contracting partners may be reviewable on the same grounds as for a statutory authority.[64]

(2) The free-standing approach has been reflected in the willingness of some judges to entertain arguments based on a number of possible "further grounds" as hinted at by Lord Diplock,[65] albeit, in cases involving statutory powers, within a theoretical framework of statutory "interpretation". The radical combined impact of the European Communities Act 1972 and the Human Rights Act 1998 in this context (and particularly with regard to the principle of proportionality) will be examined next in this section.

(3) Finally, the free-standing approach has been reflected in the suggestion (discussed in Chapter 7) that Parliament's power wholly to exclude judicial review may no longer exist,[66] a suggestion which has been said to "smack of judicial supremacism".[67]

2   INFRINGEMENTS OF COMMUNITY AND CONVENTION RIGHTS PROPORTIONALITY

(a) The principle of proportionality[68]

It will be useful at this stage to give some explanation of lack of "proportionality" as a basis for review of official decisions.

[57] Lord Bridge in *Hammersmith and Fulham L.B.C. v. Environment Secretary* [1990] 3 All E.R. 589 at 637b.
[58] [1996] 4 All E.R. at 756a.
[59] *Brind v. Home Secretary* [1991] 1 All E.R. 720.
[60] *R. v. Ministry of Defence, ex p. Smith* [1996] 1 All E.R. 257, *sub-section 2c* below.
[61] *Section C 3 b* above.
[62] *R. v. Parliamentary Commissioner for Administration, ex p. Dyer* [1994] 1 All E.R. 375: see Chap. 10, *section A 1.*
[63] Irvine (1996 *Wed.*), pp. 63 *et seq.*
[64] Oliver (1987), pp. 551 *et seq.*
[65] *Subsection b* above.
[66] Woolf (1995), pp. 67–71.
[67] Irvine (1996 *Wed.*), pp. 75–78.
[68] Craig, *AL*, pp. 586–603; de Smith, *JRAA*, pp. 593–606.

Whenever a public authority decides to act in a way which restricts an individual's rights it will no doubt be satisfied that the specific public interest (purpose or objective) which is relied upon as necessitating the restriction is proportionate to, and therefore sufficient in the circumstances to override, the individual's interest in maintaining his rights. In short, the decision-maker will judge that in the particular circumstances public benefit outweighs individual or private detriment. But where (as in both E.C. and Convention law — but not in English administrative law outside these fields[69]) lack of "proportionality" is a ground for legal challenge to an official decision, the court or tribunal in which the challenge is brought must review the decision-maker's judgment as to the balance between public benefit and individual or private detriment. It may be stated at the outset that lack of proportionality, as it has developed as a ground for review of official decisions, is somewhere between "merits" appeal[70] and review for error of law on the *Wednesbury/Padfield* "wrong considerations" basis.[71] The matter may be put simply as follows.

What is presupposed is a legal challenge to an official decision causing some individual detriment which is, in the view of the decision-maker, the necessary cost of the public benefit achieved. If the reviewing authority has "merits" jurisdiction, it must ask (see *TABLE 4*): "Do I agree with the decision-maker's view on the balance between public benefit and individual detriment?" **If the reviewing authority is required to apply the principle of proportionality, it must ask: "Is the decision (irrespective of whether or not I agree with it) one which can be regarded as striking a proper balance between public benefit and individual detriment?"** If the reviewing authority has jurisdiction to correct only error of law, it must ask: "Is the decision (irrespective of whether or not I regard it as striking a proper balance between public benefit and individual detriment) based only on "proper considerations"?

TABLE 4

PROPORTIONALITY AND OTHER LEVELS OF REVIEW: BALANCING PUBLIC BENEFIT AGAINST INDIVIDUAL DETRIMENT			
LEVEL OF REVIEW	**MERITS**	**PROPORTIONALITY**	**ERROR OF LAW**
REVIEW TRIBUNAL OR COURT MUST ASK . . .	*Did the decision maker strike the right balance?*	*Did the decision maker strike a proper balance?[(1)]*	*Did the decision maker consider all proper issues when striking the balance?*

[(1)] *Commonly judged by reference to "utility", "minimum harm" and "ends-means" criteria — see text.*

[69] *Brind v. Home Secretary* [1991] 1 All E.R. 720.
[70] Chap. 2, *section B 1 et seq.*
[71] *Section C above.*

Now, it will be immediately obvious that the notion of "a proper (*i.e.* proportionate) balance" is in itself entirely lacking in content. On the one hand, if used as a "hard-edged" review tool it could amount to merits appeal.[72] On the other hand, if given a "soft edge" it could amount to no more than error of law review by another name. But, if operated with a genuine deference to the special competence of the decision-making authority in its own field, the principle of proportionality can allow a greater degree of independent judicial scrutiny than is permissible under the *Wednesbury/Padfield* wrong considerations approach, but without amounting to merits appeal. Three criteria which are commonly used to assess propriety in this context are:

(1) Is the challenged action reasonably likely to achieve the public benefit sought? (Hereafter, the "utility" criterion.)

(2) Could that public benefit have been achieved by means less detrimental to individual rights than those actually adopted? (The "minimum harm" criterion.)

(3) Is the public benefit (the "end") sought sufficiently important to justify the means chosen — the individual detriment complained of? (The "ends-means" criterion.)

As will appear below[73] by reference to the doctrine of proportionality as developed in both E.C. and Convention law, one or more of these criteria is often used as a bench-mark to judge whether a particular infringement of individual or private right is "necessary" in the pursuit of the public good. Certainly the minimum harm criterion and the ends-means criterion could be said to make "proportionality review" more intensive than "wrong considerations" review. A decision which failed the utility (sometimes referred to as "suitability") criterion would almost certainly be based on wrong considerations; not necessarily so a decision which failed the minimum harm or the ends-means criterion.

(b) Community individual rights: "general principles of law"

As explained in Chapter 1,[74] in England and Wales a legal challenge to an official decision on the basis that it infringes directly effective E.C. individual rights may be mounted by what in the circumstances is the most appropriate avenue of challenge — be it statutory appeal, collateral defence to criminal proceedings, AJR or ordinary civil proceedings. The point to be made in this examination of grounds for judicial review is that Community law incorporates a number of "general principles of law"[75] derived principally from the Community Treaties, the legal systems of Member States and such international treaties as the Convention. These general principles include the protection of fundamental human rights, proportionality (both as part of human rights protection and as a principle in its own right[76]), procedural fairness and legitimate expectation.[77] Breach of these principles by Member State[78] public authority action affecting E.C. individual rights will constitute an infringement of those rights. In other words, in E.C. law (as incorporated in United Kingdom law by the European Communities Act 1972), breach of fundamental human rights, proportionality etc. are free-standing grounds upon which to challenge the lawfulness of official action — but only in so far as it affects E.C. individual rights.[79]

---

[72] See *e.g.* Lord Ackner in the *Brind* case (above) [1991] 1 All E.R. at 735; Lord Lowry at 737–739; *cf.* Lord Roskill at 724–725; Lord Bridge at 724f. Also see Boyron (1992); *cf.* Jowell and Lester (1988).

[73] *Sub-sections b* and *c.*

[74] *Section B 3 a.*

[75] Hartley *Foundns*, Chap. 5.

[76] *ibid.*, p. 148.

[77] *ibid.*, p. 145. "Legitimate expectation" is considered in *section E 2 b* below.

[78] For legal challenges to official action of Community institutions see Hartley, *Foundns*, Part Four: [E.C.] Administrative Law.

[79] *R. v. Ministry of Agriculture, Fisheries and Food, ex p. First City Trading Ltd, The Times,* December 20, 1996.

Some indication will now be given of how these E.C. general principles of law may be invoked by persons seeking to challenge the lawfulness of United Kingdom official action in national courts or tribunals. Then will follow an examination of the extent to which the incorporation of the Convention has extended breach of human rights and of the principle of proportionality as free-standing grounds of challenge to the lawfulness of official action in England and Wales.

(i) *Human rights protection under Community law at national level*

In *R. v. Kirk*[80] K, a Danish trawler operator, was charged in England with the offence, created by United Kingdom legislation, of unauthorised fishing within 12 miles of the United Kingdom coast. An E.C. regulation on fishing rights permitted member States temporarily to derogate from (*i.e.* to act inconsistently with) general Community law rules against discrimination between nationals of Member States. The regulation covered the date on which K's alleged offence was committed, but in the event the derogation scheme had not been promulgated until after that date. The ECJ (on a preliminary reference[81] from the English Crown Court) held that in criminalising fishing by Community nationals prior to the promulgation of the E.C. scheme permitting such prohibition, the English legislation had breached the general principle of E.C. law against retrospective penal legislation — a principle enshrined in Article 7 of the Convention.[82] Accordingly, the English legislation could not be invoked against K in these circumstances.

The operation of another general principle of Community law derived from the Convention is illustrated by *Johnston v. Chief Constable of the RUC*.[83] The security situation in Northern Ireland required that officers undertaking street patrols should be routinely armed. The Chief Constable thought it inappropriate that women should undertake armed patrols and since in 1980 there were sufficient full-time women officers to undertake non-patrol duties he decided not to recruit any more women to the RUC Reserve. J, a woman Reservist whose contract was on this basis not renewed, complained to an industrial tribunal, invoking the E.C. "Equal Treatment" directive[84] which prohibits sex-discrimination in the employment field. As permitted by the directive, the domestic implementing legislation allowed discrimination for the purpose of safeguarding national security, public safety or public order. The Home Secretary certified that the ban was for these purposes. The legislation provided that such certificate was to be "conclusive evidence" that this was so. On a preliminary reference the ECJ held that in attempting to prevent judicial scrutiny of the Home Secretary's decision, the "conclusive evidence" provision was inconsistent with the directive which itself reflected a general principle of Community law that a person is entitled to a judicial determination of the question whether his or her E.C. individual rights have been transgressed and to an effective judicial remedy if they have. The ECJ observed[85] that this principle of "effective judicial control" reflected Article 6(1) of the Convention which guarantees a right to a fair trial before an independent and impartial tribunal for the "determination of civil rights and obligations." On this basis the industrial tribunal was not prevented by the "conclusive evidence" provision from considering whether or not the ban was lawful.

(ii) *Proportionality under Community law at national level*

Community legislation (paralleling the approach taken in the Convention[86]) permits state authorities in defined circumstances to derogate from E.C. individual rights on such grounds as public morality, public policy, public security, or public health. Prominent examples are:

[80] [1985] 1 All E.R. 453.
[81] See Chap. 1, *section B 3 a.*
[82] See [1985] 1 All E.R. at 462c.
[83] [1986] 3 All E.R. 135.
[84] Directive 76/207; Rudden and Wyatt, *BCL*, p. 618.
[85] [1986] 3 All E.R. at 156d.
[86] See Chap. 1, *section A 3 a.*

- Article 30 (ex 36) of the E.C. Treaty qualifying the prohibitions in Articles 28 (ex 30) and 29 (ex 34) on quantitative restrictions on imports and exports within the Community.

- Articles 39(3) (ex 48(3)) and 46 (ex 56) derogating from the rights (in Articles 39 (ex 48), 43 (ex 52) and 49 (ex 59)) to, respectively, freedom of worker movement, freedom of establishment and freedom to provide services.

- Article 2(2) of the Equal Treatment directive[87] permitting derogations where "the sex of the worker constitutes a determining factor".

Moreover, ECJ case law has developed and applied in many areas covered by E.C. law the principle[88] that derogations from individual rights are permissible where a Member State can establish that they are necessary ("mandatory requirements") in order to protect values enshrined in E.C. law such as health and safety in employment, fair trade, consumer protection and "national socio-cultural characteristics" such as the maintenance of Sunday as a day of rest from commercial activity.[89]

A key feature of the approach to proportionality in E.C. law is the "minimum harm" criterion referred to above. This criterion is now in effect imposed by the Treaty itself upon Community action[90] and is reflected also in the case law on Member State action. In *Cassis de Dijon*,[91] for example, Germany sought to justify a ban on the sale of an imported French blackcurrant liquor by arguing that consumers might be misled into supposing that it contained a higher alcohol content than was in fact the case. But the import restriction was held disproportionate to the object of consumer protection which could be achieved in a way less detrimental to the French exporters, *i.e.* by labelling.

The European Communities Act 1972 has the effect that under English law the ECJ doctrine of proportionality may be invoked to challenge the lawfulness of any derogation from E.C. individual rights caused by official action in England ·or Wales. So, *e.g.*, in *R. v. Human Fertilisation and Embryology Authority, ex p. Blood*,[92] B succeeded in her AJR of the HFEA's refusal to authorise the export of her deceased husband's sperm to an E.C. country where she could be inseminated with it. The authority had failed to consider whether the public-policy-based ban could be justified (by reference to criteria of proportionality[93]) as a derogation from an individual's right under Article 59 **[Amst 49]** to receive medical treatment in another Member State. Similarly in *R. v. Employment Secretary, ex p. Equal Opportunities Commission*[94] the Commission, on AJR, obtained a declaration that English statutory provisions on redundancy payments and unfair dismissal compensation which discriminated indirectly against women were inconsistent with E.C. law. The House of Lords held that the provisions were not "objectively justified" by the Government's legitimate economic aim of encouraging the creation of more part-time jobs by keeping down employers' overheads.[95] The House held in effect that because of their discriminatory effect, the provisions breached both the utility and ends-means criteria of proportionality.[96]

---

[87] Directive 76/207; Rudden and Wyatt, *BCL*, p. 619.
[88] See *e.g. Cassis de Dijon* case: Case 120/78 *Rewe-Zentral AG v. Bundesmonopolverwaltung für Branntwein* [1979] E.C.R. 649; [1979] 3 C.M.L.R. 494.
[89] See the U.K. Sunday Trading law cases, below.
[90] EC Treaty Art. 5 (ex 3b).
[91] *ibid.*
[92] [1997] 2 All E.R. 687.
[93] See *ibid.*, at 700g.
[94] [1994] 1 All E.R. 910.
[95] *ibid.*, at 921–922.
[96] *ibid.*

These successful E.C. proportionality-based challenges at national level may be compared with the unsuccessful series of challenges mounted by retailers to the validity of the (now repealed) Sunday Trading legislation. Ultimately, in *Stoke-on-Trent C.C. v. B&Q plc*[97] it was held that the infringement of Article 30 **[Amst 28]** of the E.C. Treaty[98] constituted by legislation prohibiting retailers from trading on Sunday was proportionate to (*i.e.* was justified by) the aim of preserving the special character of Sunday.

PROPORTIONALITY — CLOSER SCRUTINY THAN *WEDNESBURY*?

It was said above that, if operated with a genuine deference to the special competence of the decision-making authority in its own field, the principle of proportionality can allow a greater degree of independent judicial scrutiny than is permissible under the *Wednesbury/Padfield* wrong considerations approach. Do the reported cases illustrate this?

Almost certainly, the challenge in the *Equal Opportunities* case (see text) would have succeeded on the *Wednesbury/Padfield* wrong considerations approach as well as under proportionality. But the Divisional Court in the *ITF* case[99] held that the exporters' challenge failed in so far as it was based on domestic law (*Wednesbury/Padfield*) but succeeded under proportionality. Suppose also that in *ex p. Blood* the HFEA had ultimately refused to permit the sperm export (in fact it was permitted). Refusal would not necessarily have been based on "wrong considerations" but might well have been disproportionate. The same would no doubt be true of many official decisions to achieve a legitimate public purpose by one means where the same purpose could be achieved in a manner which would occasion less harm to individual interests, *e.g.*, perhaps, a Government attempt to discourage very heavy lorries from using United Kingdom roads by imposing on any such lorry entering the country a flat-rate annual road tax (administratively simple but not distinguishing between individual levels of use) rather than, say, a use-related tax (administratively complicated but fairer as between different users).

(c) Human Rights Act 1998: challenging official action on the ground of incompatibility with Convention rights

As already noted[1] section 6(1) of the Human Rights Act 1998 provides that "It is unlawful for a public authority to act in a way which is incompatible with a Convention right". Again as explained earlier,[2] a person claiming to be the victim of a breach of this provision may assert his or her claim in any appropriate court or tribunal proceedings.

(i) *The test of incompatibility: proportionality and the margin of appreciation*

By reference to what criteria should tribunals or courts determine claims that particular official action is incompatible with Convention rights? As stated earlier,[3] the Strasbourg authorities have developed a doctrine of proportionality in determining the lawfulness of any restrictions upon Convention rights. It seems plain that English tribunals and courts will have to apply this doctrine in determining incompatibility claims under section 6 (and, indeed, for the purpose of their duty

---

[97] [1993] 1 All E.R. 481.
[98] *ibid.*
[99] *R. v. Sussex Chief Constable, ex p. ITF Ltd* [1995] 4 All E.R. 364, reversed on appeal: see *section C 2 c* above.
[1] Chap. 1, *section A 3 b.*
[2] Chap. 1, *section B 3 b.*
[3] Chap. 1, *section A 3 a.*

under section 3 to interpret legislation, so far as possible, in a way compatible with Convention rights).[4]

What remains to some extent uncertain is how, in cases brought under the 1998 Act, proportionality will interact with the "margin of appreciation" doctrine. Again as stated earlier,[5] under this doctrine, in assessing the proportionality of the state's acts, a certain degree of deference is given by the Strasbourg authorities to the judgment of national authorities when they weigh competing public and individual interests in view of their special knowledge and overall responsibility under domestic law. It seems probable that English tribunals and courts will likewise develop a practice of according an appropriate deference to official actions which are challenged under the 1998 Act as being incompatible with Convention rights.[6] What will be "appropriate" will be likely to depend on circumstances — in particular, the nature of the alleged breach and the special competences of both decision-making authority and reviewing tribunal or court.[7] So, *e.g.*, greater deference is likely to be accorded to broad policy decisions in the area of those Convention rights which are expressed to be subject to restrictions "necessary in a democratic society"[8] than to decisions in individual cases threatening so unqualified a right as the right to life.[9] The following pre-Act cases may usefully be contrasted.

In *Brind v. Home Secretary*[10] a number of TV and radio journalists applied unsuccessfully for judicial review of a government ban, mentioned above,[11] on broadcasting the voices of Irish terrorist organisations and their sympathisers. The ban had been imposed by the Home Secretary in reliance on his statutory powers in respect of the Independent Broadcasting Authority, and on his powers under the BBC's charter, to order that certain classes of material are not broadcast. It was argued that the ban was unlawful in that it contravened the journalists' right to free speech under Article 10 of the Convention and that such breach should be presumed (in the absence of clear contrary indication) to be outside the power relied on. The House of Lords held unanimously that where (as here) discretionary power is conferred in broad and unambiguous terms there is no presumption that the discretion has to be exercised in conformity with the Convention. Section 6 of the 1998 Act, of course, would in future require a minister to exercise any discretionary power compatibly with Convention rights, in effect reversing this ruling. But on such facts as those in *Brind*, this should not affect the outcome of the case. The journalists pursued their challenge unsuccessfully before the Convention authorities in Strasbourg, and the Commission held that the restriction was justified under Article 10(2).[12] Under the 1998 Act, an English court applying the proportionality principle with appropriate deference would be likely to reach the same conclusion. Contrast *R. v. Cambridge District Health Authority, ex p. B* (the case of the leukaemia girl, discussed above[13] in the context of scarce resources). Laws J. at first instance[14] considered that the girl's right to life under Article 2 of the Convention was "assaulted" by the authority's decision not to fund treatment for the girl which, accordingly, he quashed. His ruling was reversed by the Court of Appeal,[15] but perhaps under the 1998 Act it would have been upheld.[16]

[4] *Rights Brought Home*, para. 2.5.
[5] See Chap. 1, *section A 3 a*.
[6] Pannick (1998), pp. 548–549.
[7] *ibid.*, pp. 549–551.
[8] See, *e.g.* Arts 8–11 (family life, freedom of conscience, free speech, freedom of association).
[9] Art. 2.
[10] [1991] 1 All E.R. 720.
[11] *Sub-section 1 c.*
[12] See Harris, O'Boyle and Warbrick, p. 408.
[13] *Section C 3 b.*
[14] *The Times*, March 15, 1995.
[15] [1995] 2 All E.R. 129.
[16] For Convention case law see Harris, O'Boyle and Warbrick, pp. 40–41.

It should be understood that an appropriate deference in applying proportionality is different from (though akin to) the deference encapsulated in the *Wednesbury*/*Padfield* doctrine. Under proportionality, the reviewing tribunal must apply (albeit with appropriate deference) free-standing substantive criteria such as ends-means and least harm.[17] This will require the court or tribunal to call for evidence which will enable it to strike the balance which proportionality requires.[18] Under *Wednesbury*/*Padfield* the level of review is governed instead by the "wrong considerations" doctrine. This doctrine requires simply that the decision-maker placed all required issues in the balance. There is no question of the reviewing court or tribunal re-striking the balance, however uneven.

The difference between the two varieties of appropriate deference may be illustrated, again, by *ex p. B*: Laws J. found himself able in this human rights context to read into the broad discretion of the authority more substantial constraints than would be possible simply by using "the crude *Wednesbury* bludgeon." The Court of Appeal, however, adopting the orthodox restrictive approach to the review of strong discretions upheld the authority's decision not only on the resource-allocation basis already explained but also on the basis that other relevant considerations such as the wishes of the child and the prospects of the treatment's success had been taken into account.

Moreover, under pre-1998 Act English law, Government assertions that a decision was compatible with the state's Convention obligations were appraised by applying ordinary *Wednesbury* principles in making the "anxious scrutiny" required in such a case.[19] In this context, a case which may[20] prove to illustrate how proportionality can produce a different outcome is *R. v. Ministry of Defence, ex p. Smith*.[21] There the Court of Appeal upheld the dismissal of an AJR of the Ministry's blanket policy, made in the exercise of prerogative powers, of banning from the armed forces any service person found to be of homosexual orientation. The human rights argument here was based on the right to respect for private and family life in Article 8. The Ministry sought to justify the ban by the need to maintain morale in the services, to protect under-18 recruits and to avoid difficulties where communal living was necessary. The applicants' counter-arguments were based on the blanket nature of the ban and the contrary practice in the armed services of other countries. While acknowledging the cogency of the latter arguments the court held that they failed to establish that the ban was irrational. "The threshold of irrationality is a high one. It was not crossed in this case."[22] Whether the Strasbourg authorities will find that the ban can be justified as proportionate under Article 8(2) remains to be seen.

(ii) *Incompatibility claims: appeal, review, merits and law*

Where an official decision is challenged in a court or tribunal with appeal or review jurisdiction in respect of the decision, that court or tribunal will, under the 1998 Act, acquire jurisdiction to overturn the decision if it finds it to be incompatible with a Convention right. Such incompatibility would require a court or tribunal with merits appeal jurisdiction to re-take the decision with an outcome compatible with the Convention right. A court or tribunal with jurisdiction (whether statutory appeal or common law supervisory review) confined to correction of error of law[23] would

---

[17] *Sub-section a* above.

[18] Sir Thomas Bingham M.R. in *R. v. Ministry of Defence, ex p. Smith* [1996] 1 All E.R. 257 (below) at 267c–d.

[19] *R. v. Home Sec, ex p. Launder* [1997] 3 All E.R. 961 at 989–990. *Cf. R. v. Lord Saville, ex p. A, The Times*, June 27, 1999 (CA by 2:1 quashed decision of public inquiry into "Bloody Sunday" to withdraw anonymity from soldiers involved). On "anxious scrutiny" generally, see Fordham (1996).

[20] It was at the time of writing being pursued in the ECHR.

[21] [1996] 1 All E.R. 257.

[22] *ibid.*, at 266g.

[23] For whether judicial review confined to error of law fulfils the Article 6 requirement of a fair trial for the determination of civil rights and obligations (*sub-section b* above) see *section E 2 C (i)* below.

be expected to identify the incompatibility and if necessary remit the case to the decision maker for decision on the correct basis.[24]

E PROCEDURAL IMPROPRIETY

If a statute provides that it is a precondition of the legality of a public authority's exercise of a particular function that the authority must observe certain procedural requirements, *e.g.*, hearing interested parties, giving reasons for its decision, it is not difficult to see that the authority would act outside the limits of its authority, *ultra vires*, if it did not observe those requirements.

Nor is it difficult to see that the ability of a person to obtain judicial review for failure to observe such requirements — particularly a requirement that the authority give reasons — may well be the key to the exposure of some substantive defect in the decision-making process. The ability to insist on an open and fair procedure in a public authority decision-making process will often be a crucial prerequisite to exposing the decision itself as vitiated by some substantive error.

All this is easy to see. What is often not so easy is to ascertain precisely when a statute has made the fulfilment of certain procedural requirements a precondition of the legality of a public authority's acts or decisions. This section addresses that issue.

The starting-point is that sometimes a statute will make express provision regarding procedure to be followed by a public authority in its exercise of a particular function: see *sub-section 1* below. Sometimes no procedural requirements are expressly prescribed by a statute. But in some such cases the courts will hold that the statute has made provision by implication, *i.e.* that the decision-making process is subject to the so-called "rules of natural justice", or, in current terminology, the duty to act "fairly": see *sub-section 2.*

1 EXPRESS STATUTORY PROCEDURAL REQUIREMENTS[25]

In very many cases where statute creates a new type of tribunal or provides for an inquiry process or empowers an administrative authority to grant or refuse licences, permissions or benefits it will prescribe in detail for the procedure to be followed by the authority in exercising its functions. What a statute seldom does, however, is to specify the consequences of a failure by the authority to follow the procedure. In these circumstances when will the statute be taken to have made it a precondition of the legality of the authority's decisions that the procedure is followed?

(a) "Mandatory" and "directory" requirements

In responding to challenges to the legality of official action based on failure to observe express procedural requirements, the courts have classified requirements as either "mandatory" or "directory." To say that a requirement is "mandatory" means that failure to observe it makes the authority's act or decision *ultra vires*, and the court will normally exercise its discretion to grant an appropriate remedy. If, on the other hand, a requirement is classified as "directory", failure to observe it will not render the act or decision *ultra vires*, although there may be means of securing compliance, *e.g.* a statutory procedure for complaining to a minister,[26] or sanctions for failure to

---

[24] See Chap. 6, *section F* for the position where an "incompatibility" challenge is mounted collaterally (*e.g.* by way of defence to criminal proceedings).

[25] Wade and Forsyth, *AL*, pp. 253–261; de Smith, *JRAA*, pp. 265–274.

[26] *Bradbury v. Enfield L.B.C.* [1967] 3 All E.R. 434 at 441.

comply.[27] But in the absence of alternative means of enforcement it would be true to say that an authority "has a discretion not to comply with [a directory requirement] if, in its opinion, the exceptional circumstances of a particular case justify departing from it."[28]

How do the courts make the "mandatory/directory" distinction in particular cases?

(b) Statutory language or context indicating that requirement is mandatory

It may be apparent from the statutory wording that compliance is a precondition to the legality of the action concerned, *e.g.* a provision that "an [education] authority shall not do anything" towards restructuring an area's schools before completing certain public consultation procedures.[29]

But in the absence of statutory guidance the courts have taken a somewhat impressionistic approach, considering on a case to case basis "the importance of the provision that has been disregarded, and the relation of that provision to the general object intended to be secured by the Act."[30] The result is "an inextricable tangle of loose ends"[31] and a huge bulk of reported cases tending to yield guidance only in the particular statutory context concerned.

Nevertheless, "some classes of procedural requirements are so important that they will nearly always be held to be 'mandatory'."[32] Thus, where statute imposes on a public authority a duty to inform or consult or give a hearing to persons likely to be affected by proposed action, the requirement will usually be treated as mandatory. This approach is reinforced where the effect of the action on the individual concerned may be in the nature of a penal sanction or loss of property or privilege.[33]

(c) Substantial compliance / no substantial prejudice

There may be circumstances in which the breach of a mandatory procedural requirement has caused no substantial prejudice to anyone for whose protection the requirement has been imposed — often because the prescribed procedure has been substantially (albeit not wholly) complied with. In such circumstances the breach may be overlooked. For example, in *Coney v. Choyce*[34] the public notice requirements regarding school restructuring (held mandatory in the case referred to above) were substantially complied with so that all concerned were well aware of the proposals. In these circumstances an isolated failure to post a notice near a school main entrance was held not to invalidate the action taken. Even total non-compliance may, in the particular circumstances of a case, cause no prejudice — and thus will not be a ground of complaint.[35]

Despite instances of the adoption of this approach in the highest courts,[36] it remains to be seen whether it will emerge as a general principle,[37] although in 1999 the Court of Appeal suggested that it should.[38]

---

[27] *e.g.*, *Woodward v. Sarsons* (1875) 10 L.R.C.P. 733, *Margate Pier Co. v. Hannam* (1819) 3 B. & Ald. 266.
[28] Lord Diplock in *O'Reilly v. Mackman* [1982] 3 All E.R. 1124 at 1127d.
[29] *Bradbury v. Enfield L.B.C.* [1967] 3 All E.R. 434.
[30] Lord Penzance in *Howard v. Bodington* (1877) 2 P.D. 203 at 211.
[31] de Smith, *JRAA*, p. 266.
[32] *ibid.*, p. 268.
[33] For case law see Emery and Smythe, *JR*, p. 209.
[34] [1975] 1 All E.R. 979.
[35] See, *e.g. R. v. Home Secretary, ex p. Jeyeanthan* [1999] 3 All E.R. 231, CA.
[36] *e.g.* the Privy Council in *Wang v. Commissioner of Inland Revenue* [1995] 1 All E.R. 367.
[37] de Smith, *JRAA*, p. 271.
[38] *Ex p. Jeyeanthan* (above).

The courts' willingness to focus upon the effect of a breach of a procedural requirement rather than simply on the classification of the requirement as mandatory can be further illustrated by reference to the common express statutory procedural requirement to give reasons for a decision. Examples of this requirement are as follows:

- When rejecting a homeless person's housing application a local authority must give reasons for its conclusion that the applicant is homeless intentionally or has no priority need.[39]

- When excluding a person from an approved list of contractors or when not inviting, or rejecting, a tender for a contract governed by the "non-commercial considerations" provisions of the Local Government Act 1988[40] a local authority must give reasons if requested to do so by the person concerned.[41]

- Tribunals and Inquiries Act 1992, s.10 is an important general provision which requires the wide range of tribunals specified in schedule 1 of the Act, and also any Minister notifying a decision after holding a statutory inquiry, to give reasons for a decision if requested to do so.

In *Save Britain's Heritage v. Environment Secretary*[42] a conservationist group unsuccessfully sought judicial review (under a special statutory procedure[43]) of the minister's confirmation, after a public inquiry, of planning permission to demolish the Mappin & Webb building in the City of London. The group alleged that the statutory requirement to give reasons had been breached in that the reasons given failed to "deal with the substantial points that have been raised" in a manner which would "enable the reader to know what conclusion the decision-maker has reached on the principal controversial issues". Accepting these tests of compliance with the duty[44] the House of Lords said that the question turned on "whether the interests of the applicant have been substantially prejudiced by the deficiency of the reasons given".[45] As the case shows, this is often itself a matter of judgment, the House of Lords differing from the Court of Appeal.

2 Natural Justice — the Duty to Act Fairly[46]

The remainder of this section deals with the position where a person seeking to challenge official action alleges procedural unfairness but cannot point to the infringement of any express procedural provision.

- It will be shown that the courts adopt the presumption (rebuttable in certain circumstances) that official power is to be regarded as having been conferred subject to a requirement that persons are entitled to a fair hearing before action is taken which will prejudicially affect what Lord Reid referred to in the leading case of *Ridge v. Baldwin* in 1963[47] as their "property rights or privileges".[48] Action taken in breach of

---

[39] Housing Act 1996, s.184(3): see *R. v. Westminster C.C., ex p. Ermakov* [1996] 2 All E.R. 302.
[40] Ss.17–20: see Chap. 3, *section C 2 a.*
[41] 1988 Act s 20.
[42] [1991] 2 All E.R. 10.
[43] Now in Town and Country Planning Act 1990, s.288: see Chap. 7, *section A 6 a.*
[44] [1991] 2 All E.R. at 23h, 27g, 28h.
[45] *ibid.*, p. 24b.
[46] de Smith, *JRAA*, Chaps 7–12; Wade, *AL*, Pt V; Craig, *AL*, Chaps 13–14.
[47] [1963] 2 All E.R. 66.
[48] *ibid.*, at 73D.

this requirement of "natural justice" will be *ultra vires*. *Ridge v. Baldwin* is of signal importance since it re-emphasised, after a period of collective judicial amnesia, that the crucial consideration in deciding whether or not a person has a right to a hearing is "the nature of the thing [to be] done"[49] rather than whether the power under which it is to be done is "judicial" or otherwise. In the period before *Ridge v. Baldwin* some courts, emphasising the judicial overtones of the phrase "natural justice" had held that the rules applied only where a public authority could be said to be "acting judicially." *Ridge v. Baldwin* eradicated this "'judicial' fallacy."[50] In the *CCSU* case[51] in 1984 Lord Roskill said that the terminology of "natural justice" "perhaps might now be allowed to find a permanent resting-place and be better replaced by speaking of a duty to act fairly."[52]

- Additionally it has been recognised, over the last decade or so, that a person has a right to a fair hearing wherever a public authority has by promise or by conduct created a "legitimate expectation" that a hearing will be given. Moreover, the courts have indicated that there are some circumstances in which persons may claim a legitimate expectation not merely to a hearing but to the conferment of some substantive benefit or advantage.

The following issues will be addressed: (a) What are "rights" and "privileges" for the purpose of a right to a fair hearing? (b) When may a "legitimate expectation" arise, and to what? (c) What counts as a "fair hearing"? (d) In what circumstances will the presumption of a right to a fair hearing be rebutted?

(a) Rights and Privileges

As will now appear, these categories have expanded gradually on a case by case basis. Consequently their content cannot be exhaustively stated, but some indication of their current scope may be given.

(i) *Rights*

Although Lord Reid referred to "property rights" the House of Lords has more recently referred simply to "rights",[53] and many important cases in this area relate to decisions impacting on the liberty of the individual.[54] Beyond this, "property rights" include:

- Title to property, *e.g.* in *Cooper v. Wandsworth Board of Works*[55] the local authority had exercised its statutory power to demolish a house built in breach of a statutory requirement to give notice of intention to build. The owner sued successfully for damages in trespass: the authority had acted *ultra vires* in exercising its power without first hearing his side of the case.

- Tenure of a public office: in *Ridge v. Baldwin* itself a police authority had acted under a statutory power to dismiss the chief constable whom they thought unfit to discharge his duties. The authority had not heard the officer in his own defence but had proceeded on

---

[49] See *ibid.*, at 74C.
[50] Wade and Forsyth, *AL*, p. 511.
[51] *Council of Civil Service Unions v. Minister for the Civil Service* [1984] 3 All E.R. 935: see Chap. 3, *section B 2 a*.
[52] *ibid.*, at 954b.
[53] *R. v. Commission for Racial Equality, ex p. Hillingdon L.B.C.* [1982] 3 W.L.R. 159 at 165H (Lord Diplock).
[54] See, *e.g. Doody v. Home Secretary* [1993] 3 All E.R. 92 and other cases on prisoners' rights cited below.
[55] (1863) 14 C.B.N.S. 180.

the basis of remarks made by the judge during the trial of the officer on corruption charges of which he was in the event acquitted. A majority of the House of Lords declared the dismissal void on the basis that the officer had not been given the fair hearing to which, under the rules of natural justice, he was entitled.

- Legal entitlement to sums of money: in *R. v. Environment Secretary, ex p. Brent L.B.C.*[56] the minister's exercise of his statutory power to reduce the Government's rate support grant to the authority — "a right to substantial sums of money"[57] — was quashed because he had failed to invite the authority put its case before he made the decision.

(ii) *Privileges*

"Privileges" is usually taken to refer to benefits to which a person has no strict legal claim, such as:

- Official licences or permissions. "The exercise of a licensing function . . . by any authority is one to which the rules of natural justice . . . would normally apply."[58] So, for example, a person is entitled to state his case before he is refused a public entertainments licence,[59] or before a market or street trading licence is withdrawn.[60]

- A passport: in *R. v. Foreign Secretary, ex p. Everett*[61] the Court of Appeal held that fairness required the Home Secretary to explain the grounds for his refusal to renew the passport of a passport holder living in Spain and in respect of whom warrants of arrest were outstanding in the United Kingdom.

- The grant of British citizenship: in *R. v. Home Secretary, ex p. Fayed*[62] the Home Secretary had refused the Fayeds' citizenship applications because he was not satisfied that they were of good character.[63] By 2:1 the Court of Appeal quashed the refusal, holding that an express statutory provision[64] relieving the Home Secretary of a duty to give reasons did not mean that there was no duty to give the applicant an opportunity to address the Home Secretary's concerns on the good character issue before the application was refused. Woolf M.R. observed[65] that this was "classically" a situation in which procedural fairness applied.

- A place in a particular local authority residential home: in *R. v. Devon C.C., ex p. Baker, R. v. Durham C.C., ex p. Curtis*[66] the Court of Appeal held that whilst an authority has no duty individually to consult the residents of an old peoples' home before closing it down, the authority must give reasonable notice of any proposal to close a home so that residents have ample time to oppose the proposal. This duty of fairness was held to have been discharged in the *Devon* case (one year's notice of the possible closure followed by six weeks of meetings and consultations — including with residents in the homes — prior to decision) but not in the *Durham* case where the only notice of the closure was a letter to residents sent five days before the meeting when the decision was taken.

---

[56] [1983] 3 All E.R. 321.
[57] Ackner L.J., *ibid.*, at 355a.
[58] Glidewell J. in *R. v. Huntingdon D.C., ex p. Cowan* [1984] 1 All E.R. 58 at 64b.
[59] *ibid.*
[60] *R. v. Barnsley M.B.C., ex p. Hook* [1976] 3 All E.R. 452; *R. v. Wear Valley D.C., ex p. Binks* [1985] 2 All E.R. 699: see Chap. 3, *section C 2 b*.
[61] [1989] 1 All E.R. 655.
[62] [1997] 1 All E.R. 228.
[63] British Nationality Act 1981, s.6.
[64] *ibid.*, s.44(2).
[65] [1997] 1 All E.R. at 237h.
[66] [1995] 1 All E.R. 73.

(b) The doctrine of legitimate expectation[67]

It was said above that a person may claim a fair hearing wherever a public authority has by promise or by conduct ("the existence of a regular practice which the claimant can reasonably expect to continue"[68]) created a "legitimate expectation" that a hearing will be given. In one sense, the notion of a legitimate expectation of fair treatment at the hands of officialdom is used simply to articulate the proposition that privileges should not be withdrawn without a fair hearing.[69] But the concept is used in another sense, as a basis for according rights.[70] Essentially, one may assert that one's "privileges" are at stake if one can show that the previous conduct (promise or practice) of the authority has given one cause to expect that one will be given a fair hearing before it takes action of the sort in question.

(i) *Express promise of consultation*

An illegal immigrant to Hong Kong acquired a legitimate expectation that his case would be considered on its merits via the Governor's express promise to that effect.[71] From the local authority's promise of full prior consultation, Liverpool taxi owners gained a right to be heard before the authority increased the number of licences issued.[72] And the colliery review procedure (established under the 1946 nationalisation legislation and modified after the 1984 miners' strike) gave miners a right to be consulted before a government decision to close mines, thus furnishing a "classic example of legitimate expectation [of the express promise variety]".[73]

(ii) *Regular practice of consultation*

On this basis the House of Lords held that the civil servants in the *CCSU* case[74] had a legitimate expectation to consultation before being prohibited by their employer from union membership; prisoners have a legitimate expectation to a fair hearing before loss of remission for disciplinary offences[75]; and parents have a legitimate expectation that they will be consulted before the closure of their children's schools.[76]

(iii) *"Substantive" legitimate expectation*[77]

It is often asked whether it is of much use to obtain judicial review on the ground of procedural unfairness. Surely, it is said, the authority may well provide the required fair hearing and then arrive once more at precisely the same decision, as, *e.g.*, in the mine closure case just mentioned.

Even in a case of this sort it may well be that the detail of the decision may in the end be less unfavourable as a result of the publicity and argument flowing from the proper procedure. In other cases the exposure of the challenged decision to proper scrutiny may reveal that the authority was relying on unlawful considerations and so cannot in fact stand its ground.[78]

But beyond this, as said above, the courts have indicated that there are some circumstances in which persons may claim a legitimate expectation not merely to a hearing but to the conferment

---

[67] Craig, *AL*, Chap. 19; de Smith, *JRAA*, pp. 417–430, 563–576; Craig (1992); Elias (1988); Forsyth (1988).
[68] Lord Fraser in the *CCSU* case [1984] All E.R. at 944a.
[69] See Simon Brown L.J. in *Baker* (above) at [1995] 1 All E.R. 91.
[70] Craig, *AL*, pp. 611 *et seq.*
[71] *Att.-Gen. (Hong-Kong) v. Ng Yuen Shiu* [1983] 2 All E.R. 346.
[72] *R. v. Liverpool Corporation, ex p. Liverpool Taxi Association* [1972] 2 All E.R. 589.
[73] *R. v. Trade Secretary, ex p. Vardy, The Times*, December 30, 1992.
[74] *Council of Civil Service Unions v. Minister for the Civil Service* [1984] 3 All E.R. 935.
[75] *R. v. Hull Prison Visitors, ex p. St Germain* [1979] 1 All E.R. 701; approved by the House of Lords in *O'Reilly v. Mackman* [1982] 3 All E.R. 1124.
[76] *R. v. Brent L.B.C., ex p. Gunning, The Times*, April 30, 1985.
[77] Craig (1996).
[78] See, *e.g. R. v. Westminster C.C., ex p. Ermakov* [1996] 2 All E.R. 302 at 315.

of some substantive benefit or advantage. On this basis, of course, the doctrine of legitimate expectation steps outside the arena of procedural fairness and becomes, to that extent, a substantive principle of administrative law akin to proportionality and obedience to the European Convention on Human Rights (the Convention). The case law in this area is not yet fully developed, but the following points may be made.

- A person may be able to secure via judicial review a *benefit or advantage expressly promised* (albeit without contractual force) by a public authority. A number of cases relating to informal assurances given to tax payers by the revenue authorities indicate that if an assurance is unequivocal,[79] based on full disclosure by the tax payer, and made by a person with actual or ostensible authority to make it, the agreement must be honoured. "In [such] circumstances it is an abuse of power for the Revenue to seek to extract tax contrary to an advance clearance".[80]

- Similarly one may be able to secure via judicial review *a benefit or advantage which one might reasonably expect under a policy maintained by an authority at the relevant time*. In *R. v. Home Secretary, ex p. Khan*[81] the applicants were seeking entry clearance for a foreign child whom they wished to adopt. They had satisfied existing Home Office criteria but were refused clearance on the basis of their failure to satisfy a newly-announced criterion. In quashing the refusal Parker L.J. said: "The Secretary of State is, of course, at liberty to change the policy but in my view, *vis-à-vis* the recipient of such a letter, a new policy can only be implemented after such recipient has been given a full and serious consideration whether there is some overriding public interest which justifies a departure from the procedures stated. . . ."[82] In *R. v. Criminal Injuries Compensation Board, ex p. P*[83] the court said that claimants would have a legitimate expectation to an award of compensation under whatever was the criminal injuries scheme in place at time of the injury in question.[84]

- The courts have made it clear that the doctrine of legitimate expectation cannot be invoked in order to prevent a public authority from *changing an existing policy and applying the new policy to all subsequent cases covered by it*.[85] But suppose that in reliance on an existing policy a person has committed his time and resources to embarking on a course of conduct which would eventually yield him a benefit. If the policy is changed during the course of his reliance — in "mid-stream", as regards him — may he assert that he will nevertheless acquire a legitimate expectation to that benefit if he eventually completes the course of conduct?

In *R. v. Ministry of Agriculture, Fisheries and Food, ex p. Hamble Fisheries Ltd*[86] relying on existing ministry (MAFF) policy, Hamble had bought two vessels with MAFF fishing licences and was downsizing the engines of another, larger, vessel with the intention of securing MAFF transfer of the licences to that vessel. Before the downsizing was complete MAFF changed its licensing policy and refused the transfers. On AJR Hamble

---

[79] But *cf. R. v. IRC, ex p. Unilever plc* [1996] S.T.C. 681.
[80] Lord Browne-Wilkinson in *Matrix-Securities Ltd v. IRC* [1994] 1 All E.R. 769 at 791e, citing *R. v. IRC, ex p. Preston* [1985] 2 All E.R. 327.
[81] [1985] 1 All E.R. 40; see also *R. v. Home Secretary, ex p. Ruddock* [1987] 2 All E.R. 518 at 531.
[82] *ibid.*, p. 48f.
[83] [1994] 1 All E.R. 80.
[84] *ibid.*, at 84f.
[85] See, *e.g. Findlay v. Home Secretary* [1984] 3 All E.R. 801; *Hughes v. DHSS* [1985] A.C. 318, *R. v. Transport Sec, ex p. Richmond L.B.C.* [1994] 1 All E.R. 577; *cf.* Dotan (1997).
[86] [1995] 2 All E.R. 714.

sought to enforce the legitimate expectation which it maintained that it had acquired prior to the policy change. Although Sedley J. rejected the AJR he said that the question of the existence of a legitimate expectation is a question of balancing the value that policy should be allowed to be changed against the value of fulfilling expectations already raised. This balance was primarily for the policy-maker to strike "but if the outcome is challenged by way of judicial review . . . the court's criterion is [not] the bare rationality of the policy-maker's conclusion."[87] The question for the court (answered in MAFF's favour in *Hamble*) was whether the decision "bore a fair proportion to the end in view".[88] The Court of Appeal has however since held in *R. v. Home Secretary, ex p. Hargreaves*[89] that, on the contrary, where legitimate expectation is being relied upon as a basis to challenge the substance of a decision rather than the fairness of procedure "*Wednesbury* provides the correct test".[90] Sedley J's proportionality approach in *Hamble* was characterised as "heresy".[91] As already explained,[92] what is heresy in pure English domestic law would be required orthodoxy in cases raising issues of E.C. and Convention law.

Hargreaves applied the approach adopted by the House of Lords in *Findlay v. Home Secretary*[93] in holding (as in *Findlay*) that where parole policy is changed during a particular prisoner's term "the most that a convicted prisoner can legitimately expect is that his case will be examined individually in the light of whatever policy [prevails]".[94]

- *International Treaties* It seems that "the entering into a treaty by [a] Secretary of State could give rise to a legitimate expectation on which the public generally are entitled to rely . . . that [he] would act in accordance with any obligations which he accepted under the treaty"[95] But this is "subject to any indication to the contrary"[96] by the relevant public authority. So, *e.g.*, the United Kingdom Parliament's postponement of the coming into effect of the main provisions of the Human Rights Act 1998 until a date to be appointed by the Government[97] precluded the creation of any legitimate expectation that the DPP would exercise his prosecutorial discretions in accordance with the Convention prior to that date.[98]

- *Lawful to breach legitimate expectation?* Finally, the courts have stressed that "The existence of a legitimate expectation that a decision-maker will act in a particular way does not necessarily compel him or her to act in that way. That is the difference between a legitimate expectation and a binding rule of law."[99] Even where such expectation has been created, a decision to breach it will apparently be unlawful (in English pure domestic law) only if *Wednesbury* unreasonable.[1] In Community and Convention cases, no doubt, a proportionality approach will apply.

---

[87] *ibid.*, p. 731c.
[88] *ibid.*, p. 735j.
[89] [1997] 1 All E.R. 397.
[90] *ibid.*, at 412h (Hirst L.J.).
[91] *ibid.*
[92] *Section D2* above.
[93] [1984] 3 All E.R. 801.
[94] [1984] 3 All E.R. at 830 (Lord Scarman).
[95] Lord Woolf M.R. in *R. v. Home Secretary, ex p. Patel*, July 30, 1998 (unreported), CA; see also Hobhouse L.J.
[96] Lord Woolf M.R., *ibid*.
[97] 1998 Act. s.22(3).
[98] *R. v. DPP, ex p. Kebilene and others, The Times* March 31, 1999. *Cf.* Lester (1996).
[99] *Minister of State v. Teoh* [1995] 183 C.L.R. 273 at 291.
[1] *R. v. Home Secretary, ex p. Hargreaves* [1997] 1 All E.R. 397 (above); see also *R. v. Home Secretary, ex p. Khan* [1985] 1 All E.R. 40 (above).

(c) What counts as a "fair hearing"?

Because of the infinite variety of circumstances in which the rules of natural justice — or duty to act fairly — may apply, "[t]he requirements of natural justice must depend on the circumstances of the case, the nature of the inquiry, the rules under which the tribunal is acting, the subject-matter that is being dealt with, and so forth".[2] Nevertheless, some general indication may be given of what, in particular circumstances, will count as acting fairly.

By reference to the Latin tags "*audi alteram partem*" ("hear the other side [also]") and "*nemo iudex in causa sua*" ("no one should be judge in his own cause"), the question of the content of the duty is usually dealt with under two main heads:

(i) *The right to a hearing*

Prior Notice Of Opposing Case   Generally speaking a fair hearing will require prior notice of the proceedings at which the matter is to be considered and of the main features of the opposing case.[3] Moreover, it will be unfair for the prosecution in criminal proceedings to withhold, even inadvertently, information which would benefit the defendant (*e.g.* if the police withhold the names of witnesses who might testify in the defendant's favour).[4] The decision may be quashed as unfair even though, of course, the court's own procedure has been impeccable. But the principle does not extend to a case where a party's own advisers — or even the party himself — inadvertently fail to put forward certain points which could have been made on the party's behalf.[5] Nor, apparently, does the principle extend to the provision of unintentionally misleading evidence by a witness in tribunal proceedings.[6]

Details of procedure   The actual extent of a person's knowledge of and ability to answer an opposing case will turn very much on the details of the procedure adopted by the deciding authority, *e.g.* whether the hearing is oral or, on the contrary, by way of written submissions; if it is oral, whether or not there is a right to legal or other representation and a right to call and to cross-examine witnesses. As already observed, there is often detailed statutory provision on matters of procedure. But in cases where statute is silent the courts have refrained from any general statement beyond that "what [the] procedure is to be in detail must depend on the nature of the [authority]'.[7] And, in order that authorities may dispose of their business with due speed and efficiency, they have at common law a wide discretion in the matter of their own procedure.[8]

This said, there will be many cases where fairness will require an oral hearing, *e.g.* disciplinary proceedings carrying a severe penalty — where, also, it would be unfair to deny a party the right to legal representation,[9] although this will not necessarily be a pre-requisite of fairness in less serious cases.[10] And, especially in penal and other cases where questions of fact are in issue, a fair hearing will normally include the right to call and cross-examine witnesses.[11]

On the other hand, many decisions of a routine nature (*e.g.* on applications for firearms, entertainments, or street trading licences or for planning permissions) are properly made on the

---

[2] Tucker L.J. in *Russell v. Duke of Norfolk* [1949] 1 All E.R. 109 at 118.

[3] See, *e.g. R. v. Home Secretary, ex p. Fayed* [1997] 1 All E.R. 228 at 237–238, CA, citing *Doody v. Home Secretary* (below) [1993] 3 All E.R. at 106g, HL.

[4] *R. v. Leyland J.J., ex p. Hawthorn* [1979] 1 All E.R. 209. *R. v. Criminal Injuries Compensation Board, ex p. A, The Times*, March 26, 1999, HL.

[5] *R. v. Home Secretary, ex p. Al-Mehdawi* [1989] 3 All E.R. 843.

[6] *R. v. Criminal Injuries Compensation Board, ex p. A* [1997] 3 All E.R. 745, 764.

[7] Viscount Haldane L.C. in *Local Government Board v. Arlidge* [1914–15] All E.R. Rep. 1, 6I.

[8] See *e.g. Re Pergamon Press Ltd* [1970] 3 All E.R. 535; *R. v. Home Secretary, ex p. Tarrant* [1984] 1 All E.R. 799.

[9] *Ex p. Tarrant* (previous note) at 818b.

[10] *Hone v. Maze Prison Visitors* [1988] 1 All E.R. 321.

[11] *R. v. Hull Prison Visitors, ex p. St Germain (No. 2)* [1979] 3 All E.R. 545.

basis of written submissions, although there is commonly provision for oral hearing later by way of appeal.[12]

Reasons for decisions   Clearly the value of any hearing or consultation prior to a decision will be much diminished if the decision-maker is not obliged to explain the reasons for his decision once it is taken. A distinction is drawn between courts and other decision makers. "A professional judge should, as a rule, give reasons for his decision."[13] However, in the absence of express statutory provision[14] where reliance must be placed on the rules of natural justice, the House of Lords has reiterated that "the law does not at present recognise a general duty to give reasons for an administrative decision. Nevertheless, it is equally beyond question that such a duty may in appropriate circumstances be implied . . ."[15] The question always is whether in all the circumstances a procedure can be regarded as fair without the giving of reasons.[16] Key features of situations in which the courts have required reasons to be given as a matter of fairness are:

- Where what is at stake are a person's liberty (see *Doody v. Home Secretary*[17]: fairness requires Home Secretary to give reasons for increasing the judicially recommended period of imprisonment ("tariff") to be served by way of punishment by a prisoner awarded a mandatory life sentence) or their livelihood (see *R. v. Civil Service Appeal Board, ex p. Cunningham*[18]: fairness required civil service disciplinary tribunal to explain why it had awarded what appeared to be an unjustifiably low amount of compensation for unfair dismissal). But contrast *R. v. Higher Education Funding Council, ex p. Institute of Dental Surgery*[19]: fairness did not require the Council (HEFC) to give reasons for its decision to down-grade its assessment of the quality of the Institute's research despite the substantial funding consequences of the decision.[20]

- Where in the absence of reasons and because of the opacity of the decision-making process the decision will be impenetrable, thus negativing the value of any opportunity one may have had to state one's case. This was true in *Doody*[21] and *Cunningham*[22]; but not in *HEFC*.[23]

- Where there is "something peculiar to the decision which in fairness calls for reasons to be given",[24] as in *Cunningham*,[25] but not in *HEFC*.[26]

As to the possibility that the "no general duty to give reasons" rule might be replaced with a judge-made requirement of "general duty subject to exceptions",[27] the Privy Council has observed that it is in the context of the application of the Human Rights Act 1998 (and in particular of the

---

[12] For these decisions see Chap. 2, *section C 3*.
[13] Griffiths L.J. in *Eagil Trust Co. Ltd v. Pigott-Brown* [1985] 3 All E.R. 119 at 122, referring also to certain "well-established exceptions" to the general rule. See further Emery and Smythe, *JR*, p. 235.
[14] See *sub-section 1* above.
[15] Lord Mustill in *Doody v. Home Secretary* [1993] 3 All E.R. 92 at 110b.
[16] *ibid.*, p. 110e; *R. v. Civil Service Appeal Board, ex p. Cunningham* [1991] 4 All E.R. 310 at 318–319, 322–323, 325.
[17] [1993] 3 All E.R. 92.
[18] [1991] 4 All E.R. 310. See also *Stefan v. General Medical Council, The Times*, March 11, 1999, PC.
[19] [1994] 1 All E.R. 651.
[20] See *ibid.*, at 669b.
[21] [1993] 3 All E.R. at 110h.
[22] [1991] 4 All E.R. at 319, 325h. See also *Stefan* (above).
[23] [1994] 1 All E.R. at 669g.
[24] Sedley J. in *HEFC* [1994] 1 All E.R. at 667c.
[25] [1991] 4 All E.R. at 322h, 326b.
[26] [1994] 1 All E.R. at 670j.
[27] See Neill (1988).

right to a fair trial under Article 6 of the Convention) that such review of the common law position might take place.[28] Alternatively, a general duty to give reasons may be imposed in forthcoming freedom of information legislation.[29]

Judicial review as a fair trial for purposes of Article 6 of the Convention   As already noted[30] Article 6(1) of the Convention guarantees a right to a fair trial before an independent and impartial tribunal for the determination of civil rights and obligations. Many claims which persons may assert against public authorities have been held by the Strasbourg authorities to be "civil rights" for this purpose, *e.g.* in such fields as planning, licensing of commercial activities and social security (though not immigration or taxation).[31] Many official decisions in such areas are subject to a "merits" appeal before an independent tribunal.[32] But in the absence of such provision, is judicial review confined to error of law sufficient by itself to satisfy the Article 6(1) requirement? In essence, it appears that full merits appeal will be required under Article 6 (and thus under the Human Rights Act 1998) except where, on the facts of any particular case, either (1) review on law will allow full exploration of the complainant's case; or (2) the absence of merits appeal can be justified on the basis that questions of policy are best left to the appropriate administrative authority.[33]

(ii) The rule against bias

Ordinarily, of course, a hearing will not be fair if the decision-maker is or appears to be biased, *i.e.* to have extraneous reasons for being predisposed to decide the matter against one.

- "Any direct pecuniary interest, however small, in the subject of inquiry"[34] will automatically breach the rule against bias unless known and waived (*i.e.* not objected to) by the party affected. Likewise if a judge or other decision maker has an active role in an organisation which is a party to a case or matter and whose cause will be promoted by the decision. Therefore, in *R. v. Bow Street Metropolitan Stipendiary Magistrate, ex p. Pinochet Ugarte (No. 2)*[35] Lord Hoffmann was held to be automatically disqualified from hearing Pinochet's extradition challenge because he was chairman of a charity closely allied to Amnesty International, an intervening party to the proceedings.

- Such interests apart, the rule will be broken (again subject to waiver) when it can be shown that in the circumstances of the case a reasonable person in possession of such relevant information as he might readily have ascertained would have thought that there was a "real danger", a "possibility rather than probability of bias".[36] This test was formulated by the House of Lords in the case, *R. v. Gough*,[37] concerning possible bias of a juror in a trial on indictment, but the House indicated that the test should be the same in all contexts. In *R. v. Environment Secretary, ex p. Kirkstall Valley Campaign Ltd*[38] Sedley J. (dismissing on the merits an AJR by a community action group alleging bias on the part of a planning authority in the grant of a planning permission) confirmed that the *Gough* test "is of general application in public law and is not limited to judicial or

---

[28] *Stefan v. General Medical Council, The Times*, March 11, 1999.
[29] Sedley J. in *R. v. Criminal Injuries Compensation Board, ex p. Moore* [1999] 2 All E.R. 90 at 96e.
[30] *Section D 2 b above.*
[31] Harris, O'Boyle and Warbrick, *ECHR.* pp. 177–186.
[32] Chap. 2, *section B.*
[33] Harris, O'Boyle and Warbrick, *ECHR,* pp. 192–195. See also *Bryan v. United Kingdom* (1996) 21 E.H.R.R. 342.
[34] Blackburn J. in *R. v. Rand* (1866) L.R. 1 Q.B. 230 at 232.
[35] [1999] 1 All E.R. 577.
[36] *R. v. Gough* [1993] 2 All E.R. 724 at 737j (Lord Goff).
[37] *ibid.*
[38] [1996] 3 All E.R. 304.

quasi-judicial bodies or proceedings".[39] In every case one must decide "whether there was a real danger of bias by reference to circumstances which will include the particular nature and function of the body whose decision is impugned. In this way the necessary involvement of local elected councillors in matters of public controversy, and the probability that they will have taken a stand on many of them, limits the range of attack which can properly made upon any decision in which even a highly opinionated councillor has taken part."[40]

(d) In what circumstances will the presumption of a right to a fair hearing be rebutted?[41]

Where the duty to act fairly is held to exist, it is, as already stated, based upon a presumption adopted by the courts that official power is to be regarded as having been conferred subject to this important constraint. In *Doody*, for example, Lord Mustill said: "Where an Act of Parliament confers an administrative power there is a presumption that it will be exercised in a manner which is fair in all the circumstances."[42]

(i) *Express provision in statute*

The presumption will be rebutted by contrary statutory provision — although such provision may be ineffective in the context of E.C. law[43] and, as just seen, may be incompatible with Convention rights. Subject to these considerations, an express statutory provision may wholly exclude any "right to be heard" as, *e.g.* in the provision[44] that an inspector conducting a public inquiry into proposed changes to a local structure plan need not hear any persons other than those invited. Or it may simply exclude what, in the circumstances, would otherwise be a feature of fairness as, *e.g.* in the statutory exclusion already mentioned of any duty on the Home Secretary to give reasons for refusing a citizenship application — a duty which in that context fairness would require but for the exclusion[45]

(ii) *Implied exclusion*

A number of examples may be given of categories of case where the statutory context may exclude a duty of fairness which would appear prima facie to exist.

- To reach a decision without affording a hearing to persons prejudicially affected may not be unlawful if there is provision for an appeal on the merits at which all sides will be fully heard. Routinely no hearing is afforded to a person whose application for planning permission is refused, but a full hearing is available on appeal. And in a case where a district auditor had certified that councillors were in wilful default (and so liable to surcharge) for not setting a rate the Court of Appeal held that "what is required is examination of the hearing process, original and appeal as a whole, and a decision whether, after it has been gone through, the complainant has had a fair deal".[46] As

---

[39] *ibid.*, at p. 325b. But *cf. ex p. Pinochet* (above) [1999] 1 All E.R. at 589b, 594–595.

[40] *R. v. Environment Secretary, ex p. Kirkstall Valley Campaign Ltd* [1996] 3 All E.R. at 321a, citing *R. v. Amber Valley DC, ex p. Jackson* [1984] 3 All E.R. 501. *Cf. R. v. Local Commissioner for Administration, ex p. Liverpool C.C.* [1999] 3 All E.R. 85 at 93–94.

[41] de Smith, *JRAA*, Chap. 10.

[42] [1993] 3 All E.R. at 106d.

[43] See, *e.g. Johnston v. Chief Constable of the RUC* [1986] 3 All E.R. 135, *section D 2 b above.*

[44] TCPA 1990, s.35(6).

[45] *R. v. Home Secretary, ex p. Fayed* [1997] 1 All E.R. 228 at 241g, 251h.

[46] *Lloyd v. McMahon* [1987] 1 All E.R. 1118 at 1136e (Dillon L.J.), 1147d (Woolf L.J.).

mentioned in Chapter 2,[47] surcharged councillors have a full merits appeal from the auditor's finding.

• Where a statute confers power to act in an emergency situation it may be "a reasonable [or] almost inevitable inference . . . that the intention must have been to exclude the principles of natural justice."[48] Lord Reid was here speaking of war-time legislation but the principle may apply also in a peace-time context as, *e.g.*, in *R. v. Transport Secretary, ex p. Pegasus Holidays*[49] where the Secretary of State had exercised a power provisionally to suspend the United Kingdom operating permit of a Romanian airline whose pilots had failed a test on flight rules and procedures.

• There are some circumstances in which "to have afforded a hearing to [an individual] would have been a useless formality because whatever he might have said could have made no difference."[50] This dictum was applied by the Court of Appeal in *Cinnamond v. British Airports Authority*[51] in holding that the authority acted lawfully in summarily banning from the airport a number of taxi drivers who persistently and incorrigibly flouted airport byelaws. But the principle should be applied with the greatest caution: the question is not "*would* the authority actually have changed its mind?" but "*could* it properly have done so?" Could the applicant's arguments have provided a basis upon which a different decision could properly have been reached? Cases where, without hearing the other side, one can confidently answer "no" will be "of great rarity".[52]

• Procedural impropriety in the making of delegated legislation is considered in *section F*, below.

F GROUNDS FOR JUDICIAL REVIEW OF DELEGATED LEGISLATION[53]

It will now be shown that the grounds of illegality, irrationality and procedural impropriety apply with some qualifications when judicial review is sought of delegated legislation.

1 STATUTORY POWERS TO MAKE DELEGATED LEGISLATION

Statute very commonly confers on central and local government and other public authorities power to make legally enforceable rules or regulations — "delegated" or "subordinate" legislation. Government departments and other authorities operating nationwide will commonly be empowered to legislate by "statutory instrument" under the procedural regime of the Statutory Instruments Act 1946. Examples appear below. Local authorities and others with a localised jurisdiction will be empowered to make "byelaws"[54] on such matters as public health, safety and amenity in the locality.

---

[47] *Sub-section C 3.*
[48] Lord Reid in *Ridge v. Baldwin* [1963] 2 All E.R. at 76F.
[49] [1989] 2 All E.R. 481. See also *R. v. Birmingham C.C., ex p. Ferrero Ltd* [1993] 1 All E.R. 530 (consumer protection): Chap. 5, *section C 2 a.*
[50] Lord Reid in *Malloch v. Aberdeen Corporation* [1971] 2 All E.R. 1278 at 1283a.
[51] [1980] 2 All E.R. 368 at 377b; see also at 375j.
[52] Bingham L.J. in *R. v. Chief Constable Thames Valley, ex p. Cotton* [1990] I.R.L.R. 344: see [1991] P.L. 72.
[53] Wade and Forsyth, *AL*, pp. 874–889; Craig, *AL*, pp. 384–388.
[54] "By[e]" means "secondary", as in "by-product", "by-election": Wade and Forsyth, *AL*, p. 138.

2 EXAMPLES OF DELEGATED LEGISLATION BEING HELD *ULTRA VIRES*

Any statutory power to make delegated legislation is limited by the terms of the empowering statute. If a statutory instrument, byelaw or other provision goes beyond what is authorised, it, like any other exercise of statutory power, may be the subject of judicial review.

Regulations may be held *ultra vires* because the rule-maker has made an error of "pure statutory construction"[55] in interpreting the extent of his powers. In *R. v. Transport Secretary, ex p. Richmond L.B.C.*[56] Laws J. held that new regulations for controlling night flights at Heathrow were *ultra vires* because based on error of interpretation of the statutory power in question: the power was to limit numbers of aircraft take-offs and landings, not (as the new regulations in effect did) to permit operators to determine numbers within a global allocation of "points" based on the noise impact of particular types of aircraft. In *R. v. IRC, ex p. Woolwich Equitable Building Society*[57] the building society obtained a declaration that an Inland Revenue regulation prescribing new arrangements for payment of tax on interest and dividends paid to investors was *ultra vires*: the whole regulation was infected by the revenue's erroneous belief that they were empowered to extend the regulations to a period for which tax had already been paid.

In these cases the successful challenge was mounted by AJR, but a well-known earlier case, *Customs and Excise Commissioners v. Cure & Deeley Ltd*,[58] shows that (in common with many categories of official decision[59]) delegated legislation may be challenged indirectly or "collaterally", *e.g.* by way of defence to ordinary civil proceedings — here a debt claim by the revenue. The Commissioners were empowered to make such regulations as "appear[ed] to them necessary" to give effect to Purchase Tax legislation. But regulations empowering the revenue to determine conclusively, and to the exclusion of challenge in the courts, what tax was due were held *ultra vires* this power: there is a presumption that statute does not authorise the imposition of tax by delegated legislation.

3 COURTS AND PARLIAMENT

(i) *The United Kingdom Parliament*

Statutes conferring power to make regulations will very commonly provide for some degree of parliamentary scrutiny of the regulations while still in draft form, *e.g.* requiring laying before Parliament[60] and perhaps being subject to annulment by resolution of either House[61] or, in particularly controversial cases, requiring parliamentary approval before taking effect.

As the cases cited above show, government departments can err in law in the interpretation of their rule-making powers. The fact that rules made under such misapprehension have been subject to some degree of parliamentary scrutiny does not immunise them from judicial review in respect of such error.[62] But in *Nottinghamshire C.C. v. Environment Secretary*[63] the House of Lords expressed the view that it was not "constitutionally appropriate, save in very exceptional circumstances for the courts to intervene on the ground of 'unreasonableness'". In referring to a

---

[55] Lord Bridge in *Chief Adjudication Officer v. Foster* [1993] 1 All E.R. 705 at 712g.
[56] [1994] 1 All E.R. 577.
[57] [1991] 4 All E.R. 92.
[58] [1961] 3 All E.R. 641.
[59] See Chap. 6, *Collateral Challenge*.
[60] Statutory Instruments Act 1946, s.4.
[61] *ibid.*, s.5.
[62] See, *e.g. Cure and Deeley* [1961] 3 All E.R. at 655I.
[63] [1986] 1 All E.R. 199 at 202d.

decision "so absurd that [the decision-maker] must have taken leave of his senses", Lord Scarman signalled a kind of "ultra soft-edged"[64] approach justified by the courts' sensitivity to the constitutional implications of branding "unreasonable" or "irrational" delegated legislation which has been subjected to some degree of parliamentary scrutiny and approval. There is apparently no reported case of a successful challenge of this kind,[65] and the indications are that, outside the Community and Convention[66] law context, challenge to such legislation is restricted to errors of interpretation (as in the cases discussed above) and "where the procedure followed departed from the requirements of the enabling statute."[67] This "constitutional propriety" point does not apply to byelaws made at local level and subject to no parliamentary scrutiny: here, successful "unreasonableness" challenges are not uncommon.[68]

Note, however, that in the context of review of delegated legislation which is subject to parliamentary scrutiny, "errors of interpretation" include "*Wednesbury/Padfield*" wrong considerations.[69] So, in *R. v. Social Security Secretary, ex p. Joint Council for Welfare of Immigrants*[70] regulations made under a 1992 social security statute which withdrew asylum seekers' income-related social security benefit rights were held *ultra vires* by the Court of Appeal. By threatening such persons with destitution (and so discouraging requests for asylum) the regulations frustrated the purpose of the 1993 Asylum and Immigration Appeals Act which was to facilitate the proper consideration of asylum requests. The Asylum and Immigration Act 1996[71] reinstated the cuts with statutory force but in *R. v. Hammersmith and Fulham L.B.C., ex p. M*[72] the Court of Appeal held that the 1996 Act did not affect local authorities' duties under section 21 of the National Assistance Act 1948 to provide the basic necessities of life for destitute people in their area. Section 21 "was a provision of last resort" which should be construed broadly in accordance with the common law presumption that Parliament intends to protect fundamental human rights.[73] If Parliament were now to remove this provision it would be, the court said, "almost certainly" in breach of the European Convention on Human Rights.

A further example of regulations being held *ultra vires* because in breach of the presumption that in the absence of clear statutory words delegated legislation may not encroach on fundamental "constitutional rights" — in this case, an individual's right of access to the courts — is *R. v. Lord Chancellor, ex p. Witham*.[74] The case concerned rules abolishing both the specific existing right of litigants in person in receipt of income support to commence civil proceedings without paying court fees and the general court discretion to waive fees on the ground of financial hardship in exceptional circumstances. The Divisional Court held that the rules were *ultra vires*.

Finally, it should be noted that delegated legislation (and action taken thereunder) is within the scope of section 6(1) of the Human Rights Act 1998[75] except to the extent that it is protected by sections 3(2)(c) and 6(2)(b) whose effect was mentioned earlier.[76]

---

[64] For "hard-" and "soft-edged" judicial review of official discretion, see *section C 2* above.
[65] Lord Bridge in *Foster* (above) [1993] 1 All E.R. at 712c.
[66] *i.e.* under the Human Rights Act 1998 (see below) when brought into force.
[67] Lord Jauncey in *Edinburgh City D.C. v. Scottish Secretary* [1985] S.C. 261, cited by Lord Bridge, *ibid.*
[68] See, *e.g. Munro v. Watson* (1887) 57 L.T. 366, *Nicholls v. Tavistock UDC* [1923] 2 Ch. 18 and other cases cited by Wade and Forsyth, pp. 879–880.
[69] See Lord Bridge in *Hammersmith L.B.C. v. Environment Secretary* [1990] 3 All E.R. 589 at 636–7.
[70] [1996] 4 All E.R. 385.
[71] Ss.9–11 & Sched. 1.
[72] *The Times*, February 19, 1997.
[73] See Chap. 1, *section A 3 b.*
[74] [1997] 2 All E.R. 779.
[75] Chap. 1, *section A 3 b.*
[76] *ibid.*

(ii) *The Welsh Assembly*

The Government of Wales Act 1998 (GWA) makes detailed provision[77] for the manner in which the Assembly is to exercise its delegated (*i.e.* devolved) legislative powers.[78] Schedule 8 provides for the resolution of "devolution issues",[79] *i.e.* legal challenges to the validity of Assembly action in the exercise or purported exercise of the devolved powers. The provisions are complex[80] but provide for both pre- and post-enactment challenges to Assembly measures.

- The machinery of challenge will be outlined in Chapter 6[81] since it incorporates a system of reference of issues, from courts or tribunals in which they arise, to the superior courts — a procedure which, as will be explained there, might with benefit be applied more generally to *vires* challenges.

- As for grounds of challenge, the courts "will be on relatively familiar ground, since they are accustomed to reviewing secondary legislation."[82] What particular constitutional perspective the courts will bring to reviewing the measures of the Assembly as distinct from measures enacted under the Westminster regime (above) remains to be seen.[83]

4 PROCEDURAL IMPROPRIETY

Since delegated legislation may affect a huge number of individuals it would be unrealistic for the courts to presume that in the absence of express provision[84] Parliament intends as a general rule that persons liable to be affected are entitled to be heard or consulted before such legislation is made. So, in *Bates v. Lord Hailsham*[85] an association of solicitors unsuccessfully challenged a statutory instrument abolishing conveyancing scale fees on the ground that it, unlike the Law Society, had not been consulted. But where a statutory instrument will directly affect only a small group of persons, fairness may require consultation as a pre-requisite of its validity. For example, in *R. v. Lord Chancellor, ex p. Alexander*[86] the government conceded that for it to fix legal aid levels without adequate consultation of those practitioners concerned would be unlawful.

---

[77] GWA, Pt III (see esp. s.66).
[78] See Chap. 3, *section B 1 a*.
[79] Sched. 8, para. 1(1).
[80] See Craig and Walters (1999), pp. 277–281.
[81] *Section G*.
[82] Craig and Walters (1999), p. 288.
[83] See Craig and Walters, *ibid*.
[84] As to which see, *e.g. Agricultural etc. Training Board v. Aylesbury Mushrooms Ltd* [1972] 1 All E.R. 280.
[85] [1972] 3 All E.R. 1019.
[86] *The Times*, March 27, 1986.

Chapter 5

APPLICATIONS FOR JUDICIAL REVIEW — PERMISSION, STANDING, REMEDIES AND CHOICE OF PROCEDURE

The judicial review jurisdiction described in the previous two chapters may be invoked "directly" by way of the High Court procedure of application for judicial review (AJR) described in this chapter. Alternatively it may be invoked "indirectly" (or "collaterally") as described in Chapter 6.

The procedure of AJR was created in 1977 by a new Order 53 of the Rules of the Supreme Court (RSC)[1] made by the judges themselves[2] in the exercise of their statutory powers to make rules of court.

Section 31 of the Supreme Court Act 1981 gave statutory recognition to the new Order 53 procedure (allaying any doubts that in replacing the pre-1977 judicial review procedure by the new AJR procedure the rule committee might have overstepped its powers). The current provisions governing AJR are thus to be found by reading together section 31 and Order 53 (as amended).[3]

- *Section A* of this chapter examines key features of the AJR procedure — the need to obtain the High Court's permission to make an AJR; the need ordinarily to apply within three months of the challenged action; and the need for an applicant to demonstrate a "sufficient interest" to give him standing to mount the challenge in question.

- *Section B* explains what remedies are available on AJR, focusing both on the particular functions of different remedies and on the fact that the remedies are available only subject to the court's discretion.

- *Section C* considers "procedural exclusivity", *i.e.* the rule that AJR rather than ordinary civil proceedings (ordinary civil claim) must be used to invoke judicial review jurisdiction in "pure public law" cases; and the obverse rule that ordinary civil proceedings, and not AJR, must be used when initiating a "pure private law" claim against a public authority. Finally it explains how persons should choose between AJR and appeal when considering mounting a challenge by one or other of those avenues.

---

[1] S.I. 1977 No. 1955.
[2] Following the 1976 Law Commission Report (LCR 73), *Remedies in Administrative Law*.
[3] See now Civil Procedure Rules 1998, (S.I. 1998 No. 3132) (L.17), Sched. 1, RSC Rules.

It was explained at the start of Chapter 3 that the public interest requires that those exercising public power must, on the one hand, be subjected to special controls and, on the other, be granted sufficient latitude to fulfil their intended functions. This chapter will show how at the procedural level the "special control" requirement is reflected in the availability of AJR to any person adjudged to have a sufficient interest in mounting the challenge: unlike ordinary civil proceedings AJR is not restricted to individuals with a private cause of action but is available to any member of the public with a "sufficient interest" in attacking the legality of the official action in question: see *section A 3* below. The "special latitude" requirement is reflected in the "public authority protection" features of AJR: the requirement of permission (*section A 1*); the flexibility of "sufficient interest" which may be used to restrict as well as to amplify the availability of judicial review; the very short time limit (*section A 2*); discretion as to remedies (*section B 4*) and procedural exclusivity (*section C*).

The public interest nature of AJR is reflected also in the fact that all applications (like most criminal prosecutions) are nominally made **by** the Crown **against** the public authority in question (the "respondent") **on behalf of** ("*ex parte*") the actual applicant: *e.g. R. v. Home Secretary, ex p[arte]. Fire Brigades Union & others*; *R. v. Barnsley Metropolitan Borough Council, ex p. Hook*.

A MAKING AN AJR — PERMISSION, DELAY AND STANDING

1 PERMISSION[4]

Section 31(3) of the Supreme Court Act 1981 provides that no AJR shall be made unless the leave of the High Court has been obtained in accordance with rules of court. The rules[5] now refer to "permission" rather than "leave" and no doubt section 31 will be amended in due course. Application for permission is to a single High Court (Crown Office list) judge and is initially *ex parte, i.e.* by the applicant alone and without reference to the public authority respondent, to whom however a "letter before action" should have been sent, thus enabling him to make submissions, helping to highlight hopeless cases quickly.[6] The application will be dealt with on the papers unless the applicant requests an oral hearing or seeks interlocutory relief or the judge thinks it desirable to order an *inter partes* hearing.[7]

If permission is refused, the application can be renewed to another judge who will hold an oral hearing[8] and, if he refuses, to the Court of Appeal.[9] Once permission is granted, substantive civil AJR hearings are usually before a single judge[10] but complex cases may be heard by a Divisional Court.[11]

2 DELAY

Order 53, r.4(1) requires that "an application for permission to apply for judicial review shall be made promptly and in any event within three months from the date when grounds for the

---

[4] Le Sueur and Sunkin (1992). For detailed treatment of the AJR procedure see Gordon, *JRLP*.
[5] RSC, Ord. 53, rr.3(1) *et seq.*.
[6] See Brooke J. in *R. v. Horsham D.C., ex p. Wenman* [1994] 4 All E.R. 681 at 710f.
[7] Gordon, *JRLP*, para. 7–004.
[8] *ibid.*, para. 7–018.
[9] *ibid.*, para. 7–021.
[10] Ord. 53, r.5(2).
[11] Gordon, *JRLP*, para. 9–011.

application first arose unless the Court considers that there is good reason for extending the period . . .". Section 31(6) of the 1981 Act appears to take a more relaxed and purposive approach to delay, providing that in the event of "undue delay" in making an application the court may refuse either leave or relief (*i.e.* a remedy) if it considers that the granting of relief "would be likely to cause substantial hardship to, or substantially prejudice the rights of, any person or would be detrimental to good administration". But this is expressed to be "without prejudice" to the Order 53 time limit.[12]

The combined effect of these provisions appears to be as follows.[13] When seeking permission outside the three month period the onus is placed on the applicant to persuade the court that there is good reason for breaching the three month limit in rule 4. Delaying an AJR while seeking legal aid[14] or while seeking to resolve a dispute by alternative means[15] may count as good reasons. Becoming aware of a ground for judicial review only after the three month limit has expired might be a good reason,[16] but, like other good reasons, will be of no avail if the respondent authority or, as in *R. v. Health Secretary, ex p. Furneaux*,[17] a third party joined as respondent[18] can establish hardship, prejudice or detriment to good administration under section 31(6). This is because:

> "whenever there is a failure to act promptly or within three months there is 'undue delay' [for section 31(6) purposes]. Accordingly, even though the court may be satisfied in the light of all the circumstances . . . that there is good reason for that failure, nevertheless the delay, viewed objectively, remains 'undue delay'. The court therefore still retains a discretion to refuse to grant permission for the making of the application or the relief sought on the substantive application on the grounds of undue delay, if it considers that the granting of the relief sought would be likely to cause [hardship, prejudice or detriment to good administration]".[19]

In *Furneaux* in refusing a rural medical practice consent to dispense medicines the Health Secretary had taken account of representations (on which the applicant practice doctors were not invited to comment) from two pharmacists. Six months later the doctors obtained permission to AJR the refusal. At the hearing a third pharmacist was granted leave to intervene in the proceedings. This pharmacist had established a business in the locality in reliance on the minister's refusal. The Court of Appeal held that the doctors' AJR should be dismissed: they had not applied promptly, and to grant relief would have prejudiced the third pharmacist's rights.

The *Furneaux* case demonstrates that even if permission to AJR is granted despite delay and, at the hearing of the application, grounds for relief are made out, a respondent may still be able to persuade the court to deny the applicant a remedy on the "individual hardship or prejudice" or "detriment to good administration" grounds in section 31(6).[20] But at the hearing stage, delay in seeking permission cannot justify refusal of relief in the absence of one or more of these grounds; and the court has no jurisdiction to re-consider the grant of permission based on a finding of "good reason" for the delay.[21]

---

[12] Supreme Court Act (SCA) 1981, s.31(7).

[13] But *cf.* Lindsay (1995).

[14] *R. v. Stratford-on-Avon D.C., ex p. Jackson* [1985] 3 All E.R. 769.

[15] *R. v. Port Talbot B.C., ex p. Jones* [1988] 2 All E.R. 207, 214–216.

[16] See, possibly, *R. v. Employment Secretary, ex p. Equal Opportunities Commission* [1994] 1 All E.R. 910. where no delay point was taken.

[17] [1994] 2 All E.R. 652.

[18] On third parties in AJR see *subsection 3 d* below.

[19] Ackner L.J. in *ex p. Jackson* (above) at 774.

[20] See *R. v. Stratford-on-Avon D.C., ex p. Jackson* (above) and *R. v. Dairy Produce Quota Tribunal, ex p. Caswell* [1990] 2 All E.R. 434, below, *section B 2 c.*

[21] *R. v. Criminal Injuries Compensation Board, ex p. A The Times*, March 26, 1999, HL.

The Law Commission has recommended[22] that this approach to time limits should be in substance retained, essentially by reference to "the need for speed and certainty in administrative decision-making in cases where the whole community, or large sections of it, will be affected by the decisions of public law bodies".[23] But not all AJRs are cases of this type. At any rate, the period of delay before a case is heard, criticised by the Commission,[24] has now been reduced to six or seven months and in urgent cases to "a matter of days".[25]

Time limit for proceedings under the Human Rights Act, s.7(1)(a)

As mentioned earlier,[26] section 7(5) of the Human Rights Act 1998 provides that proceedings under section 7(1)(a) (*i.e.* by a person claiming to be the victim of official action incompatible with his Convention rights) must be brought within one year of the date on which the act complained of took place or within such longer period as the court or tribunal considers equitable having regard to all the circumstances. But this is "subject to any rule imposing a stricter time limit in relation to the procedure in question". Most section 7(1)(a) proceedings are likely to be brought either by appeal or by AJR.[27] Statutory appeals are commonly required to be lodged within three, four or six weeks and AJRs must normally be commenced within three months. Under section 7(5), these time limits surely override the general "one year or longer" provision (which, on that basis would serve principally to subject section 7(1)(a) points raised in ordinary civil claims to a shorter time limit than the ordinary three- or six-year limitation periods). But for AJRs, at any rate, in the human rights context, the courts may be inclined to exercise generously their general jurisdiction (above) on "promptness" and "undue delay".[28]

3 STANDING[29]

(a) Sufficient interest to obtain permission for AJR

Having provided that no AJR shall be made unless the leave of the High Court has been obtained, section 31(3) continues: "and the court shall not grant leave . . . unless it considers that the applicant has a sufficient interest in the matter to which the application relates."[30] As will appear below, this linkage between permission and standing (*locus standi*) indicates that the chief purpose of the permission requirement is to weed out hopeless cases: it operates as a "sieve" — somewhat similarly to the jurisdiction of civil courts to strike out groundless or vexatious proceedings or to a finding by a criminal court of "no case to answer."

The question of what will count as a sufficient interest to obtain permission for AJR can be answered only by reference to the case law on section 31 and Order 53. Before turning to that, two preliminary points may be noted:

(i) *Jurisdiction on the issue of standing*

In *R. v. Social Services Secretary ex p. Child Poverty Action Group*[31] the Group alleged that the Social Security Department's time scale for processing claims involved unlawful delay. Because of

[22] LCR 226 (1994), para. 5.23 *et seq.*
[23] *ibid.*, para. 2.3.
[24] *ibid.*, paras 1.10, 2.22.
[25] Woolf (1998), p. 587.
[26] Chap. 1, *section B 3 b (i)*.
[27] Chap. 1, *ibid.*
[28] de la Mare (1999), p. 34.
[29] Wade & Forsyth, *AL*, pp. 696–718; Craig, *AL*, Chap. 21; de Smith, *JRAA*, Chap. 2; Justice/A-S, Chap. 8.
[30] See also RSC, Ord. 53, r.3(7).
[31] [1989] 1 All E.R. 1047.

the importance of the issue the department did not dispute the Group's standing to seek judicial review. But the Court of Appeal ruled[32] that the issue of standing contributes to determining whether or not the court has jurisdiction to hear an AJR. It follows that the parties cannot avoid the issue by agreeing not to raise it. Standing is a matter for the court alone to decide.

(ii) Standing distinguished from capacity

In *R. v. Darlington B.C., ex p. Association of Darlington Taxi Owners*[33] it was held that an unincorporated association has no capacity to apply for judicial review. The issue of capacity was held to precede and to be distinct from that of standing which accordingly could not be considered until capacity was established. Given the public interest dimension of AJR, this exclusion of unincorporated associations is unfortunate — and indeed seems to be an unintended consequence of the 1977 reforms.[34] The Law Commission has recommended that unincorporated associations should have capacity, but with due safeguards for the payment of costs by their members.[35]

Turning now to the test for standing: an applicant's "interest" may be insufficient to obtain permission for AJR because of the weakness either of his case or of his connection with, or stake in, the matter in question.

Case too weak unless "clearly arguable" In *R. v. Legal Aid Board, ex p. Hughes*[36] Lord Donaldson M.R. said:

> "It is only when there is clearly an arguable case that leave should be granted *ex parte*. Equally it is only when *prima facie* there is clearly no arguable case that leave should be refused *ex parte*. Usually *ex parte* applications fall into one or other of these categories, but not always. There is also a small 'I really need to know a bit more about it' category and in such cases the appropriate course is to adjourn the application for an *inter partes* hearing."[37]

Reported examples of refusals of permission in clearly unarguable cases are: *Re Walker's application*[38] where the applicants' baby required hole-in-the-heart surgery. To the distress of the parents but without endangering the baby, the operation had been postponed five times because of shortage of resources and "queue-jumping" by more urgent cases. The Court of Appeal refused the parents permission to apply since they plainly had no grounds.[39] And in *R. v. Highbury Magistrates' Court, ex p. Ewing*[40] the Court of Appeal rejected as "quite unarguable" a challenge to a vote taken "on the nod" at a council meeting, the challenge being based on the absence of recorded votes. It has been suggested that it would prevent waste of resources if Order 53 were amended to allow a judge hearing a permission application to refuse permission as regards unarguable grounds and to grant it only on arguable ones.[41]

Applicant has insufficient stake in case This category would clearly include cases where the applicant is a busybody (*e.g.* an attempt by a person not resident in a particular local authority

---

[32] *ibid.*, at 1056.
[33] *The Times*, January 19, 1994.
[34] LCR 226 (1994), para. 5.38.
[35] *ibid.*, para. 5.41; *cf.* Cane (1995), p. 285 identifying confusions in the Commission's approach.
[36] [1992] N.L.J. 1304.
[37] *ibid.*,, at 1305.
[38] *The Times*, November 27, 1987.
[39] *Cf. R. v. Cambridge District Health Authority, ex p. B* [1995] 2 All E.R. 129 (the leukaemia girl case discussed in Chap. 4, *section C 3 b*). See also *R. v. Panel on Take-overs and Mergers, ex p. Al Fayed, The Times* April 15, 1992.
[40] [1991] 3 All E.R. 192 at 195a.
[41] Laws J. in *R. v. Transport Secretary, ex p. Richmond L.B.C.* [1994] 1 All E.R. 577 at 600.

district to challenge the council tax level for that district) or a crank[42] (*e.g.* an attempt by an Orkney resident to challenge the grant of a sex-shop licence in Brighton) or even "quixotic".[43] But the category may include also serious applicants who nevertheless are judged to have an insufficiently close interest in the matter. For example, in *R. v. Social Security Secretary, ex p. Armstrong*[44] a woman who alleged that certain social security regulations relating to women under the age of 65 were contrary to E.C. rules against sex-discrimination was refused permission by the Court of Appeal because at the time of the application she had passed the age of 65, had been awarded the full benefit which she had originally claimed and could show no loss from the department's earlier refusal: "she had no other interest in the outcome and the secretary of state should be left to take whatever steps he thought appropriate without having to litigate the issue at the applicant's suit."[45] Perhaps over-strictly, the Divisional Court in *R. v. Home Secretary, ex p. Ruddock*[46] took the view that permission to AJR an allegedly unlawful Home Office phone tap on the vice-president of CND, while properly granted to him, should not have been granted to the chairman and secretary who merely alleged unlawful interception of their calls to him. Recent case law development of the notion of "public interest" standing[47] may mean that in future only true busybodies and cranks will fall at this hurdle. For example, in *R. v. Somerset C.C., ex p. Dixon*[48] Sedley J. granted permission to an environmentally-minded individual with no greater interest than any member of the general public to AJR a planning permission for quarrying operations which would have an irreversible environmental impact

(b) Sufficient interest not an issue confined to permission stage of AJR

In *R. v. IRC, ex p. National Federation of Self-Employed and Small Businesses Ltd*[49] the House of Lords held that the question of sufficient interest is not to be regarded solely as a preliminary or "threshold" issue but may raise questions which can be resolved only at the hearing of an application for which permission has properly been granted. The Federation had obtained permission *ex parte* to seek judicial review of what it alleged was an *ultra vires* agreement struck between the revenue and trade unions representing casual workers in the newspaper industry. The essence of the agreement was that in return for satisfactory assurances regarding future payment of income tax by the workers, the revenue would drop investigations into alleged past transgressions. The essence of the Federation's complaint was that the revenue had a statutory duty to collect taxes due and should not bow to the strength of unionised labour where in similar circumstances they would vigorously pursue claims against vulnerable self-employed persons.

At the hearing, the revenue took the preliminary point that the Federation had no sufficient interest. The point was appealed to the House of Lords which held that the Federation had properly obtained permission, but that, after closer scrutiny at the hearing, the case should be rejected for lack of sufficient interest.

On the one hand this looks strange in the face of section 31(3) which links sufficient interest only to the permission stage. On the other, given the *ex parte*, or at least summary, nature of the permission stage it is not surprising that there may be cases where what initially looked like sufficient interest turns out on closer scrutiny not to be. As Lord Wilberforce said:

---

[42] Terms used by Lord Scarman in the *Self-Employed case* (below) [1981] 2 All E.R. at 113h. Lord Diplock referred to "misguided or trivial complaints", *ibid* at 105j.
[43] Nolan L.J. in *R. v. Legal Aid Board ex p. Bateman* [1992] 3 All E.R. 490 at 496h.
[44] *The Times,* July 10, 1996.
[45] *ibid.,*
[46] [1987] 2 All E.R. 518 at 521.
[47] *Sub-section c,* below.
[48] [1997] C.O.D. 323: see Kolinsky (1997).
[49] [1981] 2 All E.R. 93.

"There may be simple cases in which it can be seen at the earliest stage that the person applying for judicial review has no interest at all, or no sufficient interest to support the application; then it would be quite correct at the threshold to refuse him permission to apply. . . . But in other cases this will not be so. In these it will be necessary to consider the powers or the duties in law of those against whom the relief is asked, the position of the applicant in relation to those powers or duties, and the breach of those said to have been committed. In other words, the question of sufficient interest cannot, in such cases, be considered in the abstract, or as an isolated point: it must be taken together with the legal or factual context."[50]

In the *Self-Employed* case the majority held that the Revenue's statutory duties are owed to the Crown rather than to other taxpayers so that "as a matter of general principle . . . one taxpayer has no sufficient interest in asking the court to investigate the tax affairs of another taxpayer or to complain that the latter has been underassessed or overassessed."[51] The majority did however take the view that the general principle would yield in a case of exceptional gravity or impropriety.[52] This has been criticised[53] as unsound in principle: the flagrancy of a breach (as opposed to the nature of the power or duty breached) should not be relevant to the right of anyone to challenge it.

(c) Sufficient interest: individual rights or public interest?

The majority ruling in the *Self-Employed* case embodies what may be described as a "rights-based" approach to standing for AJR: one must ask whether the statute "gives any express or implied right to persons in the position of the applicant to complain . . .".[54] There is however a counter-current of judicial opinion that AJR should be regarded as a public interest procedure in principle entitling anyone who can show that a public authority has acted *ultra vires* to ask the court to grant a remedy.[55] This view is strongly expressed in the *Self-Employed* case in the speech of Lord Diplock (who held that the Federation failed not on the ground of insufficient interest[56] but because they had not shown that the revenue had acted unlawfully[57]). Lord Diplock said: "It would in my view be a grave lacuna in our system of public law if a pressure group, like the federation, or even a single public-spirited taxpayer, were prevented by outdated technical rules of *locus standi* from bringing the matter to the attention of the court to vindicate the rule of law and get the unlawful conduct stopped."[58]

It seemed possible that the majority approach in the *Self-Employed* case would inhibit the development of judicial review as a means of challenging official illegality in the public interest rather than simply to protect individual rights or expectations. The rights-based approach was applied by Schiemann J. in *R. v. Environment Secretary, ex p. Rose Theatre Trust Co.*[59] in holding that a trust company formed to campaign to preserve the remains of an Elizabethan theatre in central London had no sufficient interest to obtain judicial review of the Environment Secretary's refusal to schedule the site as a monument of national importance. The judge accepted that this meant that an unlawful act by a minister might go entirely "unrebuked".[60] This observation shows, importantly, that in many circumstances AJR will be the only means of challenging unlawful government action.

---

[50] *ibid.*, at 96h.
[51] Lord Wilberforce, *ibid.*, at 99a; see also Lord Fraser at 108, Lord Roskill at 120.
[52] *ibid.*, at 99b, 108h, 120d.
[53] Justice/A-S, p. 196; LCR 226 (1994), para. 5.18.
[54] Lord Fraser [1981] 2 All E.R. at 108c.
[55] For remedies available on AJR, see *section B* below.
[56] [1981] 2 All E.R. 106j; see also Lord Scarman at 114b.
[57] *ibid.*, at 101j; see also Lord Scarman at 114a.
[58] *ibid.*, at 107a.
[59] [1990] 1 All E.R. 754 at 766e, 768b.
[60] *ibid.*, at 768a.

- It is true that the Attorney-General (representing the Crown as guardian of the public interest) always has standing to seek a declaration or injunction to restrain "unlawful conduct that would cause public harm"[61] — including *ultra vires* action. And he may in effect confer that standing upon any member of the public by agreeing to allow his name to be used as nominal claimant in a "relator" action — an action in reality brought and funded by the member of the public in question. But the mechanism is of limited value as a means of facilitating public interest challenges because (a) the Attorney's decision whether or not to lend his name will not be reviewed by the courts[62]; and (b) by convention he never lends his name for proceedings against the Crown (*i.e.* the central government).

- It is also true that statute may confer standing to bring cases before the courts in the public interest. This may be by express provision for a particular form of procedure as, *e.g.*, in the Local Government Act 1972, s.222 of which provides that where a local authority consider it expedient for the promotion or protection of the interests of the inhabitants of their area, the authority may prosecute or defend or appear in any legal proceedings and in the case of civil proceedings may institute them in their own name. Or the provision may be implied from the statutory remit of a particular body such as the Equal Opportunities Commission whose duty to work towards the elimination of sex discrimination was held to confer on it a sufficient interest to seek a declaration of inconsistency between United Kingdom and Community law on that matter.[63]

Of course, such sporadic provisions do not address the need for a general avenue of public interest challenge in appropriate cases. However, on the question of public interest standing for AJR, recent case law has focused more upon the acceptance by the House of Lords in the *Self-Employed* case that the question of standing must be decided on a case-by-case basis[64] than upon the requirement that an applicant must demonstrate "a greater right or expectation than any other citizen . . . to have [a] decision taken lawfully."[65]

In *R. v. Pollution Inspectorate, ex p. Greenpeace Ltd (No. 2)*[66] Otton J. held that Greenpeace had a sufficient interest to AJR the Government's decision to authorise British Nuclear Fuels to test the THORP reprocessing plant at Sellafield in Cumbria. It is true that the judge treated Greenpeace as having what may be termed "associational standing"[67] to represent the interests of local people as well as standing to represent the public interest at large: "The fact that there are 400,000 [Greenpeace] supporters in the U.K. carries less weight than the fact that 2,500 of them come from the Cumbria region."[68] And he distinguished the *Rose Theatre* case on the basis that, apparently unlike Greenpeace's Cumbria supporters, "no individual member [of the Rose Theatre company] could show any personal interest in the outcome."[69] But it has been observed that "The issues at stake in the application did not relate specifically to the personal interests of any members of Greenpeace but more widely to the public interest in the running of the Sellafield plant."[70] In any event it has since been held that where an important issue is raised by an applicant

---

[61] *Gouriet v. Union of Post Office Workers* [1977] 3 All E.R. 70 at 99d (Lord Diplock).

[62] *Gouriet* (previous note).

[63] *R. v. Employment Secretary, ex p. Equal Opportunities Commission* [1994] 1 All E.R. 910 at 918–919.

[64] See *R. v. Pollution Inspectorate, ex p. Greenpeace Ltd (No. 2)* [1994] 4 All E.R. 329 at 351e; *R. v. Foreign Secretary, ex p. World Development Movement Ltd* [1995] 1 All E.R. 611 at 620c.

[65] Schiemann J. in the *Rose Theatre* case (above) at 768b.

[66] [1994] 4 All E.R. 329.

[67] "Associational" and "public interest" standing may be regarded as varieties of "representative" (as opposed to individual) standing: see Cane (1995), p. 276.

[68] [1994] 4 All E.R. at 350c.

[69] *ibid.*, at 351h.

[70] Cane (1995), p. 281.

playing a prominent role in the field in question, the importance of vindicating the rule of law may give that applicant a sufficient interest for AJR in the absence of any personal right or interest. This was the basis on which in *R. v. Foreign Secretary, ex p. World Development Movement Ltd*[71] the applicant, an established "non-partisan pressure group",[72] was held to have a sufficient interest to mount a challenge to the Foreign Secretary's decision to grant some £80 million from the United Kingdom overseas aid budget to assist construction of the Pergau Dam in Malaysia in fulfilment of undertakings earlier given to the Malaysian Government by Prime Minister Thatcher. The challenge succeeded on the basis that statute[73] required aid to be for the purpose of promoting the aided country's economy, whereas the scheme was "so economically unsound that there [was] no economic argument in favour of the case."[74]

Public interest standing had already been permitted in such cases as *R. v. HM Treasury, ex p. Smedley*[75] where the Government did not strongly contest the standing of Mr Smedley as a taxpayer to raise "a serious question"[76] as to the legality of government expenditure of substantial sums of tax revenue on new contributions to the E.C. budget; and *R. v. Foreign Secretary, ex p. Rees-Mogg*[77] where the Government did not challenge Lord Rees-Mogg's interest, which the court characterised as based on "his serious concern for constitutional issues".[78] But standing was strongly contested in the *Greenpeace* and Pergau Dam cases, and the latter in particular clearly confirms that public rather than individual interest can suffice. In both cases the courts took account of the suitability of the means and expertise of the applicants. Whether such considerations should limit public interest standing,[79] and, on the contrary, whether an applicant claiming associational standing should be required to show some evidence of support from those he claims to represent (a "democratic stake" in the matter[80]) are matters which await authoritative resolution. The Law Commission has recommended the statutory recognition of public interest standing[81] but have left it to the courts to articulate principles on which to exercise what would otherwise be an unacceptably broad discretion.[82]

Public interest standing and Human Rights Act AJRs

Section 7(3) of the Human Rights Act 1998 provides that if proceedings under section 7(1)(a) (*i.e.* by a person claiming to be the victim of official action incompatible with his Convention rights) are brought by AJR, the applicant is to be taken to have a sufficient interest only if he is, or would be, a victim of that act. As already noted,[83] under section 7(7) "victim" has the same meaning as in the Convention[84] which, as interpreted by the ECHR, requires that a claimant must be "directly affected in some way by the matter complained of".[85] This plainly excludes, as it was intended to,[86] AJRs by persons asserting only public interest standing. But it seems unlikely to have much of an inhibiting effect on human rights challenges, for victims can be supported (financially and otherwise[87]) in their

[71] [1995] 1 All E.R. 611 at 620d–g.
[72] *ibid.,* at 617g.
[73] Overseas Development, etc. Act 1980, s.1(1).
[74] Rose L.J. [1995] 1 All E.R. at 626j.
[75] [1985] 1 All E.R. 589.
[76] *ibid.,* at 595h.
[77] [1994] 1 All E.R. 457: see Chap. 3, *section B 2 a.*
[78] *ibid.,* at 461j.
[79] Cane (1995), p. 285 argues that they should not.
[80] *ibid.,* p. 278.
[81] LCR 226 (1994), para. 5.22.
[82] Schiemann (1990), pp. 350–353; Schiemann (1996), reviewing Justice/PLP, *PI,* which at p. 13 proposes criteria for inclusion in a future Practice Statement.
[83] Chap. 1, *section B 3 b (i).*
[84] Art. 34.
[85] Harris, O'Boyle and Warbrick, *ECHR,* p. 632; on "indirect victims" see *ibid,* p. 637.
[86] de la Mare (1999), p. 33.
[87] See *sub-section d,* below.

AJRs by public interest groups. And, in any event, many human rights points can be presented in terms of domestic[88] or E.C. law[89] where the "victim" restriction has no application.[90]

(d) Sufficient interest: third party respondents and interveners

(i) *Third party respondents*

Following the grant of permission to AJR, the application must be made by the issue of a claim form which, under Order 53, r.5(3) "must be served on all persons directly affected". This provision requires, of course, that the authority whose act or decision is impugned be made a respondent. Beyond that, its scope is narrow, including only a limited range of third party respondents: "That a person is directly affected by something connotes that he is affected without the intervention of any intermediate agency".[91] This would include, *e.g.*, the maker of regulations whose validity was being attacked in an AJR of a decision applying them in a particular case; but not a minister obliged to fund benefit claims payable by an authority whose decision to refuse them is being attacked.[92]

(ii) *Third party "own interest" intervention against an AJR*

Order 53, r.9(1) does, however, empower the court to hear ". . . any person who desires to be heard in opposition to [an AJR] and appears to the Court to be a proper person to be heard". The minister in the last example "might be regarded by the court as a proper person to be heard [under rule 9(1)]"[93] but, not being a party, would have no right of appeal. It appears anomalous[94] that the rule applies only to a person with an interest in opposing an AJR and not to one who might wish to support the application.

(iii) *Third party public interest intervention*

"This [rule 9(1)] procedure for interventions has been traditionally relevant to those wishing to intervene in their own interests, rather than in the public interest. However, recent decisions indicate that the courts may be broadening the interpretation of who may be 'a proper person' to include a public interest intervention."[95] In *R. v. Bow Street Metropolitan Stipendiary Magistrate, ex p. Pinochet Ugarte (No. 2)*[96] Lord Browne-Wilkinson recorded[97] that Amnesty International and two other human rights bodies together with three individuals were granted permission to intervene on this AJR appeal to the House of Lords. Given the development of public interest standing to apply for judicial review[98] it seems desirable for the court to be able to grant requests by third parties to intervene in AJRs on a matter of public interest in which they appear likely to be able to assist the court. Proposals on these lines have been made, incorporating safeguards against possible prejudice to the parties (*e.g.* delay, extra costs) flowing from such interventions.[99]

---

[88] See *e.g.* Chap. 4, *section F 3*.
[89] Chap. 4, *section D 2 b*.
[90] de la Mare (1999), p. 33.
[91] Lord Keith in *R. v. Rent Officer Service, ex p. Muldoon* [1996] 3 All E.R. 498 at 500d.
[92] *ibid.*
[93] *ibid.*, at 500c.
[94] Justice/PLP, *PI*, p. 21.
[95] *ibid.*, at 20, citing the intervention of an animal welfare organisation in *R. v. Coventry C.C., ex p. Phoenix Aviation* [1995] 3 All E.R. 37 at 40a (for this case, see Chap. 4, *section C 2 c*); see also *R. v. Chief Constable North Wales Police, ex p. A B* [1998] 3 All E.R. 310.
[96] [1999] 1 All E.R. 577 (see Chap. 4, *section E 2 c ii*)). See also *R. v. IAT, ex p. Shah (UN High Commissioner for Refugees intervening)* [1999] 2 All E.R. 545 (above, Chap. 4, *section B 3 b*).
[97] *ibid.*, at 580g.
[98] *Sub-section c* above.
[99] Justice/PLP, *PI*, pp. 21–29 and appendix.

A further danger to be avoided in the trend towards making judicial review a multi-party process is "blur[ring] the boundary between legal and political processes".[1]

B REMEDIES AVAILABLE ON AJR[2]

1 THE PREROGATIVE REMEDIES: MANDAMUS, PROHIBITION, CERTIORARI

Under section 31(1) of the Supreme Court Act 1981[3] an application for an order of mandamus, prohibition or certiorari "shall be made" by AJR which is thus the only procedure by which these so-called "prerogative" remedies may be obtained. As will be explained, all remedies on AJR are available only subject to the court's discretion.[4]

Historically these remedies were fashioned by the High Court (Court of King's Bench[5]) specifically for the purpose of keeping public authorities within their remit. The label "prerogative" denotes that the remedies were originally available only to the Crown to enable it to keep inferior authorities within bounds.

(a) What the prerogative remedies do

Prohibition is an order of the court to a reviewable authority[6] to refrain from a particular course of *ultra vires* action. Mandamus[7] is an order to a reviewable authority to discharge some aspect of its public duty — either to consider a matter lawfully which has previously not been so considered[8]; or, if it is plain that a particular course of action is required, to act accordingly, *e.g.* to provide a house for a person who is unintentionally homeless and has a priority need.[9] The effect of certiorari[10] is to "quash" (*i.e.* to declare *ultra vires*[11]) a particular official decision or other reviewable action.

Prohibition and mandamus are equivalent in effect to (respectively) prohibitory and mandatory injunctions: disobedience to any of these orders is punishable as a contempt of court. Certiorari is a kind of "extra-strong" public law declaration, establishing authoritatively that an action is unlawful. Like a declaration[12] it has in itself no mandatory effect; but section 31(5) of the 1981 Act enables the court to strengthen an order of certiorari by remitting the matter to the authority concerned "with a direction to reconsider it and reach a decision in accordance with the [court's] findings." As will shortly be seen, injunctions and declarations may also be obtained on AJR. The equivalence of effect as between the prerogative remedies on the one hand and injunction and declaration on the other raises the question, considered below, as to why, when creating the new

---

[1] Harlow (1997) p. 255.
[2] Wade & Forsyth, *AL*, Chaps 16–17; Craig, *AL*, Chap. 22; de Smith, *JRAA*, part IV.
[3] Mirroring RSC, Ord. 53, r.1(1).
[4] See *sub-section 4* below.
[5] Chap. 3, *section A 3*.
[6] See Chap. 3, *section B*.
[7] Latin, "we order".
[8] *Padfield v. Minister of Agriculture* [1968] 1 All E.R. 694.
[9] *R. v. Eastleigh B.C., ex p. Betts* [1983] 2 All E.R. 481.
[10] Latin "to be informed": the High Court required the challenged decision to be presented for its scrutiny.
[11] For the modern expansion of *"ultra vires"* and the corresponding eclipse of the old "patent error" jurisdiction, see Chap. 4, *section B 2*.
[12] See Chap. 3, *section C 1 b*.

AJR procedure, it was thought necessary to supplement the established public law remedies with their private law analogues.

(b) Availability of the prerogative remedies

Consistently with the courts' modern expansion of the ambit of judicial review,[13] old technical rules restricting (in different ways for the different remedies) the availability of the prerogative remedies have been swept away. Subject to one qualification, all the remedies appear now to be available against either any authority exercising statutory functions, or "any other body of persons having legal authority to determine questions affecting the common law or statutory rights or obligations of other persons . . ."[14] This may be confirmed by reference to case law examples of successful AJRs already met in previous discussion of review jurisdiction (Chapter 3) and grounds for review (Chapter 4).[15]

The qualification just mentioned is that the prerogative remedies, being technically sought by the Crown, cannot be granted against the Crown. But this limitation is more theoretical than real because the courts "regularly"[16] grant the remedies against ministers of the Crown adjudged to have acted beyond their or their departments' statutory powers. Even where ministerial or departmental action relies on "prerogative" power (in its current broad meaning[17]), as regards the availability of the prerogative remedies "a distinction probably no longer has to be drawn between duties which have a statutory and those which have a prerogative source."[18]

2 INJUNCTION AND DECLARATION

Under section 31(2) of the Supreme Court Act 1981[19] injunctions or declarations may be granted on AJR. In exercising this jurisdiction the court is required to have regard to: (a) the nature of the matters in respect of which relief may be granted by orders of mandamus, prohibition or certiorari; (b) the nature of the persons and bodies against whom relief may be granted by such orders; and (c) all the circumstances of the case. While this indicates that the remedies are to be granted on AJR only in respect of reviewable action by a reviewable authority,[20] it underscores the question, already identified, of the value of making provision in the AJR procedure for the grant of what appear to be overlapping remedies.

(a) Why injunction and declaration in addition to the prerogative remedies?

To answer the question requires some reference to the deficiencies in the procedural law of judicial review to remedy which the new Order 53 procedure was created in 1977. Prior to the 1977 reform,

---

[13] See generally Chap. 3, section A 2 b.
[14] O'Reilly v. Mackman [1982] 3 All E.R. 1124 at 1129h (Lord Diplock).
[15] Statutory functions — **mandamus**: R. v. Legal Aid Board, ex p. Donn and Co. [1996] 3 All E.R. 1, Padfield v. Minister of Agriculture [1968] 1 All E.R. 694; **prohibition**: R. v. Liverpool Corporation, ex p. Liverpool Taxi Association [1972] 2 All E.R. 589; Att.-Gen. (Hong Kong) v. Ng Yuen Shiu [1983] 2 All E.R. 346; **certiorari**: R. v. Environment Secretary, ex p. Brent L.B.C. [1983] 3 All E.R. 321; R. v. Barnsley M.B.C., ex p. Hook [1976] 3 All E.R. 452. Non statutory functions — R. v. Liverpool C.C., ex p. Employment Secretary [1989] C.O.D. 404, R. v. Norfolk C.C., ex p. M [1989] 2 All E.R. 359, R. v. Lewisham L.B.C., ex p. Shell U.K. Ltd [1988] 1 All E.R. 938 (all **certiorari** but for the prerogative remedies generally "the existence of statutory power is no longer the sole touchstone", Wade & Forsyth, AL, pp. 627, 659–667).
[16] Lord Woolf in M v. Home Office [1993] 3 All E.R. 537 at 560a.
[17] Chap. 3, section B 2 a.
[18] Lord Woolf in M (above) at 560c.
[19] Mirroring RSC, Ord. 53, r.1(2).
[20] See Chap. 3.

there were many procedural anomalies and inconveniences which discouraged litigants from using the old Order 53 to seek prerogative remedies (then as now available only via the Order 53 procedure) to correct unlawful official action. Apart from the different and technically restrictive rules for different prerogative remedies already referred to, the principal deficiencies of the old procedure were the absence of any provision either for "discovery" of documents (*i.e.* for enabling parties to require their opponents to disclose relevant documentation) or for the cross-examination of persons upon whose written (affidavit) evidence a case turned.[21]

Consequently, instead of applying for one or more of the prerogative remedies under the pre-1977 Order 53 procedure litigants were inclined to use ordinary civil proceedings (then[22] commenced by "writ" or "originating summons") to seek injunctions or declarations to challenge *ultra vires* action. The courts recognised the unjust limitations of the Order 53 procedure and permitted this, even though it allowed claimants to side-step the special "public authority protection" features of AJR discussed above, *i.e.* the requirement to obtain permission and to demonstrate "sufficient interest", and the very short time limit. The *Anisminic* and *Wednesbury* cases are well-known examples of declarations being sought by ordinary civil proceedings against public authorities to remedy what was alleged (successfully in *Anisminic*) to be *ultra vires* action. And in *Bradbury v. Enfield L.B.C.*[23] ratepayers brought ordinary civil proceedings and obtained an injunction to prevent the *ultra vires* re-structuring of local schools before the completion of certain public consultation procedures. The requirement of standing to bring ordinary civil proceedings (*i.e.* that the claimant has a private "cause of action", *e.g.* in contract or tort) was dealt with by a dubious[24] reliance on *Boyce v. Paddington B.C.*[25] for the proposition that a claimant has standing to bring ordinary civil proceedings for an injunction or declaration if he is asserting an "actual or threatened infringement of public rights [which] would cause him special damage."[26]

The new Order 53 procedure removed the anomalies and inconveniences of the existing procedure[27] and, as will be explained in *section C* below, the House of Lords swiftly ruled in *O'Reilly v. Mackman*[28] that the procedural tolerance described in the last paragraph should thenceforth be withdrawn, the need for it having disappeared. The question to be pursued at this juncture, however, is why it was necessary in 1977 to allow in Order 53 for the granting on AJR of injunctions and declarations in the new circumstances — in which their public law analogues, the prerogative remedies, were regarded as being available whenever justice required. The answer to this question is provided by an examination of the role which the remedies of injunction and declaration have actually played, and do today play, in the AJR procedure. As will now appear, there are circumstances in which those remedies may still play an important part in supplementing the relief available through the prerogative remedies.

(b) The role of the injunction in AJR

The chief role of the injunction in AJR seems to be to provide effective interim relief, *i.e.*, in an urgent situation to enable the court at any stage of AJR proceedings prior to their conclusion to

---

[21] Lord Diplock in *O'Reilly v. Mackman* [1982] 3 All E.R. 1124 at 1130.

[22] Now, under r.7.2 of the Civil Procedure Rules 1998 ordinary civil proceedings are commenced by the issue of a "claim form": see further, *section C 1* below.

[23] [1967] 3 All E.R. 434: see Chap. 4, *section E 1*.

[24] Emery and Smythe, *JR*, p. 250.

[25] [1903] 1 Ch. 109.

[26] Lord Browne-Wilkinson in *R. v. Employment Secretary, ex p. Equal Opportunities Commission* [1994] 1 All E.R. 910 at 926e, citing *Gouriet v. Union of Post Office Workers* [1977] 3 All E.R. 70 where at 110e Lord Edmund-Davies founded this proposition upon *Boyce*.

[27] See Lord Diplock in *O'Reilly v. Mackman* [1982] 3 All E.R. at 1131–1132.

[28] Previous note.

order a respondent authority to do or refrain from some action. The courts have not developed interim versions of any of the prerogative remedies nor of the declaration — although the Civil Procedure Rules 1998[29] do now provide[30] for the grant (in civil proceedings generally, including AJR) of interim declarations. The Law Commission had recommended statutory provision on these lines[31]; whether the change can be achieved by subordinate legislation remains unclear. Moreover, there is doubt as to the scope of the provision in Order 53[32] for a stay of proceedings seeking prohibition or certiorari.[33]

This leaves only the injunction, the grant of an interim version of which on AJR is plainly contemplated by Order 53, r.3(10)(b). In *M v. Home Office*[34] Lord Woolf said: "So far as respondents other than ministers are concerned, the provisions of rule 3(10)(b) have always been treated as giving the court jurisdiction to grant interim injunctions. This is confirmed to be the position by the decision of the Court of Appeal in *R. v. Kensington L.B.C., ex p. Hammell*"[35] in which an interim mandatory injunction was granted requiring the council to house a homeless person pending a full hearing of her AJR.

As to ministers of the Crown: until the House of Lords' decision in *M v. Home Office* in 1993 it appeared that in purely domestic law cases the High Court had no jurisdiction to grant any (therefore including interim) injunctive relief against the Crown or a minister. As related in Chapter 1,[36] in *Factortame Ltd v. Transport Secretary*[37] Spanish fishing vessel owners invoked Community law in applying for judicial review of provisions of the Merchant Shipping Act 1988 designed to stop the practice of "quota-hopping". To avoid business collapse while legal issues shuttled between the English courts and the ECJ, the applicants first sought an interim injunction restraining the minister from enforcing the impugned United Kingdom legislation. The House of Lords held that section 21 of the Crown Proceedings Act 1947[38] precluded the award of any injunction against either the Crown or a minister of the Crown but sought a ruling from the ECJ on the attitude of Community law. The ECJ held[39] that the Community law requirement of effective judicial remedy[40] demands that national courts be able to give interim relief where state breaches of E.C. individual rights are alleged, and that any contrary domestic rule (such as section 21) should be disapplied by the courts. The House of Lords accordingly granted[41] the interim injunction claimed.

The position thus appeared to be that injunctive relief against the Crown was available in AJR cases with a Community law element but not in purely domestic cases. But in *M v. Home Office*[42] the House of Lords gave section 21 a far more limited interpretation than that adopted by the House in *Factortame* and held that the section simply preserved the pre-1947 immunity of the Crown and ministers from the grant of injunctions to remedy civil (private law) wrongs consisting of breaches of statutory duty laid expressly upon the Crown rather than a named minister, an

---

[29] See *section C 1* below.
[30] r.25.1(1)(b).
[31] LCR 226 (1994), para 6.27.
[32] r.3(10)(a).
[33] LCR 226 (1994) para. 6.23, citing *Minister of Foreign Affairs v. Vehicles, etc. Ltd* [1991] 4 All E.R. 65 at 71, PC; *cf. R. v. Education Secretary, ex p. Avon C.C.* [1991] 1 All E.R. 282, CA.
[34] [1993] 3 All E.R. 537 at 563j.
[35] [1989] 1 All E.R. 1202.
[36] *Section A 2.*
[37] [1989] 2 All E.R. 692.
[38] " . . . in any [civil] proceedings against the Crown . . . the court shall not grant an injunction . . . " (s.21(1)) " . . . or make any order against an officer of the Crown if the effect . . . would be to give . . . any relief against the Crown which could not have been obtained in proceedings against the Crown" (s.21(2)).
[39] *Factortame Ltd v. Transport Secretary (No. 2)* [1991] 1 All E.R. 70.
[40] Chap. 4, *section D 2 b* above. Hartley, *Foundns*, pp. 220–226.
[41] *Factortame (No. 2)* (above).
[42] [1993] 3 All E.R. 537. Sedley (1998).

uncommon situation[43] and thus of limited practical importance. The point of central practical importance in *M v. Home Office* is that the House held that under the unqualified language of section 31(2) of the Supreme Court Act 1981 (above), injunctions are available in judicial review proceedings against ministers of the Crown acting in their official capacity.[44] Moreover, "because of the scope of the remedies of mandamus and prohibition the availability of injunctions against ministers [will] only be of any significance in situations where it would be appropriate to grant interim relief."[45] The House took the view that *M* itself was such a case[46]: thus when the Home Secretary disobeyed an interim injunction requiring him to procure the return to the United Kingdom of an asylum-seeker who was being deported, the minister was, in his official capacity,[47] guilty of contempt of court.

(c) The role of the declaration in AJR

As explained above, the effect of certiorari is essentially declaratory. Examples were given above of the availability of the declaration in ordinary civil proceedings seeking a remedy for *ultra vires* action. But this was prior to the 1977 procedural reforms after which, as also explained, certiorari and the other prerogative remedies were regarded as having become available on AJR whenever justice required. In these circumstances why was it thought necessary in 1977 to make the declaration also available as a remedy on AJR?

- The breadth of availability of certiorari was much less clear in 1977 than it is today. The inclusion of the declaration in Order 53 militated against any risk of reducing the range of remedy previously available for *ultra vires* action.[48]

- Indeed it was apparent in 1977 that there were circumstances in which a declaration would be the only, or at least the best, remedy for an *ultra vires* official decision — as *e.g.* in the *Pyx Granite* case[49] mentioned in Chapter 3[50] where a minister had decided wrongly that planning permission was required for certain quarrying operations on a company's land. Even if certiorari could quash such a decision, a declaration could more clearly spell out the true extent of the landowner's rights.

- Moreover there are circumstances in which it has become clear since 1977 that only a declaration will be regarded as an appropriate remedy. Principal among these is where a court holds that an English statute is inconsistent with Community law and thus should be "disapplied" as, *e.g.*, in two cases already referred to in this chapter: *R. v. Employment Secretary, ex p. Equal Opportunities Commission*[51] and *Factortame Ltd v. Transport Secretary (No. 2)*.[52] Constitutional propriety would not countenance the quashing of a statutory provision by certiorari: a declaration is the only appropriate remedy.[53]

---

[43] *ibid.*, 556c.
[44] *ibid.*, 564f.
[45] *ibid.*, 561b.
[46] *ibid.*, 565.
[47] *ibid.*, 568j.
[48] Lord Browne-Wilkinson in *R. v. Employment Secretary, ex p. Equal Opportunities Commission* [1994] 1 All E.R. 910 at 927j.
[49] *Pyx Granite Co. Ltd v. Ministry of Housing and Local Government* [1959] 3 All E.R. 1.
[50] *Section C 1 b.*
[51] [1994] 1 All E.R. 910: *section A 3 c* above.
[52] [1991] 1 All E.R. 70 (above).
[53] [1994] 1 All E.R. at 928f.

- The remedy of declaration may also be used where the court could, but is unwilling to, grant a prerogative remedy. No doubt with an eye to the mandatory potential (already mentioned) of section 31(5) of the Supreme Court Act 1981, certiorari tends to be regarded as "more mandatory" than the declaration which may thus be granted in circumstances where the court wishes to indicate that an authority has acted *ultra vires* but deems it inappropriate to precipitate corrective action by the authority. This view is reflected in the observation of Donaldson M.R. in the *Datafin* case[54] that on AJR the court always has "an ultimate discretion whether to set [a reviewable decision] aside and may refuse to do so in the public interest[55] notwithstanding that it holds and declares the decision to have been made *ultra vires*". Consider also *R. v. Dairy Produce Quota Tribunal, ex p. Caswell*.[56] C, a dairy farmer, applied to the Tribunal in 1985 for a milk quota allocation which would reflect his intention to increase the size of his herd in the following few years. The Tribunal refused the application on what subsequently proved to be the erroneous basis that the 1985 quotas could be adjusted in later years. When C discovered the error he applied for judicial review of the Tribunal's ruling more than two years after it had been made. The House of Lords eventually held that C had been properly granted both permission out of time and a declaration that the Tribunal had erred in law. But the House upheld the refusal of the courts below to grant either mandamus or certiorari. Because this was a test case and would have precipitated a flood of like challenges, to grant these remedies would have been "detrimental to good administration" given the undue delay in mounting the challenge.[57]

- The declaration has an inherent flexibility which certiorari lacks. Thus, the *Royal College of Nursing*[58] and *Gillick*[59] cases (discussed in Chapter 3[60]) may be regarded as examples of "advisory" declarations, *i.e.* declarations as to "what the law is" on a particular point, even though no legally effective official act or decision is being challenged. In public law "the need for citizens and authorities to 'know where they stand'" qualifies "the long-standing tradition [grounded principally in private law[61]] that the courts do not enter into purely hypothetical questions."[62]

Again, a declaration may amount to merely "prospective" relief, *i.e.*, a court, while refusing any mandatory relief, may use a declaration to indicate that an authority has acted *ultra vires* and to indicate also that, if the error is repeated, mandatory relief may be granted in future.[63]

3   DAMAGES ON AJR

A person seeking judicial review may be able to establish not merely that the respondent authority has acted *ultra vires* but also that the *ultra vires* action, or some action consequent upon it, amounts to a tort or other civil wrong against him, entitling him to damages. A straightforward example would be if an authority had demolished a house in reliance upon what turns out to be an

---

[54] [1987] 1 All E.R. 564 at 578b.
[55] Here the need for City confidence in the reliability of the Panel's adjudications.
[56] [1990] 2 All E.R. 434.
[57] See above, *section A 2.*
[58] *Royal College of Nursing v. Department of Health and Social Security* [1981] 1 All E.R. 545.
[59] *Gillick v. West Norfolk, etc. HA and Department of Health and Social Security* [1985] 3 All E.R. 402.
[60] *Section C 1 b.*
[61] *cf. R. v. Home Secretary, ex p. Salem* [1999] 2 All E.R. 42 at 46f, 47c.
[62] LCR 226 (1994), paras 8.9 - 8.12 recommending statutory recognition of this advisory jurisdiction; see also Beatson (1998), pp. 243–251.
[63] LCR 226 (1994), para. 8.22.

ultra vires decision under the dangerous building legislation.[64] If in such circumstances the claimant makes an AJR of the *ultra vires* decision and joins with his application his claim for damages for the civil wrong, the court may award the damages within the AJR proceedings.[65]

The relationship between *ultra vires* action and civil liability will be explored, and further examples given, in *section C* of this chapter and in Chapters 6, 8 and 9. But it must be emphasised here that in order to obtain damages on AJR it is necessary but not sufficient to establish that the respondent authority has acted *ultra vires*:

- On AJR "unless judicial review would lie, damages cannot be given".[66] AJR is a special public law procedure by which the judicial review jurisdiction described in Chapters 3 and 4 may be invoked. If a person's claim has no public law dimension it should be pursued by ordinary civil proceedings, not by AJR.[67]

- *Ultra vires* action causing damage does not by itself give rise to a claim for damages. As just indicated, an applicant must establish not merely that the authority has acted *ultra vires* and caused him damage but also that the causation of damage constitutes a recognised tort or other civil wrong.

4 THE COURT'S DISCRETION AS TO REMEDIES

The prerogative remedies and the remedies of injunction and declaration are all discretionary. This does not mean that they may be granted or refused at the whim of the court. But the case law shows that even where an applicant is able to establish that there are grounds for judicial review the court may decline to award any of these remedies by reference to one or more of a number of factors.

It has already been explained that either undue delay[68] or lack of sufficient interest[69] may be a basis upon which the court on AJR will refuse to grant a remedy to an applicant who has not only obtained permission but has also established grounds for review. Courts do sometimes treat delay and lack of standing as "discretionary" factors grounding a refusal of remedy.[70] But it has been cogently argued that these issues should be regarded as matters of "judgment" rather than "discretion".[71] The distinction may be explained as follows. Whether an applicant has a sufficient interest is a matter of judgment, applying criteria which are, or should be, clearly articulated in the case law. If the answer to the question is unfavourable to the applicant the judge has no discretion to grant any remedy. The same may be true of the question whether an applicant has delayed unduly in applying and the grant of a remedy would cause hardship, prejudice or detriment to good administration — although the terms of section 31(6) of the Supreme Court Act 1981 are permissive ("may" refuse . . .): compare the mandatory "shall not grant" in section 31(3).

Refusal of a remedy on grounds of lack of standing or of delay may be contrasted with the clearly "discretionary" bases upon which relief has been refused by reference to the particular circumstances of a case. The following are examples.

---

[64] Building Act 1984, ss.77 *et seq. cf. Cooper v. Wandsworth Board of Works* (1863) 14 C.B.N.S. 180, above Chap. 4, *section E 2 a.*

[65] SCA 1981, s.31(4); RSC, Ord. 53, r.7.

[66] Lord Wilberforce in *Davy v. Spelthorne B.C.* [1983] 3 All E.R. 278 at 286j.

[67] *Section C 1 d* below.

[68] *Section A 2* above.

[69] *Section A 3 b* above.

[70] See, *e.g. R. v. Transport Department, ex p. Presvac Ltd, The Times,* July 10, 1991.

[71] Bingham (1991), pp. 68–69.

(a) Passage of time

An AJR may have been made promptly, so that no issue of delay arises. But the length of time between the impugned act or decision and the ruling of the court in the applicant's favour may cause the court to exercise its discretion to withhold any remedy. In *R. v. Devon and Cornwall Chief Constable, ex p. Hay*[72] the Chief Constable was held to have erred in law in discontinuing disciplinary proceedings against an officer in respect of his part in a police siege in which the applicant's brother had been shot dead. The basis of the discontinuance was the officer's mental ill-health. The officer had then retired. Sedley J. held that because of the medical evidence and the six month time lapse since the officer's retirement the court would not "wind the film back"[73] by granting any remedy against the decision.

(b) Conduct of the applicant

The court may in its discretion refused a remedy on AJR if the applicant's conduct is judged unmeritorious. A plain example would be where the applicant presents his case in such a way as to mislead and deceive the court.[74] "It may no doubt be reasonable to give a court the power to deny relief to an applicant who has tried to deceive it or has abused its process . . . [but] the rules governing the exercise of the discretion should be narrow and perhaps more clearly defined than they are at present."[75] This view is perhaps illustrated by *R. v. Education Secretary, ex p. Birmingham D.C.*[76] in which the minister had made a school closure order at the request of the council. After local elections the newly-constituted council sought to reverse the process by itself seeking judicial review on the basis that its decision to seek the closure was vitiated by unlawful delegation. The court refused to grant any remedy to the council because of its "unattractive" behaviour, but granted certiorari to the school's governors who also had applied.

(c) No useful purpose

A remedy will be refused if in the circumstances it would serve no useful purpose. For example, in *R. v. Inner London Education Authority, ex p. Ali*[77] the authority (ILEA) acknowledged that it was in breach of its statutory duty to provide schooling for the applicants following a large increase in the school-aged population in the area. The court refused to grant a declaration to the applicants: any declaration would merely reiterate the existence of a duty which ILEA acknowledged and was taking steps to rectify. "No useful purpose" was also, in effect, the basis on which in *R. v. Employment Secretary, ex p. Seymour-Smith*[78] the House of Lords discharged a declaration that the two year statutory qualifying period for unfair dismissal rights was contrary to E.C. sex discrimination law in 1991. The evidence suggested that by virtue of a change in employment patterns this might no longer have been the case by the time of the judgment in 1995. The declaration would in those circumstances have served no useful purpose.[79]

---

[72] [1996] 2 All E.R. 712.
[73] *ibid.*, at 726e.
[74] As *e.g.* in *R. v. Kensington General Commissioners, ex p. Polignac* [1917] 1 K.B. 486.
[75] Bingham (1991) p. 71.
[76] *The Times*, July 18, 1984.
[77] *The Times*, February 21, 1990.
[78] [1997] 2 All E.R. 273.
[79] *ibid.*, at 279g–280g.

(d) No substantial prejudice

Another situation (already met[80]) in which a remedy may be refused on the ground that it would serve no useful purpose is where a decision has been taken unfairly but a hearing "could have made no difference." Also in the context of unfair procedure, the court may refuse any remedy where it finds that the applicant suffered no substantial prejudice. In *R. v. Foreign Secretary, ex p. Everett*[81] Everett's application for renewal of his passport had not been fairly dealt with; but in the exercise of its discretion the court declined to grant any remedy. There was a warrant out for Everett's arrest. This justified the refusal, and by the time the AJR was heard the Foreign Office had given Everett details of the warrant: so he had not in the event been prejudiced by the earlier unfair refusal.

It is impossible to catalogue exhaustively the types of circumstance which may be held to make the grant of any remedy inappropriate. The open-endedness of the court's discretion to base a refusal of remedy on the particular circumstances of the case may suggest that, as with the "conduct of the applicant" ground, the rules governing its exercise should be narrow and perhaps more clearly defined. But the Law Commission found "little disagreement with the factors said to be taken into account by the courts at present"[82] and proposed neither statutory definition nor the adoption of any new criteria.[83]

C CHOICE OF PROCEDURE — AJR AND OTHER FORMS OF ATTACK
(SEE *TABLE 5*)

1 AJR OR ORDINARY CIVIL PROCEEDINGS? THE PROBLEM OF PROCEDURAL EXCLUSIVITY[84]

Civil proceedings in England and Wales are now governed by the Civil Procedure Rules 1998.[85] Prior to the new rules, ordinary civil proceedings ("civil actions") were commenced either by writ or (less commonly) by originating summons which no longer exist. Instead, under the 1998 Rules,[86] ordinary civil proceedings take the form of what in this book is referred to as an ordinary civil claim.[87] The adjective "ordinary" is used to distinguish this from special types of civil claim, of which, under the Rules,[88] AJR is one. An AJR claim, unlike an ordinary civil claim, can be made only after permission[89] of the High Court has been obtained under Order 53 of the Rules of the Supreme Court.[90]

[80] Chap. 4, *section E 2 d.*
[81] [1989] 1 All E.R. 655 (see Chap. 3, *section B 2 a*).
[82] LCR 226 (1994) para 8.21 (listing them).
[83] *ibid.,* at para. 8.19.
[84] Wade & Forsyth, *AL*, Chap. 18; Craig, *AL*, Chap. 23; de Smith, *JRAA*, pp. 191–201; Woolf (1986); Beatson (1987).
[85] S.I. 1998 No. 3132 (L.17) - effective from April 26, 1999.
[86] r.7.2.
[87] See Chap. 1, *section B 2.*
[88] Sched. 1 to the RSC (Rules of the Supreme Court) Rules, Ord. 53, r.5(2A).
[89] *Sub-section A 1* above.
[90] This is the effect of Order 53 r.5(1), (2) and (2A) read together. See further Practice Direction on AJR, May 5, 1999.

TABLE 5

WHEN TO APPLY FOR JUDICIAL REVIEW

NOTE: "TARGET ACTION" = OFFICIAL ACT OR DECISION AGAINST WHICH PERSON "C" SEEKS TO MOUNT LEGAL CHALLENGE

HAS C A RIGHT OF APPEAL AGAINST THE TARGET ACTION? *(See Chap. 2)*

— Yes →

IS APPEAL CAPABLE OF YIELDING A "CONVENIENT" REMEDY, i.e. ONE WHICH C SEEKS? *(See Chap. 2, s.E; Chap. 5, s.C 2)*

— Yes → **C SHOULD APPEAL**[1]

— No →

HAS C A PRIVATE LAW CLAIM ARISING FROM THE TARGET ACTION? *(See Chap. 5, s.C; Chap. 8; Chap. 9)*

— Yes → **C SHOULD COMMENCE ORDINARY CIVIL CLAIM**[2]

— No →

IS TARGET ACTION REVIEWABLE? *(See Chap. 3 & Table 3)*

— Yes →

HAS C ANY GROUNDS FOR REVIEW? *(See Chap. 4)*

— Yes →

HAS C SUFFICIENT INTEREST AND IS HE ACTING SUFFICIENTLY PROMPTLY FOR AJR? *(See Chap. 5, s.A)*

— Yes → **C SHOULD SEEK PERMISSION TO AJR**

— No → **C SHOULD NOT AJR**

NOTES

(1) Where C is challenging a discretionary decision on the ground that it is *ultra vires* because failing properly to apply an established policy (*i.e.* alleging Wednesbury/Padfield "wrong considerations"), the *vires* point may be treated as collateral and outwith the appeal tribunal's jurisdiction. *(See Chap. 6, s.E.)* In these circumstances, C should seek permission to AJR.

(2) In "mixed" public law/private law cases C may usually choose between AJR and ordinary civil claim. *(See Chap. 5, s.C 1 c.)* Because AJR must be commenced in the High Court, requires permission and is subject to much shorter time limit than ordinary civil claim, C will often prefer latter.

(a) The rule in *O'Reilly v. Mackman*

In *O'Reilly v. Mackman*[91] four prisoners commenced ordinary civil proceedings by writ seeking a declaration that their prison disciplinary authorities had acted *ultra vires* (in breach of natural justice) in sentencing them to loss of remission following their conviction for rioting in the prison. The House of Lords ruled that the prisoners could not attempt to vindicate their "public law right" to a fair hearing by use of ordinary civil proceedings. Their only proper course was AJR, a procedure crafted precisely to deal with public law issues, and they were well out of time for that. Lord Diplock said:

> "[I]t would . . . as a general rule be contrary to public policy, and as such an abuse of the process of the court, to permit a person seeking to establish that a decision of a public authority infringed rights to which he was entitled to protection under public law to proceed by way of an ordinary action and by this means to evade the provisions of [RSC] Order 53 for the protection of such authorities."[92]

O'Reilly thus yields the rule that it is generally an abuse of process to use ordinary civil proceedings rather than AJR to complain of a breach of public law rights.

As already explained,[93] the Order 53 procedure introduced in 1977 had removed the anomalies and inconveniences of the old procedure, thus also removing the basis on which the courts had permitted the use of ordinary civil proceedings to challenge *ultra vires* action. Under the post-1977 procedural regime the "abuse of process" prohibited by the *O'Reilly* rule thus consists in public law litigants using ordinary civil proceedings in an attempt to side-step the AJR features of permission, sufficient interest and strict time limits "imposed in the public interest against groundless, unmeritorious or tardy attacks on the validity of decisions made by public authorities in the field of public law."[94] The sanction for this abuse has been that such ordinary civil action will be struck out (rejected) without any consideration of its merits. If a litigant has an arguable public law point he can of course consider re-launching his challenge by AJR. But he may very well find that, like the prisoners in *O'Reilly*, he is out of time. And he will in any event have incurred the costs of the abortive proceedings. How this position will be affected by the Civil Procedure Rules 1998 remains (at the time of writing in July 1999) unclear. The 1998 Rules followed Lord Woolf's *Access to Justice* report[95] which contains proposals, as yet not fully implemented, for dealing with the problems flowing from the rule in *O'Reilly*. These proposals will be considered below.[96] Now it is necessary to look in more detail at the *O'Reilly* prohibition on using ordinary civil proceedings rather than AJR to complain of breach of public law rights.

- The case law indicates that if on analysis a challenge raises only "public law" issues, *i.e.* is solely concerned to invoke the judicial review grounds and remedies discussed above and in Chapters 3 and 4, it falls within the *O'Reilly* rule: *sub-section b*, below.

- If, on the contrary, a challenger is able to demonstrate that *ultra vires* action has caused him damage so as to constitute a tort or other civil ("private law") wrong against him, the *O'Reilly* rule will not usually apply: *sub-section c* below.

---

91 [1982] 3 All E.R. 1124.
92 [1982] 3 All E.R. at 1134e.
93 *Section B 2 a* above.
94 Lord Diplock in *O'Reilly* at 1131j.
95 Woolf, *Access.*
96 *Sub-section f.*

(b) "Pure public law" cases brought wrongly by ordinary civil proceedings

(i) Clear and less clear cases of "pure public law" challenge

Some challenges are almost self-evidently what for convenience may be labelled "pure public law", *e.g.* the those (discussed above[97]) based purely on public interest standing. But very many challenges to the legality of official action are brought by persons seeking to obtain some form of benefit personal to themselves. How is the public law/private law dividing-line to be drawn in such cases?

(ii) Decision-making functions as public law functions

In *O'Reilly* itself Lord Diplock said that the prisoners had no private law rights, only a "legitimate expectation", because ". . . under the Prison Rules remission of sentence is not a matter of right but of indulgence".[98] The prisoners had a public law right to a lawful and fair decision on remission of sentence, but no private law claim to remission itself. Their case was pure public law. The concept of public law rights was further elaborated in *Cocks v. Thanet D.C.*[99] decided by the House of Lords on the same day as *O'Reilly*. In *Cocks*, C applied to his local authority for housing under the homeless persons legislation. Before he had received any decision on his application he sued the authority in the local county court seeking a declaration that he was unintentionally homeless with priority need and that the council was in breach of their statutory duty[1] to house him; he also sought damages for the tort of breach of statutory duty. On appeal, the House of Lords struck out C's action as an abuse of process: C's complaint was in substance that he had not received the decision on his application to which he claimed he was entitled. Lord Bridge said that decision-making functions requiring an authority to decide whether they have reason to believe and whether they are or are not satisfied of certain matters "are essentially public law functions".[2] C thus had no private law claim against the authority, and the rule in *O'Reilly* applied.

Later cases, in particular *X v. Bedfordshire C.C., E v. Dorset C.C.*[3] decided by the House of Lords in 1995, have elaborated this approach as follows. There are many circumstances in which an individual's access to some benefit such as housing or services (*e.g.* health or welfare or education), or a money benefit, is dependent on the exercise by a public authority of judgment or discretion. In these circumstances the individual has a public law right to a lawful decision but no private law right to damages if he does not obtain the decision to which he claims he is entitled. In the absence of any appeal mechanism, judicial review is the appropriate means by which to challenge a decision based on unlawful criteria, and AJR is the appropriate procedure by which to mount the challenge. Thus, as will be more fully explained in the chapter on official liability in tort,[4] in the case just mentioned, the House held that breaches of local authorities' decision-making duties in respect of child protection and special educational provision do not constitute the torts of breach of statutory duty or negligence. Thus under the rule in *O'Reilly*, any challenge in the courts must be mounted by AJR and not ordinary civil proceedings — unless the

---

[97] *Section A 3 c.* Particularly *R. v. HM Treasury, ex p. Smedley* [1985] 1 All E.R. 589, *R. v. Foreign Secretary, ex p. Rees-Mogg* [1994] 1 All E.R. 457; *R. v. Foreign Secretary, ex p. World Development Movement Ltd* [1995] 1 All E.R. 611.
[98] [1982] 3 All E.R. at 1126h.
[99] [1982] 3 All E.R. 1135.
[1] Now under Housing Act 1996, Pt VII. The "full" housing duty claimed by Cocks is now in s.193 of the 1996 Act.
[2] [1982] 3 All E.R. at 1137–1138.
[3] [1995] 3 All E.R. 353.
[4] Chap. 8, *sections B 3* and *C 2 d.*

complainant can show that the authority has acted in bad faith, in which case he may bring an ordinary civil claim alleging the tort of misfeasance in public office.[5]

This approach would apply equally to claims against public authorities for the payment of money benefits, as illustrated by *Cato v. Minister of Agriculture*.[6] C, the owner of a fishing vessel brought a civil action for breach of statutory duty against the minister for his failure to make a payment under an E.C. vessel-decommissioning compensation scheme. The Court of Appeal held that, like the claimant in *Cocks*, C had no cause of action. The minister had never reached the point of deciding that C fulfilled the criteria for payment of the compensation, so C had only public law rights and his action was barred by the rule in *O'Reilly*.

(iii) *Private law rights flowing from favourable decisions?*

Defining the notion of a public law right by reference to decision-making functions involving judgment or discretion does provide a workable test in many cases: wrong decisions as to entitlements to state benefits will usually not breach any private law right. This analysis does not, however, address the question of the nature of an individual's right to such benefit once it has been decided or accepted, in a particular case, that he or she is entitled to it. In *Cocks v. Thanet D.C.*[7] Lord Bridge said that after a local housing authority has decided that a particular applicant fulfils the criteria for housing it has an "executive" duty to provide housing. The applicant has a corresponding private law right to be housed and may sue for damages if housing is not provided.[8] But 15 years later, in *O'Rourke v. Camden L.B.C.*[9] in 1997, the House of Lords disapproved these observations.

In *O'Rourke*, O had applied for housing as a homeless person. He claimed damages for breach of the authority's statutory duty[10] to provide him with temporary accommodation pending the conclusion of their inquiries. The House of Lords struck out O's claim on the basis that at no stage of the relationship between an applicant and an authority does the authority owe the applicant any private law housing duty. Lord Hoffmann (in effect giving the judgment of the House) observed that "The concept of a duty in private law which arises only when it has been acknowledged to exist is anomalous. It means that a housing authority which accepts that it has a duty to house the applicant but does so inadequately will be liable in damages, but an authority which perversely refuses to accept that it has any such duty will not. This seems to me wrong."[11]

Strictly the ruling in *O'Rourke* covers only the temporary duty, but the reasoning of the House plainly extends to all the homeless person duties, and, indeed, very much further. Under this reasoning it seems likely, that most or all social welfare benefits will be regarded as conferring only public law rights on those entitled to them: this is based on the proposition that welfare provision is to be regarded as made primarily for the benefit of the public at large rather than to confer private rights on individual recipients.[12] Lord Hoffmann did refer to "benefits in kind", but the thrust of his argument would cover all social welfare benefits. If in later cases this approach is applied broadly, most or all such benefits, whether in cash or in kind, and whether or not the authority has at some stage made a decision that a particular person is entitled, will count as public law rights only. They may be vindicated by way of any appeal mechanism provided, but subject to that, AJR will be the only remedy for bona fide breach. AJR is subject to the limitations

---

[5] *ibid., section D.*
[6] *The Times,* June 23, 1989.
[7] [1982] 3 All E.R. 1135.
[8] *ibid.,* at 1138c.
[9] [1997] 3 All E.R. 23.
[10] Now under Housing Act 1996, s.188.
[11] [1997] 3 All E.R. at 29c.
[12] [1997] 3 All E.R. at 26. See further Chap. 8, *section B 4 a.*

(1) that it must be sought within a very short time-limit; (2) that it cannot go into the merits of a wrong decision; and (3) that damages are not available for breach of a purely public law right.

(iv) *No private law rights to any state benefits?*

Does the reasoning in *O'Rourke* extend beyond the area of social welfare benefits and apply to any right to a sum of money or other benefit which an individual can claim only after an administrative decision that he is entitled to it? This would include not only welfare benefits but also, *e.g.*, a statutory right to compensation (such as that claimed in *Cato*[13] or in the *Anisminic* case,[14]) or some form of money grant outside the social welfare area.[15] Does *O'Rourke* mean that such benefit, even when acknowledged by the relevant authority to be due, cannot be claimed by ordinary civil proceedings?

That the reasoning in *O'Rourke* may extend so far is suggested by Lord Hoffmann's above-quoted observation that "The concept of a duty in private law which arises only when it has been acknowledged to exist is anomalous." On the other hand, as will shortly be seen, a public authority's failure to make money payments which under statute must be paid on compliance by a claimant with statutory conditions has been treated by the House of Lords[16] as breaching the claimant's (albeit conditional) private law rights and as thus being challengeable by ordinary civil proceedings.

(v) *Summary on "pure public law" challenges*

It appears that official decisions that one is not entitled to a particular state benefit are matters of pure public law to which the *O'Reilly* rule applies. Similarly it applies where one is considering bringing court proceedings to challenge a failure to confer any social welfare benefit, even where the relevant authority has decided or accepts that the benefit is due. And this is possibly true also of any other state benefit which an individual can claim only after an administrative decision that he is entitled to it.

Further difficulties with the application of the *O'Reilly* rule flowing from uncertainty as to the boundary between public law and private law rights will be encountered shortly. But it is now convenient to consider two exceptions which Lord Diplock identified to the general rule in *O'Reilly*.

(vi) *The "no objection" exception to* O'Reilly

The basis of the *O'Reilly* rule is that litigants should not be permitted to proceed by ordinary civil action in an attempt to side-step the public authority protection features of AJR. On this basis Lord Diplock said that if in a particular public law case "none of the parties objects to the adoption of the procedure by writ or originating summons",[17] the court would not strike out the action as an abuse of process.

This "no objection" exception probably explains *British Amusement Catering Trade Association v. Westminster C.C.*,[18] ordinary civil proceedings brought by a trade association and one of its members, a video games arcade owner, seeking a declaration that the council were wrong in law in their view that a games arcade required a cinema licence. The House of Lords upheld the grant of a declaration to both claimants without reference to the fact that, at any rate as far as the

---

[13] See above.

[14] *Anisminic Ltd v. Foreign Compensation Commission* [1969] 1 All E.R. 208: see Chap. 4, *section B 3 a*.

[15] *e.g.* as in *R. v. Transport Secretary, ex p. Sherriff and Sons Ltd The Times,* December 18, 1986.

[16] In *Roy v. Kensington, etc. Family Practitioner Committee* [1992] 1 All E.R. 705: *sub-section c,* below.

[17] [1982] 3 All E.R. at 1134f. Under the Civil Procedure Rules 1998, "writ" and "originating summons" are replaced by ordinary "claim": see *sub-section a* above.

[18] [1988] 1 All E.R. 740.

association was concerned, this was plainly a pure public law issue. The exception has been applied in a number of pure public law cases;[19] but in one such case,[20] while not striking out the civil proceedings as an abuse of process, the court indicated that, despite the absence of objection by the defendant, AJR should have been used. Indeed, it is not obvious why a rule which is imposed in the public interest for the protection of public authorities should be capable of waiver in a particular case at the unfettered discretion of an authority.

(c) The "collateral issue" exception to *O'Reilly*: "mixed" public law/private law cases

(i) *Scope and rationale of the exception: mixed cases brought by ordinary civil proceedings*

The second exception which Lord Diplock identified to the general rule in *O'Reilly* was ". . . where the invalidity of the decision arises as a collateral issue in a claim for infringement of a right of the plaintiff[21] arising under private law . . ."[22]

The leading case on the scope of this exception is the 1992 decision of the House of Lords in *Roy v. Kensington, etc. Family Practitioner Committee*.[23] R was a GP who had been on the Committee's NHS list since 1954. Under statutory regulations he was thus entitled to be paid a certain stipend (a "practice allowance") if the Committee considered that he was devoting a "substantial amount of time" to NHS work. Having formed the view that he was not doing so, the Committee reduced R's stipend by 20 per cent from January 1, 1985. R brought an ordinary civil action alleging breach of what he said was his private law right to the full amount. The success of this claim (characterised by Lord Lowry as "the very important private law right to be paid for the work that he has done"[24]) depended, of course, upon R's ability to show that the Committee's decision was *ultra vires*. A case such as this, where a person asserts **an existing private law cause of action** but where that assertion stands or falls upon his ability to establish that an act or decision of a public authority is *ultra vires* (a public law issue) may for convenience be termed a "mixed" public law/private law case.

The *Roy* case went to the House of Lords on the question whether the rule in *O'Reilly* precluded R from challenging the Committee's decision in ordinary civil proceedings. The House held that it did not, for the following reasons[25]:

- the private law right which R was asserting "dominated" the proceedings;

- R's claim was of a sort where issues of fact might (although they did not in the case) arise;

- the order for payment sought by Roy could not be granted on AJR, not being strictly a damages claim;[26]

- it was joined with another claim (re payment to reimburse R for his employment of ancillary staff) which had been successfully prosecuted;

---

[19] *e.g. Securities and Investments Board v. FIMBRA* [1991] 4 All E.R. 398 at 402h; *Kent* case, n.20.
[20] *Kent v. University College London, The Times,* February 18, 1992.
[21] *i.e.* "claimant" in the terminology of the Civil Procedure Rules 1998. The term "plaintiff" is no longer used.
[22] [1982] 3 All E.R. at 1134f.
[23] [1992] 1 All E.R. 705.
[24] *ibid.,* at 725h.
[25] *ibid.,* at 729 (Lord Lowry, with whom the other four law lords agreed).
[26] See Lord Lowry, *ibid* at 726b. For damages on AJR, see *section B 3* above.

- an action should be allowed to proceed unless it is plainly an abuse of process;

- "When individual rights are claimed, there should not be a need for leave or a special time limit, nor should the relief be discretionary".[27]

The last-mentioned reason will exist, of course, in every mixed public law/private law case — which suggests that the rule in *O'Reilly* should never be applied in such a case. Although expressing a preference for that approach in *Roy*,[28] the House declined to lay down so broad a rule. Subsequent cases have shown that some uncertainty as to the applicability of *O'Reilly* in mixed cases still persists.

On the one hand there are cases which appear to be mixed cases but which have been treated as pure public law cases. In *The Great House at Sonning Ltd v. Berkshire C.C.*[29] retail traders sued the local authority alleging the tort of nuisance. The nuisance was said to arise from an allegedly *ultra vires* road closure order. Although apparently squarely within the *Roy* principle, the action was struck out under *O'Reilly*. Similarly, in *British Steel plc v. Customs and Excise Commissioners*[30] Laws J. struck out a restitution[31] action for re-payment of excise duty allegedly unlawfully demanded, although he was subsequently reversed by the Court of Appeal,[32] apparently applying *Roy*.

The position thus appears to be that mixed cases may usually be brought by ordinary civil proceedings but that it may sometimes still be possible for a defendant to persuade a court to strike out a mixed case brought by ordinary civil proceedings on the basis that AJR was the only proper form of procedure. This uncertainty can hardly be regarded as satisfactory.

On the other hand in *Trustees of the Dennis Rye Pension Fund v. Sheffield City Council*[33] what might have been thought to be a pure public law case was treated by the Court of Appeal as a mixed case: the court rejected the council's argument that a challenge to its refusal to pay housing improvement grants[34] in respect of work done by the claimants to render premises fit for human habitation could be brought only by AJR. Lord Woolf M.R. said that, as in *Roy*, the claimants had "conditional rights to payment" which could be asserted in ordinary civil proceedings. But the council had taken the view that the claimants had not satisfied the statutory conditions for the payment of grant, and it is difficult to see that as regards the assertion of established private law rights the claimants were in a different position from the claimants in *Cocks*, *O'Rourke* or *Cato*.[35]

(ii) *Mixed cases brought by AJR*

As already seen, damages are available on AJR in a mixed case.[36] Even though a mixed case claimant may have the option to use ordinary civil proceedings, it would appear that he may alternatively proceed by AJR if that seems appropriate. This might be so, *e.g.*, in a case where the public law issue seems difficult or prominent and where, consequently, it is likely to be cheaper and swifter to proceed by AJR rather than to commence civil proceedings (perhaps in a county court) with the probability that the matter will anyway proceed ultimately to the Court of Appeal or House of Lords. On the other hand, "judicial review is not a fact-finding exercise"[37] and should

---

[27] *ibid.*, at 729d.
[28] *ibid.*, at 728j.
[29] *The Times*, March 25, 1996.
[30] [1996] 1 All E.R. 1002.
[31] See Chap. 9, *section B 1 f (ii)*.
[32] [1997] 2 All E.R. 366.
[33] [1997] 4 All E.R. 747.
[34] Under Local Government and Housing Act 1989, s.113.
[35] *Sub-section b* above.
[36] Above, *section B 3*.
[37] Jowitt J. in *R. v. Chief Constable of Warwickshire, ex p. F* [1998] 1 All E.R. 65 at 80c.

not be used in mixed cases where difficult issues of fact arise. Moreover, "the court should be cautious in supplying a remedy by way of judicial review where a[n ordinary civil] claim would be anything other than obvious and certain."[38]

(iii) *Summary on procedure in mixed cases*

Subject to the uncertainties canvassed above about the scope of *Roy* in mixed public law/private law cases and to considerations just mentioned, it seems that in mixed cases "the rule applies that the [claimant] may choose the court and procedure which suit him best".[39]

(iv) *Challenging the withdrawal of an official licence or permission by ordinary civil proceedings?*

Cocks v. Thanet D.C.[40] shows that one must use AJR rather than ordinary civil proceedings to attack an official decision that one is not entitled to a particular state benefit.[41] *Roy v. Kensington, etc. Family Practitioner Committee*[42] shows that one may generally use ordinary civil proceedings rather than AJR to attack an official decision to withdraw a private law benefit once conferred. As seen, the House of Lords in *Roy* was inclined to the broad view that civil proceedings to vindicate existing "individual rights"[43] should not be struck out under *O'Reilly*, even though their vindication depends upon the successful assertion of a public law, *vires*, point.

Many official licences (*e.g.* road tax or television licences or local authority trading or entertainments licences) or permissions (*e.g.* planning permissions) are regarded as "individual rights" by those upon whom they are conferred. It appears from the reasoning in *O'Rourke*[44] that such licences are unlikely to be regarded as conferring private law rights upon holders. It would follow that an *ultra vires* decision to withdraw such licence or permission would not (in the absence of bad faith on the part of the public authority concerned) be tortious. But would it be an abuse of process under *O'Reilly* to challenge such withdrawal by ordinary civil proceedings seeking a declaration? Certainly such proceedings were permitted in the pre-1977 era, as in *Congreve v. Home Office*[45] where in ordinary civil proceedings the Court of Appeal declared *ultra vires* a decision by the Home Office to revoke television licences which the holders had purchased shortly before their existing licences were due to expire so as to avoid a fee increase which took effect on the expiry date. It may be that such proceedings would be permitted today — either under a relaxed application of the "collateral issue" exception to *O'Reilly* or as one of the "other exceptions" which Lord Diplock anticipated might develop "on a case to case basis".[46]

In this connection consider *Mercury Communications Ltd v. Director General of Telecommunications*[47] in which Mercury (M) had brought ordinary civil proceedings seeking a declaration that the Director General (DG) had erred in his interpretation of a statutory "contract" between M and British Telecom thus prejudicing M's existing rights to participate in national telecommunications provision. The case went to the House of Lords on DG's contention that M was seeking, in breach of the rule in *O'Reilly*, to vindicate public law rights in private law proceedings. The House held that ordinary civil proceedings were proper. Lord Slynn, giving in effect the judgment of the

---

[38] *R. v. Barnet Magistrates' Court, ex p. Cantor* [1998] 2 All E.R. 333 at 342j.

[39] *Davy v. Spelthorne B.C.* [1983] 3 All E.R. 278 at 287d (Lord Wilberforce); See also *Gillick v. West Norfolk, etc. Health Authority and Department of Health and Social Security* [1985] 3 All E.R. 402 at pp 416e (Lord Scarman), 405e (Lord Fraser); *Andreou v. Institute of Chartered Accountants* [1998] 1 All E.R. 14 at 21c.

[40] [1982] 3 All E.R. 1135: *sub-section b*, above.

[41] As will be explained in *subsection 2* below, where there is an adequate appeal procedure, that rather than AJR should be used.

[42] [1992] 1 All E.R. 705 (above).

[43] [1992] 1 All E.R. at 729d.

[44] Sub-section *b* above.

[45] [1976] 1 All E.R. 697.

[46] [1982] 3 All E.R. at 1134f.

[47] (1995) [1996] 1 All E.R. 575.

House, said[48] that it was important "to retain some flexibility as the precise limits of what is called 'public law' and what is called 'private law' are by no means worked out. . . . [T]he overriding question is whether the proceedings constitute an abuse of the process of the court". Civil proceedings in the Commercial court were well-suited to decide the dispute and so were proper: "[T]he dispute in substance and form is as to the effect of the terms of the contract even if it can also be expressed as a dispute as to the terms of the licence".[49]

M's "contractual rights" here seem more like a statutory licence than the paradigm contractual bargain. While concerned with a licence of a very different kind from those mentioned above, the *Mercury* case may thus indicate an increasingly lenient approach to the application of the *O'Reilly* rule and its collateral issue exception where what is challenged is an allegedly unlawful decision to withdraw or reduce benefits flowing to an individual under an official licence.[50] But the matter further illustrates the uncertainty as to the boundary between public and private law.

Whether "mixed" public law/private law cases may be brought by ordinary civil proceedings raises questions other than that of abuse of process. Moreover, it is not only claimants in civil proceedings who may wish to raise *vires* points other than on AJR: defendants in both civil and criminal proceedings and persons bringing administrative appeals may also wish to do so. These matters will be considered in Chapter 6.

(d) "Pure private law" cases brought wrongly by AJR

Eighteen months after the House of Lords laid down the rule in *O'Reilly v. Mackman*, the Court of Appeal in *R. v. East Berkshire Health Authority, ex p. Walsh*[51] applied what Donaldson M.R. described as the "obverse"[52] rule: that a person might not proceed against a public authority by way of AJR when his complaint raised only issues of private law. The effect of this rule has been that in these circumstances an AJR will be rejected outright, leaving the complainant to proceed by ordinary civil proceedings if he chooses.

The *Walsh* rule is not truly the obverse of that in *O'Reilly*, for they are differently based.[53] Under *O'Reilly* it is an abuse of process to use civil proceedings in order to avoid the public authority protection features of AJR in a pure public law case. Under *Walsh*, what is forbidden is to use AJR (accepting those protective constraints) in an attempt to import into the area of civil (private law) liability the rules or remedies of public law simply because in the circumstances they will afford more extensive protection to the applicant. Thus in *R. v. Disciplinary Committee of the Jockey Club, ex p. Aga Khan*[54] (considered in Chapter 3[55]) the Aga Khan applied for certiorari to quash the jockey club's disqualification of his horse (and thus to achieve its re-instatement as the Oaks winner). But his AJR was rejected under the *Walsh* rule, the Court of Appeal holding that the matter was one purely within the private law of contract.

While it is plain that public law rules and remedies should be confined to their proper sphere, it was suggested in Chapter 3[56] that the formalistic and rigid exclusion of all contractual activity from public law scrutiny is unsatisfactory. This proposition is further illustrated by cases in the area of public authority employment contracts. In the *Walsh* case itself an NHS nurse was

[48] *ibid.*, at 581e.
[49] *ibid.*, at 582a.
[50] See also *Andreou v. Institute of Chartered Accountants* [1998] 1 All E.R. 14.
[51] [1984] 3 All E.R. 425.
[52] *ibid.*, at 427d.
[53] Tanney (1994), p. 66; Fredman and Morris (1994), p. 71.
[54] [1993] 2 All E.R. 853.
[55] *Sub-section B 2 b.*
[56] *ibid.*

prevented from using AJR to seek certiorari to quash his dismissal and thus to obtain reinstatement. The health authority was under a statutory duty to employ only on pre-negotiated terms which included provisions governing the procedure for dismissal[57] which Walsh asserted had been breached. Notwithstanding this statutory dimension, the court held that a nurse's employment contract was an ordinary "master and servant" (*i.e.* employer and employee) contract and was therefore governed solely by the private law of employment contracts. Most of the reported cases on the *Walsh* rule, like *Walsh* itself, have involved unsuccessful attempts by public authority employees to avail themselves of protections not available to employees in the private sector.[58] It is true that where a particular public employment relationship is directly regulated or "underpinned" by a statutory regime, the courts have accepted that public law standards apply and challenges may be mounted by AJR. Thus in *R. v. Home Secretary, ex p. Benwell*[59] a prison officer was allowed to challenge his dismissal by AJR because his employment was governed by a statutory disciplinary code imposing special statutory duties and conferring special powers on the employer. Recall also the mine closure case mentioned in Chapter 4[60] where on AJR the Divisional Court rejected the Government's argument that miners threatened with redundancy had a claim only in private law: the court held that the Coal Industry Nationalisation Act 1946 had provided a unique statutory regime governing the case. However, the general message from the case law is that "the courts are wary of expanding indirect job security rights by allowing potentially large categories of employees into [AJR]".[61] The approach has been criticised for its over-rigid exclusion of public law scrutiny in this area,[62] a line of criticism which, as explained in Chapter 3, has begun to bear fruit in the imposition of some degree of public law control upon public authorities' choice and treatment of contracting partners. Specifically in the employment context, *R. v. Crown Prosecution Service, ex p. Hogg*[63] should be noted. There, the Court of Appeal applied *Walsh* in refusing permission for AJR to a probationary Crown Prosecution Service prosecutor seeking to challenge his dismissal. But the court did say that if a case were to arise in which the dismissal were "for reasons which impugned his independence . . . such issue might properly fall within the public law area".

The *Walsh* rule that pure private law cases cannot be litigated by AJR is further illustrated, outside the contract field, by *R. v. Home Secretary, ex p. Dew*.[64] D had been convicted and imprisoned for armed robbery. He had been shot by the police during his arrest and now alleged breach of the prison authorities' duty to provide proper medical treatment for his injury. He sought mandamus on AJR (as noted above,[65] injunctions are not available against the Crown to remedy private law wrongs) and damages. By the time the case was heard, treatment had been provided, so only the damages claim remained. Applying the *Walsh* rule McNeill J. held that the case "was in private law from the beginning"[66] and should have been brought as an ordinary civil claim for medical negligence.

---

[57] [1984] 3 All E.R. at 431d.

[58] *e.g. R. v. Derbyshire C.C., ex p. Noble* [1990] I.R.L.R. 332 (police surgeon); *R. v. Lord Chancellor's Department, ex p. Nangle* [1992] 1 All E.R. 897 (civil service clerical officer); and see also *R. v. Crown Prosecution Service, ex p. Hogg* (text below).

[59] [1984] 3 All E.R. 854.

[60] *R. v. Trade Secretary, ex p. Vardy, The Times,* December 30, 1992: Chap. 4, *section E 2 b.*

[61] Craig, *AL*, p. 768.

[62] See Fredman and Morris (1991).

[63] *The Times,* April 14, 1994.

[64] [1987] 2 All E.R. 1049.

[65] *Section B 2 b.*

[66] *ibid.,* at 1061f.

(e) Case transfer as an alternative to striking out?

The basis of the ruling in *Dew* seems to be[67] that an unqualified statutory duty to confer a defined benefit (here proper medical treatment) does not impose, in *Cocks v. Thanet D.C.* terms,[68] a "decision-making" duty. One can perhaps see that the rules, remedies and procedure of judicial review are not well-designed to determine challenges to day-to-day executive or operational or managerial[69] decisions as to how, rather than whether, to confer such benefits. Similarly, there may be something to be said for restraint in subjecting the contractual activities of public authorities to the public law regime of judicial review. Moreover, one can see that a deliberate attempt by a litigant to prosecute a case by what could be said in advance of the proceedings to be the wrong procedure may properly be struck out as an abuse of process. But it is surely indefensibly harsh to strike out proceedings raising substantial issues by (under *Walsh*) applying to them at a preliminary stage the label "private" or (under *O'Reilly*) "public" where the question of the appropriate remedies and procedures is, in advance of the litigation, quite unanswerable and is, indeed, at the heart of the proceedings. The courts should surely have jurisdiction to transfer such cases into the correct procedure rather than striking them out.

Under Order 53, r.9(5), where a declaration, injunction or damages are sought on AJR and the court considers that the remedy should not be granted on AJR but might have been granted in an ordinary civil claim, the court may, instead of refusing (*i.e.* striking out) the AJR, order the proceedings to continue as if they had been brought as an ordinary civil claim.

(i) *Transfer possible in mixed cases*

This jurisdiction has been used in mixed cases where, *e.g.*, the public law issue has been resolved in the applicant's favour leaving "issues of fact which [can] not suitably be resolved in judicial review proceedings"[70]; or where the AJR "is academic in the sense that its sole or main purpose is merely to prime the pump for [a] damages claim."[71]

(ii) *No transfer in pure private cases*

Unfortunately, in *Walsh* and *Dew* the courts took the strict view that rule 9(5) applies only in mixed cases and only where the applicant has actually claimed a declaration, injunction or damages in addition to one or more of the prerogative orders.[72] The rule thus does not assist in a case like *Walsh* or *Dew* where what might reasonably be thought to have been a mixed case is held to be a pure private law case. In these circumstances AJRs have been struck out (with whatever costs consequences follow) and the applicants have been left to decide whether or not to re-commence proceedings by way of ordinary civil claim.

(iii) *No transfer in pure public cases*

Not only is rule 9(5) thus deficient in its provision for transfer from AJR into ordinary civil proceedings but also there is no reverse provision, allowing an ordinary civil claim to be converted into an AJR in an appropriate case. Such provision certainly seems necessary in order to avoid injustice to a claimant in a case such as *Cocks* who is held on analysis, but unpredictably, to be asserting a pure public law case.

---

[67] See [1987] 2 All E.R. at 1056h-1061f. See also *Ettridge v. Morrell The Times*, May 5, 1986, Chap. 8, *section B 4 b.*
[68] See *sub-section b* above.
[69] [1987] 2 All E.R. at 1056h.
[70] Nolan L.J. in *R. v. Lancashire Chief Constable, ex p. Parker and McGrath* [1993] 2 All E.R. 56 at 58f.
[71] Taylor L.J. in *R. v. Blandford JJ., ex p. Pamment* [1991] 1 All E.R. 218 at 224e.
[72] [1984] 3 All E.R. at 432c, 441j; [1987] 2 All E.R. at 1064j.

The Law Commission have recommended the amendment of Order 53 to deal with both these problems.[73]

(f) Procedural exclusivity — problems and solutions

The rules in *O'Reilly*[74] and *Walsh*[75] embody the proposition that the AJR procedure created in 1977 should be used for, and only for, the type of case for which it was designed, *i.e.* for assertions promptly made by persons with a sufficient interest that an exercise of official power was illegal, irrational or unfair. Such cases may be referred to as "pure public law" cases. The availability of damages as a remedy on AJR suggests, and the *Roy*[76] line of case law confirms, that a case which combines a public law challenge with a private law damages suit (a "mixed" case) may be brought by AJR as an alternative to an ordinary civil claim. This approach to defining the province of AJR has generated two major problems for litigants and for the satisfactory development of judicial review. But before turning to those problems, and to possible solutions, it is important to acknowledge the values which are intended to be served by the existing arrangements.

(i) *Values served by* O'Reilly/Walsh *procedural exclusivity*

It will now be understood that, as stated earlier,[77] the special procedural features of AJR (permission, the short time-limit and the flexible notion of sufficient interest) together with the fact that remedies on AJR are available subject to the court's discretion rather than (as with civil damages or debt claims) "as of right" are designed with the following aim. The aim is to enable the court to balance (a) the public interest in subjecting public authorities to the rule of law and in enabling individual litigants to obtain a remedy for their grievances, against (b) the (sometimes conflicting) public interest in achieving speed and certainty in administrative decision making affecting the whole community or large sections of it.

If there are cases which require this balance to be struck in the public interest, those cases should obviously be brought by AJR rather than by ordinary civil claim which lacks the features which enable it to be struck. There will, of course, be disagreement as to which cases require the balance to be struck. It might be widely agreed that cases based purely on public interest standing[78] do normally require this, whereas actions against public authorities in respect of personal injuries inflicted by their employees or for non-payment of ordinary trading debts do not. But between any paradigms which might be agreed would be many cases where the need for the special procedural features would be highly controversial. The test established by the *O'Reilly* line of case law for identifying cases where the need does arise is any case where what is asserted is solely that an exercise of official power was illegal, irrational or unfair, *i.e.* any case which invokes only judicial review principles. Leaving aside the fact that it is by no means obvious that public authorities need the procedural protections of AJR always and only in judicial review cases,[79] the first of the major problems referred to above stems from the uncertainty of the *O'Reilly* test.

(ii) O'Reilly/Walsh *procedural exclusivity may unfairly prejudice litigants*

The cases discussed above[80] demonstrate that it is by no means always clear in advance of a court ruling whether an issue is one of public or, on the contrary, of private law. Thus, under the

---

[73] See *sub-section f,* below.
[74] *Sub-sections a and b* above.
[75] *Sub-section d* above.
[76] *Roy v. Kensington, etc. Family Practitioner Committee* [1992] 1 All E.R. 705: *sub-section c* above.
[77] Chap. 3, *section A 3 c.*
[78] *Section B 3 c* above.
[79] Beatson (1987), pp 43–44; Fredman and Morris (1994), pp. 70–71.
[80] See *e.g. sub-section b: Cocks, O'Rourke* (public); *sub-section d: Walsh, Dew* (private).

O'Reilly/Walsh rules, even a well-advised litigant may find that he has selected the wrong procedure. Even if he can commence and win new proceedings, the costs of the abortive proceedings are likely to fall on him.

The solution to this problem is relatively straight-forward, *i.e.* to equip the courts with far more wide-ranging and flexible procedures than they currently enjoy to transfer deserving cases from AJR to ordinary civil proceedings and vice-versa. *The current Law Commission proposals to this end are outlined in the boxed section below.*

LAW COMMISSION "CASE TRANSFER" SOLUTION TO PROBLEMS OF PROCEDURAL EXCLUSIVITY

(References are to Law Commission Report No. 226, *Administrative Law: Judicial Review and Statutory Appeals* (1994))

- AJR should be retained as a separate procedure (para 3.5). The *O'Reilly* principle of procedural exclusivity and its *Walsh* counterpart should continue to operate with regard to (respectively) pure public law and pure private law cases (para 3.15 (*O'Reilly*); 3.18 (*Walsh*)).
- In order to "eliminate the uncertainty and potential for litigation over procedural issues and the risk of being non-suited where . . . the applicant/litigant is not sure in which jurisdiction to commence proceedings" (para 3.16) the Commission recommend the amendment of Ord. 53, r.9(5) for transfer of cases from AJR into civil proceedings (para 3.19) and the creation of a new High Court power to transfer cases from civil proceedings into AJR (para 3.21). In 1997 in *Trustees of the Dennis Rye Pension Fund v. Sheffield City Council*[81] Lord Woolf suggested that even under then existing arrangements the courts could achieve this sort of procedural flexibility. But it is uncertain whether "the constant unprofitable litigation over the divide between public and private law proceedings"[82] can now be stopped simply by a change in the courts' approach to this vexed issue.
- Following the "broad" approach in *Roy*,[83] mixed cases should not generally be governed by the principle of procedural exclusivity (para 3.15.) But where the court considers it appropriate that a particular mixed case begun by ordinary civil proceedings should be dealt with on AJR the case should be transferable under the new transfer provisions (para 3.20. Presumably it is contemplated that in appropriate circumstances mixed cases begun by AJR may continue to be transferred into ordinary civil proceedings).

COMMENT[84]

These proposals will remove the unfairness to litigants described in the text, provided that:

- transfer rather than striking out will always be available where a litigant's wrong choice of procedure is not culpable (*i.e.* reflects uncertainty in whatever is the existing state of the public law/private law distinction);
- where the transfer is from ordinary civil proceedings into AJR, the AJR time limit is not, in general, applied and is never applied in mixed cases.

---

[81] [1997] 4 All E.R. 747.
[82] *ibid.*, at 754f.
[83] *Sub-section c* above.
[84] See further, Emery (1995 Tr.).

A satisfactory case-transfer mechanism could ensure that in future good cases are not struck out because of non-culpable errors in choosing between public law and private law procedures. The second problem, however, is more fundamental and more intractable.

(iii) O'Reilly/Walsh *procedural exclusivity distorts the development of the substantive law of judicial review*

The classification of an issue as "public law" or "private law" carries with it important consequences for a litigant's rights and remedies. If "public", judicial review principles apply and public law remedies are available; if "private", neither is true: but for private law wrongs damages will be available as of right, which they are not in pure public law cases.

The effect of *O'Reilly/Walsh* procedural exclusivity is that these critical questions have to be decided as preliminary issues whereas they often form the very heart of the case. Moreover, it has been pointed out that "the doctrine of procedural exclusivity requires the courts to attempt to devise means of categorising issues as exclusively public or private"[85] whereas, particularly in the era of the "contract state", many issues should be treated as hybrid, requiring a mix of public and private law principles and remedies. For example, should not public authority contracting be governed by a mix of judicial review and contract law principles? And should not public authorities whose *ultra vires* decisions cause damage be liable in tort for breach of public duty?[86]

In short, procedural exclusivity may be said to distort the development of administrative law by treating central issues as preliminary and by requiring all issues to be treated as either public or private whereas in reality many issues are hybrid. This has led a number of commentators[87] to argue that *O'Reilly/Walsh* procedural exclusivity should be abandoned by replacing the separate public and private law procedures with a single unified civil procedure. This, it is said, would mean that the public law/private law question need not be treated as a preliminary matter, and would leave open the possibility of treating appropriate issues as hybrid, thus facilitating a more satisfactory development of administrative law principle.

Whether or not these beneficial results would flow from the creation of a unified procedure would, of course, depend on the detail of the new procedure.[88] The Law Commission took the view that "any 'unified procedure' would prevent the expeditious disposal of public law cases by specialist judges and could increase complexity and cost".[89] However, the 1996 Woolf Report[90] did recommend a form of unified procedure which, when fully implemented, may contribute to the solution of the problems generated by the current procedural divide. *For details and assessment of the Woolf proposals, see boxed section and accompanying chart, TABLE 6.*

---

[85] Fredman & Morris (1994) at 71.
[86] *e.g.* Justice/A-S, Chap. 11.
[87] *e.g.* Fredman and Morris (above); Harlow (1995).
[88] Emery (1995 Pub.) pp. 454–455.
[89] LCR 226 (1994), para. 3.5.
[90] Woolf, *Access*, chap. 18.

WOOLF UNIFIED CIVIL PROCEDURE AND THE PUBLIC LAW/PRIVATE LAW DIVIDE

(References are to Lord Woolf, *Access to Justice — Final Report*, July 1996)

- Woolf proposed that "all [civil] proceedings should be begun by means of a claim. There should be a single claim form which could be used for every case".[91]
- "It is nevertheless important that the safeguards of the three month time limit and of standing, which are necessary in a judicial review claim, should not be bypassed, but these can be retained without making it an abuse of process to adopt the wrong procedure".[92]
- For this reason AJR will remain as a separate procedure albeit commenced (once permission has been granted[93] by the universal standard claim form.
- If a claimant does not seek judicial review but the defendant asks for the case to be struck out under *O'Reilly* "[I]t will be possible to transfer the claim to the Crown Office for a case management conference, at which the same filtering process [as for a case begun as a judicial review claim], without the court having to consider whether the issues are ones of public or private law, will apply, unless the answer is obvious or unless the issue needs to be resolved for substantive as opposed to procedural reasons. If the case . . . has merit the judge can direct it to proceed without determining whether it is a public or private law case. Furthermore, if the court thinks this is the best course to adopt in all the circumstances, it will be possible to leave consideration of standing and time limits until the final hearing".[94]

COMMENT[95]

Under the Woolf proposals the public-private question in difficult or marginal cases would not normally be answered as a preliminary issue, but would be left for resolution at the hearing of the case in the judicial review list. As explained in the text, this is likely to prove beneficial provided that:

- AJR time limits are not over-stringently applied to difficult or marginal cases held ultimately to be appropriate for AJR — and are never applied to such mixed cases;
- defendants do not misuse their ability to send a case to the Crown Office by raising the "public law bar" (see *TABLE 6*) with the result either that the AJR procedure becomes overloaded or that claimants are cowed into submission by the prospect of High Court litigation in low value cases with a public law dimension.

Much will turn on new Crown Office rules (yet to be published) for judicial review under the Woolf regime; on any Practice Statements which may be issued; and on the flexibility with which the Crown Office judges apply both.

---

[91] Chap. 12, para. 3.
[92] Chap. 18, para. 26.
[93] See above: *sub-section 1*, opening paragraph.
[94] *ibid.*, para. 27.
[95] See further, Emery (1997).

TABLE 6

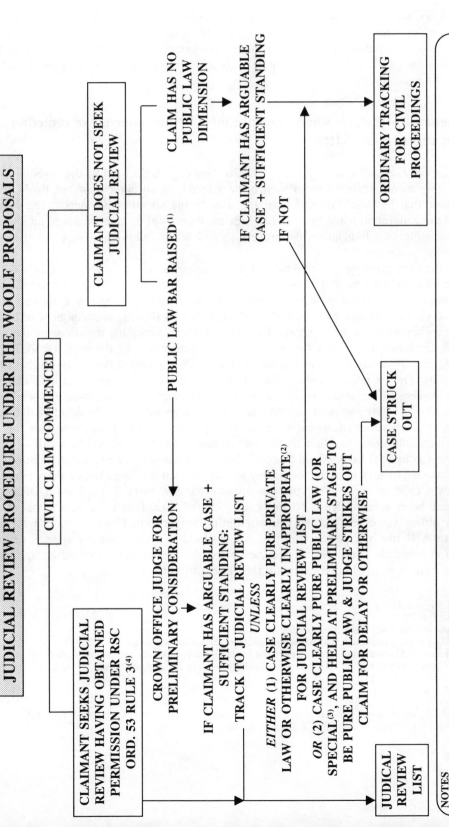

JUDICIAL REVIEW PROCEDURE UNDER THE WOOLF PROPOSALS

CIVIL CLAIM COMMENCED

CLAIMANT SEEKS JUDICIAL REVIEW HAVING OBTAINED PERMISSION UNDER RSC ORD. 53 RULE 3[4]

CLAIMANT DOES NOT SEEK JUDICIAL REVIEW

CROWN OFFICE JUDGE FOR PRELIMINARY CONSIDERATION

PUBLIC LAW BAR RAISED[1]

CLAIM HAS NO PUBLIC LAW DIMENSION

IF CLAIMANT HAS ARGUABLE CASE + SUFFICIENT STANDING: TRACK TO JUDICIAL REVIEW LIST

UNLESS

IF CLAIMANT HAS ARGUABLE CASE + SUFFICIENT STANDING

IF NOT

EITHER (1) CASE CLEARLY PURE PRIVATE LAW OR OTHERWISE CLEARLY INAPPROPRIATE[2] FOR JUDICIAL REVIEW LIST

OR (2) CASE CLEARLY PURE PUBLIC LAW (OR SPECIAL[3], AND HELD AT PRELIMINARY STAGE TO BE PURE PUBLIC LAW) & JUDGE STRIKES OUT CLAIM FOR DELAY OR OTHERWISE

ORDINARY TRACKING FOR CIVIL PROCEEDINGS

CASE STRUCK OUT

JUDICAL REVIEW LIST

NOTES
[1] *i.e. a (substantial?) question as to whether proceedings should be brought by judicial review is raised.*
[2] *It may be appropriate to track some "mixed" cases (e.g. those raising no difficult public law issue) as ordinary civil proceedings at High Court or county court level.*
[3] *i.e. if there is some substantive reason for deciding the public/private issue at the preliminary stage.*
[4] *If judge hearing permission application is of the view that case is pure private law and that claimant has arguable case + sufficient standing, he should transfer it for ordinary civil tracking; cf. ex p. Walsh.*

2 AJR OR APPEAL?[96]

As explained in Chapter 2, statutory rights of appeal against official decisions are widely available. There will be many situations where a person has a right of appeal against a decision which is also in principle subject to judicial review. If in these circumstances the decision under challenge is alleged to be wrong in law, the challenger appears to have a choice between appeal and AJR. Which should be chosen?

(a) The general principle: where appeal and AJR are alternative remedies, use appeal rather than AJR

In *R. v. IRC, ex p. Preston*[97] a taxpayer used AJR to challenge a decision by the revenue to raise certain tax assessments against him in breach, he alleged, of an agreement not to do so. The revenue argued that he should instead have appealed to the tax commissioners.[98] The House of Lords stated the general principle that "Judicial review should not be granted where an alternative remedy is available. . . . Judicial review process should not be allowed to supplant the normal statutory appeal procedure."[99]

In *Preston* itself the principle was held not to apply because the statutory avenue of appeal against the substance of a tax assessment did not extend to a challenge to a decision to raise an assessment: AJR was thus the appropriate procedure.[1] However, the *Preston* principle was applied in *R. v. Birmingham C.C., ex p. Ferrero Ltd.*[2] A child had died after swallowing a component of a toy kit contained in a chocolate egg manufactured by F Ltd. Without consulting the company the council had issued a Consumer Protection Act notice banning further sale of the eggs. On AJR by the company, alleging unfairness in issuing the notice, Hutchison J. quashed the notice on that ground. But applying the *Preston* principle, the Court of Appeal reversed the judge and held that F Ltd should have challenged the notice by appeal to the magistrates: "the real issue was whether the goods contravened a safety provision and the . . . appeal was geared exactly to deciding that issue."[3]

It appears that wherever an appeal mechanism is geared to deal adequately with the issues raised by a particular challenge that mechanism, rather than AJR, should be used — as when challenging, *e.g.*, a Special Educational Needs Tribunal's decision to amend a statement of special educational needs,[4] or a local authority's delay in carrying out its duties under the Children Act 1989 towards a child in need.[5] The rule can operate harshly, as in *R. v. Home Secretary, ex p. Swati*[6]: S had been refused leave to enter the United Kingdom as a visitor because the immigration officer suspected that he was attempting longer-term illegal entry. S was refused permission to AJR the refusal: the Court of Appeal held that the statutory appeals procedure provided an appropriate alternative remedy, even though the statute[7] required an appellant to return to his country of origin and to mount the appeal from there.

---

[96] Wade and Forsyth, *AL*, pp. 718–729; Craig, *AL*, pp. 806–809; Lewis (1992).

[97] [1985] 2 All E.R. 327.

[98] For tax commissioners, see Chap. 2, *section B 2 b.*

[99] *ibid.*, at 337g–j (Lord Templeman, with whose speech the other law lords agreed).

[1] *ibid.*, The question of choice between appeal and AJR has been found especially problematical where appellants have sought to raise points which may be regarded as particularly suitable for disposal by way of AJR. This problem is considered in Chap. 6, *section E.*

[2] [1993] 1 All E.R. 530.

[3] *ibid.*, at 539a.

[4] *R. v. Special Educational Needs Tribunal, ex p. South Glamorgan C.C., The Times* December 12, 1995, CA.

[5] *R. v. Birmingham C.C., ex p. A The Times,* February 19, 1997.

[6] [1986] 1 All E.R. 717.

[7] See Chap. 2, *section B 2 d.*

(b) The exceptions: use AJR where appeal is not equally effective and convenient

In *R. v. Chief Constable of Merseyside, ex p. Calveley*[8] five police officers who had been dismissed from the force for misconduct were permitted by the Court of Appeal to challenge their dismissals by AJR without having exhausted the statutory police appeal procedure. While emphasising that the *Preston* principle would normally make AJR impermissible in such circumstances,[9] the court said that the case was exceptional because two years had elapsed between the start of the investigations against the officers and their being informed of the matter. So serious a procedural defect made AJR appropriate. In these exceptional circumstances the appeal was not "equally effective and convenient".[10]

Circumstances in which AJR is likely to be permitted, even though the decision under challenge is also subject to a right of appeal, include the following:

- Where (if the grounds of challenge are substantiated) the decision in question will be plainly invalid and would certainly be quashed. In such circumstances, to use an appeal mechanism (which may well itself lead ultimately to the High Court) would be unnecessarily cumbersome and a waste of adjudicative resources. This was essentially the position in *Calveley*; see also *R. v. Wandsworth JJ., ex p. Read*,[11] in which it was said that it would be "ludicrous" to initiate a formal appeal in order to rectify a glaring and admitted error by magistrates in convicting the applicant without proper consideration of the evidence.

- Where a successful AJR, by quashing an unlawful decision, would give a person a "fresh start" and the full range of fair hearing and re-hearing to which he is entitled, whereas an appeal would in effect constitute the only fair hearing obtained.[12]

- Where a case raises a new point of general importance, AJR is likely to be the swiftest and most efficient avenue to an authoritative resolution of the point. Thus in *R. v. Huntingdon D.C., ex p. Cowan*[13] the applicant was permitted to challenge his local authority's refusal of a public entertainments licence by AJR rather than appeal because he was seeking a novel ruling that rules of natural justice applied to such decisions. The court must ask which of alternative remedies "is the most effective and convenient in all the circumstances, not merely for the applicant but in the public interest".[14]

- Where the appeal procedure will not provide an adequate remedy. The range of remedy available under a particular statutory appeal provision may be crucially narrower than what is available on AJR. For example, in *Bone v. Mental Health Review Tribunal*[15] a mental health patient appealed to the High Court against a refusal of the Mental Health Review Tribunal to direct his discharge. The Tribunal had failed to give reasons as required. The appropriate remedy would have been to quash the decision and to remit

---

[8] [1986] 1 All E.R. 257.
[9] See *e.g. R. v. Chief Constable of Merseyside, ex p. Merrill* [1989] 1 W.L.R. 1077.
[10] [1986] 1 All E.R. at 262b, 264c, citing Lord Widgery in *R. v. Hillingdon L.B.C., ex p. Royco Ltd* [1974] 2 All E.R. 643 at 648.
[11] [1942] 1 K.B. 281.
[12] *R. v. Hereford Magistrates' Court, ex p. Rowlands, The Times,* February 17, 1997.
[13] [1984] 1 All E.R. 58.
[14] *ibid.,* at 63h (Glidewell J.).
[15] [1985] 3 All E.R. 330.

the case to the Tribunal for proper determination, possible under AJR but not under the appeal procedure which empowered the court only to confirm or reverse the Tribunal's ruling. In these circumstances the court's only proper course was to confirm the ruling, stating that in future such challenges should be brought by AJR.[16]

---

[16] As in *R. v. Mental Health Review Tribunal, ex p. Clatworthy* [1985] 3 All E.R. 699: certiorari granted.

Chapter 6

COLLATERAL CHALLENGE — JUDICIAL REVIEW OTHER THAN BY AJR[1]

A DEFINITION AND TYPES OF COLLATERAL CHALLENGE

1 DEFINITION; COLLATERAL ATTACK IN ORDINARY CIVIL PROCEEDINGS

One type of collateral challenge was encountered in the previous chapter. That is the situation (exemplified by the *Roy* case[2]) where a person brings ordinary civil proceedings to assert an existing private law cause of action but where that assertion stands or falls upon his ability to establish that a particular act or decision of a public authority is *ultra vires*. If a public law (*vires*) point is raised and determined within such proceedings, the *vires* challenge is said to be "collateral" within those proceedings. The proceedings in which it is raised are designed, and are being used, to determine an issue of civil liability. They are not designed, but are nevertheless being used, to determine — "collaterally" — a *vires* issue.

A *vires* challenge may thus be described as "collateral"[3] when:

(1) The determination of a case requires the resolution of both *vires* and other issues; and

(2) The case is brought not by AJR but by a form of procedure which is designed to resolve the non-*vires* issues which arise.

In short, the notion of collateral *vires* challenge envisages a "mixed" public law/non-public law case brought other than by AJR. In contrast, a *vires* challenge mounted by AJR (whether in a mixed or a pure public law case) would be described as a "direct" *vires* (or public law) challenge.

2 OTHER TYPES OF COLLATERAL CHALLENGE

A case such as *Roy*, *i.e.* a case of *Collateral Attack in ordinary civil proceedings*, may be described as a "mixed" public law/private law case because it raises points both of public and of private law.

---

[1] Wade and Forsyth, *AL*, pp. 655–660, 756–767; Craig, *AL*, pp. 655–660, 756–767; de Smith, *JRAA*, pp. 262–265, and see Index under "Collateral Challenge"; Rubinstein, *JI*, Chap. III; Emery (1992); Emery (1993).

[2] *Roy v. Kensington, etc. Family Practitioner Committee* [1992] 1 All E.R. 705: Chap. 5, *section C 1 c.*

[3] See the classic definition of collateral challenge in Rubinstein, *JI*, pp. 37–38.

But there are other types of "mixed" case — cases rasing both *vires* issues and other issues of liability or entitlement.

(a) Collateral defence to ordinary civil proceedings

In *Wandsworth L.B.C. v. Winder*[4] the council took county court proceedings for possession of a council house on the basis of the tenant's refusal to pay a rent increase. The tenant sought to defend the council's claim by arguing that the rent increase was *ultra vires*, so that his failure to pay was not a breach of his tenancy agreement which, accordingly, could not be terminated by the council. The council argued that to raise the *vires* point by way of defence to the civil proceedings was an abuse of process within the rule in *O'Reilly v. Mackman*.[5] As will be explained later,[6] the House of Lords held that it was not.

(b) Collateral defence to criminal proceedings

In *R. v. Reading Crown Court ex p Hutchinson*[7] two anti-nuclear protestors had been convicted of breaching a byelaw forbidding unauthorised entry of a military "protected area", but the Crown Court had refused to permit the defendants to argue that the byelaw was *ultra vires* and that, therefore, they had committed no offence. On the defendants' AJR of the Crown Court's refusal, the Divisional Court issued a mandamus ordering the Crown Court to entertain the *vires* defence.

(c) Collateral attack in administrative appeals

In *Chief Adjudication Officer v. Foster*[8] a social security claimant, F, appealed against the decision of a local adjudication officer to discontinue the payment of a benefit to her. The decision was based upon amendments to regulations which the claimant argued (before the Social Security Commissioner) were *ultra vires*, so that the benefit remained payable. The Department of Social Security argued that the *vires* of regulations could be attacked only on AJR; but the House of Lords (overturning the Court of Appeal) held that F was entitled to mount her *vires* challenge collaterally before the Commissioner.

3 WHEN WILL PERSONS CHALLENGING OFFICIAL ACTION BE PERMITTED TO RAISE *VIRES* POINTS COLLATERALLY?

As the above examples show, there are circumstances in which the courts have permitted each of the identified types of collateral *vires* challenge to be mounted. However, as already explained in Chapter 5,[9] the circumstances in which collateral attack in civil proceedings will be permitted are by no means clearly defined. As will be seen in this chapter, the same is true with regard to the other types of collateral challenge identified above. This uncertainty in the law is largely explained by the need to re-appraise the law on collateral challenge in the light of the modern expansion of judicial review[10] and by reference to a range of public policy considerations, some of which argue

---

[4] [1984] 3 All E.R. 976.
[5] [1982] 3 All E.R. 1124: see Chap. 5, *section C 1*.
[6] *Section C 2*, below.
[7] [1988] 1 All E.R. 333.
[8] [1993] 1 All E.R. 705.
[9] *Section C 1 c.*
[10] Lord Nicholls in *R. v. Wicks* [1997] 2 All E.R. 801 at 804f; Woolf L.J. in *Bugg v. DPP* [1993] 2 All E.R. 815 at 822.

for, and some against, permitting collateral challenge. As will appear, these different considerations may be differently balanced with respect to different types of collateral challenge.

4 PLAN OF THIS CHAPTER

The range of public policy arguments for and against permitting collateral *vires* challenges to be mounted will be considered in *section B*. The position with regard to collateral challenge in ordinary civil proceedings will be reviewed in *section C* in the light of this range of arguments. *Sections D* and *E* will deal respectively with collateral defence to criminal proceedings and collateral attack in administrative appeals. *Section F* explains how the application of pure domestic English law on collateral challenge is affected where a case raises issues of Community or Convention law. *Section G* considers how the existing law on collateral challenge might be improved.

B PUBLIC POLICY ARGUMENTS FOR AND AGAINST COLLATERAL CHALLENGE[11]

1 ARGUMENTS FOR PERMITTING COLLATERAL CHALLENGE

Three categories of argument are commonly advanced in favour of permitting collateral *vires* challenges to be mounted. For ease of reference they will be labelled the "lock-out", "one-stop litigation" and "European law" arguments:

- The *lock-out argument* is that persons should not be barred (locked out) from mounting claims or defences in mixed cases by subjecting such claims or defences to the procedural constraints (particularly the time limits) of the AJR procedure: public law considerations should not "trump" other distinct claims and defences.

- The *one-stop litigation argument* is that a mixed case claimant or appellant, or a defendant to criminal or civil proceedings, should be permitted to raise his public law point collaterally within proceedings commenced by him or against him. He should not be required (in order to raise the public law point) to seek an adjournment of those proceedings in order to commence a separate AJR.

  This argument is perhaps at it weakest when advanced on behalf of a claimant in a mixed civil case, for it can be said that he could have chosen to proceed by AJR in the first place. The argument is stronger for a defendant (who has not chosen to proceed at all), or for an appellant before an administrative tribunal (who has used a procedure provided by statute apparently for the very purpose of challenging the decision in question).

- The *European law argument* is based on the wide availability of collateral challenge in cases with a Community law or Convention law element.[12] The argument, which will be considered below,[13] is that collateral challenge should not be less widely available in English courts and tribunals simply because a case has no European law element.

[11] Emery (1995 Pub.) p. 455.
[12] *Section F* below.
[13] *ibid.*

2 ARGUMENTS AGAINST PERMITTING COLLATERAL CHALLENGE

Three frequently-met categories of counter-argument may be labelled the "skills", "tools" and "legal certainty" arguments:

- The *skills argument* is that the expertise required to resolve difficult or novel points of public law lies with those High Court judges hearing cases in the Crown Office list[14] and the appeal courts above them. According to this argument, county courts, criminal trial courts, administrative tribunals and other authorities lack this expertise and may, indeed, lack jurisdiction to entertain *vires* points — points invoking the supervisory review regime developed and exercised by the High Court. So, public law issues in these categories should be dealt with on AJR and not collaterally.

- The *tools argument* is that even if it were conceded that courts or tribunals other than the superior courts have the skills to tackle these public law issues, they do not have the tools: only under Order 53 is there the remedial and procedural flexibility for matching remedies to wrongs which is necessary to ensure a balance between individual rights and good administration. In *Waverley B.C. v. Hilden*[15] Scott J. said that a successful collateral challenge "cannot be dealt with with the same flexibility [as a direct challenge on AJR]. It either succeeds or fails."[16] This underlines the important point that the only "remedy" for *ultra vires* action when challenged collaterally is that the court or tribunal will decide the individual case on the basis that the action is *ultra vires, i.e.* devoid of legal effect. The discretionary prerogative and other public law remedies are available only on AJR, not by way of collateral challenge.

  Why is this lack of remedial flexibility an argument against permitting collateral challenge? Consider an example based on *R. v. Paddington Valuation Officer, ex p. Peachey Ltd*[17] Suppose that a local authority rating (*e.g.* Council Tax) list has been compiled on the basis of an error of law that affects a substantial part of the list. In *Peachey* the Court of Appeal said that in those circumstances on AJR it would refuse to quash the list until a new one was prepared. This would enable the valid part to be enforced *pro tempore*. But suppose that two individual charge-payers (one from the valid part of the list and one from the invalid) were to raise collateral defences to county court claims for unpaid charges: it seems from Scott J.'s dictum in *Waverley* that a county court could not treat the two cases differently. If the error renders the list *ultra vires*, the claim against both defendants must fail, an outcome plainly at variance with the flexible approach envisaged by the Court of Appeal in *Peachey* and illustrating one facet of the tools argument against permitting collateral challenge.

  Another facet of the tools argument which, as will appear, has surfaced in the cases on criminal defences, is that the Order 53 time limit should apply as much in mixed as in pure public law cases.

- The *legal certainty* argument is essentially that one can only achieve the required certainty and consistency in public law by restricting judicial review to AJR. The basis of the argument is that a collateral ruling on a *vires* issue by, say, a magistrates' or county court or by an administrative tribunal would be binding in no other case. Such court or tribunal is not "a competent authority to strike down [an official] decision in the sense

---

[14] See Chap. 5, *section A 1*.
[15] [1988] 1 All E.R. 807 (below, *section C 2*).
[16] *ibid.*, at 819c.
[17] [1965] 2 All E.R. 836.

of declaring it invalid for all purposes."[18] It follows, it is said, that the issue may arise again in different proceedings in a different court or tribunal which might reach a different conclusion.

This argument is much weakened by the very widespread availability of appeal on law from courts and tribunals to the superior courts.[19] This means that wherever a *vires* point, particularly one of general importance, arises in a magistrates' or county court or in an administrative tribunal, it may well arrive — on appeal — for authoritative determination in the High Court or Court of Appeal as the case may be.[20] The argument is stronger where (as is likely, *e.g.*, in the case of a challenge to byelaws or other delegated legislation) the authority whose action is challenged is not a party to the case.[21] No doubt the authority might bring an AJR seeking a declaration of validity, but absent such proceedings it would, it seems, be obliged to accept the *ultra vires* ruling.[22]

As will now be shown, the arguments for and against permitting collateral challenge apply with differences of nuance and emphasis in the different contexts in which collateral challenges may be attempted. But, as will appear, there is in the case law on different types of collateral challenge a tendency for courts to focus heavily on one or other argument or set of arguments (be they for or against) and to pay insufficient attention to the counter-arguments.

C COLLATERAL CHALLENGE IN ORDINARY CIVIL PROCEEDINGS

1 COLLATERAL ATTACK

Where, as in *Roy v. Kensington, etc. Family Practitioner Committee*,[23] a claimant is permitted to bring a mixed public law/private law case by ordinary civil proceedings rather than by AJR, the lock-out and one-stop litigation arguments are allowed to trump the arguments against permitting collateral *vires* challenge. In *Roy* the former arguments were in substance articulated by the House of Lords as reasons for permitting collateral challenge in that case.[24] But, as already noted,[25] the House declined to adopt the broad rule that collateral attack will always be permitted to claimants in mixed public law/private law cases. It remains to be seen whether there will be circumstances in which the skills and/or tools arguments will trump the counter-arguments. In *Roy* itself the private law right was said to dominate the proceedings, suggesting that the House regarded the *vires* point as neither specially complex nor of general importance. Moreover, if a mixed public law/private law case were commenced at county court (rather than, as in *Roy*, High Court) level, the question of the jurisdiction of county courts to deal with *vires* issues[26] would arise. Further, in *Mercury Communications Ltd v. Director General of Telecommunications*[27] where the House of Lords took a flexible approach to procedural exclusivity[28] Lord Slynn said, somewhat cryptically, that "In dealing with the originating summons the trial judge can have regard to, even if he is not strictly

---

[18] *Plymouth City Council v. Quietlynn Ltd* [1987] 2 All E.R. 1040 at 1044h.
[19] Chap. 2, *section C*.
[20] See [1992] C.L.J. at 318–319.
[21] See *Bugg v. DPP* [1993] 2 All E.R. at 826j.
[22] *Defence Secretary v. Percy* [1999] 1 All E.R. 732 at 742–743.
[23] [1992] 1 All E.R. 705: *section A*, above.
[24] See Chap. 5, *section C 1 c*.
[25] *ibid.*
[26] See *sub-section 2* following.
[27] [1996] 1 All E.R. 575.
[28] See Chap. 5, *section C 1 c*.

bound by, the procedural protection [of Order 53]".[29] Does this mean that in civil proceedings the court in a mixed case could exercise a public law style discretion to decline a remedy by reference to the public authority protection values embodied in AJR?

These questions remain unresolved, indeed largely unidentified, in the case law on collateral attack by claimants. As will now be seen, the cases on the raising of public law defences to civil proceedings also display an unresolved tension between arguments for and against collateral challenge.

2 COLLATERAL DEFENCE

As already stated,[30] in *Wandsworth L.B.C. v. Winder*,[31] a council tenant was permitted to defend a possession action for non payment of a rent increase by arguing that the increase was *ultra vires*: the House of Lords held that to raise a *vires* point by way of defence to civil proceedings could not be regarded as an abuse of process within the rule in *O'Reilly v. Mackman*.[32] Lord Fraser observed: "It would . . . be a very strange use of language to describe the [tenant's] behaviour in relation to this litigation as an abuse or misuse by him of the process of the court. He did not select the procedure to be adopted. He is merely seeking to defend the proceedings brought against him by the appellants. In so doing he is seeking only to exercise the ordinary right of any individual to defend an action against him. . . ."[33] The critical point in *Winder* was that the defendant tenant would have committed no breach of her tenancy agreement (and would therefore not have been liable to the possession order sought) had the rent increase been, as she maintained, *ultra vires*. Lord Fraser said that "the arguments for protecting public authorities against unmeritorious or dilatory challenges to their decisions have to be set against the arguments for preserving the ordinary rights of private citizens to defend themselves against unfounded claims."[34] In short, if by showing that a public authority has acted *ultra vires* a defendant to ordinary civil proceedings would establish that he is therefore not liable to the private law remedy claimed against him, he should be permitted (subject to contrary statutory provision[35]) to raise the *vires* point by way of defence to those proceedings. He should not be required to seek an adjournment of the proceedings in order to mount his own AJR on the *vires* issue.

Under the *Winder* approach, then, the lock-out and one-stop procedure arguments trump not only the tools but also, by inference, the skills counter-arguments, for the proceedings in *Winder* were commenced in a county court. The jurisdiction of county courts to entertain *vires* points appears simply to have been assumed,[36] even though it is plain that the county court has no jurisdiction to hear an AJR.[37] There are, however, some problematic cases.

Contrast *Winder* with *Avon C.C. v. Buscott*[38] in which the council sought possession of its land from gypsies who were trespassing there. The gypsies' defence was that the council's decision to bring the possession proceedings was *Wednesbury* unreasonable since the council (as it did not dispute) was in breach of its statutory duty[39] to provide sites for the gypsies' caravans. The Court

---

[29] [1996] 1 All E.R. at 582c.
[30] *Section A* above.
[31] [1984] 3 All E.R. 976.
[32] [1982] 3 All E.R. 1124: see Chap. 5, *section C 1*.
[33] *ibid.*, at 981c.
[34] *ibid.*, at 981b.
[35] *cf. section D 3* below.
[36] *cf.* Lord Donaldson M.R. in *Chief Adjudication Officer v. Foster* [1991] 3 All E.R. 846 at 854d.
[37] Courts and Legal Services Act 1990, s.1(10). See Emery (1993), p. 667.
[38] [1988] 1 All E.R. 841.
[39] Caravan Sites Act 1968, s.6; duty now replaced with power: Criminal Justice and Public Order Act 1994, s.80.

of Appeal held that the gypsies could not raise the *vires* point by way of defence because they would still be trespassers even if the *Wednesbury* point could be made good and the trespass action quashed on AJR — as happened in *R. v. Welsh Secretary, ex p. Gilhaney*.[40] How is *Avon* to be distinguished from *Winder*?

In both the *Winder* and the *Avon* situations the defendant will escape liability if his *vires* challenge succeeds: in *Winder* because he has not committed any civil wrong; in *Avon* because, although he has committed a civil wrong, it is in the circumstances unlawful (*ultra vires*) for the authority to pursue him for it. On this basis it may seem unduly technical to allow the *vires* point to be raised collaterally in the *Winder* case but not in the *Avon* case — where the defendant would have to seek an adjournment of the civil proceedings in order to seek AJR.[41] But in *Avon* the Court of Appeal applied the reasoning of Scott J. in the earlier case of *Waverley B.C. v. Hilden*[42] which raised a similar point. Scott J. invoked the tools argument as the basis for prohibiting collateral defence where the defence consisted of a challenge to the *vires* of the authority's decision to bring the civil proceedings: circumstances could change between the date of the challenged decision and the date of the challenge (*e.g.* the council might have cured its breach of its public law duty to accommodate the gypsies). The court needed the flexibility of remedy on AJR in order to respond to any such change.

In *Avon* and *Waverley*, unlike *Winder*, the defendants' conduct would have remained unlawful even had they been permitted to advance the *vires* defence. But in *Tower Hamlets L.B.C. v. Abdi*[43] the Court of Appeal seems to have distinguished *Winder* on inadequate grounds. In *Abdi*, Mrs A was occupying temporary accommodation provided for her by the council in discharge of its duties under the homeless persons legislation.[44] The council had offered her permanent accommodation which she considered unsuitable. She sought to defend county court proceedings for possession of the temporary accommodation by arguing that she remained entitled to possession unless the council had a lawful basis to terminate her lawful occupation. If, as she alleged, the council's decision on the suitability of the permanent accommodation was *ultra vires*, it had no such lawful basis. Rejecting the defence as an abuse of process, the Court of Appeal distinguished *Winder* on the ground that Mrs A had no private law right to the temporary accommodation. But, surely, Mrs A was and would remain lawfully in possession as licensee until her licence was lawfully terminated. The alleged breach by the council of its public law duty to provide suitable accommodation would deprive the council of any ground for such termination. Mrs A, like the tenant in *Winder*, but unlike the gypsies in *Avon* and *Waverley*, was advancing a "substantive"[45] defence to the council's action and should have been permitted to do so collaterally.

3 CONCLUSION

As regards both collateral attack and collateral defence in ordinary civil proceedings, the main thrust of the case law is towards allowing the public policy arguments for collateral challenge to trump those against. But there are tensions in the case law which reflect the strength of the counter-arguments. The current law is unsatisfactory both because of the uncertainties identified above and, more importantly, because whenever collateral challenge is either permitted or prohibited, some substantial policy counter-argument is overridden. As will be seen in *sections D* and *E* following, these observations apply no less strongly in the context of criminal trials and

---

[40] [1987] 1 All E.R. 1005.
[41] As in *South Hams DC v. Shough*, *The Times*, December 8, 1992.
[42] [1988] 1 All E.R. 807.
[43] *The Times*, October 26, 1992; Gordon and Barlow (1992).
[44] Now under Housing Act 1996, ss.190–193.
[45] Scott J. in *Waverley* [1988] 1 All E.R. at 818a.

administrative appeals. A procedural reform which could improve the current situation will be considered in *section G*.

D COLLATERAL DEFENCE TO CRIMINAL PROCEEDINGS

Suppose that you are charged with a criminal offence consisting of the breach of regulations or byelaws, or the breach of an administrative order or licence condition. Suppose that your defence is that the regulations or byelaws are, or that the order or condition is, *ultra vires*. You maintain that breach of an *ultra vires* rule or order is no offence. But is this unqualifiedly true of all *ultra vires* rules or orders? Can the criminal court (magistrates' or Crown court) hearing your case consider and determine your *vires* defence; or, on the contrary, is the best you can hope for an adjournment of the criminal proceedings to permit you to embark on the uncertain and expensive course of seeking AJR in order to mount your *vires* challenge? And how would such AJR fare if made well outside the Order 53 time limit?

> "[T]he proper starting point"[46] in answering these questions seems to be that:
> . . . Prima facie one would expect, surely, that in the criminal proceedings an accused should be able to challenge, on any ground, the lawfulness of an order the breach of which constitutes his alleged criminal offence."[47]

How far does this represent English law?

1 EMERGING PRINCIPLES

Unfortunately, in the decade before 1997 the case law in this area became extremely unclear. In 1997 in *R. v. Wicks*,[48] the House of Lords began the process of clarification. The House continued the process in 1998 in *Boddington v. British Transport Police*.[49] But a number of important questions still remain unanswered.

The approach which emerged from *Wicks* and was endorsed in *Boddington* is as follows. Whether or not a defendant will be able to raise a *vires* defence in criminal proceedings "must depend entirely upon the construction of the statute under which the prosecution is brought. The statute may require the prosecution to prove that the act in question is not open to challenge on any ground available in public law, or it may be a defence to show that it is. In such a case, the [criminal court] will have to rule upon the validity of the act. On the other hand, the statute may upon its true construction merely require an act which appears formally valid and has not been quashed by judicial review. In such a case, nothing but the formal validity of the act will be relevant to an issue before the [criminal court]."[50]

This extract from Lord Hoffmann's speech in *Wicks* indicates that in every case where a *vires* defence is raised the following question should be considered: **on the proper construction of the relevant legislation, is it a defence to show that the rule or order whose breach constitutes the offence is *ultra vires* on any (*i.e.* no matter what) basis?** If so, the defendant may raise the *vires*

---

[46] Lord Nicholls in *R. v. Wicks* [1997] 2 All E.R. 801 at 805f.
[47] *ibid.*
[48] *ibid.*
[49] [1998] 2 All E.R. 203.
[50] *Wicks* [1997] 2 All E.R. 801 at 815h (Lord Hoffmann). See similarly *Boddington* [1998] 2 All E.R. at 208e–209b, 215c (Lord Irvine L.C.).

defence and the criminal court (magistrates' or Crown court) must determine whether or not the challenged rule or order is *ultra vires*. If not, the legality of the rule or order cannot be challenged unless it is "formally invalid". Is it possible to formulate any general principles which will indicate whether a particular case is (1) one where it is a defence to show that the act in question is *ultra vires* on any basis ("open to challenge on any ground available in public law" in Lord Hoffmann's words); or, on the contrary, is (2) one where (if the act has not been quashed on AJR) only "formal invalidity" may be raised by way of *vires* defence?

As will shortly appear, *Wicks* was held to be a case of type (2) above; and their Lordships took the view[51] that it was unnecessary there to rule definitively on general principles. The opportunity to do so, however, arose in *Boddington*. B was charged with the offence of smoking in a "non-smoking" railway carriage. The rail company was empowered by byelaws to regulate smoking on trains; in purported exercise of that power the company had prohibited smoking in all carriages. B's defence was that the company's decision to impose a total ban on smoking was *ultra vires* the power in the byelaws which permitted "regulation" but not total prohibition. Reversing the Divisional Court which had upheld the stipendiary magistrate's ruling that he had no jurisdiction to entertain the challenge, the House of Lords held unanimously that it would be a defence for B to show that the decision was *ultra vires* on any ground and that the trial court had jurisdiction to rule on the point. The House decided, however, that B's challenge failed: the company's decision was not *ultra vires* since, in the context, "regulation" permitted a total smoking ban.

In terms of general principle, as will now be explained, it seems that the *vires* defence will almost invariably be available without restriction where the prosecution is for breach of a byelaw or other delegated legislation or (as in *Boddington*) of an administrative order of general application made thereunder. On the other hand, it seems likely that the statutory context which led to the conclusion in *Wicks* will be found to be replicated in very many cases of prosecution for breach of an order or licence condition or other restriction contained in a decision addressed to a defendant individually.

2 CASES WHERE THE *VIRES* DEFENCE MAY BE RAISED ON ANY PUBLIC LAW GROUND

In 1987 in *R. v. Reading Crown Court, ex p. Hutchinson*,[52] anti-nuclear protestors who had been convicted of breaching a byelaw forbidding unauthorised entry of a military "protected area" were held on appeal to the Divisional Court to have been entitled to raise the defence that the byelaw was *ultra vires*. Observing that "justices have always had jurisdiction to inquire into the validity of a byelaw",[53] Lloyd L.J. held that despite the modern expansion and increased complexity of the notion of *ultra vires*, the skills and other public policy arguments against collateral challenge should not lock out defendants from escaping liability for action which (if the byelaw is *ultra vires*) is not criminal. *Hutchinson* may thus be seen as exemplifying in the context of criminal proceedings the same values as *Winder*[54] in civil proceedings.[55]

But in 1992 in *Bugg v. DPP*,[56] a differently-constituted Divisional Court applied the skills and legal certainty arguments to qualify the general right of collateral byelaw challenge endorsed in *Hutchinson*. In *Bugg*, also a case of collateral challenge to the validity of military installation byelaws, the Divisional Court held that a *vires* defence might be raised within the criminal

---

[51] *ibid.*, at 808c (Lord Nicholls), 814f (Lord Hoffmann).
[52] [1988] 1 All E.R. 333: see *section A* above.
[53] [1988] 1 All E.R. at 336g.
[54] *Wandsworth L.B.C. v. Winder* [1984] 3 All E.R. 976; *section C 2* above.
[55] Lord Hoffmann in *Wicks* at 813h; Lord Irvine in *Boddington* at 212c.
[56] [1993] 2 All E.R. 815.

proceedings only where a byelaw was either invalid "on its face"[57] or, possibly, made in bad faith.[58] Woolf L.J. said that a byelaw would be invalid on its face if "either it is outwith the power pursuant to which it was made because, for example, it seeks to deal with matters outside the scope of the enabling legislation, or it is patently unreasonable. This can be described as substantive invalidity."[59] Other *vires* points (constituting "procedural invalidity") could not be raised by way of defence: "A member of the public is required to comply with byelaws even if he believes they have a procedural defect unless and until the law is held to be invalid by a court of competent jurisdiction. If before this happens he contravenes the byelaw, he commits an offence and can be punished."[60]

The *Bugg* distinction between "substantive" and "procedural" invalidity was intended essentially to distinguish between *vires* matters within and those beyond the competence of magistrates and other criminal trial courts to deal with.[61] But in *Boddington* the House of Lords (following dicta in *Wicks*) endorsed *Hutchinson* and overruled *Bugg*. Subject only to clear contrary statutory provision,[62] "a man commits no crime if he infringes an invalid byelaw and has the right to challenge the validity of the byelaw before any court in which he is being tried."[63] The presumption[64] in favour of the availability of collateral defence in criminal proceedings is particularly strong where the prosecution is for breach of a byelaw or other delegated legislation or (as in *Boddington*) of an administrative order of general application made thereunder. This is because "the first time an individual may be affected by that legislation is when he is charged with an offence under it . . . Such an individual would have had no sensible opportunity to challenge [its] validity . . . until he was charged."[65] The same appears to be true of an administrative order addressed to a third party, as in *DPP v. Head*.[66] In *Boddington* the House rejected the *Bugg* distinction between "substantive" and "procedural" invalidity as being both unworkable, and, because of its uncertainty of operation, contrary to the rule of law.[67] Such distinction could not be justified by invoking skills or tools arguments against collateral challenge and produced consequences "too austere and indeed too authoritarian to be compatible with the tradition of the common law."[68]

Despite the resounding endorsement in *Boddington* of collateral defence to criminal charges as a constitutional fundamental, it is critically important to realise that, however wide the right to challenge byelaws collaterally, this right, as Lord Hoffmann said in *Wicks*, cannot "be extrapolated to enable a defendant to challenge the *vires* of every act done under statutory authority".[69] As already noted, Lord Hoffmann said that in other cases — such as *Wicks* itself — "the statute may upon its true construction merely require an act which appears formally valid and has not been quashed by judicial review."[70] In what circumstances is a statute likely to be interpreted in this way?

---

[57] *ibid.,* at 822d.
[58] *ibid.,* at 827j.
[59] *ibid.,* at 822d.
[60] *ibid.,* at 827g.
[61] [1993] 2 All E.R. at 826h. See also Lord Hoffmann in *Wicks* at 815b.
[62] Lord Irvine in *Boddington* [1998] 2 All E.R. at 217f.
[63] Lord Browne-Wilkinson, *ibid,* at 219a.
[64] Lord Irvine, *ibid.,* at 216d.
[65] Lord Irvine, *ibid.,* at 216h.
[66] [1958] 1 All E.R. 679: see [1998] 2 All E.R. at 208f–209f.
[67] Lord Steyn, *ibid.,* at 225d.
[68] *ibid.,* at 227c.
[69] [1997] 2 All E.R. at 815g.
[70] *ibid.,* at 815h.

3 CASES WHERE THE STATUTORY CONTEXT RESTRICTS THE *VIRES* DEFENCE TO CASES OF FORMAL INVALIDITY

In *Wicks* the defendant, W, was charged with failing to comply with a planning law enforcement notice in respect of alterations to a storehouse in a residential area. The notice was formally valid in that it specified the breach of planning control complained of, the steps required to be taken to remedy the breach, and the period for compliance. W appealed unsuccessfully against the notice. When eventually prosecuted for non-compliance he sought to raise the defence that the notice was *ultra vires* because "the council had acted in bad faith and had been motivated by immaterial considerations."[71] The House of Lords held that this would be no defence: the offence was committed by breach of a notice "which on its face complies with the requirements of the Act and has not been quashed on appeal or by judicial review."[72]

Vires issues of the type which W sought to raise were not included within the statutory grounds of appeal against an enforcement notice because they were "quite unsuitable for decision by a planning inspector. The question then is whether Parliament regarded them as suitable for decision by a criminal court."[73] In concluding that it did not, Lord Hoffmann endorsed the reasoning of the Divisional Court in *Plymouth City Council v. Quietlynn Ltd*[74] where, by reference to skills and legal certainty arguments, the company was not permitted to raise by way of defence to criminal proceedings its argument that the authority's refusal of a sex-shop licence was *ultra vires* because in breach of fair procedure. Lord Hoffmann observed that not only are criminal courts ill-equipped to decide *vires* matters such as those raised in *Wicks* and *Quietlynn*, but to permit defendants to raise them by way of defence to criminal proceedings would prejudice the prompt and effective enforcement of planning control.

In many other cases[75] of prosecutions for offences consisting of acts or omissions following an official order addressed to the defendant, the defendant will have chosen not to avail himself of either a statutory appeal or, in the absence of appeal provision, AJR. *Wicks* indicates that in such situations the court will be likely to conclude that the purposes of the regulatory regime in question will be frustrated by permitting defendants to mount collateral *vires* defences. On this basis the court will be likely to construe the statute as providing that an offence is committed if the official notice or determination in question is formally valid and has not been quashed by judicial review.[76]

4 CONCLUSION

After *Boddington* one may say that where a person is charged with a criminal offence consisting of the breach of a rule or order, there is a strong presumption that it will be a defence to the charge to show that the rule or order is *ultra vires*. The presumption will not be easily displaced where the prosecution is for breach of a rule or order of general application (*e.g.* byelaws, statutory instruments). But the courts may well infer that Parliament intended the presumption not to apply where the prosecution is for breach of an order or notice addressed to the defendant individually (*e.g.* planning enforcement notice, licence refusal). The following points may be made.

---

[71] *ibid.,* at 811a.
[72] *ibid.,* at 820g.
[73] *ibid.,* at 818f.
[74] [1987] 2 All E.R. 1040. See [1992] C.L.J. at 316–319.
[75] See *e.g. R. v. Davey* [1899] 2 Q.B. 301.
[76] *IRC v. Aken* [1990] 1 W.L.R. 1374 takes a similar approach in the context of *vires* defences to ordinary civil proceedings.

- There remains obvious uncertainty as to precisely when, in particular statutory contexts, this inference will or will not be drawn. So, *e.g.*, in *Dilieto v. Ealing L.B.C.*,[77] the Divisional Court distinguished *Wicks* in holding that the statutory context showed that it is a defence to a charge of breaching a planning law "breach of condition notice" that the notice was served outside the statutory time-limit; or that the condition is void for uncertainty. Given this uncertainty in the law, the rule of thumb must be: if in doubt as to the validity of a formally valid official order or notice whose breach may precipitate criminal proceedings, one should either appeal or AJR (as appropriate[78]) or comply.

- Whether the "no *vires* defence" inference (when drawn) can be regarded as justifiable is open to discussion.

  It is true that in most cases where the inference is drawn, as in *Wicks*, the defendant will have been fully apprised of the order and the grounds for challenging it in time for appeal or AJR. And in a case where there is good reason for delay in making an AJR (*e.g.* because the ground of challenge emerged long after the order was made) the delay might not prove fatal. Indeed, in an appropriate case, a defendant might hope to obtain an adjournment of the criminal proceedings to enable him to make an AJR.

  But there must be doubts as to the constitutional propriety of judicial inferences that Parliament has intended that persons may be punished for breach of *ultra vires* official orders, including orders made in bad faith. As Lord Irvine said in *Boddington*: "It would be a fundamental departure from the rule of law if an individual were liable to conviction for contravention of some rule which is itself liable to be set aside by a court as unlawful."[79] Moreover, whether a person should ever be put to the expense and uncertainty of AJR in order to escape future criminal liability for breach of an *ultra vires* order may be questioned. Civil legal aid (for an AJR) is much less widely available than legal aid to defend criminal proceedings. And there may be a "fair trial" point under the European Convention on Human Rights.[80]

  A possible legislative reform (referred to by Lord Nicholls in *Wicks*[81] and by Lords Slynn and Steyn in *Boddington*[82]) which is designed to accommodate the skills, tools and legal certainty arguments against collateral challenge while protecting the right of collateral challenge would be the creation of a procedure allowing reference of *vires* points by trial courts to the High Court. As will be explained later,[83] such procedure might apply also to non-criminal cases of collateral challenge.

- Finally, in *Boddington* the majority of the House of Lords left open the difficult issue of whether "an *ultra vires* act is incapable of having any legal consequences during the period between the doing of that act and the recognition of its invalidity by the court."[84] This is one element of the rarefied "void or voidable?" question[85]; but the clear indications are that the courts today will not feel themselves constrained by juristic concepts such as "voidness", "nullity" and "voidability" to reach a particular result.[86]

---

[77] [1998] 2 All E.R. 885.
[78] See Chap. 5, *section C 2*.
[79] [1998] 2 All E.R. at 209e.
[80] [1992] CLJ at 333–335.
[81] [1997] 2 All E.R. at 807a.
[82] [1998] 2 All E.R. at 219e, 229f.
[83] *Section F* below.
[84] [1998] 2 All E.R. at 218h (Lord Browne-Wilkinson); see also 219f (Lord Slynn), 225j (Lord Steyn); *cf.* 210h (Lord Irvine).
[85] Emery and Smythe, *JR*, pp. 61–65.
[86] But compare Forsyth (1998) with Cooke (1998).

They will instead adopt a pragmatic approach to determining the different consequences of invalidity in different contexts. For example, one should not infer from the approach adopted by the House of Lords in *Boddington* that a successful challenge to the validity of a byelaw in one case will automatically mean that all previous convictions under that byelaw are to be regarded as legally baseless.[87] On the other hand, a prisoner detained on the basis of what is later held to be a misunderstanding of the law governing the deduction of periods spent in custody on remand may obtain damages for false imprisonment. The correction of the earlier error operates retrospectively in favour of the prisoner.[88]

E COLLATERAL ATTACK IN ADMINISTRATIVE APPEALS

As already stated, in *Chief Adjudication Officer v. Foster*[89] a social security appellant was permitted by the House of Lords to attack the validity of regulations collaterally on appeal to a Social Security Commissioner. It was common ground that the *O'Reilly v. Mackman*[90] rule had no application "since there can be no abuse of process by a party who seeks a remedy by the very process which statute requires him to pursue."[91] The question was whether the Commissioners had jurisdiction to determine the validity of regulations. The House held that they did. The Commissioners are empowered by statute to correct decisions which are wrong in law, and a decision based on *ultra vires* regulations is wrong in law. The jurisdiction extended equally to social security appeal tribunals and adjudication officers,[92] although the latter would be expected to refer such points to a tribunal.[93]

It is quite clear however, that *Foster* does not enshrine a general principle that any administrative appeal authority with jurisdiction to correct decisions which are wrong in law can entertain all collateral *vires* challenges. As a matter of general principle, the question of the availability of collateral attack in appeal proceedings will turn on the correct construction of the statutory appeal provisions in question. Moreover, in *Foster* itself the *vires* issue was a point of "pure statutory construction unaffected by evidence"[94] But Lord Bridge, referring to *Bugg v. DPP*,[95] declined "to determine whether a comparable distinction between substantive and procedural invalidity should be made in relation to the jurisdiction of the commissioners. . . . [This] can be safely left for decision if and when it arises." Although, as seen, the House of Lords in *Boddington*[96] has jettisoned the *Bugg* distinction, that distinction does seek to address the fact that some *vires* points are, and some are not, suitable for determination by courts and tribunals other than the Crown Office judges on AJR. As will now be seen, there is a burgeoning case law which shows that the courts will often invoke the skills argument as the basis for a restrictive interpretation of the jurisdiction of appeal authorities to rule on *vires* issues.

---

[87] See *e.g. Percy v. Hall* [1996] 4 All E.R. 523.
[88] *R. v. Brockhill Prison Governor, ex p. Evans (No. 2)* [1998] 4 All E.R. 993.
[89] [1993] 1 All E.R. 705, *section A* above.
[90] [1982] 3 All E.R. 1124: see Chap. 5, *section C 1*.
[91] [1993] 1 All E.R. at 709a.
[92] For current social security appeal arrangements under Social Security Act 1998, see above, Chap. 2, *section B 2 c*.
[93] [1993] 1 All E.R. at 709d–f.
[94] *ibid.*, at 712g.
[95] [1993] 2 All E.R. 815: *section D* above.
[96] [1998] 2 All E.R. 203: *ibid.*

In *Aspin v. Estill*[97] a tax-payer appealed to the General Commissioners against an income tax assessment. One ground of the appeal was that his local tax office had advised him unequivocally (but wrongly in law) that he was not liable to tax. On that basis, he argued, the Revenue had acted *ultra vires* (had "abused its power") in raising the assessment. The Court of Appeal held that the Commissioners had been right to decline to entertain this argument and that the tax-payer's only possible route to a remedy on this basis was by AJR. To the argument that the Commissioners had jurisdiction to decide the *vires* point Sir John Donaldson M.R. reacted ". . . with surprise bordering on horror, because I did not believe that it was the intention of Parliament that the General Commissioners of income tax, worthy body though they are, should exercise a judicial review jurisdiction."[98] The status of this decision remains unclear after *Foster*, but more recent case law has indicated that there remain many circumstances in which public law challenges may not be mounted in administrative appeal proceedings but can be made only by AJR.

For example, on a (merits) appeal to magistrates against a local authority's refusal to register the appellant as a child-minder, it seems that the magistrates may not entertain an argument that the refusal to register should be overturned because the policy on which the refusal was based was *ultra vires*.[99] On the basis that appeal proceedings are designed to test the application of rules and policies rather than their lawfulness, an allegation that the authority's policy was *ultra vires* would be collateral in such proceedings. But other reported cases go further.

These other cases indicate that where a discretionary decision is being challenged by way of an administrative appeal procedure on the ground that the decision is *ultra vires* because failing properly to apply an established policy (*i.e.* alleging *Wednesbury/Padfield* "wrong considerations"[1]), the *vires* point may be treated as collateral and outwith the appeal tribunal's jurisdiction. In *R. v. Leeds C.C., ex p. Hendry*[2] H sought AJR of the local authority's refusal to grant him a taxi licence. The authority argued unsuccessfully that H should have challenged the refusal by way of appeal to magistrates and that the AJR should be dismissed on the *Preston* principle[3] that judicial review should not be granted where an alternative remedy is available. In that H was contending that the authority's refusal was *ultra vires* because inconsistent with its stated policy, one can see that AJR might be a more "convenient"[4] way to dispose of this public law point so that the *Preston* principle would not apply. But Latham J. indicated that, in any event, magistrates would have had no jurisdiction to entertain the *vires* point: "If [the council officer] was acting outside his authority, then going before justices was not the appropriate forum". Nor, on an appeal against a Child Support Agency (CSA) deduction-from-earnings order, may magistrates entertain a *Wednesbury/Padfield* challenge to the order based on the Agency's alleged failure to take proper account of the children's welfare. In *B v. Secretary of State for Social Security*[5] the main ground of the father's appeal was that in making the order the CSA had failed to consider the welfare of children as the legislation required. The magistrates found no evidence of such failure and dismissed the appeal. But on the father's appeal to the High Court, Thorpe J. held that the magistrates had no jurisdiction to consider the matter, which could be raised only on AJR.

---

[97] (1987) 60 T.C. 549.
[98] *ibid.*, at 556F. See also *R. v. Home Secretary, ex p. Malhi* [1990] 2 All E.R. 357 at 361f (Dillon L.J.), 366 (Stuart-Smith L.J.).
[99] *Sutton L.B.C. v. Davis* [1995] 1 All E.R. 53 at 60j (Wilson J.).
[1] See Chap. 2, *section D 6 a.*
[2] *The Times*, January 20, 1994.
[3] *R. v. IRC, ex p. Preston* [1985] 2 All E.R. 327: see Chap. 5, *section C 2 a.*
[4] Chap. 5, *section C 2 b.*
[5] *The Times*, January 30, 1995.

The last two cases appear unjustifiably restrictive of the appeal jurisdictions in question. But these and other cases[6] do indicate that, in the context of *vires* challenges raising issues other than of "pure statutory construction unaffected by evidence",[7] many tribunals and other bodies with functions of administrative adjudication are regarded as not competent to determine public law issues arising (whether collaterally or otherwise) within cases brought before them.

F COLLATERAL CHALLENGE — THE EUROPEAN LAW DIMENSION

1 COLLATERAL CHALLENGE IN COMMUNITY LAW CASES

As the ECJ made clear in the *Simmenthal* case,[8] the Community law doctrine of the supremacy of Community law over the domestic law of Member States[9] requires that "every national court must, in a case within its jurisdiction, apply Community law in its entirety and protect rights which the latter confers on individuals". What are the implications of this doctrine for the law of collateral challenge?

(a) Collateral attack

(i) *Collateral attack in administrative appeals*

As more fully explained elsewhere,[10] the effect of the *Simmenthal* doctrine in the context of administrative appeals is that if a case is properly brought before a particular administrative tribunal but the case raises collaterally (or otherwise) a *vires* issue governed by Community law, that issue automatically falls within the jurisdiction of the tribunal. The tribunal must thus entertain and determine the *vires* point.[11] The tribunal (or, on appeal from it, the court) may or may not find it necessary to make a preliminary reference[12] to the ECJ Article 234 (ex 177) of the E.C. Treaty.[13]

(ii) *Collateral attack in ordinary civil proceedings*

As will be explained in Chapter 8,[14] there are some circumstances in which official breach of Community law individual rights will constitute a private law (civil) wrong for which damages may be recovered. In these circumstances, even if public law issues arise, the rule in *O'Reilly v. Mackman*[15] should not be applied so as to terminate proceedings on the basis that they should have been commenced by AJR. To restrict a claimant's remedies in such a case by invoking the public authority protection features of AJR could hardly satisfy the *Simmenthal* requirement (above) of applying Community law in its entirety and protecting rights which the latter confers on individuals.[16]

---

[6] See Emery (1995 Pub.) p. 460.
[7] Lord Bridge in *Foster* (above).
[8] Case 106/77 *Amministrazione delle Finanze dello Stato v. Simmenthal SpA* [1978] E.C.R. 629; [1978] 3 C.M.L.R.263.
[9] Chap. 1, *section A 2.*
[10] Emery (1993), p. 662.
[11] *Shields v. Coomes (Holdings) Ltd* [1979] 1 All E.R. 462. For the E.C. law perspective see Anderson, *Ref.*, pp. 45–48.
[12] Chap. 1, *section B 3 a*. And see further *sub-section c* below.
[13] For case law see Emery (1993), p. 664.
[14] *Section E.*
[15] [1982] 3 All E.R. 1124: see Chap. 5, *section C 1.*
[16] Emery (1993), pp. 660–662.

(b) Collateral defence

The effect of the *Simmenthal* doctrine in the defence context is that it is always open to a defendant to challenge domestic official action, including primary legislation, on the ground that it is inconsistent with Community law individual rights.[17] Examples of the "Euro-defence" already met are the Sunday trading cases[18] and *R. v. Kirk*.[19]

(c) The role of the preliminary reference procedure

The apparent strangeness of administrative tribunals or magistrates' courts being asked to grapple with complex issues of E.C. law is very much offset by the availability and operation of the preliminary reference procedure.[20] Under this procedure, as already noted,[21] any national court or tribunal may, if it considers that a decision on a question of interpretation of E.C. law is necessary to enable it to give judgment, request the ECJ to give a ruling thereon.

Commonly, a trial court will not make a reference itself "before the facts of the alleged offence have been ascertained . . .", for "[i]t is generally better . . . that the question be decided by [the trial court] in the first instance and reviewed thereafter if necessary through the hierarchy of the national courts."[22] The same could be said of first-tier administrative tribunals. So, *e.g.*, *Marshall v. Southampton etc Health Authority*,[23] the case of successful Euro/*vires* collateral challenge mentioned earlier,[24] was commenced in an industrial tribunal and was referred to the ECJ by the Court of Appeal hearing M's appeal from the Employment Appeal Tribunal.

The availability of the preliminary reference procedure, of course, largely destroys the skills argument and other arguments against permitting collateral challenge in these contexts.

2 Collateral challenge in Convention law cases

As stated in Chapter 1,[25] under section 7(1) of the Human Rights Act 1998 a person claiming that he is a victim of official action which is unlawful[26] because incompatible with his Convention rights may either:

(a) bring proceedings against the authority under this Act in the appropriate court or tribunal, or

(b) rely on the Convention right or rights concerned in any legal proceedings.

The effect of this provision is to permit unrestricted collateral challenge in such cases:

---

[17] Emery (1992), pp. 335–338.

[18] Culminating in *Stoke-on-Trent C.C. v. B&Q plc* [1993] 1 All E.R. 481, ECJ. See Chap. 1, *section B 3 a*; Chap. 4, *section D 2 b*.

[19] [1985] 1 All E.R. 453. See Chap. 4, *ibid*.

[20] Emery (1992), pp. 338–339.

[21] Chap. 1, *section B 3 a*.

[22] Lord Diplock in *R. v. Henn* [1980] 2 All E.R. 166 at 196. See *e.g. R. v. Kirk* [1985] 1 All E.R. 453 (above); but *cf. R. v. Plymouth J.J. ex p. Rogers* [1982] 2 All E.R. 175.

[23] [1986] 2 All E.R. 584.

[24] Chap. 1, *section B 3 a*.

[25] *Section B 3 b (i)*.

[26] *i.e.* under s.6(1): see Chap. 1, *section A 3 b*.

(a) Collateral attack

If, *e.g.*, an appellant within the immigration, employment or social security appeals systems[27] wished to challenge the *vires* of a statutory instrument[28] on the basis of its incompatibility with a Convention right, that challenge could, under section 7(1)(a), be mounted collaterally within the appeal proceedings. Note, however, that the compatibility of primary legislation[29] with Convention rights may be challenged only by way of the section 4 "declaration of incompatibility" procedure considered earlier.[30]

(b) Collateral defence

If, *e.g.*, a person is prosecuted for a criminal offence he may, under section 7(1)(b), rely on a Convention right by way of defence. An example was given earlier[31] based on the Osteopaths Act 1993 where the defendant sought to rely on Articles 8 and 14 of the Convention. A successful collateral defence will negative any criminal liability of the defendant.

(c) No reference procedure

Whether the absence of a reference procedure of the kind which is available in E.C. cases (above) will cause difficulties in tribunal and criminal collateral challenges alleging incompatibility of official action with Convention rights remains to be seen.

3 Conclusion: the "European law argument" for Collateral Challenge

To the extent that the right to collateral challenge is more extensive in cases with an E.C. or Convention law component, the arguments against allowing/extending collateral challenge in domestic law are plainly much weakened — except, of course, that in E.C. cases, there is the possibility of a preliminary reference to the ECJ. Without a domestic reference mechanism the European law argument[32] loses some of its force. The case for creating a domestic reference procedure will now be considered.

G Collateral Challenge — Improving the Law

It will now be apparent that the English law on collateral challenge (whether in civil or criminal proceedings or in administrative appeals) is beset with unresolved tensions and consequent uncertainties.

As already explained, when a claimant, defendant or appellant is permitted to raise a *vires* issue other than by AJR, the public interest in individuals being permitted to assert rights and defences

---

[27] For details see Chap. 2, *section B 2.*
[28] Other than one protected by ss.3(2)(c) or 6(2)(b): see Chap. 1, *section A 3 b.*
[29] And of subordinate legislation protected by ss.3(2)(c) or 6(2)(b).
[30] Chap. 1, *sections A 3 b, B 3 b (ii).*
[31] Chap. 1, *section B 3 b (i).*
[32] *Section B 1* above.

within a single set of proceedings and without the procedural restraints of AJR, in effect trumps the public interest in confining the exercise of judicial review jurisdiction to courts which are best-equipped (in terms of both skills and tools) to exercise it. When, on the contrary, this is not permitted, the assertion of individual rights and defences is restricted, or even barred, by the application of the countervailing public interest considerations just mentioned. The uncertainty in the law on collateral challenge reflects the fact that legislature and judiciary have not yet fully settled the principles upon which these tensions may best be resolved in the context of the modern expansion of judicial review.

A procedural reform which could contribute to the accommodation of opposed values and to some extent prevent arguments for collateral challenge overriding (or being overridden by) arguments against, would be, as already mentioned, the creation of a procedure allowing reference of *vires* points by civil and criminal courts and appeal tribunals to the High Court.

1 THE ARGUMENT FOR A REFERENCE PROCEDURE

- Under the Woolf proposals for bridging the divide between public law and private law claims discussed in Chapter 5[33] a defendant to an ordinary civil claim would be able to have the claim transferred to the Crown Office by arguing that public law issues arise which make the case appropriate for AJR. The Crown Office judge would track the case to the appropriate procedure. Presumably also a claimant faced with a *Winder*-style *vires* defence[34] would be able to seek a transfer.

- But wholesale case transfer will surely not always be appropriate, particularly in mixed cases. There are likely to be mixed civil cases raising both public law points suitable for determination in the Crown Office list and private law points and/or issues of fact suitable for determination in ordinary civil proceedings (at High Court or county court level as appropriate). This is all the more true of mixed cases arising by way of criminal defence or in administrative appeal proceedings. What is needed is a procedural regime which, so far as possible, will ensure that difficult public law points are dealt with by the right court at the right stage in the proceedings. In civil proceedings wholesale case transfer will sometimes be the answer. Alternatively, if authoritative guidance on a public law point appears desirable at an early stage of civil, criminal or administrative appeal proceedings, it may well be possible under existing arrangements for a party to obtain an adjournment in order to initiate a separate AJR. But the following observations of Lord Nicholls in *R. v. Wicks*[35] surely apply in substance to mixed cases generally:

  "[C]ircumstances in individual cases vary infinitely. . . . For instance, not all questions of invalidity . . . are sophisticated and complex. And sometimes a short point of disputed fact, concerning what happened when a local authority was deciding to make the impugned order, might be determined as easily, or better, in a criminal court than in judicial review proceedings in the Divisional Court. If a discretion as to the more suitable forum were to exist, factors to be taken into account would include the extra expense involved for an accused in having to initiate separate proceedings of his own in the Divisional Court (the 'cumbrous duplicity of proceedings' mentioned by Lord Bridge in *Chief Adjudication Officer v.*

---

[33] *Section C 1 f.*
[34] *Wandsworth L.B.C. v. Winder* [1984] 3 All E.R. 976: *section C 2 above.*
[35] [1997] 2 All E.R. at 806g.

Foster[36]), and the greater difficulty of the accused in obtaining legal aid in civil proceedings."

A reference procedure would thus be a useful supplement to other existing and proposed ways of dealing with mixed cases.

2 THE E.C. PRELIMINARY REFERENCE PROCEDURE AS A MODEL

- Using the E.C. preliminary reference procedure[37] as a model it could be enacted that, subject to express contrary statutory provision, where a question as to whether a person or body exercising a public function has erred in law arises in proceedings before any court or tribunal in England and Wales, that court or tribunal may, if it considers that a decision on the question is necessary to enable it to give judgment, either determine the question or request the High Court to give a ruling thereon.

- The High Court should have jurisdiction to accept or to decline the reference, treating the request somewhat similarly to an application for permission to apply for judicial review. As with the Woolf proposals on case transfer, the detailed procedure and practice on the application of time limits would be critical. Plainly different considerations will apply in different types of case: *e.g.*, compare the House of Lords' approach in *Roy*[38] and *Winder* (suggesting that AJR time provisions should not normally apply in mixed civil cases) with that in *Wicks* (suggesting that they should commonly apply in the context of prosecutions for breach of orders or restrictions contained in decisions addressed to individuals). Time apart, the judge could consider the reference application with regard both to the appropriateness of the decision to seek the reference and to the likelihood of the success of the *vires* challenge. If the judge declined to accept the reference, the requesting court or tribunal would then be obliged to attempt a determination of the *vires* point. In most cases, of course, an error would be subject to correction in the ordinary course of any appeal which might later be pursued.[39]

---

[36] [1993] 1 All E.R. at 712.
[37] *Section F* above.
[38] *Roy v. Kensington etc Family Practitioner Committee* [1992] 1 All E.R. 705: *section C 1* above.
[39] See further, Emery (1992), at pp. 344–348, (1993), pp. 667–668, (1995 Pub.) pp. 457–458.

REFERENCE OF "DEVOLUTION ISSUES" UNDER GOVERNMENT OF WALES ACT 1998, SCHED. 8

An interesting prototype of "issue reference" has been enacted in Schedule 8 to the Government of Wales Act 1998 (GWA). Devolution issues[40] can be raised before the Judicial Committee of the Privy Council in proceedings instituted for the purpose by the Attorney-General.[41] Additionally, challenges may be mounted by individual parties to proceedings in which a devolution issue arises:

- **Direct attack by AJR** will no doubt be a common mode of proceeding. The judge or Divisional Court may decide the devolution issue or may refer it to the Court of Appeal.[42]
- If a devolution issue arises **collaterally in criminal proceedings** the trial court may refer it to the High Court (summary proceedings) or Court of Appeal (proceedings on indictment).[43]
- If a devolution issue arises **collaterally in ordinary civil proceedings** at county court or High Court level, it may be referred to the Court of Appeal.[44]
- **Tribunals** from which there is no appeal are obliged to refer devolution issues to the Court of Appeal; other tribunals may make such a reference.[45]
- *Note also:* the Attorney General or the Assembly (1) may require any court or tribunal to refer to the Judicial Committee any devolution issue which has arisen in any proceedings before the court or tribunal to which he or it is a party[46]; or (2) may refer to the Judicial Committee any devolution issue which is not already the subject of proceedings.[47]

It is implicit in these issue reference provisions that the case will be disposed of by the referring court or tribunal once it has received a ruling on the referred issue. It seems probable that a court or tribunal on which a *power* to refer an issue is conferred may opt (subject to contrary provision, as *e.g.* re. tribunals, above) instead to decide the issue itself. An error could be corrected on appeal in due course.

---

[40] Chap. 3, *section B 1 a;* Chap. 4, *section F.*
[41] GWA, Sched. 8, para. 4.
[42] *ibid.,* para. 7(1): AJRs are civil proceedings — see para. 1(2)(b).
[43] *ibid.,* para. 9.
[44] *ibid.,* para. 7(1).
[45] *ibid.,* para. 8.
[46] *ibid.,* para. 30.
[47] *ibid.,* para. 31.

Chapter 7

RESTRICTIONS ON LEGAL CHALLENGE

Suppose a particular case in which one would conclude that, under the rules and principles dealt with in the preceding chapters, certain official action can successfully be challenged — whether directly or collaterally. How may that conclusion be upset by an argument on behalf of the authority concerned that, in the circumstances of the case, the rules or principles relied upon cannot be invoked?

Such argument might be based either on express statutory restriction of avenues of challenge or on restriction to be implied from the nature or context of the action in question.

A EXPRESS STATUTORY RESTRICTION: OUSTER CLAUSES[1]

An express statutory provision designed to restrict or remove an avenue of challenge to official action is known as an "ouster clause".

- *Express restriction of appeal*
  In some situations, Parliament has enacted that a right of appeal which would otherwise have been available under a statutory appeal provision should not be available in particular circumstances.

- *Express restriction of judicial review*
  In other situations Parliament (sometimes in addition to removing a right of appeal) has restricted the availability of the common law supervisory judicial review jurisdiction which, as already explained,[2] is otherwise in principle available to challenge the validity of any reviewable official action.

The courts' approach to different forms of ouster clause will be examined below. But their general stance is indicated in the following observation of Lord Reid in the *Anisminic* case[3]: "it is a well-established principle that a provision ousting the ordinary jurisdiction of the courts must be construed strictly — meaning, I think, that if such a provision is reasonably capable of having two meanings, that meaning shall be taken which preserves the ordinary jurisdiction of the court."[4]

---

[1] Wade and Forsyth, *AL*, pp. 729–749; Craig, *AL*, Chap. 24; de Smith, *JRAA*, pp. 231–249.
[2] Chap. 1, *section B 2*; Chap. 3, *section A*.
[3] *Anisminic Ltd v. Foreign Compensation Commission* [1969] 1 All E.R. 208: see Chap. 4, *section B 3*.
[4] [1969] 1 All E.R. at 213A.

1 "Finality" clauses

One often encounters statutory provisions that particular types of order or decision are to be "final" or "final and conclusive". The case law shows that these "finality" clauses do not in any way affect the availability of AJR but, subject to contrary indication, will be treated as removing (ousting) any right of appeal which would otherwise have been available. An example of "contrary indication" would be the provision in the Supreme Court Act 1981[5] that the a High Court order awarding a prerogative remedy "shall be final, subject to any right of appeal therefrom." This is plainly intended not to remove any right of appeal but simply to confirm that only final, as opposed to interim, prerogative remedies may be awarded.[6]

(a) Finality clause removing existing right of appeal

The ousting effect of a finality clause is illustrated in *Pearlman v. Keepers of Harrow School*.[7] P was a tenant who claimed to have a statutory right to buy the freehold of his property. Whether or not he had such a right turned upon the rateable value of the property. That, in turn, depended on whether his installation of gas central heating counted as a "structural alteration". If it did, the increase in the property's rateable value flowing from the installation was to be disregarded, thus keeping the value of property within the right-to-buy provisions. The statute provided that a county court ruling on the structural alteration issue was to be "final and conclusive". The county court judge decided against P who applied, under the pre-1977 Order 53 procedure,[8] for certiorari alleging that the judge had erred in law. By a majority, the Court of Appeal overturned the High Court's rejection of P's application. The Court of Appeal accepted unanimously that the "final and conclusive" provision ousted the appeal which would otherwise have been available from the county court to the Court of Appeal. P's only avenue of challenge was thus under the Order 53 procedure. The court's ruling on the extent of its supervisory review jurisdiction in these circumstances will be examined below, following consideration of "no certiorari" clauses — another type of ouster clause which also featured in the *Pearlman* case.

(b) Effect of finality clause where no right of appeal to remove

The courts' interpretation of finality clauses as precluding appeal but not affecting judicial review may possibly be justified on the basis that parliamentary draftsmen have over the centuries developed other forms of provision ("no certiorari" clauses — see below) which plainly do aim to restrict the availability of the prerogative remedies. But the courts have applied the same limiting interpretation to finality clauses even where there is in the circumstances no appeal to oust. In *R. v. Medical Appeal Tribunal, ex p. Gilmore*[9] a statute provided that a person whose claim to industrial injury benefit was rejected by a medical board might appeal to a tribunal whose decision was to be final. The purpose of this finality clause is difficult to see. In *Pearlman* the finality clause was plainly intended to remove the usual right of appeal from the county court to the Court of Appeal. But in *Gilmore* there was no right of appeal at all against decisions of the tribunal: there was no appeal for the finality clause to oust. What, then, did Parliament intend by providing that the tribunal's decision was to be "final"? In *Gilmore* the Divisional Court held that the provision

---

[5] s.29(2).
[6] See Chap. 5, *section B 2 b*.
[7] [1979] 1 All E.R. 365.
[8] Chap. 5, *section B 2 a*.
[9] [1957] 1 All E.R. 796.

was to be regarded simply as an express statement of the fact that no further appeal was available. On this basis the claimant's right to invoke the supervisory review jurisdiction was unaffected. The court quashed the tribunal's decision for patent error ("error on the face of the record"[10]).

In *Gilmore* the finality clause was treated as a statement that no appeal was available beyond what had been expressly provided. Parker L.J. indicated, moreover, that in a situation where no appeal provision at all had been made, a finality clause would be treated simply as a statement that no appeal was available.[11] In both types of situation these interpretations deprive the finality clause of any effect since it is axiomatic that there is no appeal in the absence of express statutory provision.[12] The propriety of such judicial "construction" may thus be questioned. Its only possible justification is that finality clauses have, by long statutory usage in the light of established judicial interpretation, acquired a fixed, limited meaning.

2 "SHALL NOT BE QUESTIONED" CLAUSES

(a) Origins: "no certiorari" clauses

As early as 1670[13] some statutes contained provisions which on a straightforward reading seemed plainly to prohibit judicial review of the decisions of specified authorities by certiorari or the other prerogative remedies. A standard form of provision was that "No determination [or, as the case might be, conviction, order, etc.] under this Act shall be . . . removed by certiorari or otherwise into any of Her Majesty's Superior Courts of Record". As mentioned in Chapter 4,[14] the courts interpreted these "no certiorari" clauses as ousting only patent error ("face of the record") review, not jurisdictional (*vires*) review.

The basis for this restrictive interpretation was as follows.[15] At the time when Parliament began to enact no certiorari clauses, certiorari was regarded as a remedy for error on the face of the record but not for *ultra vires* action which, at that time, was remediable by tort damages rather than via judicial review.[16] In those circumstances it was plain that a no certiorari clause was intended to oust patent error review but was not intended to restrict remedies for *ultra vires* action. However, during the eighteenth century no certiorari clauses were enacted with increasing frequency. The courts reacted to this curtailment of their judicial review jurisdiction by gradually extending the ambit of *ultra vires* and, crucially, by granting certiorari and the other prerogative remedies by way of judicial review of such action. Unsurprisingly though, the courts adhered to the established doctrine that no certiorari clauses were not intended to restrict remedies for *ultra vires* action. The result was that no certiorari clauses were largely emasculated: they ousted review for patent error; but that ouster was often side-stepped by the expansion of the *ultra vires* jurisdiction.

So, in *Ex p. Bradlaugh*[17] a magistrate had invoked a statutory power to order the destruction of a book on the ground of obscenity. But the statute provided that the power could not be used unless a magistrate took the view also that the publication would be a criminal offence. The magistrate had not considered the issue of criminality. There was no provision for appeal against an order, and there was a no certiorari clause. The Divisional Court nevertheless quashed the

---

[10] See Chap. 4, *section B 2*.
[11] [1957] 1 All E.R. at 805A.
[12] Chap. 1, *section B 2*.
[13] Rubinstein, *JI*, p.72.
[14] *Section B 3 b*.
[15] For a detailed account, see Rubinstein, *JI*: summarised in Emery (1993), p. 652.
[16] Today, as will be seen in Chap. 8, *ultra vires* action causing damage is not in itself tortious.
[17] (1878) 3 Q.B.D. 509.

order by certiorari on the basis that it was *ultra vires* on account of the magistrate's failure to take account of the criminality issue. As Mellor J. observed, the consequence of holding that a no certiorari clause prevented judicial review of *ultra vires* action "would be that a . . . magistrate could make any order he pleased without question."[18] He could, for example order the destruction of a book which he considered "distasteful" rather than obscene.

Now, the courts' constitutional duty to uphold the rule of law no doubt justifies an unwillingness to interpret ouster clauses as being intended to make public authorities "laws unto themselves". But for 300 years the courts have sheltered behind that impeccable constitutional stance in order to preserve and extend their review jurisdiction by the device of constantly expanding the ambit of *ultra vires*. No doubt, as it is often said in the cases,[19] Parliament should not be taken to be protecting from judicial review official action which is devoid of legal authority — a "nullity". But, in the cases, the notion of "nullity" — of *ultra vires* action — has been expanded precisely to preserve a review jurisdiction which Parliament was often intending to oust by enacting a no certiorari clause.[20] This process is well-illustrated in modern times by the *Anisminic* case.

(b) Contemporary "shall not be questioned" clauses

In modern times Parliament has ceased to use old-style no certiorari clauses. Instead, a common form of ouster clause has been to provide that "a decision [or] determination [*of a specified authority*] shall not be called in question in any court of law". In the *Anisminic* case[21] the House of Lords confirmed that such provision, like old-style no certiorari clauses, did not preclude challenge to *ultra vires* decisions.[22] It followed that, as already described in Chapter 4,[23] Anisminic Ltd was permitted to challenge the adverse ruling of the Foreign Compensation Commission (FCC) as *ultra vires* notwithstanding the "shall not be called in question" provision. The "determination" of Anisminic's claim, being *ultra vires*, was in reality not a determination but a nullity: and the ouster clause did not protect nullities from judicial review.

What was new and controversial in the *Anisminic* case was not this restrictive interpretation of the ouster clause but, as explained in Chapter 4, the creation of the presumption of statutory interpretation that every error of law in the exercise of statutory power carries an authority *ultra vires*. This gave the court a review jurisdiction over the FCC which it would not otherwise have had and was probably intended not to have. For even if the Commission's error in interpreting the phrase "successor in title" was patently erroneous, it would, prior to *Anisminic*, probably have been regarded as *intra* [within] *vires* and thus as protected from challenge by the ouster clause. (Section 11 of the Tribunals and Inquiries Act 1958[24] had diluted existing "shall not be questioned" clauses by providing in effect that they should operate only as finality clauses.[25] But decisions of the FCC and of inferior courts were expressly excluded.)

The constitutional propriety of the creation of the *Anisminic* presumption was considered in Chapter 4.[26] What must now be considered is whether the courts have displayed a willingness to accept statutory indications in particular circumstances that the presumption is not to apply and that, accordingly, the courts' jurisdiction to review errors of law is in these circumstances restricted or removed by an ouster clause.

---

[18] *ibid.,* at 513.
[19] See *e.g.* Lord Reid in the *Anisminic* case [1969] 1 All E.R. at 213.
[20] See *e.g. Bunbury v. Fuller* (1853) 156 ER 47; *R. v. Bradford* [1908] 1 K.B. 365.
[21] *Anisminic Ltd v. Foreign Compensation Commission* [1969] 1 All E.R. 208.
[22] [1969] 1 All E.R. 208 at 213, 237.
[23] *Section B 3 a.*
[24] See now Tribunals and Inquiries Act 1992, s.12.
[25] Emery and Smythe, *JR*, p. 51.
[26] *Section B 3 b.*

3 WHEN AN OUSTER CLAUSE WILL REBUT THE *ANISMINIC* PRESUMPTION

The question may be approached by considering the following hypothetical example. Suppose that social security amending legislation provides that decisions of an appeal tribunal (UAT[27]) on appeals against refusals of a specified class of benefit shall be final and shall not be questioned in any court. If it can be shown that in rejecting a claim the UAT has erred in law, can the claimant challenge the ruling? Plainly the usual law appeal to a Social Security Commissioner[28] is ousted by the finality clause. Can the claimant instead invoke the *Anisminic* presumption and hope to obtain judicial review of the UAT decision? On both principle and authority the answer is that the UAT decision is immune from challenge except if it can be shown to be *ultra vires* in the pre-*Anisminic* "boundary" sense.[29]

The principle is as follows. In removing (by the finality clause) the otherwise existing appeal on law, Parliament has indicated that error of law alone is not in this case to ground a challenge. It is true that the "shall not be questioned" clause does not oust judicial review of action which is *ultra vires*. But for a court in these circumstances to apply the *Anisminic* presumption that all errors of law take an authority *ultra vires* and then to review the decision on that basis would be to nullify the plain intent of the finality clause. In this context judicial review must be restricted to cases of "boundary" *ultra vires*: the *Anisminic* presumption is in effect rebutted.

This argument is reflected in the case law. It will be recalled that in *Pearlman v. Keepers of Harrow School*[30] the usual right of appeal from the county court to the Court of Appeal had been ousted by a finality clause. In addition, there was a no certiorari clause.[31] In these circumstances could the tenant seek judicial review of what he alleged was the county court judge's error of law in his decision on the "structural alteration" point? A majority of the Court of Appeal held (1) that the no certiorari clause did not oust the court's jurisdiction to review *ultra vires* action; and (2) that *Anisminic* had decided that all errors of law take an authority *ultra vires*. Thus, the judge's error of law in misconstruing "structural alteration" was reviewable on that basis. But in later cases the House of Lords has disapproved this reasoning and endorsed that of Lane L.J. who dissented in *Pearlman*. Lane L.J. took the view that the *Anisminic* presumption was rebutted in circumstances like those in *Pearlman* where Parliament (by the finality clause) had expressly taken away a right of appeal on law which would otherwise have existed. In such circumstances, it was plain that error of law alone was not intended to ground a challenge: to adopt the contrary presumption would be to traduce the plain intention of the statutory provisions. Thus, Lane L.J. held, county court decisions protected by a finality clause would be reviewable only if they could be shown to be *ultra vires* in the pre-*Anisminic* "boundary" sense — which was not the case in *Pearlman*.

The House of Lords has on a number of subsequent occasions[32] approved Lane L.J.'s approach, thus indicating that wherever Parliament has expressly removed a right of appeal on law which would otherwise have existed, the legislature must be taken also as indicating that judicial review is not available to correct any error of law but only such errors as take the authority *ultra vires* in the pre-*Anisminic* "boundary" sense. The courts thus demonstrate a willingness to accept that Parliament has restricted their review jurisdiction in cases where that is plainly intended. A

---

[27] See above, Chap. 2, *section B 2 c.*
[28] *ibid.*
[29] See Chap. 4, *section B 1.*
[30] [1979] 1 All E.R. 365, *sub-section a* above.
[31] County Courts Act 1959, s.107: repealed by Supreme Court Act 1981, s.152(4).
[32] See *e.g. Re Racal Communications Ltd* [1980] 2 All E.R. at 639h, 644h; *Page v. Hull University Visitor* [1993] 1 All E.R. at 100d, 108–109.

further example of this constitutionally orthodox stance is *R. v. Home Secretary, ex p. Malhi*,[33] a case arising from restrictions imposed by the Immigration Act 1988 on appeals against deportation for breach of limited leave to remain in the United Kingdom. The 1988 Act[34] replaced the existing broad right of appeal on law with a narrow right to appeal on the basis that the minister had "no power to make the deportation order". The Court of Appeal held that "no power" was not used in the post-*Anisminic* "wider" sense of "wrong in law" but in the pre-*Anisminic* "narrower" sense of "trying to do something which in reality it could not do"[35] Here again, therefore, the *Anisminic* presumption was held to have been rebutted.

4 OUSTER CLAUSES AND COLLATERAL CHALLENGE

The above cases on finality clauses and "shall not be questioned" clauses are cases of direct challenge. The principle that neither type of ouster clause precludes *vires* review would seem to apply equally when the challenge is collateral. So, if in a case governed by a "shall not be questioned" clause a party wished to bring or defend proceedings involving a collateral *vires* challenge, the clause should not prevent that: it should prevent neither the collateral *vires* challenge nor the assertion of a cause of action. For example, suppose that a statute conferred on a nuclear waste disposal authority a power to make test excavations on private land in order to determine whether the land might be suitable for storing waste. Suppose also that decisions of the authority to exercise the power were protected by a "shall not be questioned" clause. If the authority, without hearing objections, or *Wednesbury/Padfield* unreasonably, decided to excavate and did excavate P's land, P could, it would seem, apply for judicial review alleging that the decision was *ultra vires* and adding a claim for trespass damages. The ouster clause would not preclude the *vires* challenge. Alternatively (and within *Roy* limits[36]) P could bring ordinary civil proceedings for trespass and mount a collateral attack on the *vires* of the authority's decision.

This analysis casts doubt on the Court of Appeal decision in *Jones v. Department of Employment*.[37] J had appealed successfully against a refusal of his claim to unemployment benefit. He subsequently sued the department, alleging negligence against its employee, the adjudication officer who had initially refused J's benefit application. J claimed damages in respect of the inconvenience caused to him by the delayed payment. One basis upon which the Court of Appeal struck out J's negligence action was that social security benefit decisions are protected by a finality clause once any avenues of appeal have been pursued. The court held that this clause prevented J from challenging the initial decision collaterally in negligence proceedings.[38] But this is difficult to understand. J was alleging that the decision was bad in law (*i.e. ultra vires*). It was accepted (as it had to be on the authority of *Gilmore*[39]) that the finality clause would not prevent AJR of the decision in an appropriate case. Why then should it prevent collateral *vires* challenge?

The ruling in *Jones* that a finality clause will oust collateral *vires* challenge must be regarded as doubtful in principle and inconsistent with the general tendency of the courts to interpret ouster clauses restrictively. It is of course possible for Parliament expressly to oust collateral challenge of a particular category of decision. For example, the Local Government Finance Act 1992 provides that a range of matters relating to liability to pay Council Tax (including the setting of charge

---

[33] [1990] 2 All E.R. 357.

[34] s.5(1).

[35] [1990] 2 All E.R. at 363f (Mustill L.J.); approved by the House of Lords in *R. v. Home Secretary, ex p. Oladehinde* [1990] 3 All E.R. 393.

[36] *Roy v. Kensington, etc. Family Practitioner Committee* [1992] 1 All E.R. 705: Chap. 5, *section C 1 c*.

[37] [1988] 1 All E.R. 725.

[38] [1988] 1 All E.R. at 733g-734e.

[39] *R. v. Medical Appeal Tribunal, ex p. Gilmore* [1957] 1 All E.R. 796, *sub-section 1 b* above.

TABLE 7

COMMON TYPES OF OUSTER CLAUSE AND THEIR EFFECT

CLAUSE PROVIDES:

EFFECT:

Decision shall be final

> OUSTS (OR CONFIRMS ABSENCE OF) ANY RIGHT OF APPEAL *(Section A 1)*

Decision shall not be questioned

> - OUSTS ANY EXISTING RIGHT OF APPEAL. BUT DOES NOT OUST JUDICIAL REVIEW OF *ULTRA VIRES* ACTION *(Section A 2)*
> - HOWEVER, WHERE EFFECT OF CLAUSE IS TO REMOVE EXISTING APPEAL ON POINT OF LAW, ONLY "BOUNDARY" *ULTRA VIRES* MAY BE CHALLENGED *(Section A 3)*

Certificate shall be conclusive

> - PRECLUDES ANY CHALLENGE TO FACTS STATED IN CERTIFICATE *(Section A 3)*
> - QUERY WHETHER IT PRECLUDES CHALLENGE TO **DECISIONS RECORDED** IN CERTIFICATE *(ibid.)*

Decision may be challenged only on specified grounds and within prescribed time limit

> PRECLUDES ANY CHALLENGE ON OTHER GROUNDS OR OUTSIDE TIME LIMIT *(Section A 6)*

Decision, including decision "as to [decision-making authority's] jurisdiction" shall not be questioned

> ARGUABLY PRECLUDES ANY CHALLENGE *(Section A 7 a)*

NOTE OUSTER CLAUSES UNDER E.C. AND CONVENTION LAW
- An ouster clause in a U.K. statute must be disapplied (ignored) by an English court or tribunal if it would prevent the grant of an effective remedy for breach of an E.C. individual right *(Section A 8 a)*
- If it is not possible to interpret an ouster clause compatibly with Convention rights, High Court, Court of Appeal or House of Lords may make a declaration of incompatibility *(Section A 8 b)*

levels and the calculations on which the levels are based) "shall not be questioned except by an application for judicial review."[40] This would clearly exclude both collateral *vires* attack (*e.g.* in a restitutionary claim for unlawfully demanded tax) and defence to either civil or criminal proceedings for non-payment — although, as *Wicks*[41] shows, it is likely that the courts would anyway infer that, "formal invalidity" apart, a *vires* defence was not available in criminal proceedings. The approach adopted in the 1992 Act has been criticised on the basis that "if Parliament considers that judicial review is something to be conferred in precise terms, we are a brief step away from legislation seeking to shape review as the Government wishes to see it. . . . The availability of judicial review is a constitutional fundamental. Undue limits upon its scope imposed by national law are not going to survive scrutiny at the European level."[42] The European point is taken up below.[43]

5 "CONCLUSIVE EVIDENCE" CLAUSES

The effects of two common types of ouster clause have now been examined. (*TABLE 7* summarises the effects of all the common types of ouster clause dealt with in this chapter.) Another commonly used form of clause provides not (as a finality clause[44] does) that an **act or decision** is final and conclusive but that a particular official **document** shall be treated as "conclusive" or as "conclusive evidence" of matters stated in it. As seen above, a provision that a decision etc is "final and conclusive" or "shall not be called into question in any court" does not prevent judicial review of an *ultra vires* decision which, in law, is a "non-decision", a nullity. Moreover, since *Anisminic*,[45] there is a rebuttable presumption that any decision vitiated by an error of law is *ultra vires*. It follows that in general a decision vitiated by error of law is not immunised from judicial review by a "shall not be questioned", still less by a finality clause. What is the effect of a "conclusive evidence" clause? One analysis which immediately suggests itself is that if the document in question contains an error of law, the document is a nullity and so will not be immunised from judicial review. The argument would be that a clause providing that a document is conclusive of matters stated in it would not protect a document vitiated by error of law, just as a clause providing that a decision is conclusive, or not subject to legal challenge, will not protect a decision vitiated by error of law.

R. v. Registrar of Companies, ex p. Central Bank of India[46] concerned a statutory provision relating to certificates issued by the Registrar of Companies to persons registering charges against companies' assets. The statute[47] provided that a certificate was to be "conclusive evidence that the requirements of . . . [the] Act as to registration had been complied with". The Court of Appeal held that, at any rate in the absence of any allegation of bad faith against the registrar, no evidence might be brought to attack the validity of the certificate by showing that a time limit for registration had in fact been breached. "The whole point of creating the register . . . is to give security to persons relying on the certificate. If it were possible to go behind the certificate . . . no lender . . . could be secure. . . ."[48] This decision is, however, of limited scope. It shows that a statutory provision to the effect that certain facts are to be conclusively presumed to be as stated

---

[40] s.66(1). See also the "certified contract" provisions of the Local Government (Contracts) Act 1997: Chap. 9, *section B 1 f.*

[41] *R. v. Wicks* [1997] 2 All E.R. 801: Chap. 6, *section D 3.*

[42] Bradley (1991), p. 390.

[43] *Sub-section 8.*

[44] *Sub-section 1* above.

[45] *Anisminic Ltd v. Foreign Compensation Commission* [1969] 1 All E.R. 208, *sub-section 2 b* above.

[46] [1986] 1 All E.R. 105.

[47] Companies Act 1948, s.98(2); see now Companies Act 1985, s.401(2).

[48] Harman L.J. in *Re C L Nye Ltd* [1970] 3 All E.R. 1061, cited by Lawton L.J. at [1986] 1 All E.R. 116.

in an official document means what it says. But it leaves unanswered the question of the effect of a statutory provision which on its face seems to immunise from challenge not a documentary statement that facts are as are they are certified to be but, instead, a decision-making process of the types to which finality and "shall not be questioned" clauses commonly apply.

Consider, *e.g.*, section 1(3) of the European Communities Act 1972 which provides that an Order in Council declaring that a treaty is a Community Treaty "shall be conclusive that it is to be so regarded." In *R. v. HM Treasury, ex p. Smedley*[49] Slade L.J. said that the subsection would not "empower [the Crown] to purport to bring into the ambit of the 'Community Treaties' an international agreement which demonstrably had no connection whatever with 'the Treaties' as defined. . . ."[50] The purpose of the "conclusive" provision was to avoid judicial intervention "in borderline cases." Its purpose was not to empower the Crown to confer the legal status of a Community Treaty upon, say, a United Kingdom trade agreement with Saudi Arabia. In this politically sensitive area, judicial review may be confined to the correction of *e.g.* regious errors, but the critical point is that the clause does not wholly preclude judicial review.

Similar observations, surely, could be made about the purpose of section 40(3) of the Crown Proceedings Act 1947. This provides that "A certificate of a Secretary of State: (a) to the effect that any alleged liability of the Crown arises otherwise than in respect of His Majesty's Government in the United Kingdom [thus preventing any proceedings being taken[51]] . . . shall, for the purposes of this Act, be conclusive as to the matter so certified." Suppose that a hiker who had been shot near a British military establishment in the United Kingdom by a member of the British armed services were to sue in tort, alleging that the Crown was vicariously liable for the act of its servant. Surely Parliament did not intend the above provision to empower the Foreign or Home Secretary to issue (albeit in good faith) an unchallengeable certificate immunising the Crown from liability. Unfortunately, in *R. v. Foreign Secretary, ex p. Trawnik*[52] the Court of Appeal seems to have ruled to the contrary. The court dismissed an AJR of a section 40(3)(a) certificate relating to prospective liability of the Crown in nuisance for the establishment of a machine gun range in West Berlin. May L.J. (with whom Gibson L.J. agreed) said: "[A]n application for judicial review . . . if based upon the proposition that that which has been certified is so clearly wrong that the certificate must be a nullity, would be bound to fail because the evidence which counsel would wish to call to prove this very thing could not be adduced." The reasoning in *Trawnik* seems inconsistent with that in *Anisminic*. In *Trawnik* the court distinguished *Anisminic*, apparently on the basis that the ouster clause there referred to a "determination" whereas in *Trawnik* what was protected was a certificate. Surely, though, where a certificate is the legal vehicle of a decision, it is inconsistent with *Anisminic* to hold that a certificate which can be shown to be a nullity is immunised from challenge by a conclusiveness provision.

6 TIME-LIMITED OUSTER CLAUSES

A type of ouster clause will now be considered which is essentially different from those types already encountered, both in its statutory purpose and in the judicial interpretation it has received.

(a) The standard formula

In certain areas of official decision-making Parliament has taken the view that if there is to be any challenge to the validity of decisions, it must come very quickly or not at all. Prominent examples

---

[49] [1985] 1 All E.R. 589.
[50] *ibid.*, at 598e.
[51] s.40(2)(b).
[52] *The Times*, February 21, 1986.

are planning[53] and compulsory purchase.[54] Essentially, the standard form of statutory provision in these and other areas[55] permits the validity of certain specified types of decision to be challenged only:

- on specified grounds,
- by application to the High Court by any person aggrieved,
- within six weeks of the decision being made.

This mechanism of challenge apart, such decisions "shall not be questioned in any legal proceedings whatsoever".[56]

Before examining the courts' interpretation of this type of ouster clause it may be noted that the grounds on which decisions can be challenged under these standard time-limited clauses are either:

- that the order is not within the powers of the Act; or
- that any requirement of the Act has not been complied with, to the substantial prejudice of the applicant.

It seems[57] that "not within the powers" embraces all categories of *ultra vires* action, *i.e.*, since *Anisminic*[58] all varieties of error of law which are now reviewable under the common law supervisory review jurisdiction. The second limb of the statutory formula (failure to comply with any requirement of the Act) plainly includes *ultra vires* action but seems also[59] to permit challenges for breach of "directory" procedural requirements[60] whose breach can be shown substantially to have prejudiced the applicant although not rendering the action in question *ultra vires*.

(b) Judicial interpretation

(i) *The* East Elloe *case*

In *Smith v. East Elloe RDC*[61] S's house had been demolished by the council in reliance on a compulsory purchase order (CPO) made in 1948. Almost six years later S sued the council for trespass, alleging that the CPO had been procured by the deceit of the clerk to the council. S also sued the clerk for misfeasance in public office.[62] The House held by 3:2 that the trespass action should be struck out: the ouster clause meant what it said, and so precluded any attack upon the validity of the CPO outside the six week period. Lords Reid and Somervell dissented on the basis that the clause should not be construed to protect an order tainted by bad faith. (It may be noted that the trespass action involved a collateral attack upon the validity of the CPO similar to that which succeeded, though based on unfairness rather than deceit, in *Cooper v. Wandsworth Board*

---

[53] Town and Country Planning Act 1990, ss.284, 288.
[54] Acquisition of Land Act 1981, ss.23–25.
[55] Annex 2 of LCCP 126 (1993) contains a comprehensive survey of all such clauses in force on September 1, 1992.
[56] See *e.g.* Town and Country Planning Act 1990, s.284(1); Acquisition of Land Act 1981, s.25.
[57] See Wade and Forsyth, *AL*, pp. 749–756 analysing the sometimes confused case law on both grounds and standing under the standard-form clause.
[58] *Anisminic Ltd v. Foreign Compensation Commission* [1969] 1 All E.R. 208, *sub-section 2 b* above.
[59] Wade and Forsyth, *AL*, pp. 750–751.
[60] See Chap. 4, *section E 1.*
[61] [1956] 1 All E.R. 855.
[62] See Chap. 8, *section D.*

of Works[63] under nineteenth century legislation not containing a modern time-limited ouster clause.) The House was unanimous that since the misfeasance action against the clerk did not impugn the validity of the order it was not affected by the ouster clause so should be permitted to proceed.

It should be observed that the standard-form time-limited ouster clause prohibits not only any challenge outside the six week period; but also any challenge within that period by any other form of proceedings. On this basis, *e.g.*, a collateral trespass action seeking an injunction against implementing an *ultra vires* CPO would fail even if it were commenced within the six week period. But within that period an adjournment would no doubt be permitted, so as to permit a direct challenge to be mounted by the statutory procedure.[64]

(ii) *Same words, different effect?*

Why should a statutory provision that an order "shall not be questioned" in the courts have a radically different effect according to whether the prohibition (as in *East Elloe*) is preceded by a six-week period in which a challenge can be made, or (as in *Anisminic*) is absolute? In the latter case the "shall not be questioned" provision was held not to oust judicial review of an *ultra vires* order; in the former, the provision was held to oust judicial review totally after the expiry of the six week period. Can the different approaches be reconciled?

In *Anisminic* the House of Lords appeared to cast doubt on the *East Elloe* case, observing that the authorities on the effect of no certiorari clauses had not been cited there.[65] This disapproval suggested that the *Anisminic* approach might in the future be held to apply as much to the time-limited type of "shall not be questioned" clause as to the absolute type. But subsequently in *R. v. Environment Secretary, ex p. Ostler*[66] and in *R. v. Cornwall C.C., ex p. Huntington*[67] the Court of Appeal has reconciled the approaches on the basis that:

> "In the *Anisminic* case the ... Act ousted the jurisdiction of the court altogether. It precluded the court from entertaining any complaint at any time about the determination. Whereas in *Smith v. East Elloe* the statutory provision has given the court jurisdiction to inquire into complaints so long as the applicant comes within six weeks. The provision is more in the nature of a limitation period than of a complete ouster."[68]

Moreover, in the *Huntington* case the court made it clear that the standard time-limited clause will not merely rebut the *Anisminic* presumption that all errors of law take an authority *ultra vires* but will, as indicated in the *East Elloe* case, preclude judicial review even of orders which are *ultra vires* in the pre-*Anisminic* "boundary" sense.[69] It seems, then, that under the standard time-limited clause the courts will treat themselves as having no jurisdiction to entertain any challenge whatever outside the time limit, just as they have no jurisdiction to hear actions time-barred under the Limitation Act 1980.

One can see that there is a public interest in imposing a time limit on the courts' jurisdiction to quash or reverse official action in areas such as planning or compulsory purchase. It is perhaps not sensible to contemplate the restoration by judicial order of cottages or green fields where shopping malls or motorways now stand. Moreover, as the *East Elloe* case itself shows, a person

---

[63] (1863) 14 C.B.N.S. 180: see Chap. 4, *section E 2 a*.
[64] See also *R. v. Smith* (1984) 48 P.C.R. 392 (adjournment of criminal proceedings).
[65] [1969] 1 All E.R. at 213G, 238G, 246G.
[66] [1976] 3 All E.R. 90.
[67] [1994] 1 All E.R. 694.
[68] [1976] 3 All E.R. at 95c; [1994] 1 All E.R. at 699h.
[69] See Chap. 4, *section B 1*.

damaged by an order or decision made in bad faith can sue in tort (misfeasance in public office) unaffected by the six-week limitation period. On the other hand, for Parliament to rule out after six weeks any other form of damages action may be regarded as unjustifiably restrictive. It is true, of course, that in cases not governed by time-limited ouster clauses AJR must normally be commenced within three months, and statutory appeals are commonly required to be lodged within three, four or six weeks. But tort actions raising *vires* issues collaterally are governed by private law limitation periods, not by short public law time limits.[70] No obvious compelling public interest is served by a rule that a person whose house has been demolished in reliance upon an *ultra vires* compulsory purchase order may not obtain trespass damages unless he sues within six weeks of the order being made.

7 CAN PARLIAMENT OUST JUDICIAL REVIEW ENTIRELY?

(a) In particular situations

There are many public authorities whose acts and decisions are not subject to any appeal or other statutory mechanism of challenge. If Parliament were to enact an ouster clause which provided that all the actions of a particular such authority were to be totally immune from judicial review, one would surely have to accept that Parliament had intended to create an authority with "full and autonomous powers to fix its own area of operation".[71] In the *Anisminic* case in 1968 Lord Wilberforce said that "although in theory perhaps [this] may be possible", it had "so far not been done in this country".[72] Is this still true today?

The Interception of the Communications Act 1985 regulated the issue of government warrants for the interception of communications sent by post or via public telecommunication systems. The Act[73] set up an independent tribunal of five experienced lawyers to investigate individual complaints of alleged government contraventions of the statutory regime. The tribunal has powers to quash unlawful warrants and to order compensation. But, because of the sensitivity of this area of government operations, the statute provides that "decisions of the Tribunal (including any decisions as to their jurisdiction) shall not be subject to appeal or liable to be questioned in any court".[74] The same clause has been used in subsequent statutes in similarly sensitive areas.[75] Do these words wholly oust judicial review of the determinations of the tribunal in question?

The statute prohibits judicial review not simply of the tribunal's "decisions" (which, on the *Anisminic* reading, would not cover *ultra vires* decisions) but, expressly, of their "decisions as to their jurisdiction." This seems to mean "decisions as to how far the tribunal's jurisdiction (*vires*) extends", and so appears to give the tribunal (in Lord Wilberforce's words) "autonomous powers to fix its own area of operation". It thus seems most unlikely that the tribunal's decisions (even if *ultra vires* on ordinary principles) can be challenged for illegality (including *Wednesbury/Padfield* wrong considerations) or procedural impropriety. But would a "decision which is so outrageous in its defiance of logic or of accepted moral standards that no sensible person who had applied his mind to the question to be decided could have arrived at it"[76] be regarded as a (bona fide) "decision as to jurisdiction" and thus immunised from judicial review by this wording?

---

[70] Chap. 5, *section C 1 c.*
[71] Lord Wilberforce in *Anisminic* [1969] 1 All E.R. at 244B.
[72] *ibid.*
[73] s.7.
[74] s.7(8).
[75] Security Service Act 1989, s.5(4); Intelligence Services Act 1994, s.9(4); Police Act 1997, s.91(10).
[76] Lord Diplock in the *CCSU* case (*Council of Civil Service Unions v. Minister for the Civil Service*) [1984] 3 All E.R. at 951: see Chap. 4, *section D 1 b.*

Such egregious decisions are perhaps unlikely from the tribunals set up by the 1985 and subsequent statutes in which this form of ouster clause has been employed. Moreover, the courts' unwillingness to review government invocations of danger to national security[77] suggests that in these contexts the courts may take the view (expressed obiter in a case governed by the law prior to the 1985 Act) that they have "no supervisory or investigative function".[78] But if ouster clauses of this nature came to be used in government statutes in contexts where the arguments for judicial restraint were felt to be less compelling, it is possible that the courts would take the view that Parliament "could not have intended" to immunise from review decisions for which no rational basis could be perceived in the empowering legislation.

(b) Abolishing judicial review generally

The words in inverted commas in the previous sentence are a formula by which the courts acknowledge the legislative supremacy of Parliament. The courts have not questioned the power of Parliament, by statute, to oust their jurisdiction to review particular categories of official decision. But, as the case law discussed in this chapter shows, the effect and extent of any particular ouster clause can be largely determined by the courts themselves, so long as their general supervisory review jurisdiction remains unchallenged by Parliamentary enactment.

This observation does prompt the question "What happens if a party with a large majority in Parliament uses that majority to abolish the courts' entire power of judicial review in express terms?"[79] The orthodox answer, based on the doctrine of *ultra vires*, is that in legal as distinct from political or constitutional terms, the courts could neither entertain any challenge to the validity of the abolishing statute nor (while the statute remained unrepealed) in any circumstances exercise the judicial review jurisdiction which the statute had abolished.[80] And in modern times this has been the view invariably expressed by judges when deciding cases in which the question of the reviewability of statutory provisions has arisen.[81] Recently, however, a number of judges have suggested extra-judicially that the doctrine of the legislative supremacy, or sovereignty, of Parliament should be understood in a more limited sense, in which legal sovereignty is somehow shared between Parliament and the Courts.[82] On this approach, legislation abolishing the courts' entire power of judicial review would not be applied by the courts. In 1995, extra-judicially, Lord Woolf expressed the view that in these circumstances "I myself would consider there were advantages in making it clear that ultimately there are even limits on the supremacy of Parliament which it is the courts' inalienable responsibility to identify and uphold."[83] It has even been suggested that the new approach would enable the courts in judicial review proceedings to characterise as unlawful a statutory provision abolishing certain fundamental rights such as free speech and other rights protected in the European Convention on Human Rights and similar instruments.[84] These suggestions were made prior to the incorporation of the Convention by the Human Rights Act 1998, the effect of which in this context is considered below.[85]

---

[77] See Chap. 3, *section B 2 a.*

[78] *R. v. Home Secretary, ex p. Ruddock* [1987] 2 All E.R. 518 at 527 (Taylor J.); but question left open in *R. v. Security Service Tribunal, ex p. Harman* February 14, 1992 (unreported).

[79] Woolf (1995), at p. 69.

[80] Chap. 4, *section B 3 a.*

[81] See Irvine (1996 *Wed.*) pp. 75–76.

[82] Sedley (1995), pp. 389 *et seq.*; Woolf (1995), n.83 below, and, judicially, in *R. v. Parliamentary Commissioner for Standards, ex p. Al Fayed* [1998] 1 All E.R. 93, 94j.; *cf.* Woolf (1998) pp. 581, 590, 592.

[83] Woolf (1995) p. 69; likewise, Cooke (1997), p. 79.

[84] Laws (1995), pp. 81 *et seq.*

[85] *Sub-section 8 b.*

As regards statutory abolition of judicial review, it is true that "If there were ever such an assault [upon the basic tenets of democracy], it would surely be on the political battlefield that the issue would be resolved. [One may] wonder whether it is not extra-judicial romanticism to believe that judicial decision could hold back what would, in substance, be a revolution."[86] However, the articulation of these views by serving judges not only shows that clauses ousting review in particular contexts will continue to receive the most limited possible construction but also has a certain resonance with the willingness today of Parliament itself to contemplate the subjection of its enactments to judicial review in the Community law context — and, to a more limited extent (via "declarations of incompatibility") under the Human Rights Act 1998.[87]

The operation of ouster clauses in the Community law and Convention law contexts will now be considered.

8 OUSTER CLAUSES IN THE COMMUNITY AND CONVENTION LAW CONTEXTS

(a) Community law: European Communities Act 1972

An ouster clause in the Community law context will have the same effect as in the context of pure domestic law, with the very important proviso that the clause will not be applied where its effect would be to prevent the grant of an effective remedy for breach of an E.C. individual right. The reasoning is as follows.

Under section 2(4) of the European Communities Act 1972 all United Kingdom statutes, whether enacted before or after the 1972 Act, are subject to directly effective Community law.[88] As already explained,[89] it is a general principle of Community law that a person is entitled to a judicial determination of the question whether his or her E.C. individual rights have been transgressed and to an effective judicial remedy if they have. It follows from this that an ouster clause in a United Kingdom statute must be disapplied (ignored) by an English court or tribunal if it would prevent the grant of an effective remedy for breach of an E.C. individual right. This proposition may be illustrated by two cases discussed earlier: *Factortame Ltd v. Transport Secretary (No. 2)*[90] in which the House of Lords disapplied a statutory provision in so far as it precluded the grant of interim relief in respect of an alleged breach of E.C. individual rights; and *Johnston v. Chief Constable of the RUC*[91] in which a conclusive evidence clause was disapplied so as to permit judicial scrutiny of an executive ruling that a particular instance of sex discrimination in the employment field was justified on public interest grounds.

As explained above, the orthodox view in the purely domestic English law context is that Parliament can wholly oust judicial review either in particular cases or, even, generally. An indication of the far more limited potential of ouster clauses in the Community law context may be gained by contrasting *Johnston* with the *Trawnik* case,[92] discussed above. The outcome in *Johnston* contrasts sharply with that in *Trawnik* where the "conclusive evidence" clause was held to preclude judicial review entirely. Moreover, *Johnston* demonstrates that the courts' unwillingness in the purely domestic context to review government invocations of danger to national security cannot be sustained in the Community law context.[93]

---

[86] Irvine (1996 *Wed.*) p. 77.
[87] s.4: see Chap. 1, *section A 3 b.*
[88] Chap. 1, *section A 2.*
[89] Chap. 4, *section D 2 b.*
[90] [1991] 1 All E.R. 70: Chap. 5, *section B 2 b.*
[91] [1986] 3 All E.R. 135: Chap. 4, *section D 2 b.*
[92] *R. v. Foreign Secretary, ex p. Trawnik, The Times,* February 21, 1986.
[93] See further, Chap. 3, *section B 2 a.*

COMMUNITY LAW: ENTRENCHMENT AND PARLIAMENTARY SOVEREIGNTY

The *Factortame* and *Johnston* cases show that the effect of section 2(4) of the European Communities Act 1972 is to empower courts and tribunals to override statutory restrictions in order to protect E.C. individual rights. But is this effect of the 1972 Act irreversible? No doubt (say following a referendum) a future United Kingdom government could withdraw from the European Union. In these circumstances Parliament could surely repeal the 1972 Act which, together with E.C. individual rights, would cease to have effect in English law. But, while the United Kingdom remains within the Union, how should English courts and tribunals react if faced with a statutory provision — perhaps an ouster clause — which states that it is to apply notwithstanding the provisions of the 1972 Act? Are these provisions "entrenched", *i.e.* is the legal protection conferred by section 2(4) itself irremovable by statute? Or would the later Act prevail over the 1972 Act provisions?

The latter alternative clearly represents orthodox United Kingdom constitutional theory and appears implicit in Lord Bridge's explanation in *Factortame Ltd v. Transport Secretary*[94] of the effect of section 2(4) as requiring United Kingdom courts and tribunals to proceed on the basis that all previous and subsequent statutes are to be read as incorporating a statement that their provisions are to operate without prejudice to directly effective E.C. individual rights. On this analysis, a contrary provision in a later statute would prevail. However Sir William Wade has asserted[95] that in *Factortame Ltd v. Transport Secretary (No. 2)*[96] Lord Bridge adopted a fundamentally different approach when he stated that in enacting the 1972 Act Parliament had voluntarily limited its sovereignty.[97] This conclusion might be based on the proposition that the United Kingdom's decision to join the European Community was an act of political autonomy which (because of the Community law doctrine of the supremacy of Community law over the national, *i.e.* domestic, law of Member States)[98] entailed a voluntary partial surrender of legal sovereignty. Short, at any rate, of United Kingdom withdrawal from the EC, this partial surrender would be irreversible. The answer to the question posed at the end of the last paragraph thus remains unclear.

(b) Convention law: Human Rights Act 1998

Under the Human Rights Act 1998, legislation must, so far as possible, be interpreted in a way which is compatible with Convention rights.[99] One of the Convention rights is the right (under Article 6(1)) to a fair trial before an independent and impartial tribunal for the determination of civil rights and obligations. As explained earlier,[1] many claims which persons may assert against public authorities have been held by the Strasbourg authorities to be "civil rights" for this purpose, *e.g.* in such fields as planning, licensing of commercial activities and social security. It is difficult to see that it would be possible for English courts or tribunals to interpret common-form ouster clauses of the types discussed in this chapter differently in the context of the 1998 Act. A statutory ouster clause which, on this basis, produced a situation incompatible with Article 6

---

[94] [1989] 2 All E.R. 692 at 700–701.
[95] Wade (1996).
[96] [1991] 1 All E.R. 70.
[97] *ibid.*, at 107j–108c.
[98] Chap. 1, *section A 2.*
[99] s.3(1): see Chap. 1, *section A 3 b.*
[1] Chap. 4, *section E 2 c (i).*

would remain fully effective,[2] but the High Court, Court of Appeal or House of Lords could, under section 4(5) of the 1998 Act make a declaration that the clause was incompatible with the Convention right. As already mentioned,[3] under section 4(6) such declaration does not affect the provision's validity, continuing operation or enforcement and is not binding on the parties to the proceedings in which it is made. It would nevertheless be likely to precipitate corrective legislation.[4]

CONVENTION LAW: ENTRENCHMENT AND PARLIAMENTARY SOVEREIGNTY

The power of courts to pronounce on the compatibility with Convention rights of ouster clauses and other statutory provisions does not, of course, come close to their power under the 1972 Act to disapply statutory provisions in order to protect E.C. individual rights. But the question still arises, as with E.C. individual rights, whether such protection as is afforded by the 1998 Act to Convention rights may be regarded as entrenched, preventing Parliament in future from withdrawing that protection. On analysis[5] the provisions of the 1998 Act, in particular section 4(6), do seem to fulfil the Government's stated intention[6] to avoid entrenchment — and, in this context at least, not to erode Parliamentary sovereignty. But in the area of fundamental rights the doctrine was being questioned even prior to the 1998 Act,[7] and it has been asked "[h]ow far the courts will continue to respect [the doctrine] if the Act succeeds in fostering a rather stronger culture of legal rights than has hitherto existed in the U.K."[8] Against this, Lord Woolf M.R. said extra-judicially in 1998 that in not empowering the courts to strike down statutes, the Act "reflects the views of the vast majority of, if not possibly all, the senior judiciary".[9]

B IMPLIED RESTRICTION

When, in the absence of any statutory avenue of challenge, will an attempt to invoke judicial review fail on the basis that the jurisdiction is treated by the court as restricted not expressly, by an ouster clause, but impliedly, by the nature or context of the action in question?

1 THE UNCERTAIN AND FLEXIBLE BOUNDARIES OF JUDICIAL REVIEW

One may briefly recall and collect here the many circumstances, met in earlier chapters, in which it will not be clear without litigation whether certain acts or decisions may be challenged by judicial review.

As explained in Chapter 3, an act or decision may be immune from judicial review because it is held not to be an exercise of official power. This may be so even though at first sight the case

---

[2] 1998 Act, s.3(2)(b).
[3] See Chap. 1, *section A 3 b.*
[4] *Rights Brought Home,* para. 2.10.
[5] Bamforth (1998).
[6] *Rights Brought Home,* paras. 2.10–2.16.
[7] *Subsection 7b* above.
[8] Bamforth (1998), p. 582.
[9] Woolf (1998), p. 592.

might appear to fall within the extensions of review jurisdiction initiated by, *e.g.*, the *CCSU*,[10] *Datafin*,[11] *Gillick*[12] or *Lewisham*[13] cases. Where the courts decline to continue to extend the reach of judicial review in a particular direction they do so essentially on the basis that the nature or context of the action in question makes it unsuitable for review. This judicial self-restraint, where it occurs, may be regarded as an important variety of implied restriction of judicial review.

Chapters 4 and 5 provide numerous other examples of implied restrictions reflecting judicial self-restraint:

(1) Under the orthodox *Wednesbury/Padfield* approach to review of discretionary power the courts have refused to weaken "strong" (broadly-expressed) discretions by presuming that Parliament "must have intended" certain substantive limitations such as conformity with the European Convention on Human Rights or a general principle of proportionality.[14] This approach will be much changed under the Human Rights Act 1998.

(2) The courts have often invoked the nature or statutory context of particular official action as the basis either for holding that there is no duty to act fairly[15] or for minimising the content of such duty, *e.g.* by not requiring reasons to be given for a decision.[16]

(3) The law on standing for judicial review[17] and the discretionary nature of public law remedies[18] affords great scope for the courts to decline to review reviewable action in what are regarded as (for one reason or another) inappropriate contexts.

2 INTERNAL OR EXTERNAL REVIEW PROCEDURES?

Chapter 5 concludes with a further instance of implied restriction of judicial review, *i.e.*, under the operation of the *Preston* "alternative remedy" principle.[19] It may be said, of course, that here the restriction does not deprive a person of a remedy for unlawful official action but simply channels the complaint to a more appropriate form of independent review in the appeals process.

Recently, however, in a number of situations, central government has set up internal review procedures designed substantially to restrict judicial review of the official decisions in question. As will now be explained, where the judges accept that such decisions are indeed immune from judicial review, one encounters a further category of implied restriction of judicial review.

A prime example of this government strategy is the internal review process created as the avenue of challenge to decisions as to payments out of the discretionary part of the social fund.[20] These payments (from a cash-limited fund) comprise "budgeting" and "crisis" loans and community care grants. The internal review process is provided[21] instead of the usual appeal process in the social security field.[22] Hadfield[23] explains how this internal process is aimed at

---

[10] *Council of Civil Service Unions v. Minister for the Civil Service* [1984] 3 All E.R. 935: Chap. 3, *section B 2 a.*
[11] *R. v. Panel on Take-overs and Mergers, ex p. Datafin plc* [1987] 1 All E.R. 564: *ibid, B 2 b.*
[12] *Gillick v. West Norfolk, etc. HA and Department of Health and Social Security* [1985] 3 All E.R. 402: *ibid., C 1 b.*
[13] *R. v. Lewisham L.B.C., ex p. Shell U.K. Ltd* [1988] 1 All E.R. 938: *ibid, C 2 a.*
[14] Chap. 4, *section D 1 c.*
[15] *ibid., E 2 d.*
[16] *ibid., E 2 c.*
[17] Chap. 5, *section A 3.*
[18] *ibid., B 4.*
[19] *R. v. IRC, ex p. Preston* [1985] 2 All E.R. 327: *ibid., C 2.*
[20] Social Security Contributions and Benefits Act (SSCBA) 1992, s.138(1)(b).
[21] Social Security Act 1998, s.38 replacing Social Security Administration Act 1992, s.66.
[22] See Chap. 2, *section B 2 c.*
[23] Hadfield (1995).

"judge-proofing" what are plainly in principle reviewable decisions of the social security authorities in the administration of this fund. Essentially, fund-allocation decisions are made by departmental officers on behalf of the Secretary of State. The officers themselves and, then, Social Fund Inspectors (SFIs) have a broad power to review such decisions. This does "facilitate an extensive re-examination" and "goes a not insignificant way towards meeting the . . . Franks criteria[24] of openness, fairness and impartiality as deemed appropriate for tribunal adjudication. This is not to say, however, that SFI determinations are truly comparable with a tribunal hearing, nor that SFIs are as well equipped (in terms of training, knowledge or expertise) to deal with judicial review principles as are the courts."[25]

Neither this nor other instances of internal review procedure,[26] contain provisions expressly ousting judicial review. But the more extensive a procedure and the nearer it approaches to the paradigms just mentioned, the less the judges will be inclined to intervene. Hadfield observes that "There have been very few judicial reviews of SFIs' decisions . . . and in general terms, the courts have indicated (whilst not necessarily always finding for the respondent) a 'hands-off' approach."[27] In this sense, therefore, the provision of internal review mechanisms may constitute a de facto restriction on judicial review.

3   UNREVIEWABLE EXECUTIVE RULE-MAKING POWERS?

The social fund legislation referred to above exemplifies another and more worrying method of de facto ouster of judicial review. SFOs are required to determine any question regarding applications for Social Fund benefits "in accordance with any general directions issued by the Secretary of State . . ."[28] These may include directions not to make awards or determine applications in circumstances specified by the Secretary of State.[29] In *R. v. Social Services Secretary, ex p. Stitt*[30] the Court of Appeal accepted that these provisions were sufficiently wide to authorise directions excluding whole categories of benefit such as the domestic assistance and respite care sought by the applicant.

Thus, ministerial "directions" under the 1992 Act, as Feldman points out "have all the effects of statutory instruments without [the] democratic safeguards"[31] which, as explained earlier,[32] have led the courts to adopt a restrained approach to judicial review of such instruments. Here, the de facto ouster of judicial review is achieved by the extraordinary breadth of the legislative power; a power which is thus in effect subject to neither judicial control nor Parliamentary scrutiny. Although in *Stitt* the judges expressed doubts as to the constitutional propriety of such an approach,[33] the court rejected the argument that Parliament must be presumed to have authorised such broad legislative powers only on the basis that directions should (like statutory instruments) be laid before Parliament.

Arguments of constitutional propriety were however to an extent heeded in the enactment of Part I of the Deregulation and Contracting Out Act 1994 which confers on ministers power to repeal by statutory instrument a wide range of existing statutory provisions. The purpose of Part I of the Act is to empower ministers to remove what they consider to be over-burdensome statutory

---

[24] Franks, paras 23, 41–42.
[25] Hadfield (1995), p. 268.
[26] *e.g.* Housing Act 1996, ss.164–165 (council housing allocation); 202–203 (homeless persons applications).
[27] Hadfield (1995), p. 267.
[28] SSCBA 1992, s.140(2).
[29] *ibid.,* ss.(3), (4).
[30] *The Times,* July 5, 1990.
[31] Feldman (1991), p. 41.
[32] Chap. 4, *section F 3.*
[33] Feldman (1991), p. 42.

regulations upon trade and business, *e.g.* in fields such as retail, tourism, food and drink, agriculture, construction and engineering, chemicals and pharmaceuticals, transport (*e.g.* bus services), financial services, charities.

The chief enabling provision is section 1(1) which empowers any minister by statutory instrument to amend or repeal any statutory provision whose effect, in his opinion, is to impose a burden affecting any person in the carrying on of any trade, business or profession or otherwise if such amendment or repeal would reduce the burden without removing any necessary protection.

Given the breadth of this provision and the courts' restrictive approach to reviewing delegated legislation, this is a clear further example of de facto ouster. But constitutional propriety is to some extent preserved by sections 3 and 4 which provide for consultations and a specially extended process of Parliamentary scrutiny before a statutory instrument is made under section 1. Particularly important is the requirement[34] that a minister must lay before Parliament details of the background and rationale for any proposed change. Nevertheless, the point remains that the conferment by statute on ministers of wide legislative powers is a highly effective indirect means of restricting judicial review.[35] It is a means which, if widely used, could side-step the efforts of the courts to preserve their review jurisdiction in the face of direct assault by ouster clauses.

[34] s.3(4).
[35] See *e.g.* Ganz (1997).

Chapter 8

OFFICIAL TORT LIABILITY[1]

A INTRODUCTION: GENERAL PRINCIPLES, "INEVITABLE INJURY", PUBLIC LAW RIGHTS AND PRIVATE LAW RIGHTS

1 GENERAL PRINCIPLES

(a) Application of ordinary tort law

In general, public authorities, like private individuals, may be liable under the ordinary law of tort — trespass, nuisance, negligence, defamation, etc. For example, a public authority would be liable to a person whose property was damaged by an explosion or land subsidence negligently caused by the authority's workmen, or by nuisance flowing from the authority's unreasonable use of its land. Likewise an authority would be liable for negligent infliction of personal injury if a pedestrian were knocked down by a vehicle driven by an employee of the authority in the course of his employment; or, if the authority were responsible for repairing the highway, and a pedestrian fell into an inadequately fenced hole dug in the road by employees of the authority.

Commonly, as these examples suggest, public authority tort liability will be vicarious liability for the torts of authority employees committed in the course of their employment. The employees themselves will be personally liable on ordinary principles but often only the authority will have the resources to satisfy a damages judgment. Contrastingly, a public authority may be directly rather than vicariously liable in tort where, e.g., via the acts or omissions of its members, employees or agents, it fails to discharge a statutory duty laid upon it and in the circumstances breach of that duty is tortious according to principles to be discussed below. The liability of public authorities for the actions of persons to whom functions of the authority have been "contracted-out" is considered in Chapter 9.[2]

To the extent just explained it may be said that public authorities[3] are subject to the ordinary law of tort. But there are two major respects in which public authorities are in a special position as regards tort liability.

---

[1] See generally Arrowsmith, *Civ. Liab.*, Chaps 5–9; Harlow, *CGT*; Weir (1989). For treatment in Administrative Law texts, see section headings below.

[2] *Section C 2 a.*

[3] Judges, however, enjoy wide immunity from tort liability when acting in good faith: see Wade and Forsyth, *AL*, p. 796; Emery and Smythe, *JR*, p.71.

(b) Special position of public authorities

(i) *Public powers overriding private rights*

Public authorities often have special statutory powers or duties to act in a way which would be tortious if a private individual were to act thus. In consequence, many actions which if done by a private individual would be tortious, are not so if done by a public authority authorised by statute to act in this way. This issue will be considered briefly in *sub-section 2*, under the heading *Inevitable injury*.

(ii) *Unlawful official action and the individual's claim to compensation*

Public authorities have a vast range of special powers and duties (mostly statutory) to make decisions or take actions having a direct impact on individuals — particularly decisions to grant, or withhold or withdraw, benefits and services of many different types. If a particular such decision or action is *ultra vires* or otherwise unlawful (*e.g.* a criminal breach of duty) it may cause loss or injury ("damage") to individuals. It will be seen in *sub-section 3*, **Public law rights and private law rights**, that *ultra vires* action (like other unlawful, *e.g.* criminal, action[4]) causing damage does not in itself give a right to damages. It is of course true that an *ultra vires* decision may lead the authority to commit a tort by unlawfully damaging an existing private law right, *e.g.* by demolishing a person's house on the basis of an *ultra vires* order.[5] But an *ultra vires* decision may by itself cause injury or loss, *e.g.* by depriving a person of a benefit which should be conferred. In these circumstances, as will be seen, the victim of the *ultra vires* decision will be able to claim tort damages only if he can satisfy the criteria of a recognised tort, whether **breach of statutory duty**, **negligence**, or **misfeasance in public office** (a special tort, which can be committed only by public authorities or other persons exercising public functions). The courts have taken an approach designed to balance the sometimes conflicting public interests in (on the one hand) compensating individuals damaged by unlawful official action and (on the other) not draining the public purse by damages awards in respect of unlawful but bona fide official action. Moreover, the availability of AJR as a remedy for *ultra vires* action compounds a general unwillingness of the courts to impose damages liability on the public purse.

(c) A note on suing the Crown in tort

Until 1947, victims of torts committed by government ministers or civil servants were subject to sometimes insuperable difficulties in recovering damages from the Government ("the Crown") as distinct from the individual wrongdoer. These difficulties were largely overcome by the Crown Proceedings Act 1947, s.2 which, in general, subjects the Crown to the same liabilities for the torts of its "servants or agents"[6] paid out of central funds[7] as if the Crown were "a private person of full age and capacity". And the Crown is made liable in respect of torts committed by "an officer of the Crown" in the performance of his official functions even where the functions are formally those of the officer (*e.g.* conferred by statute on a minister or other official) rather than the Crown.[8]

2 INEVITABLE INJURY

"A public authority will . . . not be liable in tort where [an] injury is the inevitable consequence of what Parliament has authorised."[9] This principle is illustrated by a line of cases on nuisance. For

---

[4] See further *section B 3 c* below.
[5] As *e.g.* in *Cooper v. Wandsworth Board of Works* (1863) 14 C.B.N.S. 180: see Chap. 5, *section B 3*.
[6] s.2(1).
[7] s.2(6).
[8] s.2(3).
[9] Wade and Forsyth, *AL*, p. 765.

example, in *Allen v. Gulf Oil Refining Ltd*[10] a statute had empowered the defendant company to build an oil refinery and to build and operate an access railway. The statute did not expressly authorise the operation of the refinery itself. Pollution from the operation of the refinery inevitably damaged land owned by the plaintiffs.[11] They sued in nuisance arguing that the statute's failure expressly to authorise the operation of the refinery was deliberate and was intended to leave unaffected any liability of the operator in nuisance. But the House of Lords held that the express statutory authority to build the refinery impliedly authorised its operation so that no nuisance claim lay in respect of damage inevitably caused.

Notice, however, that under the Land Compensation Act 1973 even inevitable injury is compensable to the extent that "physical factors caused by the use of public works"[12] (*e.g.* noise, smell, fumes, etc.) cause depreciation in land value, provided that the claimant did not "come to the nuisance". But this redress is much inferior to that available by way of a nuisance claim, *i.e.* either an injunction to prevent the nuisance, or damages in lieu. Nuisance damages are not limited to land value depreciation but may reflect also the distress and loss of amenity of living in the shadow of a huge installation such as an oil refinery.[13]

The principle exemplified in *Allen* relates to "inevitable" injury. Any injury beyond the inevitable may thus result in liability. So in *Manchester Corporation v. Farnsworth*[14] the House of Lords held the corporation liable in nuisance for sulphurous contamination of the claimant farmer's land by fumes from a power station it operated: these were held in the circumstances not to have been inevitable. But Lord Dunedin did say that "the criterion of inevitability is not what is theoretically possible but what is possible according to the state of scientific knowledge at the time, having also in view a certain common sense appreciation, which cannot be rigidly defined, of practical feasibility in view of situation and of expense."[15] This test is plainly designed to avoid burdening public authorities with cripplingly expensive steps to avoid private harm from public works. But if on this test an injury is not inevitable, the authority cannot plead "necessity in the public interest" as a defence to a nuisance claim. In *Pride of Derby Angling Association Ltd v. British Celanese Ltd*[16] the Corporation was held liable in nuisance for discharging untreated sewage into a river, damaging the claimants' fishing rights. It was no defence to the claim that the discharge was necessary because the town's growth had outstripped the capacity of the existing sewage works. But an injunction was suspended for 16 months to allow the corporation to expand its sewerage facilities.

3 PUBLIC LAW RIGHTS AND PRIVATE LAW RIGHTS

In *X v. Bedfordshire C.C., E v. Dorset C.C. and other appeals*[17] (the *Bedford/Dorset* case) Lord Browne-Wilkinson said:

> "It is important to distinguish . . . actions to recover damages, based on a private law cause of action, from actions in public law to enforce the due performance of statutory duties, now brought by way of judicial review. *The breach of a public law right by itself gives rise to no claim for damages. A claim for damages must be based on a private law cause of action.*"[18]

[10] [1981] 1 All E.R. 353.
[11] *i.e.* "claimants" in the terminology of the Civil Procedure Rules 1998. The term "plaintiff" is no longer used.
[12] s.1.
[13] See Lord Denning's graphic description in the Court of Appeal judgment in *Allen* [1979] 3 All E.R. 1008 at 1011.
[14] [1929] All E.R. Rep. 90.
[15] *ibid.*, at 95F.
[16] [1953] 1 All E.R. 179.
[17] [1995] 3 All E.R. 353.
[18] *ibid.*, at 363h, emphasis added.

(a) "The breach of a public law right" — the *Bedford/Dorset* case

As explained in Chapter 5,[19] the House of Lords has used the phrase "public law right" to describe claims or interests which can be vindicated by judicial review. Thus, a person who asserts a public law right is ordinarily founding his claim on an allegation of *ultra vires* action.[20] Moreover, it is plain from the context in which Lord Browne-Wilkinson used the phrase in the *Bedford/Dorset* case that a person's "public law rights" may be breached not only by *ultra vires* omission (*i.e.* where a public authority fails to confer a benefit which it has a statutory duty to confer) but also by *ultra vires* commission (*i.e.* where a public authority acts to a person's detriment in circumstances where it has no power so to act). The principle enshrined in the above extract from the *Bedford/Dorset* case is thus as follows. If a person has suffered injury or loss as a consequence of an *ultra vires* decision or action, the authority concerned is not liable to compensate for the loss unless the victim can demonstrate not only that the act or decision is *ultra vires* but also that the authority's actions give rise to a private law cause of action.

The *Bedford/Dorset* case actually comprised appeals in five separate tort claims. The House of Lords dealt with the five appeals together and thus provided authoritative guidance on the principles governing tort liability of public authorities for *ultra vires* decisions causing damage to persons for whose benefit the decisions were intended to be taken. The judgment of the House was delivered substantially by Lord Browne-Wilkinson with whom the other four law lords agreed, except that Lord Nolan dissented on one particular point which did not affect the outcome of the case. References below are to the speech of Lord Browne-Wilkinson unless otherwise stated. For details of the five claims in the case see the boxed text below.

THE CLAIMS IN THE *BEDFORD/DORSET* CASE

- Two claims (*Bedford* and *Newham*) in which local authorities were sued in tort (breach of statutory duty and negligence) for injury sustained by parents and children as a result of alleged breaches of the authorities' duties under the Child Care Act 1980 (and other statutes) to safeguard the welfare of children.

The claims alleged both **omissions** (failing to identify child abuse — *Bedford*) and **commissions** (wrongly identifying a child abuser and removing a child from its home as a consequence — *Newham*).

- Three claims (*Dorset*, *Hampshire* and *Bromley*) for breach of statutory duty and negligence (*Hampshire*, negligence only) in respect of damage to children's educational development as a result of alleged breaches of the authorities' duties under the Education Acts 1944 and 1981 to provide for children with special educational needs (SEN).

The claims alleged both **omissions** (failure to identify SEN — *Dorset*, *Hampshire*) and **commissions** (providing inappropriately for particular SEN by placing a child in special rather than ordinary schools — *Bromley*: also alleging consequential omission to supply ordinary education).

---

[19] *Section C 1.*
[20] Chap. 4, *section B 1, 3 a.*

The case reached the House of Lords on the preliminary issue of whether the statements of claim should be struck out as disclosing no cause of action: the question before the House was thus whether, if the facts alleged could in due course be proved, the defendants would be liable.

(b) When the breach of a public law right amounts also to the breach of a private law right

The *Bedford/Dorset* judgment will be examined below, but the point to be made here is that the central issue was in effect whether, on the facts alleged, the claimants had any private law, as opposed to public law, rights. In other words, the question was whether the alleged breaches of statutory duty could be remedied only via the principles and remedies of judicial review, or whether, on the contrary, the damage suffered by the claimants as a consequence of those breaches was recoverable on the basis that, *vis-à-vis* those claimants, the breaches constituted the torts.

(4) PLAN OF THIS CHAPTER

The remainder of this chapter focuses upon the question of when unlawful official action in the exercise of public functions constitutes a tort against a person to whom damage is thereby caused:

(a) Breach of statutory duty

As will now be apparent, by no means all breaches by public authorities of their special statutory duties constitute torts, *i.e.* entitle the persons damaged by such breaches to claim compensation (damages). But if the breach of a particular duty is held to be tortious, the claimant is required only to show that the breach has occurred and has damaged him.

The basis upon which the breach of particular statutory duties of public authorities may be held to be tortious will be considered in *section B*.

(b) Negligence

If, however, a breach is held not to be in itself tortious, the claimant may seek to show that the defendant authority acted carelessly and, in the circumstances, owed the claimant a "duty of care" which has thus been breached. In these circumstances the claimant may recover damages for the tort of negligence.

Negligence liability of public authorities in the exercise of their public functions will be considered in *section C*.

(c) Misfeasance in public office

Section D will examine the tort of misfeasance in public office which, as already mentioned, is a tort which can be committed only by public authorities or other persons exercising public functions. It consists of deliberate abuse of official power causing damage to the claimant.

(d) Official torts — the European law dimension

Finally, *section E* will consider the circumstances in which persons exercising public functions may be liable in tort for breach of E.C. individual rights or Convention rights.

B BREACH OF STATUTORY DUTY[21]

This category of tort liability "comprises those cases where the statement of claim alleges simply (i) the statutory duty, (ii) a breach of that duty, causing (iii) damage to the claimant. The cause of action depends neither on proof of any breach of the claimants' common law rights nor on any allegation of carelessness by the defendant."[22]

In what circumstances will such a claim succeed?

1 EXPRESS STATUTORY PROVISION

In some statutes Parliament does expressly recognise that breach of a particular statutory duty will give rise to damages liability. Examples are the liability of a highway authority in respect of personal injury[23] sustained as a result of its failure to maintain a highway (unless the authority can prove it has taken reasonable care in all the circumstances)[24]; the liability of public gas suppliers in respect of loss or damage sustained by a person as a result of the supplier's breach of an order by the Director General[25]; and the liability of local authorities in respect of breaches of the statutory "non-commercial considerations" provisions governing their award of contracts.[26]

It is, however, uncommon to find such express provision, Parliament preferring, apparently, to leave the question for decision by the courts.

2 NO EXPRESS PROVISION: THE GENERAL APPROACH

In the absence of express provision, "a private law cause of action will arise if it can be shown, as a matter of construction of the statute, that the statutory duty was imposed for the protection of a limited class of the public and that Parliament intended to confer on members of that class a private right of action for breach of the duty."[27] The difficulty is, however, that "There is no general rule by reference to which it can be decided whether a statute does create such a right of action but there are a number of indicators."[28] This, perhaps, is a temperate way of saying what Lord Denning once said more bluntly: that the dividing line between breaches of statutory duty which are and are not tortious "is so blurred and so ill-defined that you might as well toss a coin to decide it."[29]

How then can one attempt to predict whether or not the courts will hold that an official breach of a particular statutory duty will amount to a tort?

The case law shows that it is necessary but not sufficient to establish that "the statutory duty was imposed for the protection of a limited class of the public" and that the claimant belongs to that class and suffered a detriment in consequence of the breach. In *Hague v. Deputy Governor Parkhurst Prison*[30] H, a prisoner at Parkhurst, had been transferred to Wormwood Scrubs and punished with 28 days' solitary confinement for offences against prison discipline. On AJR he

---

[21] Wade and Forsyth, *AL*, pp. 847–849; Craig, *AL*, pp. 847–849; Arrowsmith, *Civ. Liab.* Chap. 7; Buckley (1984); Cane (1981).

[22] *Bedford/Dorset* case [1995] 3 All E.R. at 364c.

[23] *cf. Wentworth v. Wiltshire C.C.* [1993] 2 All E.R. 256 (below).

[24] Highways Act 1980, s.58. *Goodes v. East Sussex C.C., The Times*, January 7, 1999.

[25] Gas Act 1986, s.30(6): see Chap. 3, *section B 2 b*.

[26] Local Government Act 1988, s.19(7)(b): Chap. 3, *section C 2 a*.

[27] *Bedford/Dorset* case [1995] 3 All E.R. at 364e.

[28] *ibid.*

[29] *Ex p. Island Records Ltd* [1978] 3 All E.R. 824 at 829a.

[30] [1991] 3 All E.R. 733.

sought and obtained a declaration that his punishment was contrary to statutory prison rules; but the House of Lords held that he had no claim for breach of statutory duty. The infringed rules were of course intended to protect prisoners; but the purpose of this protection was to achieve effective regulation of the prison population, not to confer private rights on individual prisoners.[31]

The "fundamental question [is]: 'Did the legislature intend to confer on the claimant a cause of action for breach of statutory duty?'"[32]; "The fact that a particular provision was intended to protect certain individuals is not of itself sufficient to confer private law rights of action upon them, something more is required to show that the legislature intended such conferment."[33] To discover what "more is required" one may begin by considering what, from the case law, must be regarded as "counter-indications", *i.e.* as indications that the breach of a particular statutory duty is not in itself tortious.

3 "COUNTER-INDICATIONS"

(a) Regulatory systems and schemes of social welfare

In the *Bedford/Dorset* case Lord Browne-Wilkinson said that

> "it is significant that your Lordships were not referred to any case where it had been held that statutory provisions establishing a regulatory system or a scheme of social welfare for the benefit of the public at large had been held to give rise to a private right of action for damages for breach of statutory duty. Although regulatory or welfare legislation affecting a particular area of activity does in fact provide protection to those individuals particularly affected by that activity, the legislation is not to be treated as being passed for the benefit of those individuals but for the benefit of society in general."[34]

(b) Judgment and discretion left to authority

In *O'Rourke v. Camden L.B.C.*,[35] as recounted in Chapter 5,[36] the House of Lords held that breaches by local authorities of their statutory duties towards homeless persons applying to them for housing do not constitute the tort of breach of statutory duty. Lord Hoffmann observed that the existence of a duty to provide accommodation is "dependent upon a good deal of judgment on the part of the housing authority . . . If a duty does arise, the authority has a wide discretion in deciding how to provide accommodation and what kind of accommodation it will provide. The existence of all these discretions makes it unlikely that Parliament intended errors of judgment to give rise to an obligation to make financial reparation."[37]

Obversely, as remarked by Lord Browne-Wilkinson in the *Bedford/Dorset* case, "The cases where a private right of action for breach of statutory duty has been held to arise are all cases in which the statutory duty has been very limited and specific as opposed to general administrative functions imposed on public bodies and involving the exercise of administrative discretions."[38]

---

[31] *ibid.*, at 742c, 751a. See also *Calveley v. Chief Constable of Merseyside* [1989] 1 All E.R. 1025 (breach by police authorities of police discipline regulations: no claim for breach of statutory duty).
[32] *ibid.*, at 741c (Lord Bridge).
[33] *ibid.*, at 750h (Lord Jauncey).
[34] [1995] 3 All E.R. at 364j.
[35] [1997] 3 All E.R. 23.
[36] *Section C 1 b.*
[37] [1997] 3 All E.R. at 26–27.
[38] [1995] 3 All E.R. at 365a.

(c) Alternative remedy

It is well-established that "If the statute does provide some other means [than a claim for tort damages] of enforcing the duty, that will normally indicate that the statutory right was intended to be enforceable by those means and not by private right of action".[39]

- A common "other means" which will be taken as such indication is the imposition of criminal liability for breach as, *e.g.* in *Cutler v. Wandsworth Stadium Ltd*[40] where the House of Lords held on this basis that breach of the statutory duty of licensed dog-track proprietors to provide bookmakers with the facilities to operate was not a tort against the bookmakers.

- A similar approach has been applied with regard to the special statutory machinery of complaint to the Secretary of State alleging failure of a health authority to provide after-care services for discharged mental patients[41]; and of complaint to the Crown Court alleging that a highway authority is in breach of its duty to maintain a highway.[42] In *Wentworth v. Wilts C.C.*[43] the Court of Appeal held that this was the sole recourse available to a person who suffered economic loss when lorries could not pass over an unrepaired highway to his premises.

- Judicial review is, of course, a common law rather than a statutory remedy; but its availability as a means of challenging an official breach of statutory duty is often given by the courts as a reason for concluding that the breach is not in itself tortious. When imposing a statutory decision-making duty upon a public authority Parliament must be taken not only to be aware that AJR is available as a remedy for its breach but also, usually, to imply that this and not damages is the appropriate remedy.[44]

As will be seen, however, the existence of an alternative remedy will not always rule out a claim for breach of statutory duty.

4 CASE LAW EXAMPLES

It should be borne in mind that in many of the reported cases relating to public authority tort liability the claimant is alleging both the tort of breach of statutory duty and the tort of negligence. This section is concerned only with the former. The question of negligence liability will be considered in the next section.

(a) No liability

The performance of the child care duties of local authorities for breach of which the claimants sued in the *Bedford* and *Newham* cases[45] depended on the exercise of subjective judgment by the

---

[39] *ibid.*, at 364f.
[40] [1949] 1 All E.R. 544. See also *Lonrho Ltd v. Shell Petroleum Co. Ltd* [1981] 2 All E.R. 456.
[41] *Clunis v. Camden & Islington H.A.* [1998] 3 All E.R. 180 at 190h.
[42] Highways Act 1980, s.56.
[43] [1993] 2 All E.R. 256.
[44] See *e.g. Hague* (above) [1991] 3 All E.R. at 752j; *O'Rourke* (above) [1997] 3 All E.R. at 27; *Olotu v. Home Office and Crown Prosecution Service* [1997] 1 All E.R. 385 at 393–4; *Clunis* (above) [1998] 3 All E.R. at 190h.
[45] See *section A 3 a* above.

authorities. The claims for breach of statutory duty failed on this basis.[46] Such duties are in effect duties to take decisions by reference to proper considerations. The duty is discharged by the authority taking a proper decision, even if the authority's judgment proves to have been incorrect. But it may fairly be asked why a child who suffers abuse following a decision which is both incorrect and based on wrong considerations is debarred from claiming such damages as can be shown to have been caused by the breach. The answer is essentially, if not convincingly, that the courts will almost invariably regard the availability of judicial review to correct unlawful exercises of discretion as an indication that the duty is "public" rather than "private", *i.e.* that damages are not available.

In the *Bromley* education case[47] the claim for damages for breach of statutory duty to provide appropriate schooling failed on very much the same analysis. Under the statutory provisions, whether special educational needs exist, and if so how they should be catered for, "leaves so much to be decided by the authority".[48] On that basis, and also because the statute contained "machinery whereby the minister can enforce any duties imposed by the Act on the education authority"[49] the breach of statutory duty claim failed. An alternative claim for breach of the broad statutory duty imposed by the Education Act 1944[50] on local education authorities to provide "sufficient schools" for their area was also dismissed. The claim was held to have been based on a misinterpretation of earlier case law[51] in which breaches of this paradigmatically public law duty (involving discretionary allocation of state educational resources) were alleged in ordinary civil proceedings. The House held that this was simply an example of the pre-1977 willingness of the courts to allow public law challenges to be brought in this fashion because of the inadequacies of the then judicial review procedure.[52]

These cases, and also *O'Rourke*[53] to the extent that the absence of a private law duty to homeless persons was based on the judgment and discretion issue, illustrate, if they do not convincingly explain, the operation of counter-indications *b* and *c* above. More difficult still to explain is the proposition (see counter-indication *a*) that, in general, regulatory and welfare legislation, even though obviously benefiting individuals within its scope, "is not to be treated as being passed for the benefit of those individuals but for the benefit of society in general." One can perhaps see the basis on which prison or police disciplinary regulatory schemes are held not to confer individual rights of action for their breach.[54] But it would be difficult to accept that statutory child protection and educational duties were not imposed for the benefit of children. Indeed, in the *Bedford/Dorset* case Lord Browne-Wilkinson said that the former were "introduced primarily for the protection of a limited class, namely children at risk"[55]; and he was "prepared to assume that the claimant, as a child having special educational needs, was a member of a class for whose protection the statutory [education] provisions were enacted".[56] However, as seen, the breach of statutory duty claims failed for other reasons.

In *O'Rourke* Lord Hoffmann said[57]:

---

[46] [1995] 3 All E.R. at 378–379.
[47] The only one of the three education cases in the *Bedford/Dorset* case in which the breach of statutory duty claim was pursued before the House of Lords.
[48] [1995] 3 All E.R. at 398h.
[49] *ibid.*
[50] s.8.
[51] *e.g. Meade v. Haringey L.B.C.* [1979] 2 All E.R. 1016.
[52] [1995] 3 All E.R. at 397–398. See Chap. 5, *section B 2 a.*
[53] *O'Rourke v. Camden B.C.* [1997] 3 All E.R. 23.
[54] See the *Hague* and *Calveley* cases cited above.
[55] *ibid.,* at 378h.
[56] *ibid.,* at 398f.
[57] [1997] 3 All E.R. at 26.

"[T]he [homeless persons legislation] is a scheme of social welfare, intended to confer benefits at the public expense on grounds of public policy. Public money is spent on housing the homeless not merely for the private benefit of people who find themselves homeless but on grounds of general public interest: because, for example, proper housing means that people will be less likely to suffer illness, turn to crime or require the attention of other social services. The expenditure interacts with expenditure on other public services such as education, the National Health Service and even the police. It is not simply a private matter between the claimant and the housing authority. Accordingly, the fact that Parliament has provided for the expenditure of public money on benefits in kind such as housing the homeless does not necessarily mean that it intended cash payments to be made by way of damages to persons who, in breach of the housing authority's statutory duty, have unfortunately not received the benefits which they should have done."

As suggested in Chapter 5,[58] this is potentially a very broad doctrine, particularly taking account of the rejection in *O'Rourke* of the *Cocks* distinction between decision-making and executive duties. *O'Rourke* suggests that incorrect (including wrongly-based) decisions on welfare benefits are never tortious breaches of statutory duty on the "public policy" reasoning in the above passage. Additionally, a breach of duty to provide a benefit which an authority has decided should be provided to a particular individual is not a tortious breach of statutory duty because "The concept of a duty in private law which arises only when it has been acknowledged to exist is anomalous."[59]

Outside the area of social welfare, it would appear that incorrect (including wrongly-based) decisions on entitlements to grants or compensation will not be tortious breaches of statutory duty if they fall within the "judgment and discretion" criterion. And, again, it seems that a breach of duty to provide a benefit which an authority has decided should be provided to a particular individual is not a tortious breach of statutory duty because such approach would be "anomalous" as above.

When, then, in the absence of express statutory provision, may a public authority be liable for the tort of breach of statutory duty?

(b) Liability

A public nuisance (*i.e.* an unreasonable use of land to the discomfort or inconvenience of a class or section of the public[60]) is a criminal offence; but it is a tort as regards any individual specially damaged.[61] A public nuisance perpetrated by a public authority in breach of a statutory duty (*e.g.*, as in *Boyce v. Paddington B.C.*,[62] to maintain particular land as an open space for public recreation) would thus constitute a tortious breach of statutory duty as against an individual specially damaged in his enjoyment of the right. An example might be if, perhaps, a neighbouring landowner were prevented from using the open space as an amenity specially benefiting his property.[63] "Special damage public nuisance" is, of course, a case of public-duty-turned-private by particular circumstances. When will statutory duties be held to have been imposed directly for the benefit of individuals who, if damaged by their breach, may thus sue on this basis?

---

[58] *Section C 1 b.*
[59] [1997] 3 All E.R. at 29c.
[60] Winfield and Jolowicz, *Tort*, p. 402.
[61] *ibid.*, at 403.
[62] [1903] 1 Ch. 109. See Lord Diplock in *Lonrho Ltd v. Shell Petroleum Co. Ltd* [1981] 2 All E.R. 456 at 461–462.
[63] *cf. Boyce* where the claim failed because the alleged damage (loss of light to the claimant's windows) did not relate to the right to enjoy the open space.

Breaches of statutory requirements that building materials in schools (*e.g.* glass in doors) shall "be such that the health and safety of the occupants shall be reasonably assured",[64] or that a water authority "shall provide . . . pure and wholesome water"[65] have been held to constitute tortious breaches of statutory duty. This reflects the approach long taken to the statutory duties imposed on all employers with regard to employees' safety on factory premises.[66] Provisions of these types could no doubt be described as "regulatory"; moreover, their breach is commonly made a criminal offence.[67] But these "counter-indications" have not prevented their breach from being held tortious. For the duties are unequivocally intended to prevent injury to individuals and the statutory duties in question are "very limited and specific as opposed to general administrative functions . . . involving the exercise of administrative discretions."[68] The latter point may explain the ruling in *Ettridge v. Morrell*[69] that the duty of a local authority to provide a parliamentary election candidate with a suitable room in one of the authority's schools for public election meetings creates a private law right for breach of which a candidate may sue. But the Court of Appeal based its decision on Lord Bridge's distinction in *Cocks* between decision-making and executive duties; the case may thus not survive *O'Rourke*.

It must be said, in any event, that in most of the modern cases in which public authorities have been held liable for breach of statutory duty, they have been held, in the alternative, liable in negligence.[70] Given the extensive liability of public authorities for "implementational" negligence[71] and the increasing[72] unwillingness of the courts to impose absolute liability for breach of statutory duty, it is difficult to cite circumstances in which the latter tort will be likely to be the sole basis of a public authority's liability in tort for failure to discharge its public functions.

C NEGLIGENCE[73]

1 NEGLIGENT EXERCISE OF STATUTORY POWERS OR DUTIES NOT IN ITSELF TORTIOUS

The House of Lords has made it clear that "in order to found a cause of action flowing from the careless exercise of statutory powers or duties, the claimant has to show that the circumstances are such as to raise a duty of care at common law. The mere assertion of the careless exercise of a statutory power or duty is not sufficient."[74]

Previously some confusion had been generated by a misunderstanding of Lord Blackburn's remark in *Geddis v. Proprietors of Bann Reservoir*[75] that "an action does lie for doing that which the legislature has authorised, if it be done negligently". It is now clear that this is not a statement of the basis for a cause of action against a public authority; it is a statement simply limiting the scope of a public authority's defence to an established cause of action. For the statement

---

[64] *Reffell v. Surrey County Council* [1964] 1 All E.R. 743.
[65] *Read v. Croydon Corporation* [1938] 4 All E.R. 631.
[66] *Groves v. Lord Wimborne* [1895–9] All E.R. Rep 147.
[67] *e.g.* as in both *Read* and *Groves*.
[68] [1995] 3 All E.R. at 365a (above).
[69] *The Times*, May 5, 1986.
[70] As *e.g.* in both *Reffell* and *Read* (above).
[71] See *section C 2 e* below.
[72] See in particular the *Bedford/Dorset* and *O'Rourke* cases discussed above.
[73] Wade and Forsyth, *AL*, pp. 771–784; Craig, *AL*, pp. 851–875; Arrowsmith, *Civ. Liab.* Chap. 6.
[74] *Bedford/Dorset* case [1995] 3 All E.R. at 367h.
[75] (1878) 3 App. Cas. 430.

apparently refers only to the situation where a public authority defends a tort claim by relying on statutory authority to do what would otherwise be tortious (*e.g.* nuisance, trespass or negligence): there is no defence if the authority has acted without "all reasonable regard and care for the interests of other persons".[76] Thus, Lord Blackburn's observation is merely a corollary of the "inevitable injury" principle:[77] since it is never inevitable that a statutory function will be negligently exercised, it follows that a public authority cannot shelter behind such exercise in order to defend action which, absent the statutory authority, would be tortious.

Thus, if as alleged in *Geddis*, the authority has been careless in exercising its statutory powers to discharge water from a reservoir, causing flooding to the adjoining land of the claimant (C), C can sue in nuisance or negligence on ordinary principles: the defendant's statutory power is no defence where exercised negligently. And in the *Bedford/Dorset* case Lord Browne-Wilkinson explained *Home Office v. Dorset Yacht Co.*[78] on this basis. In *Dorset Yacht* it was alleged that Home Office borstal officers carelessly allowed their charges to escape and to damage C's moored yacht by colliding with it in a yacht they had misappropriated. C sued the Home Office, maintaining that it was vicariously liable for the negligence of the officers. The House of Lords accepted that the borstal authorities were empowered to decide what regime was suitable for detainees. But their lordships held that this power would be no defence to a negligence claim if the regime were carelessly operated and it could be shown[79] that the officers were under an ordinary common law duty of care "to the [claimants] to take reasonable steps to control the Borstal boys so as to prevent them causing foreseeable damage to the [claimants'] property".[80]

In short, negligence in the exercise of a statutory function deprives an authority of a defence to a properly-constituted tort claim but does not in itself constitute a cause of action for a person who has suffered damage. Such cause of action must be established according to ordinary tort law principles.

2 COMMON LAW DUTY OF CARE IN EXERCISING PUBLIC POWERS OR DUTIES

When, therefore, will a public authority be held to owe a common law duty of care to avoid inflicting damage upon persons by the exercise of its statutory powers or duties? This question poses what Lord Nicholls in *Stovin v. Wise*,[81] citing 16 divergent academic treatments of the matter, described as "a knotty problem".

(a) General approach to the problem

The courts have identified a wide range of situations in which no duty of care will ever lie upon a person or body exercising statutory functions. Outside these situations a duty of care may, but not necessarily will, be imposed.

The problem will be considered by following the approach adopted by Lord Browne-Wilkinson in the *Bedford/Dorset* case and illustrated by *TABLE 8*

---

[76] Lord Wilberforce in *Allen v. Gulf Oil Refining Ltd* [1981] 1 All E.R. 353 at 356.
[77] *Section A 2* above.
[78] [1970] 2 All E.R. 294.
[79] As in the event the House held it could: see *sub-section 2 e* below.
[80] Lord Browne-Wilkinson in the *Bedford/Dorset* case at 366h, precising Lords Morris and Pearson in *Dorset Yacht*.
[81] [1996] 3 All E.R. 801 at 809f.

DUTY OF CARE AND NON-STATUTORY PUBLIC LAW FUNCTIONS

As noted in *TABLE 8*, Lord Browne-Wilkinson in the *Bedford/Dorset* case was concerned with the application of his analysis in the context of **statutory** functions of public authorities. It seems likely though that the analysis would apply equally to resolve questions of negligence liability arising from the exercise or non-exercise of **non-statutory** public functions. For example, suppose that the police or a local authority fail or decide not to notify a council tenant with a young child, C, that a convicted paedophile, S, has been granted a tenancy of the next-door council house. If S sexually assaults C, has C a cause of action in negligence against the police or the authority? If it may be said that the authorities have a power (public, but at present non-statutory[82]) to impart such information to C's parent, Lord Browne-Wilkinson's analysis would then seem in principle to apply to determining whether there may be liability in negligence for non-exercise of the power.

- As *TABLE 8* shows, if the question is whether a claimant may hope to recover negligence damages in respect of particular official action, it is sensible first to examine the criteria identifying situations in which a duty of care cannot arise and in which, accordingly, there can be no liability in negligence.

- If the action in question falls outside those limiting criteria one can then ask whether according to ordinary negligence criteria a duty of care does arise in the particular case.

(b) Situations where no duty of care can arise

(i) Non-justiciable "whether or not" decisions

When seeking to decide whether in particular circumstances a public authority owes a common law duty of care to a claimant one must first ask whether the action complained of is the *exercise of a discretion whether or not to act* or is, on the contrary, the *implementation of a decision to act*:

> "[A] broad distinction has to be drawn between: (a) cases in which it is alleged that the authority owes a duty of care in the manner in which it exercises a statutory discretion; and (b) cases in which a duty of care is alleged to arise from the manner in which the statutory duty has been implemented in practice. . . . The distinction is between (a) taking care in exercising a statutory discretion whether or not to do an act and (b) having decided to do that act, taking care in the manner in which you do it."[83]

The distinction can be illustrated by reference to the facts of the *Bedford/Dorset* case. The claims against *Bedford*, *Dorset* and *Bromley* alleged that the authorities were in breach of duties of care in exercising statutory discretions "whether or not" to do an act: in *Bedford* in deciding not to remove a child from its home despite suspicion of sexual abuse; in *Dorset* in deciding that no special educational provision was needed for a particular child; in *Bromley* in deciding wrongly that such provision was needed for another child. The *Newham* and *Hampshire* cases, on the other hand, provide examples of alleged "implementational" negligence. In these cases no claim was made directly against the authorities in respect of their wrong decisions: in *Newham* to remove

---

[82] See, *e.g. R. v. Chief Constable North Wales Police and Wrexham Police, ex p.* AB [1998] 3 All E.R. 310.
[83] *Bedford/Dorset* case [1995] 3 All E.R. at 368e.

TABLE 8

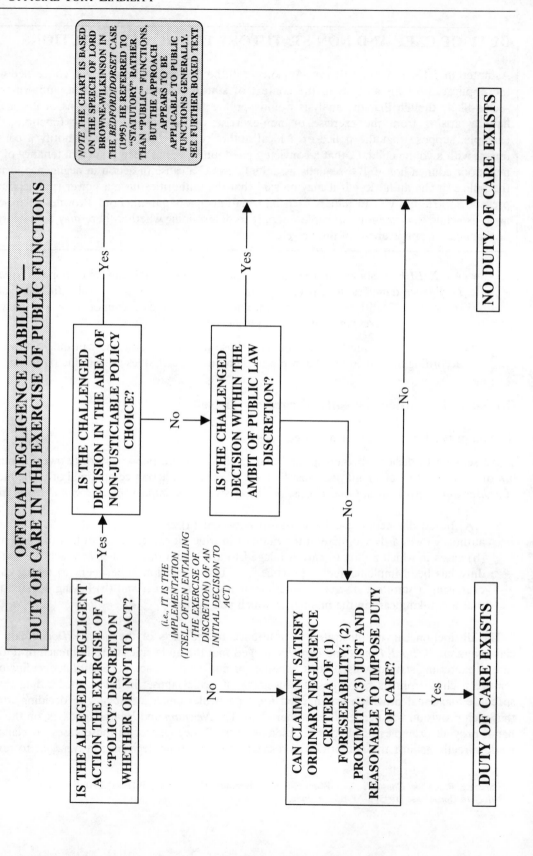

OFFICIAL NEGLIGENCE LIABILITY — DUTY OF CARE IN THE EXERCISE OF PUBLIC FUNCTIONS

NOTE THE CHART IS BASED ON THE SPEECH OF LORD BROWNE-WILKINSON IN THE *BEDFORD/DORSET* CASE (1995). HE REFERRED TO "STATUTORY" RATHER THAN "PUBLIC" FUNCTIONS, BUT THE APPROACH APPEARS TO BE APPLICABLE TO PUBLIC FUNCTIONS GENERALLY. SEE FURTHER BOXED TEXT

IS THE ALLEGEDLY NEGLIGENT ACTION THE EXERCISE OF A "POLICY" DISCRETION WHETHER OR NOT TO ACT?

—Yes→ IS THE CHALLENGED DECISION IN THE AREA OF A NON-JUSTICIABLE POLICY CHOICE?

—Yes→

—No→ *(i.e. IT IS THE IMPLEMENTATION (ITSELF OFTEN ENTAILING THE EXERCISE OF DISCRETION) OF AN INITIAL DECISION TO ACT)*

IS THE CHALLENGED DECISION WITHIN THE AMBIT OF PUBLIC LAW DISCRETION?

—Yes→

—No→

CAN CLAIMANT SATISFY ORDINARY NEGLIGENCE CRITERIA OF (1) FORESEEABILITY; (2) PROXIMITY; (3) JUST AND REASONABLE TO IMPOSE DUTY OF CARE?

—No→

—Yes→

DUTY OF CARE EXISTS

NO DUTY OF CARE EXISTS

from its home a child wrongly thought to have been sexually abused by a member of the household; in *Hampshire* that special educational provision was inappropriate for a particular child. What was claimed[84] was that the authorities' professional advisers (to whom the authorities had decided to refer the cases) provided a negligent service for which they were liable directly and the authority vicariously.

As will be immediately apparent, deciding upon "the manner in which you do an act" may well itself require the exercise of discretion. So, as will be further explained below,[85] the distinction is not between discretionary and non-discretionary action. Rather, it seems to be between the initial "policy" stance adopted by an authority in a particular case, and the subsequent decisions it takes in implementing that stance. "Policy decisions" in this sense typically "involve the weighing of competing public interests or [are] dictated by considerations which the courts are not fitted to assess."[86] The distinction is thus important because some decisions "whether or not" to act may be "matters of policy [on which] the court cannot adjudicate",[87] *i.e.* some "whether or not" decisions may be "non-justiciable". It appears, on the other hand, that any decision taken in the course of implementing a decision to act will be regarded as justiciable[88] (although, as will be seen, not necessarily as importing a duty of care).

Many decisions at a general policy level will be non-justiciable. "[N]otable examples are discretionary decisions on the allocation of scarce resources or the distribution of risks".[89] As seen in an earlier chapter,[90] decisions in individual cases, *e.g.* to reduce an existing level of provision by reference to scarcity of resource, may be justiciable by way of appeal or AJR. But general budgetary decisions to restrict or reduce funding in a particular area of service provision, *e.g.* child protection or education — will almost always be non-justiciable. Such decisions may in a political or journalistic sense be castigated as unreasonable, and may by needy individuals be thought neglectful of ("negligent" with regard to) their needs. But ". . . the courts cannot enter upon the assessment of such 'policy' matters".[91] It was also seen earlier[92] that the courts treat as non-justiciable the exercise of many Crown prerogative powers which are so broad and undefined as to make it impossible to apply legal criteria to determine the lawfulness of their exercise; and that Government assertions that the exercise of powers in sensitive areas is justified by considerations of national security are also likely to be regarded as non-justiciable.

Outside such areas, "policy" decisions, like implementational decisions and acts, will ordinarily be regarded as justiciable. In the *Bedford/Dorset* case, for example, the House of Lords held that neither the child abuse[93] nor the education[94] "whether or not" decisions referred to above were non-justiciable. The negligence claims could thus not be struck out on this basis.

(ii) *Decisions within "the ambit of the discretion conferred"*

If an allegedly negligent "policy decision" is justiciable, one must next ask if it is within the ambit of the public authority's discretion:

> "Most statutes which impose a statutory duty on local [or other public] authorities confer on the authority a discretion as to the extent to which, and the methods by which, such statutory

---

[84] See *ibid* at 379j, 394g.
[85] *Sub-section c.*
[86] Lord Hutton in *Barrett v. Enfield L.B.C.* [1999] 3 All E.R. 193 (see *sub-section d* below) at 222e.
[87] *Bedford/Dorset* case [1995] 3 All E.R. at 371b.
[88] See *ibid.*, at 380c.
[89] *Rowling v. Takaro Properties Ltd* [1988] 1 All E.R. 163 at 172 (Lord Keith).
[90] Chap. 4, *section C 3 b.*
[91] [1995] 3 All E.R. at 370b.
[92] Chap. 3, *section B 2 a.*
[93] [1995] 3 All E.R. p. 380a.
[94] *ibid.,* at 391a.

duty is to be performed. It is clear both in principle and from the decided cases that the . . . authority cannot be liable in damages for doing that which Parliament has authorised. Therefore if the decisions complained of fall within the ambit of such statutory discretion they cannot be actionable in common law. However, if the decision complained of is so unreasonable that it falls outside the ambit of the discretion conferred upon the . . . authority, there is no a priori reason for excluding all common law liability."[95]

This makes the important point that even where an exercise of "policy discretion" can be successfully challenged by judicial review (*i.e.*, is justiciable) there will be no possibility of additionally obtaining damages for negligence unless the decision complained of is so unreasonable that it falls outside the ambit of the discretion conferred.[96] Discretionary action (even though it may be *ultra vires*) falls within the ambit of statutory discretion for these purposes unless, as Lord Reid said in the *Dorset Yacht* case,[97] "the discretion [has been] exercised so carelessly or unreasonably that there has been no real exercise of the discretion." Lord Browne-Wilkinson characterised this as "*Wednesbury* unreasonableness".[98] However, the judicial pronouncements suggest that it does not include all *Wednesbury/Padfield* errors of law but only those which are egregious in the sense indicated by Lord Reid and may be described shortly as "irrational."[99]

This exclusion of negligence liability in respect of *ultra vires* "policy decisions", except those which are irrational, reflects the unwillingness of the courts to draw on public funds (via the award of negligence damages against public authorities) to remedy official decisions which, though wrong, can be regarded as genuine attempts to discharge public functions. So, for example, the decision in *Wheeler v. Leicester City Council*[1] to ban Leicester rugby club from using the municipal sports ground was wrong in law and reversible on AJR but it seems clear that the decision makers would not have been liable in negligence. The same, apparently, would be true of any refusal of an official licence or permission on a basis which might reasonably have been thought correct but is ultimately held to be wrong in law.

It may be otherwise in cases such as *Islam*,[2] *Hook*[3] or *Williams v. Giddy*[4] where the errors were far less defensible and may well have been outside the ambit of the discretion conferred upon the authority. And in the *Bedford/Dorset* case the House declined to strike out either the child abuse or the education negligence claims on the basis that they were clearly within the ambit of the authorities' discretion: in all probability these "whether or not" decisions were real attempts to exercise the discretions conferred, but that could not be determined without full trial.[5]

(c) Situations where a duty of care may arise: general considerations

Negligence liability may be ruled out by the application of the two criteria just discussed. Two broad categories of case remain in which a duty of care may, but not necessarily will, be held to exist. The two categories are:

(1) "Policy decisions" (using the phrase in the sense explained in the previous sub-section) whether or not to act which are "*Wednesbury* irrational" (as also defined above).

[95] *Bedford/Dorset* case [1995] 3 All E.R. at 368h.
[96] *ibid.*, at 369j. See also Lord Hutton in *Barrett v. Enfield* [1999] 3 All E.R. at 224f–g.
[97] [1970] 2 All E.R. at 301.
[98] [1995] 3 All E.R. at 369c.
[99] Lord Hoffmann in *Stovin v. Wise* [1996] 3 All E.R. at 828d.
[1] *ibid.*, section C 2 c.
[2] *ibid.*, section B 3 a.
[3] *ibid.*, section C 2 c.
[4] Chap. 2, *section D 6 a*.
[5] [1995] 3 All E.R. at 380d, 391c.

(2) Actions taken in the course of implementing a "policy decision" to exercise a statutory discretion.

It must be emphasised at once that the distinction between the two categories is blurred. An authority may have decided that a particular service is to be provided to a particular individual, but in the course of implementing the decision to provide the service many other "discretionary decisions to do [or not to do] some act" will have to be taken: what level of service is to be provided? for how long? by whom?, etc. Moreover, in both the *Bedford/Dorset* case[6] and, more recently, in *Stovin v. Wise*[7] and in *Barrett v. Enfield L.B.C.*[8] the House of Lords has made it clear that the dichotomy between "policy" and "operational" matters suggested by Lord Wilberforce in *Anns v. Merton L.B.C.*[9] does not (as Lord Wilberforce himself accepted) provide a litmus test for determining where a duty of care may and may not arise. Lord Browne-Wilkinson's similar distinction between "whether or not" and "implementational" decisions is plainly not intended to provide such a test, for a duty of care may be held to arise in either category. However, as will be seen, the distinction is nevertheless of significance in determining where a duty of care does arise. For, "as the part played by broad discretionary considerations in the exercise of the power grows, the less readily will a common law duty be superimposed, and vice versa".[10] In short, a duty of care is far less likely to be imposed in cases falling clearly in category (1) (see *sub-section d* below) than in cases falling clearly in category (2) (see *sub-section e*).

Subject to this, whether in any particular case a duty of care exists is to be decided by applying ordinary negligence principles "*i.e.* those laid down in *Caparo Industries plc v. Dickman*.[11] Was the damage [caused] to the [claimant] reasonably foreseeable? Was the relationship between the [claimant] and the defendant sufficiently proximate? Is it just and reasonable to impose a duty of care?"[12] However, as Lord Browne-Wilkinson observed, "the question whether there is such a common law duty and if so its ambit, must be profoundly influenced by the statutory framework within which the acts complained of were done. . . . [A] common law duty of care cannot be imposed on a statutory duty if the observance of such common law duty of care would be inconsistent with, or have a tendency to discourage, the due performance by the [public] authority of its statutory duties."[13]

The following discussion focuses on the "just and reasonable" and "proximity" issues — which have proved particularly problematic in the context of official negligence liability. Treatment of the general negligence issues of foreseeability and causation must be sought elsewhere.[14]

(d) Discretion, alternative remedies and duty of care

(i) *Factors indicating that it is not just and reasonable to impose a duty of care*

In the *Bedford/Dorset* litigation, as mentioned above, it was argued in only three of the five cases (*Bedford* — child abuse; *Dorset* and *Bromley* — education) that the authorities themselves owed duties of care directly to the claimants in making the decisions whether or not to act.

---

[6] *ibid.,* at 370–371.
[7] [1996] 3 All E.R. at 826 (Lord Hoffmann). The case dealt with the question of negligence liability for a public authority's omission to exercise a power: see *sub-section d* below.
[8] [1999] 3 All E.R. 193 at 211–212 (Lord Slynn), 222c–d (Lord Hutton): see *sub-section d* below.
[9] [1977] 2 All E.R. 492 at 500.
[10] Lord Nicholls in *Stovin v. Wise* (above) at 814a.
[11] [1990] 1 All E.R. 568 at 573–574.
[12] *Bedford/Dorset* case [1995] 3 All E.R. at 371e.
[13] *ibid.*
[14] *e.g.* Winfield and Jolowicz, *Tort*, Chap. 6.

Foreseeability and proximity were not in issue.[15] But in all three cases the argument for imposing a duty of care was rejected on the basis that it was not just and reasonable to do so.

In the *Bedford* child abuse case the following reasons were given:[16]

(1) The **inter-disciplinary** nature of the key feature of the process, the child protection conference. This body may include social workers, child psychiatrists, paediatricians, teachers, police or probation services. To impose negligence liability "on all the participant bodies would lead to almost impossible problems of disentangling as between the respective bodies the liability, both primary and by way of contribution, of each for reaching a decision found to be negligent".[17]

(2) The decision whether or not to remove a child where child abuse is suspected requires a delicate balancing of the rights of children and parents and of the desirability of not disrupting the family environment — a balance which might be upset if undue emphasis were placed simply on the question of whether or not abuse had occurred. Decisions of this type, which seek to accommodate a number of different objectives may be described as "**polycentric**".

(3) "If a liability in damages were to be imposed, it might well be that local authorities would adopt a more cautious and **defensive approach** to their duties"[18] perhaps resulting in prejudicial delay and the application of scarce resources to "negligence-proofing" decisions.

(4) If negligence damages were known to be possibly available in this highly sensitive area, ill-conceived or **vexatious litigation** might become common, again draining away scarce resources of the authority in defending them.

(5) Statutory complaints procedures and/or investigation by the local ombudsman are **alternative remedies** more appropriate than negligence liability.

(6) The courts have generally refused to impose negligence liability on **regulatory agencies** "charged by Parliament with protecting society from the wrongdoings of others."[19]

The *Dorset* and *Bromley* education rulings were based on reasons (4) and (5) above, and also on the established reluctance of the courts to impose a duty of care at the decision-making level in the social welfare, as in the regulatory context.[20] This parallels the unwillingness of the courts, as already seen, to impose liability for breach of statutory duty in these contexts.[21] As with liability for breach of statutory duty, so also on the question of duty of care: "It is one thing to provide a service at the public expense. It is another to require the public to pay compensation when a failure to provide the service has resulted in loss."[22] More generally, it has been suggested that "if the policy of the act is not to create a statutory liability to pay compensation, the same policy should ordinarily exclude the existence of a common law duty of care".[23]

---

[15] [1995] 3 All E.R. at 380f.
[16] *ibid.*, at 380j–382g.
[17] *ibid.*, at 381c.
[18] *ibid.*, at 381f.
[19] *ibid.*, at 382g.
[20] *ibid.*, at 391f–392e.
[21] *Section B 3 a* above.
[22] Lord Hoffmann in *Stovin v. Wise* [1996] 3 All E.R. at 827e. See also Weir (1989), p. 61.
[23] *ibid.*, at 827–828.

It may perhaps be felt that some of the reasons set out above for ruling out a negligence duty of care are more persuasive than others. The defensiveness and vexatious litigant arguments may seem an inadequate basis for refusing damages where negligence can be clearly shown. On the other hand, the inter-disciplinary and polycentricity arguments do indicate the difficulty of locating responsibility for error in certain types of decision-making process. However, until recently, the modern case law has indicated that even in the absence of these considerations it will seldom be held just and reasonable to impose a duty of care upon an authority charged with providing some regulatory or welfare service where an erroneous decision may be corrected on appeal or by AJR. But, as will be explained, in *Barrett v. Enfield L.B.C.*[24] the House of Lords has indicated that this restrictive approach may not be appropriate in circumstances where a public authority has, in the exercise of its statutory powers, itself undertaken responsibility for the day-to-day welfare of a particular individual.

(ii) *Regulatory systems, welfare services and alternative remedy*

When suing for negligence in respect of damage suffered as a result of a regulatory or welfare decision a claimant is alleging, essentially, that the authority has carelessly misunderstood the nature or extent of its functions. But the Privy Council in *Rowling v. Takaro Properties Ltd* observed that "anybody, even a judge, can be capable of misconstruing a statute; and such misconstruction, when it occurs, can be severely criticised without attracting the epithet 'negligent'. Obviously, this simple fact points rather to the extreme unlikelihood of a breach of duty [of care] being established in these cases."[25] So, *e.g.* it seems clear that the decision in the *Anisminic* case[26] that TEDO was successor in title to A Ltd would not have given rise to an action in negligence. Even less condonable errors will not attract liability: in *R. v. Knowsley B.C., ex p. Maguire*,[27] M obtained judicial review of the council's refusal to grant him a taxi licence. Otton J. characterised the refusal as arbitrary and unreasonable and contrary to the applicant's legitimate expectation. But on M's adjourned claim for damages Schiemann J. said that these remarks were made in a public law context and did not import negligence. On that basis the court (as in *Rowling* — concerning a refusal of a New Zealand government minister to grant a development consent) did not need to decide whether a duty of care existed. And the indications are that even in an extreme case of *Wednesbury* irrationality the courts will be reluctant to hold that a duty of care exists where, as in *Maguire*, the complainant, via appeal or judicial review, ultimately obtains the licence or ruling which he originally sought. In *Jones v. Department of Employment*,[28] as seen in an earlier chapter,[29] J sued unsuccessfully for negligence damages in respect of the allegedly careless failure of the department to accept his claim for unemployment benefit. Glidewell L.J. said: "It is a general principle that if a government department or officer, charged with the making of decisions whether certain payments should be made, is subject to a statutory right of appeal against his decisions, he owes no duty of care in private law."[30]

In the negligence context, as in that of breach of statutory duty, one may question the basis on which the courts appear largely to be ruling out damages claims for bona fide but erroneous welfare and regulatory decisions. The rejection of such claims is often buttressed by reference to the adequacy of alternative remedies.[31] But as both *Maguire* and *Jones* show, the fact that one may (via the alternative remedy) eventually obtain the licence or benefit to which one is entitled does

---

[24] [1999] 3 All E.R. 193.
[25] [1988] 1 All E.R. at 173a.
[26] Chap. 4, *section B 3 a.*
[27] [1992] N.L.J. 1375.
[28] [1988] 1 All E.R. 725.
[29] Chap. 7, *section A 4.*
[30] [1988] 1 All E.R. at 736h; see also Slade L.J. p. 739.
[31] See *e.g. Jones* (above), *Rowling* (above) at 172h.

not mean that one has not suffered serious financial loss in the meantime. And in the social welfare area, it is not clear why financial compensation for damage caused by the incompetence of social workers should be ruled out when damage caused by the incompetence of other professionals (*e.g.* teachers or doctors) may be recoverable. This was recognised by the House of Lords in *Barrett v. Enfield LBC*.[32]

In *Barrett*, B had been taken into the authority's care when 10 months old and remained in its care until the age of 17. He alleged that, over the years, the incompetence of the authority's social workers in placing him in various homes and in failing to seek adoption for him had caused him psychological damage and psychiatric illness. On this basis B claimed damages for negligence. As in *Bedford/Dorset*, the case reached the House of Lords on the preliminary issue of whether the claim should be struck out as disclosing no cause of action. Reversing the Court of Appeal which had treated the claim as covered by the child abuse ruling in *Bedford/Dorset*, the House held unanimously[33] that the claim should not be struck out. The factors (set out above) negativing liability in the child abuse cases did not necessarily have the same force "once a child is in care".[34] Where social workers (like other professionals) have taken responsibility for the day-to-day welfare of a particular individual:

> "there is a real conflict between on the one hand the need to allow social welfare services exercising statutory powers to do their work in what they as experts consider is the best way in the interests first of the child, but also of the parents and of society, without an unduly inhibiting fear of litigation if something goes wrong, and on the other hand the desirability of providing a remedy in appropriate cases for harm done to a child through the acts or failure to act of such services."[35]

In these circumstances, and taking account of the difficulty of determining issues of causation "on a preliminary issue on assumed facts",[36] it was not appropriate to strike out the claim. The House of Lords confirmed that outside the (unclearly delineated) area of "policy decisions",[37] "it is preferable for the courts to decide the validity of the plaintiff's claim by applying directly the common law concept of negligence than by applying as a preliminary test the public law concept of *Wednesbury* unreasonableness to determine if the decision fell outside the ambit of the statutory discretion."[38] Still, at trial, a claimant will face a heavy burden in establishing a duty of care in exercising discretions "in a sphere involving difficult decisions in relation to the welfare of children".[39]

Turning to an entirely different area of public authority power, even if it were accepted that a right to welfare provision does not ordinarily carry a right to damages for an authority's careless failure to reach a proper decision on entitlement, it is difficult to see why the same should be true in many licensing contexts such as those in *Maguire* or *Rowling* — where negligently not granting a licence would be in effect negligently imposing an illegal restraint on otherwise lawful activities. It has been plain for some time that the courts have not ruled out negligence claims based on *Wednesbury* irrational decisions in all such contexts. In *Lonrho plc v. Tebbit*[40] L sued T (then the

---

[32] [1999] 3 All E.R. 193.
[33] Lords Slynn and Hutton delivered lengthy opinions; Lords Browne-Wilkinson a briefer one. Lords Nolan and Steyn simply agreed with all three.
[34] Lord Slynn [1999] 3 All E.R. at 208b. See also Lord Hutton, *ibid.*, at 227j.
[35] Lord Slynn, *ibid.*, at 209e–f. See also Lord Hutton at 227–228.
[36] Lord Slynn, *ibid.*, at 214a; Lord Browne-Wilkinson at 197f.
[37] See *sub-section b* above.
[38] Lord Hutton [1999] 3 All E.R. at 225f–g; see also Lord Slynn at 211h.
[39] Lord Hutton, *ibid.*, at 230c; see also Lord Slynn at 213.
[40] [1992] 4 All E.R. 280.

Trade and Industry Secretary) alleging negligence in his delay in releasing L from an undertaking it had given on a monopolies and mergers matter, *i.e.* L in effect alleged negligent failure to license, or permit, it to engage in a lawful activity. The Court of Appeal refused to strike out the negligence claim — which suggests that had the refusal been shown at trial to be *Wednesbury* irrational, negligence liability might have been established.

In general, however, it will be extremely difficult to persuade a court that it is just and reasonable to impose a duty of care upon regulatory and welfare authorities whose erroneous decisions may be corrected on appeal or by AJR.

(iii) *Negligence liability for decisions not to exercise a power*

Given the difficulty of obtaining negligence damages in respect of even a *Wednesbury* irrational decision not to do some act in the course of discharging a statutory public duty, can a public authority ever be liable in respect of a *Wednesbury* irrational decision not to exercise a power?

In *Stovin v. Wise and Norfolk C.C.*[41] the claimant motorcyclist (C) was injured when he collided with the defendant (D) who had driven his car out of a road junction into C's path. The House of Lords held by 3:2 that the local highway authority (joined as a third party by D) owed no duty of care to highway users to exercise its power to require the removal of an earth bank which had obstructed C's view of the junction and thus contributed to his colliding with D. Lord Hoffmann, delivering the judgment of the majority, held that if (which it was not necessary to decide) there are circumstances in which "a statutory 'may' can give rise to a duty of care",[42] the claimant must satisfy two criteria: (1) the failure to exercise the power must be (as in the case of liability for breach of duty) "irrational . . ., so that there is in effect a public law duty to act", and (2) C must defeat the presumption flowing from the fact that Parliament had conferred a power rather than imposed a duty, that no compensation was intended to be paid. Hence liability will be exceptional.[43]

The majority in the House held that neither criterion was satisfied in the case: even though prior to the accident the authority had decided in principle to secure the removal of the bank, it was not in the circumstances irrational for it not to have implemented the decision.[44] In any event, the case was not exceptional — as perhaps would be a case where the claimant has been led particularly to expect that the power will be exercised, or where there is general reliance on the provision by a public authority of a "uniform identifiable benefit".[45] The minority took the view that the failure to remove the bank was irrational and that road users could reasonably rely on the highway authority to remove such dangers.[46]

The 3:2 division in the House shows that the problem of balancing public law and private law values in this field "is not going to go away."[47] At any rate, it is not obvious why it should be more difficult to establish the existence of a duty of care as regards the non-exercise of a power than as regards the failure to discharge a duty. For it is said to be a prerequisite of negligence liability in either case that the failure to discharge the duty or to exercise the power must be shown to be *Wednesbury* irrational, so that there is in effect a public law duty to act even in the power case. If there is in effect a duty to act, should not the question of the existence of a duty of care be determined on the same basis as where such duty is expressly imposed by statute — particularly as "most statutes which impose a statutory duty . . . confer on the authority a

---

[41] [1996] 3 All E.R. 801.
[42] *ibid.*, at 828b.
[43] *ibid.*, at 828d/e.
[44] *ibid.*, at 832.
[45] *ibid.*, at 829.
[46] *ibid.*, at 812, 813–814.
[47] Convery (1997), p. 559.

discretion as to the extent to which, and the methods by which, such statutory duty is to be performed"?[48]

(e) Service-provision and duty of care

As explained above,[49] the focus now shifts from cases where the claimant is alleging carelessness "in the taking of a discretionary decision to do some act" to those where what is alleged is carelessness "in the practical manner in which that act has been performed." It will be convenient first to consider cases which have turned upon the *Caparo* criterion of proximity.

(i) *Proximity*

There is a huge and complex case law on the circumstances in which a duty of care falls upon rescue and protective services: fire brigade, ambulance, police, etc. Essentially, these services are said to owe duties to the public at large rather than to particular individuals unless, in carrying out their functions, either (1) members of the service have created a **fresh danger** which has damaged the claimant; or (2) members of the service have undertaken to exercise a **special skill** for the benefit of the claimant who relies on that undertaking.[50] If one or other of these factors is not present, there is said to be insufficient proximity between claimant and defendant to generate a duty of care. On this approach, *e.g.*, the House of Lords held in *Hill v. Chief Constable of West Yorkshire*[51] that the West Yorkshire police owed no general duty of care to individual members of the public to identify and apprehend the Yorkshire Ripper even though it was foreseeable that he would commit further murders unless apprehended: a claim on behalf of his last victim was accordingly struck out. By contrast, the borstal officers in the *Dorset Yacht* case[52] were held to have created a particular danger to nearby property owners by bringing their charges into the area and to be liable in negligence to the owners if they had failed to take reasonable care in supervising the boys. Also in *Swinney v. Chief Constable of Northumbria*[53] the Court of Appeal refused to strike out a negligence claim brought by a claimant, S, who had given the police confidential information on the identity of a police killer. The police were alleged carelessly to have allowed S's identity to be discovered by the killer who had threatened S and caused her to give up her business and to become ill. The court held that it was arguable that a special relationship of proximity had been created, entitling the claimant to rely, as she had done, on the police taking special care to conceal her identity as their source of information.[54]

Turning from police to rescue services, the general "no proximity" rule is illustrated by the striking out of two claims against fire authorities.[55] In one of these cases, the brigade had attended a fire at premises adjacent to the claimant's, but failed to inspect the claimant's neighbouring premises which were subsequently destroyed by a fire generated by debris from the original fire. In the other case, the brigade had attended a fire on the claimant's premises but were unable to fight it because local water hydrants either were inadequately maintained or could not be located. But in a third case[56] the Court of Appeal held that sufficient proximity would exist where while

---

[48] *Bedford/Dorset* case [1995] 3 All E.R. at 368g.

[49] *Sub-section c.*

[50] See *Capital and Counties plc v. Hants C.C.* [1997] 2 All E.R. 865 at 879.

[51] [1988] 2 All E.R. 238.

[52] *Home Office v. Dorset Yacht Co.* [1970] 2 All E.R. 294: *sub-section 1* above.

[53] [1996] 3 All E.R. 449.

[54] Applied *Swinney v. Chief Constable of Northumbria (No. 2), The Times* May 25, 1999. See further *Costello v. Chief Constable of Northumbria* [1999] 1 All E.R. 550.

[55] *Capital and Counties plc v. Hants C.C.* [1997] 2 All E.R. 865 — the *Munroe* and *Church of Latter Day Saints* cases respectively.

[56] *ibid.*, the *Capital and Counties* case. See also *Kent v. Griffiths, The Times*, December 23, 1998 (acceptance of 999 call by ambulance service).

attending a fire in the claimant's premises a fire officer negligently ordered the building's sprinkler system to be turned off, thus creating a fresh danger.

Public authorities with regulatory functions also, of course, provide "protective" services to the public. As explained earlier,[57] breaches of statutory health and safety duties are tortious in themselves (*i.e.* negligence need not be shown) where the breach of duty causes physical injury. Where a statute confers a power rather than imposes a duty, it remains unclear to what extent if at all the principles of undertaking and reliance can be the basis of a duty of care in the context of careless exercises of *e.g.*, building regulation or food inspection powers. In *Murphy v. Brentwood D.C.*[58] the House of Lords (overruling *Anns v. Merton L.B.C.*[59] on this point) held that local authorities are not liable in negligence to persons who suffer financial loss in buying houses which are defective but have been given building regulations approval. But the basis of this ruling was that mere financial loss was not within the contemplation of the statute: building inspection functions relate to health and safety. Four of the seven Law Lords in *Murphy* left open the question of liability for personal injury. But while many persons may suffer physical injury as a result of careless inspections of one sort or another, it seems probable that few will be able to show either the particular or general reliance[60] which can lead to a finding of sufficient proximity. A case law example where particular reliance was established (and where, also, financial loss was held to be within the contemplation of the statute) is *Welton v. North Cornwall D.C.*[61] where a *Wednesbury* irrational exercise of a statutory power of inspection involved a misstatement made directly to the claimant upon which he foreseeably acted: an environmental health officer visited W's guest house unannounced and, "outside the powers of the Act and also outside the informal enforcement practice of the local authority", threatened closure unless 13 expensive building alteration requirements (made orally) were met. W spent £39,000 on the alterations and sued successfully in negligence to recover his loss when the officer's errors came to light. *Welton* was later distinguished by a differently-constituted Court of Appeal in *Harris v. Evans and Health & Safety Executive*[62] holding that the statutory purpose of the Executive's powers ("the reduction of risks to health and safety caused by dangerous business activities"[63]) would be prejudiced by the imposition of a duty of care upon inspectors in issuing, or advising other authorities to issue, notices restricting a claimant's commercial operations (in the case, the provision of bungee-jumping facilities). "Reliance" will not usually outweigh "protection of public purpose of powers of inspection" in making the duty of care calculus.

(ii) *"Public policy" as a basis for not imposing a duty of care*

In *Hill*[64] the House of Lords gave "public policy" as an alternative ground for holding that no duty of care lay upon the police "so far as concerns their function in the investigation and suppression of crime."[65] This ruling was based on the polycentric nature of policy decisions in the deployment of police resources and on the need to avoid a "defensive" approach, *i.e.* in effect reasons (2) and (3) in the *Bedford* child abuse case.[66] But this approach seems to give insufficient weight to the "whether or not"/"implementational" distinction and would create a blanket of immunity covering many operational situations where these reasons have no application and where, the blanket

[57] *Section B 4 b.*
[58] [1990] 2 All E.R. 908.
[59] [1977] 2 All E.R. 492.
[60] *Stovin v. Wise, sub-section d* (above).
[61] [1997] 1 W.L.R. 570.
[62] [1998] 3 All E.R. 522.
[63] *ibid., at 534h (Scott V.-C.).*
[64] *Hill v. Chief Constable of West Yorkshire* [1988] 2 All E.R. 238 (above).
[65] [1988] 2 All E.R. at 243h.
[66] See *sub-section d* above.

immunity apart, there might well be liability. For example, in *Osman v. Ferguson*[67] the police failed to take steps against X who was known by them to be harassing O and his father, both of whom were later shot by X. Negligence claims brought by O and by his father's estate against the police were struck out on the *Hill* public policy ground, although it was accepted that in the circumstances the proximity requirement might be fulfilled. But in *Swinney*[68] the Court of Appeal took the view that the public interest in protecting police informers might outweigh the considerations referred to in *Hill*: "Public policy in this field must be assessed in the round"[69]; and "when one is considering whether the police have an immunity from liability in negligence, to which liability otherwise they would be subject, the court must evaluate all the public policy considerations that may apply".[70] The Court's failure to do this by adopting the "blanket immunity" approach in *Osman* was subsequently characterised by the ECHR as an unlawful restriction on the claimants' right under Article 6 of the Convention: it was disproportionate to the legitimate aim of maintaining effective policing.[71] Would it not be generally more satisfactory in deciding whether a duty of care lies upon any public authority in the exercise of its public functions to identify specific public policy considerations and to treat them, as in effect the House of Lords did in the *Bedford/Dorset* case, as weights in the scales of the "just and reasonable" calculus?[72]

(iii) *Just and reasonable to impose a duty of care?*

In situations such as those arising in the *Bedford/Dorset* case where a decision has been taken by a public authority to offer or provide some service to a specific individual, proximity will commonly not be disputed by the defendant. For "once the decision is taken to offer such a service, a statutory body is in general in the same position as any private individual or organisation holding itself out as offering such a service".[73] In very many implementational situations of this sort it will be held to be just and reasonable to impose a duty of care in respect of the manner in which professional duties are carried out. The duty will fall both on the authority directly, where it is in breach of a duty laid upon it to provide the service, and on individual employees of the authority — and thus on the authority vicariously where an employee commits the tort in the course of his employment. The following are examples:

- A negligent failure by a health[74] or other (*e.g.* prison[75]) authority's doctors or other clinical staff to provide proper treatment once that duty has been assumed in a particular case.

- A negligent failure by a child's headmaster and by the local education authority's advisory service to refer the child for psychological assessment — treating this as an operational failure in dealing with the child rather than an erroneous "whether or not" decision[76]; and a negligent failure by an educational psychologist to identify special educational needs while assessing a particular child,[77] but only if the psychologist could

---

[67] [1993] 4 All E.R. 344. See also *Alexandrou v. Oxford* [1993] 4 All E.R. 328.

[68] *Swinney v. Chief Constable of Northumbria* [1996] 3 All E.R. 449 (above).

[69] [1996] 3 All E.R. at 464j (Hirst L.J.).

[70] *ibid.*, at 466e (Peter Gibson L.J.). Contrast *Leach v. Chief Constable of Gloucestershire* [1999] 1 All E.R. 215: Brooke L.J. at 229f; Henry L.J. at 234f; *cf.* Pill L.J. (dissenting) at 224j.

[71] *Osman v. United Kingdom, The Times,* November 5, 1998.

[72] On *Osman*, see further Lord Browne-Wilkinson in *Barrett v. Enfield L.B.C.* [1999] 3 All E.R. at 198.

[73] [1995] 3 All E.R. at 392j.

[74] *Gold v. Essex CC* [1942] 2 All E.R. 237; but *cf. Clunis v. Camden and Islington HA* [1998] 3 All E.R. 180 (above section B 3 c *Alternative remedy*) at 191.

[75] *R. v. Home Secretary, ex p. Dew* [1987] 2 All E.R. 1049 at 1057c: see Chap. 5, *section C 1 d.*

[76] [1995] 3 All E.R. at 394g: the *Hampshire* case.

[77] *ibid.*, at 393: the *Dorset* case.

be shown to have assumed a personal responsibility to the child in addition to performing her duty to her employer — which will be extremely unusual.[78]

- In the *Newham* child abuse case the House of Lords held by 4:1 that it would not be just and reasonable to impose upon child psychiatrists and social workers employed by public authorities to investigate child abuse a duty of care to the children concerned: "the social workers and the psychiatrist did not, by accepting the instructions of the local authority, assume any general professional duty of care to the [claimant] children. The professionals were employed or retained to advise the local authority in relation to the well-being of the [claimants] but not to advise or treat the [claimants]."[79] Lord Nolan would have based the professionals' immunity instead on public policy grounds.[80] But in other circumstances such professionals may perhaps owe a duty of care, *e.g.* to a child already taken into local authority care, when discharging its quasi-parental duties towards the child[81]; or to the children of foster parents with whom the council had placed a child who was (contrary to the council's express assurances) a known or suspected sexual abuser.[82] In the latter case the majority of the Court of Appeal held that the reasons given in the *Bedford/Dorset* case for ruling out a negligence duty of care were not there applicable and that a claim alleging negligent misstatement should be permitted to proceed.[83]

- A negligent breach of prison discipline provisions causing injury to a prisoner in the implementation of a disciplinary award.[84]

- A negligent land registry search failing to disclose an entry on the register.[85]

- A negligent breach of a housing authority's statutory duty to give advice to homeless persons. An authority was held liable in damages in respect of the personal injuries suffered by a homeless person in a fire at a boarding house at which the authority had advised him to stay despite the fact that, as the authority should have known, the house constituted a fire hazard.[86]

(f) Summary and conclusion on public authorities' duty of care in exercising powers or duties

(i) *Summary*

If one is seeking to establish that a public authority is under a common law duty of care in the exercise of a public function, the following points must be addressed:

(1) If what is alleged is carelessness in exercising a statutory (or other)[87] discretion whether or not to do an act, no duty of care can arise unless the decision is both justiciable and outside the ambit of any discretion conferred on the authority.

---

[78] *Phelps v. Hillingdon L.B.C.* [1999] 1 All E.R. 421, CA; Lord Browne-Wilkinson in *Barrett v. Enfield L.B.C.* [1999] 3 All E.R. at 197.
[79] [1995] 3 All E.R. at 384c.
[80] *ibid.*, at 400j.
[81] *Barrett v. Enfield L.B.C.* [1999] 3 All E.R. 193: *sub-section d* above.
[82] *W v. Essex C.C.* [1998] 3 All E.R. 111, reviewing the post-*Bedford/Dorset* case law.
[83] *ibid.*, at 133d–135b (Judge L.J.); 142b (Mantell L.J.).
[84] *Hague v. Deputy Governor Parkhurst Prison* [1991] 3 All E.R. 733 at 752a (Lord Jauncey).
[85] *Ministry of Housing and Local Government v. Sharp* [1970] 1 All E.R. 1009.
[86] *Ephraim v. Newham L.B.C., The Times,* January 24, 1992.
[87] See note on statutory and non-statutory public functions in *sub-section a* above.

(2) In such case, and also where what is alleged is carelessness in implementing a decision to act, a duty of care will arise if the damage caused is foreseeable, the relationship between the claimant and the defendant is sufficiently proximate and it is just and reasonable to impose a duty of care.

(3) In a "whether or not" case the courts seldom regard it as just and reasonable to impose a duty of care — whether because of the nature of the decision-making process (*e.g.* inter-disciplinary or polycentric); or the availability of an alternative remedy (*e.g.* appeal or judicial review); or the likely consequences of imposing liability (*e.g.* diversion of scarce time and resources to satisfying successful claims and defending or preventing others). Where a claim is based on an authority's failure to exercise a power rather than to discharge a duty, no duty of care will in any event arise unless the claimant can show that he reasonably relied upon the authority to exercise the power.

(4) In an "implementational" case, those providing rescue or protective services will not be in a sufficiently proximate relationship with claimants who have suffered damage unless their actions create a fresh danger or a special basis for reliance by the claimant. Even where proximity is established, a duty of care may be negatived by public policy considerations.

(5) In an implementational case where a decision has been taken by a public authority to offer or provide some service to a specific individual (so that proximity is not disputed) it will commonly be just and reasonable to impose a duty of care on the basis that in providing services of various kinds a public authority is in general in the same position as any private individual or organisation holding itself out as offering such a service. But, particularly in the social welfare field, a person providing a public service to a member of the public may owe a duty of care to the public authority on whose behalf he is working rather than to the recipient of the service.

(ii) *Conclusion*

Public authorities, like private businesses and individuals, will insure themselves against the possibility of negligence and other damages claims. But the size of insurance premiums will of course fluctuate as the possibility of liability grows or diminishes. The above survey of recent case law suggests that the courts strive, by adopting different liability-limiting criteria in different contexts, to give effect to what they conceive to be the public interest in strictly confining the extent to which scarce public funds are expended on insuring against liability arising from the provision of public services. It was suggested above that the reasoning in some of the cases, particularly the frequent invocation of the "adequacy" of alternative remedies such as judicial review, is not compelling. On the other hand, for many years now a *leitmotif* of English social and political philosophising has been how to resolve the clash between the expansion of need for public service-provision and the shrinkage of public funding available to meet that need. In these circumstances, arguably, there is much to be said for the increasingly restrictive approach adopted by the courts in the area under discussion. It may reasonably be thought that it should be for Parliament rather than the courts to decide that the public purse should compensate individuals who have suffered loss through a failure to provide services to which they are entitled.[88] Moreover, an important by-product of enacting statutory rules in this area might be a decrease in the expensive litigation which seems to be constantly necessary in order to elicit even the broad principles by which, under current arrangements, the question is to be dealt with. But unless and

---

[88] *cf.* Lord Hoffmann in *Stovin v. Wise* [1996] 3 All E.R. at 827e, cited in *sub-section d* above.

until Parliament does take up this gauntlet, persons suffering injury or loss as a consequence of breaches of official duty will often feel themselves to be without adequate remedy.

D MISFEASANCE IN PUBLIC OFFICE[89]

This tort may be shortly described as "deliberate abuse of power causing damage".[90] As stated earlier, it can be committed only by public authorities or other persons exercising public functions. The constituents of the tort are:

(1) Official action constituting an abuse of power by the defendant, D; and

(2) Damage caused thereby to the claimant, C; and

(3) *either* (a) malice by D towards C; *or* (b) knowledge or recklessness on the part of D that his act is without legal authority and likely to damage C.

There are remarkably few reported cases in English law where public authorities have been held liable for misfeasance.[91] This dearth of reported examples of the tort may account for some uncertainty in the precise boundaries of its constituent parts — particularly regarding what counts as an "abuse of power" under (1) above; and what is sufficient "knowledge" under (3)(b).

1 OFFICIAL ACTION CONSTITUTING ABUSE OF POWER

(a) Action in the course of exercising public power

It seems clear that any exercise of official power, statutory or non-statutory,[92] *i.e.* any "reviewable action",[93] may (if accompanied by sufficient wrongful intent) constitute an abuse of power for the purpose of the tort of misfeasance. For example, in *Smith v. East Elloe R.D.C.*,[94] S's house had been demolished by the council in reliance on a compulsory purchase order (CPO) made in 1948. Almost six years later S sued the council for trespass, alleging that the CPO had been procured by the deceit of the clerk to the council. S also sued the clerk for misfeasance in public office, alleging that he "knowingly acted wrongfully and in bad faith in procuring the [CPO]."[95] As explained earlier,[96] the House of Lords held that the trespass claim should be struck out because precluded by an ouster clause, but that the misfeasance claim against the clerk should be permitted to proceed.[97] Likewise, in *David v. Abdul Cader*[98] the Privy Council indicated[99] that where an applicant clearly satisfies all the criteria for the grant of a cinema licence but the licensing authority *ultra vires* and maliciously refuses to grant the licence, the applicant will have a misfeasance claim. Again, in *Bourgoin v. Ministry of Agriculture*[1] the United Kingdom Government had imposed restrictions on the import

---

[89] Wade and Forsyth, *AL*, pp. 789–796; Craig, *AL*, pp. 875–880; Arrowsmith, *Civ. Liab.* Chap. 9.
[90] Wade and Forsyth, *AL*, p. 792.
[91] *ibid.*, p. 790.
[92] Chap. 3, *section B 2*.
[93] *ibid., section C*.
[94] [1956] 1 All E.R. 855.
[95] [1956] 1 All E.R. at 860E, 861C.
[96] Chap. 7, *section A 6 b*.
[97] For possible vicarious liability of the council see *sub-section 3 b* below.
[98] [1963] 3 All E.R. 579.
[99] *ibid.*, at 582B.
[1] [1985] 3 All E.R. 585.

of French turkeys ostensibly relying on Article 36 **[Amst 30]** of the E.C. treaty which permits derogations from the general prohibition of such restrictions in Article 30 **[Amst 28]**.[2] The ministry maintained that the turkeys were carrying "Newcastle disease" virus, but the French producers sued for misfeasance,[3] alleging that the restrictions were really trade protectionism in a public health disguise. Following a rejection by the Court of Appeal of a striking-out application by the ministry, the misfeasance claim was settled out of court.

(b) Action not in the course of exercising public power

It appears probable that any official action, even if not strictly an exercise of public power for purposes of judicial review, may (if accompanied by sufficient intent) amount to an abuse of power within the definition of misfeasance. In *Jones v. Swansea City Council*,[4] J. was the tenant of commercial premises owned by the council. The council as landlord refused permission for a change of use of the premises. J alleged that the refusal was based on personal animosity against her husband, a councillor who led a political group which had previously wrested control of the council from the Labour group which had regained control at a recent election. J sued the council for misfeasance, and as explained earlier,[5] the Court of Appeal accepted that the alleged action would constitute misfeasance even though, in the absence of wrongful intent, such action would not be reviewable — it would be an exercise of private contractual rights rather than of a public power. In the Canadian case of *Roncarelli v. Duplessis*[6] the Canadian Supreme Court awarded misfeasance damages against the prime minister of Quebec personally for directing the liquor commission to revoke R's restaurant "on-licence" in order to punish R for standing bail for Jehovah's Witnesses, of whose activities the government disapproved. The prime minister had no legal power over the commission but he was nevertheless liable for misfeasance. In *Elliott v. Wiltshire C.C.*[7] the claimant, a journalist, sued for misfeasance in respect of the alleged disclosure by a police officer of the claimant's criminal record for the improper purpose of stopping him investigating police misconduct and with intention to damage him by securing his dismissal from his employment. Scott V.-C. rejected the argument that misfeasance required "the purported exercise of some power or authority": on the facts alleged, there had been an "abuse of office" even if the defendant "could not be said to have been exercising a power or authority".

These cases suggest that any actions of public office-holders or officials in their capacity as such can ground misfeasance. In *Rookes v. Barnard*[8] the House of Lords ruled that "outrageous" or "oppressive, arbitrary or unconstitutional action by the servants of the government"[9] was one of only two types of circumstance in which exemplary damages may be awarded in tort. *Rookes v. Barnard* was a private law case on conspiracy and was thus not in any way concerned with the definition of the tort of misfeasance. However the case law on misfeasance seems now to be tending towards a definition of the conduct element of that tort to include any "outrageous, oppressive, arbitrary or unconstitutional action by the servants of the government" acting as such. On this basis, it would appear that whenever exemplary damages are available under this head, the defendant can be said to be guilty of the tort of misfeasance. Thus, in *Bradford Metropolitan C.C. v. Arora*[10] the Court of Appeal upheld the ruling of an industrial tribunal that the local

---

[2] See Chap. 4, *section D 2 b*.
[3] Also for breach of statutory duty - see *section E 1* below.
[4] [1989] 3 All E.R. 162.
[5] Chap. 3, *section C 2 b*.
[6] [1952] 1 D.L.R. 680.
[7] *The Times*, December 5, 1996.
[8] [1964] 1 All E.R. 367.
[9] *ibid.*, at 408F, 410F.
[10] [1991] 3 All E.R. 545.

authority, which had been guilty of intentional racial discrimination in not employing a Sikh, was exercising a public function and so could properly be made to pay exemplary damages. It would appear that the authority's "outrageous (etc.)" conduct converted the statutory discrimination tort into the tort of misfeasance. A difficult case, however, in this context is *A B v. SW Water Services Ltd.*[11] There a (pre-privatisation) water supplier had admitted liability for illness caused by its negligent spillage of aluminium sulphate into the water supply at Camelford. On the question of exemplary damages, the Court of Appeal held that the process of supplying water "is not an exercise of executive power derived from local or central government".[12] It followed that even if, as alleged, the company's officers had acted high-handedly in dealing with the aftermath of the accident, first by ignoring complaints and later by issuing unfounded reassurances before the spillage had been properly investigated, these actions could not fall within Lord Devlin's *Rookes v. Barnard* category of outrageous, oppressive etc action by the servants of the Government. But *Jones* (above) was not cited; had it been, the court's ruling on this point might — and, surely, should — have been different.

2 DAMAGE TO CLAIMANT

On the one hand, where exemplary damages are available, damage in misfeasance cases need not necessarily be computable in financial terms. So in the old case of *Ashby v. White*,[13] A alleged that he had been fraudulently and maliciously prevented by the returning officers from voting at a Parliamentary election. The House of Lords held that he was entitled to £200 damages. Given that "anger and indignation are not proper subjects for compensatory damages,"[14] this is probably in modern terms a case of exemplary damages for misfeasance under Lord Devlin's *Rookes v. Barnard* category. On the other hand, as in the *Arora* and *Roncarelli* cases, or on the facts alleged in the *East Elloe* and *Swansea* cases, misfeasance will often cause measurable loss for which compensatory damages may be claimed. In these circumstances courts and tribunals should consider "whether the amount of compensatory damages they have awarded . . . is inadequate to punish the defendant 'for his outrageous conduct'. It is only if . . . compensatory damages are inadequate on this basis [as they were in *Arora*] that the question of exemplary damages will need to be considered at all."[15]

Plainly the amount of exemplary damages will depend on the particular circumstances of every case. But it seems probable that the courts will develop guidelines as to maximum and minimum amounts in particular classes of case, especially where damages fall to be assessed by a jury, *e.g.* as in cases of malicious prosecution and false imprisonment brought against the police. Thus in *Thompson v. Metropolitan Police Commissioner*[16] the Court of Appeal indicated that in this context exemplary damages should normally be within the range of £5000 to £25,000 or up to £50,000 in cases directly involving officers of superintendent rank or above.

3 MALICE OR KNOWLEDGE OF DEFENDANT

(a) Distinction between malice and knowledge / recklessness

As stated above, the claimant, C, in a misfeasance claim must establish either (a) malice on the part of the defendant, D; or (b) knowledge or recklessness on the part of D as to his act being (i)

---

[11] [1993] 1 All E.R. 609.
[12] *ibid., at 622h.*
[13] (1703) 2 Ld. Ray. 938; 3 *ibid* 320.
[14] *SW Water Services* case [1993] 1 All E.R. at 610e.
[15] *Arora* case [1991] 3 All E.R. at 554b (Farquharson L.J.).
[16] [1997] 2 All E.R. 762.

without legal authority and (ii) likely to damage C. One is "reckless" as to the unlawfulness of some action if one has "failed to make such inquiries as an honest and reasonable man would make"[17] as to its lawfulness. Such failure may be taken to imply at least suspicion as to the act's unlawfulness and an intention to proceed regardless.

The distinction between (a) and (b) above can be illustrated as follows. If, for example, D unlawfully revokes C's restaurant or import licence not knowing whether or not he has power to do so, but doing so in order to damage C, D acts with ("targeted"[18]) malice. But if D revokes C's licence knowing that he has no power to do so (or being reckless as to whether he has such power), but doing so to serve some extraneous purpose of his own — even perhaps what D considers to be a good public purpose such as prevention of disorderly conduct outside the restaurant, or trade protectionism — he acts with knowledge or recklessness but not with malice. (It is difficult to understand the view of the Court of Appeal in *W v. Essex C.C.*[19] that if a social worker deliberately misinforms potential foster parents that a child is not a known or suspected sexual abuser, that "does not mean he is knowingly exceeding his powers".)

To act with either malice or with knowledge/recklessness as above is deliberately to abuse one's power. To act with malice constitutes a deliberate abuse of power because public officers may be assumed to know that their powers are not given to them for the purpose of pursuing personal vendettas. To act with knowledge or recklessness is deliberate abuse because D knows that his action is legally unauthorised or is reckless as to its unlawfulness. The distinction is nevertheless significant for the following reasons:

(i) *D's knowledge of unlawfulness*

If C can establish that D acted maliciously he does not need to establish that D knew or suspected that his act was unlawful: as just explained, knowledge is assumed. Contrariwise, misfeasance liability in the absence of targeted malice requires C to prove that D knew that his act was unlawful, or that he was reckless as to its unlawfulness.

(ii) *D's liability to pay exemplary damages*

The distinction may also be significant with regard to the award of exemplary damages where malice seems likely always to deserve such epithets as "outrageous", "oppressive", or "arbitrary". Arguably, knowledge or recklessness may not, *e.g.* where D acts for what he considers to be a good public purpose.

(iii) *D's knowledge that C will be damaged*

Perhaps most importantly, if C can establish malice, he automatically establishes intent to damage or injure him and therefore knowledge that injury to C is the probable consequence. But if C founds his claim instead on D's knowledge or recklessness as to the unlawfulness of his action, it seems that C must prove also that D knew, or was reckless to the probability that, the unlawful conduct would cause the injury which it did cause and for which C is suing. Dicta in the *Bourgoin* case[20] suggested that it is enough for C to prove (1) that D knew that his conduct was unlawful and (2) that the conduct "has the foreseeable and actual consequence of injury to" C.[21] But more recently in *Three Rivers D.C. v. Bank of England (No. 3)* Clarke J.[22] and the Court of Appeal[23] have taken a different view. In the *Three Rivers* case more than 6000 claimants who had lost

[17] *Three Rivers D.C. v. Bank of England (No. 3)* [1996] 3 All E.R. 558 at 581e.
[18] *ibid.,* at 569h.
[19] [1998] 3 All E.R. 111 at 130a; *section C e* above.
[20] *Bourgoin v. Ministry of Agriculture* [1985] 3 All E.R. 585: *sub-section 1 a* above.
[21] [1985] 3 All E.R. at 624c (Oliver L.J. citing Mann J. at first instance).
[22] [1996] 3 All E.R. 558.
[23] [1999] C.L. 473.

money when a bank (BCCI) went into liquidation sued the Bank of England for misfeasance in respect of either wrongly granting or wrongly failing to revoke BCCI's licence. Clarke J. held that under the knowledge/recklessness limb C must establish that D was at least reckless both as to the unlawfulness of its action and as to the probability that the unlawful conduct would cause the injury which it did cause.[24] Since in the circumstances this was not reasonably arguable *vis-à-vis* the Bank of England, the claim was struck out.

Note: On causation, Clarke J. held that if D granted or failed to revoke BCCI's licence knowing of or reckless to the possibility that BCCI would be fraudulent, D's act or omission could be said to have caused C's loss if in fact the fraud occurred. On this basis D's unlawful action would be regarded as having caused the fraud of which C was the victim.

(b) Whose malice or knowledge? — the proper defendant

Where the operative malice or knowledge is that of an employee of a public authority, the employee will be personally liable for misfeasance and the authority may be liable vicariously. In these circumstances, of course, a claimant is advantaged by the fact that the authority is more likely than its employee to have the means of satisfying a damages award. When will a public authority be vicariously liable for misfeasance perpetrated by its employee?

(ii) *Authority vicariously liable*

In *Racz v. Home Office*[25] the House of Lords held that a misfeasance claim by a prisoner against the Home Office in respect of his allegedly unauthorised detention by prison officers in a strip cell should not be struck out. A public authority employer may be vicariously liable for the misfeasance of its employees where the misfeasance constitutes "a misguided and unauthorised method of performing their authorised duties" rather than actions "so unconnected with their authorised duties as to be quite independent of and outside those duties".[26] How will this distinction operate? From *Racz* it seems that if officers are in charge of a prisoner, lose patience and subject him to violent or other unlawfully harsh treatment, they individually and the Home Office vicariously will be liable for misfeasance. It would be otherwise in a case where officers (on or off duty) pursue a vendetta against a particular prisoner with whom, in the discharge of their duty they have no immediate concern. They, but not the Home Office, would be liable for misfeasance.

Note that in the *East Elloe* case[27] the misfeasance claim was against the council employee only. This may have been because it was at that time assumed, wrongly in the light of *Racz*, that there would be no vicarious liability for the alleged misfeasance.

(ii) *Authority directly liable*

There are circumstances in which the malice of individual members of an authority may make the authority itself (as well as the members individually) directly liable. In *Jones v. Swansea City Council*[28] J. sued the council, arguing that the Labour leader was malicious towards her and that his colleagues were tainted with his malice because they followed the party line in supporting the resolution to refuse J's request for a change of use of her premises. The trial judge found that no malice had been proved in respect of the council leader. The Court of Appeal held both that this finding could not be sustained and that the judge could have accepted the "taint" argument with

---

[24] *ibid.*, at 582j.
[25] [1994] 1 All E.R. 97.
[26] *ibid.*, at 102e–f.
[27] Sub-section *1 a* above.
[28] Sub-section *1 b* above.

regard to the leader's colleagues. But the court held that it could not itself decide the "taint" issue and, by a majority, ordered a retrial. The House of Lords reversed the Court of Appeal, holding that the judge's finding with regard to the leader was proper; and that the "taint" argument was unsound. To make the council directly liable for misfeasance in the circumstances, J would have needed to plead and prove that a majority of the councillors were maliciously disposed towards her.

(c) Case law examples

One reason for the dearth of reported cases in which an authority has actually been held liable in misfeasance may be the difficulty of showing either malice or knowledge/recklessness. Many of the cases are on a preliminary legal point, *i.e.* determining whether, **if** malice, etc. could be proved, the defendant would be liable. Examples from the cases mentioned above are the *East Elloe* case, *David v. Cader*, *Racz* and *Three Rivers. Roncarelli*, *Arora* and *Swansea* are somewhat exceptional in containing actual findings of malice — and, as just noted, in *Swansea*, the House of Lords overturned the Court of Appeal on this point and restored the trial judge's ruling that no malice had been proved.

Moreover, in *David v. Cader* Lord Radcliffe pointed out that "the presence of spite or ill-will may be insufficient in itself to render [a decision] actionable."[29] For the decision may be based on impeccable legal grounds and under the "substantial effect" doctrine[30] might well not even be reviewable, let alone ground a misfeasance claim.

E OFFICIAL TORT LIABILITY — THE EUROPEAN LAW DIMENSION

In what circumstances may persons exercising public functions be liable in tort for breach of European Community individual rights or Convention rights?

1 LIABILITY FOR BREACH OF COMMUNITY INDIVIDUAL RIGHTS

In *Bourgoin v. Ministry of Agriculture*[31] the French turkey producers sued not only for misfeasance but also, in the alternative, for breach of statutory duty. They argued that the United Kingdom Government's import ban was in itself tortious as a breach of their individual E.C. rights under Article 30 **[Amst 28]** (enshrined in English law by the European Communities Act 1972) to import products without restriction as to quantity. By a 2:1 majority the Court of Appeal rejected the breach of statutory duty claim. This was essentially on the basis that in domestic administrative law a government decision to impose such restrictions would be challengeable (misfeasance apart) only by AJR which would, moreover, provide an effective remedy for purposes of E.C. law.

But the E.C. law on the question of effective remedy has developed considerably since *Bourgoin* was decided in 1985. In 1991 in the *Francovich* litigation[32] the European Court articulated the principle that a Member State is obliged to pay damages to a person whose individual rights are infringed by a breach of Community law for which the state is responsible. This raised the possibility that where a government decision (as in *Bourgoin*) or statute (as in *Factortame*[33]) was

---

[29] [1963] 3 All E.R. at 582G.
[30] Chap. 2, *section D 6 a.*
[31] [1985] 3 All E.R. 585: *section D 1 a* above.
[32] Joined Cases C6 & C9/90, *Francovich and Bonifaci v. Italy* [1992] I.R.L.R. 84. Hartley, *Foundns*, p. 226.
[33] *Factortame Ltd v. Transport Secretary (No. 3)* [1991] 3 All E.R. 769: see Chap. 1, *section A 2.*

held to breach individual E.C. rights, the Government would thereby be fixed with "responsibility" and, therefore, under the *Francovich* principle, with liability to pay tort damages. Accordingly, the Spanish fishing-vessel owners in *Factortame* did seek *Francovich* damages in respect of their losses between the coming into effect of the unlawful provisions of the Merchant Shipping Act 1988 and the eventual grant[34] in 1990 of interim relief suspending their effect. But, on a preliminary reference in these proceedings,[35] the ECJ made clear that a Member State will be held "responsible" (and therefore liable in tort) for breach of E.C. individual rights only where the breach in question is "sufficiently serious" to constitute a "manifest and grave disregard" of E.C. law. The factors which the court may take into consideration in making this assessment include:

> "the clarity and precision of the rule breached, the measure of discretion left by that rule to the national or Community authorities, whether the infringement and the damage caused was intentional or involuntary, whether any error of law was excusable or inexcusable . . ."[36]

Whether this approach will impose more stringent liability in the E.C. context than exists in the purely domestic context under the *Bedford/Dorset*[37] approach remains to be seen. In the *Factortame* case itself the ECJ held that in some respects the unlawful provisions of the 1988 Act were "manifestly contrary"[38] to E.C. law and so should attract liability. In applying this ruling, the English courts[39] have held that this "Euro tort" is not to be equated with misfeasance and that neither intention nor negligence are prerequisites of liability.[40] To this extent, the tort is "of the character of a breach of statutory duty".[41] But the tort is in reality *sui generis*[42] and, with its emphasis upon "manifest" breach, may in substance be nearer to misfeasance than to breach of statutory duty, although (unless misfeasance is actually alleged and established) exemplary damages are apparently not available.[43]

2 LIABILITY UNDER HUMAN RIGHTS ACT 1998

As stated in Chapter 1,[44] section 8 of the 1998 Act gives guidance as to when damages may be awarded to remedy infringements of Convention rights. In determining whether to award damages (and, if so, the amount) an English court must take into account the principles applied by the ECHR in relation to the award of compensation under Article 41 of the Convention.[45] This provision, which empowers the ECHR to "afford just satisfaction" to a person whose Convention rights have been violated, has been interpreted by the ECHR as conferring upon it a discretion to award damages.[46] "The application of Article [41] is dependent on the establishment of a violation of the Convention and the absence of full domestic reparation."[47] "On many occasions the Court has held that no award should be made since the finding of violation constituted sufficient just

---

[34] *Factortame Ltd v. Transport Secretary (No. 2)* [1991] 1 All E.R. 70: Chap. 5, *section B 2 b.*
[35] *Factortame Ltd v. Transport Secretary (No. 4)* [1996] All E R (EC) 301, ECJ. Craig (1997).
[36] *ibid.,* at 365b.
[37] *X v. Bedfordshire C.C.; E v. Dorset C.C.* [1995] 3 All E.R. 353: *sections A, B, C* above.
[38] *ibid.,* p. 365j.
[39] *Factortame Ltd v. Transport Secretary (No. 5)* [1997] Eu.L.R. 475, DC; [1998] Eu.L.R. 456, CA. See also, case C–5/94 *R. v. Ministry of Agriculture, Fisheries and Food, ex p. Hedley Lomas* [1996] All E.R. (E.C.) 493.
[40] [1998] Eu.L.R. at 475H.
[41] [1997] Eu.L.R. 475.
[42] *ibid.*
[43] *ibid.*
[44] *Section B 3 b.*
[45] s.8(4).
[46] Harris, O'Boyle and Warbrick, *ECHR,* p. 683.
[47] *ibid.,* p. 684.

satisfaction. [And] the Court's judgments give little guidance as to how this discretion is exercised".[48]

How in these circumstances English courts will apply their damages jurisdiction under section 8 of the 1998 Act remains to be seen. Enough has been said above[49] in dealing with the domestic law on official negligence liability to make it clear that English law might reasonably be said in many cases to provide less than "full reparation" for loss caused to individuals by unlawful official action. Whether the courts' tendency strictly to limit the extent to which scarce public funds are expended on insuring against damages liability arising from the provision of public services will extend into the area of Human Rights violations will appear in time. Meanwhile it remains unclear whether there will be many circumstances in which a victim of an unlawful act under section 6 could obtain damages under section 8 where he could not, irrespective of the Convention right point, obtain damages under the English domestic law of tort dealt with in this chapter.

3 Choice of procedure

Finally, it is to be observed that upon the application of the above principles of liability turns not only the availability of damages but also the choice of procedure in pursuing in England an allegation of official breach of E.C. individual rights or Convention rights. Where damages are not available, the matter is one of public law and, under the rule in *O'Reilly v. Mackman*,[50] should be pursued by AJR rather than by ordinary civil claim.

---

[48] *ibid.*, p. 685.
[49] See *section C 2 f.*
[50] Chap. 5, *section C 1.*

Chapter 9

OFFICIAL CONTRACTUAL AND RESTITUTIONARY LIABILITY[1]

A INTRODUCTION: OFFICIAL CONTRACTS AND PUBLIC LAW

1 "ORDINARY" OFFICIAL CONTRACTS

At first sight it might seem that there is nothing special about very many everyday official contracts. Central or local government departments or government agencies[2] are constantly buying or — less often — selling, land or manufactured products or components or materials. Consider the following examples:

- generally, routine purchases by official bodies of office premises or equipment, or of vehicles or building materials;
- more specifically, purchases of operational equipment such as weapons or weapons components by the Ministry of Defence;
- sales of official publications or computer software.

Likewise, public bodies are constantly entering into service or employment contracts, *e.g.*:

- contracts with the providers of services such as refuse collection, catering, or maintenance;
- contracts employing civil servants or local authority or agency staff.

All these contracts are "ordinary" in a number of senses:

(1) Mostly they are the kinds of contract made every day by private individuals and firms with no government connection.

(2) They have the ordinary contractual elements of agreement and consideration.

(3) They are enforceable via the same legal procedures and remedies as non-official contracts. That said, however, "[i]n practice it is unusual for disputes on [central]

---

[1] See generally Arrowsmith, *Civ. Liab.*, Chaps 2, 3, 11. For treatment in Administrative Law texts, see section headings below.

[2] On agencies, see Chap. 3, *section B 1 b*.

government contracts to be litigated in the courts".[3] For "the relationship between government and its contractors is often more in the nature of a long-term cooperative venture for mutual advantage than a one-off commercial deal. Within such a relationship, recourse to the courts to settle disagreements will often seem inappropriate and possibly counter-productive."[4] But, as will be seen, outside the area of central government procurement and supply, issues as to the validity and effect of official contracts, particularly local authority contracts, regularly do reach the courts.

2 HOW ORDINARY ARE "ORDINARY" OFFICIAL CONTRACTS?[5]

On closer inspection, even everyday official contracts can be seen to raise a number of special legal considerations:

(a) Special public law rules for official contracts

(i) *Contractual capacity and the* ultra vires *doctrine*

The special principles and rules of public law rest ultimately on the premise that government and other public authorities exist solely for the benefit of the public.[6] On this basis one would expect that government departments (central or local) and agencies would be permitted to enter into only such contracts as would further their legitimate public purposes. This raises issues as to the legal limits of official power (or capacity) to contract. The question of the relationship between the public purposes of public authorities and their capacity to make valid contracts is considered in *section B* below.

(ii) *Applicability of public law standards to public authorities' choice and treatment of contracting partner*

The "public authority/public benefit" premise prompts consideration also of the extent to which public law standards do and should govern the various stages of the contracting process: listing of approved contractors, tendering and award of contracts, and the conduct of the contractual relationship once established. This question has been dealt with in Chapter 3, *section C 2*.

(b) Legal issues of "contracting-out"

The legal relationships of purchaser, contractor and consumer

Under the prevailing government policy of "contracting-out"[7] (or "out-sourcing"), public authorities now often contract with third parties for the provision of services to sections of the public rather than, as previously, providing the services themselves. Examples are: refuse collection, schools catering, advertising; and more controversially, aspects of health care, education provision, and the prison service. Here the "purchaser" of the service is not the recipient (*i.e.* the consumer) but the public authority acting on the consumer's behalf. This raises issues as to the legal relationships of purchaser, contractor and consumer. These are dealt with in *section C* below.

---

[3] Turpin, *GPC*, p. 222.
[4] Cane, *Intr AL*, p. 264.
[5] Craig, *AL*, pp. 121–146.
[6] See Chap. 3, *section A 3 a*.
[7] Chap. 3, *section B 1 b*.

3 FURTHER AWAY FROM "ORDINARY" CONTRACTS: FROM "COMMERCIALISATION" TO "PRIVATISATION"

Possible public law control of privatised utilities in their (quasi) contractual dealings with customers

Contracting-out reflects a government policy of "commercialisation" — the partial transfer of responsibility for service provision from public authorities to private businesses. The questions it raises overlap with those raised by privatisation — the wholesale transfer of such responsibility (for the provision, *e.g.*, of electricity, gas and water) from public authorities or state-owned undertakings to commercial companies subject to statutory regulation. These questions have been considered in Chapter 3, *section B 2 b*.

B THE VALIDITY OF OFFICIAL CONTRACTS[8]

1 CONTRACTS OF STATUTORY PUBLIC AUTHORITIES

(a) The "express or implied authority" doctrine

(i) *The doctrine and its relevance to the contractual capacity of statutory authorities*

As explained in Chapter 4,[9] for public authorities created by statute the courts have established the "express or implied authority" doctrine. Under this doctrine, statutory authorities can do only what statute authorises them to do, together with "whatever may fairly be regarded as incidental to, or consequential upon, those things which the legislature has authorised".[10] As mentioned earlier,[11] for local authorities this "incidental/consequential" test was broadened by section 111(1) of the Local Government Act 1972 to include ". . . any thing (whether or not involving the expenditure, borrowing or lending of money or the acquisition or disposal of any property or rights) which is calculated to facilitate, or is conducive or incidental to, the discharge of any of their functions."

In general, statutes conferring functions on public authorities do not expressly confer power to enter into contracts. In general, therefore, such power exists only within the parameters of the "express or implied authority" doctrine. The effect of that doctrine on the contractual capacity of statutory authorities is that they can make only such contracts as "relate to functions which [they are] authorised expressly or impliedly to perform."[12] Essentially, capacity to enter into contracts for the purpose of discharging statutory functions (whether express or implied) is itself regarded as being implicitly conferred by the statute in question. Any other contract is *ultra vires*. *Ultra vires* contracts are void from the outset, as stated by Clarke J. in *Morgan Grenfell Ltd v. Sutton L.B.C.*[13] Although it follows that such contracts cannot be enforced, it will be seen that the law of restitution may afford some relief to contractors who have dealt with public authorities in good faith and in ignorance of the invalidity of contractual arrangements.

---

[8] Wade and Forsyth, *AL*, pp. 366–378, 801–807, 832–836; Craig, *AL*, pp. 146–154, 159–162, 526–534.
[9] *Section B 1*.
[10] Lord Selborne in *Att.-Gen v. Great Eastern Railway Co.* (1880) 5 App. Cas. 473, 478.
[11] Chap. 4, *ibid*.
[12] Chitty, *Con.* para. 723.
[13] *The Times*, March 23, 1995 (below).

(ii) *Local Government (Contracts) Act 1997, s.1*

Further, as will be explained below, during the last decade or so in a number of high-profile cases, courts have held a range of local authority contracts *ultra vires* applying the approach outlined in the previous paragraphs. The Local Government (Contracts) Act 1997 was designed by the Government to rekindle the willingness of private financial and commercial enterprises to collaborate with local authorities in public service provision. The so-called "certified contract" provisions of the Act (sections 2–9) will be examined in context below. Here, however, it is important to note section 1 of the Act. Sub-section 1 provides:

> "Every statutory provision conferring or imposing a function on a local authority confers power on the local authority to enter into a contract with another person for the provision or making available of assets or services, or both, (whether or not together with goods) for the purposes of, or in connection with, the discharge of the function by the local authority."

It appears that this provision was simply intended to place the existing law as to the contractual capacity of local authorities on a statutory footing.[14] But it may do more than this. Unlike section 111(1) of the 1972 Act, section 1 of the 1997 Act expressly confers a power to enter into contracts. Under this provision, contracting is itself a statutory function. True, section 1(1) gives power to contract only "for the purposes of, or in connection with, the discharge of" another function. But it may be that a contract could be entered into "in connection with" the discharge of a function (express or implied) without necessarily being directly related to (*i.e.*, "for the purposes of") achieving that discharge.

(iii) *Operation of "express or implied authority" doctrine in contractual context*

Subject to the as yet un-tested effect of section 1 of the Local Government (Contracts) Act 1997 (which, of course, has no application to authorities other than local authorities), what functions public authorities are authorised to discharge (or perform) — and thus what contracts they are authorised to make in relation to discharging those functions — will depend on the existing general law. In other words, it will depend upon the construction of all relevant statutory provisions in the light of the "incidental/consequential" rule or, in the case of local authorities, section 111 of the Local Government Act 1972. Not uncommonly, as will be seen, the validity of a public authority's contract has been held to turn upon the resolution of an issue as to whether a function to which the contract relates is itself an authorised function within the parameters just mentioned. If a particular course of action upon which a statutory authority is embarked is *ultra vires*, any contract relating thereto will also be *ultra vires*.

It is important to note that the enabling provisions of section 111(1) of the 1972 Act are expressly subject to any contrary statutory provision — "subject to the provisions of this Act and any other enactment passed before or after this Act". Also, section 111(3) adds the caveat that section 111(1) does not permit raising or lending money "except in accordance with the enactments relating to those matters". As will be shown, these provisions have recently played a prominent role in the avoidance of certain categories of local authority contract.

Illustrations will now be given of the operation of the "express or implied authority" doctrine in different contractual contexts:

- where a contract is made in breach of statutory procedural requirements or is otherwise outside the boundaries of a statutory power (*sub-section b*, below);

---

[14] 1997 Current Law Statutes annotation (Colin Crawford) p. 65–5 refers.

- where a public authority undertakes contractual obligations which are incompatible with its performance of its statutory functions (*sub-section c*).

(b) Contracts in breach of statutory procedural requirements or otherwise outside the boundaries of a statutory power

(i) *Breach of statutory procedural requirements*

Rhyl U.D.C. v. Rhyl Amusements Ltd[15] is an example of a contract held void because it was made in breach of statutory requirements. The Council leased a lake and pleasure ground to the company in mistaken reliance on a local Act of Parliament. In the circumstances their only power of letting was under the Public Health Act 1875, subject to ministerial consent which had not been sought. In proceedings brought by the Council, Harman J. granted a declaration that the lease was void and that the council's notice to quit the premises was thus valid.

Statute may, of course, provide expressly that breach of particular procedural requirements will not invalidate a contract, as, *e.g.* with regard to breach of local government standing orders providing for competitive tendering[16] or of E.C. procurement procedures.[17]

(ii) *Outside boundaries*

In recent years central government legislation has aimed to curb local authority expenditure, in particular by imposing statutory limits upon the amount of money which authorities may raise via local taxation. Local authorities have responded by seeking indirect ways of raising funds and financing services. Much reliance, often unfounded, has been placed on the enabling effect of section 111 of the Local Government Act 1972.

Unauthorised borrowing In *Hazell v. Hammersmith & Fulham L.B.C.*[18] the House of Lords held unanimously that section 111 did not empower a local authority to enter into "interest rate swap transactions" as a method of servicing its debts so as in effect to increase its borrowing capacity. Under an interest rate swap, the parties agree to pay interest for a certain period on a notional sum, one party at a fixed rate, the other at a floating market rate. Benefit accrues to the party whose rate turns out to be lower over the agreed period. One form of swap agreement which became popular with local authorities involved an initial "upfront" capitalised interest payment to the authority. Subsequent interest shifts would either increase or diminish the capital sum outstanding. In *Hazell* the House of Lords held that such transactions were *ultra vires* because legitimate means of borrowing were set out elsewhere in the statute: Schedule 13 "establishes a comprehensive code which defines and limits the powers of a local authority with regard to its borrowing".[19]

In a number of reported cases since *Hazell*, lending banks have relied unsuccessfully on section 111 as authorising local authorities to guarantee the debts of other bodies incurred in the course of their provision of facilities which the authorities themselves have power to provide.

Contracts guaranteeing loans to bodies unconnected with authority In *Morgan Grenfell Ltd v. Sutton L.B.C.*[20] the bank (MG) failed in its claim to enforce against the Council its contractual guarantee of a loan made by MG to an unregistered housing association. The loan was intended

---

[15] [1959] 1 All E.R. 257.
[16] Local Government Act 1972, s.135(4).
[17] Arrowsmith, *Civ. Liab.*, p. 90.
[18] [1991] 1 All E.R. 545.
[19] *ibid.*, at 558d (Lord Templeman).
[20] *The Times,* March 23, 1995 (above); *The Times* November 7, 1996, CA.

for the purchase of housing which was to be leased to the council for use in discharging its statutory duties to house homeless persons. The guarantee of the loan thus certainly facilitated the discharge of the council's homelessness duties. But since the legislation provided that an authority could guarantee a loan only to a registered association, the guarantee was void: reliance on section 111 was defeated by this contrary statutory provision.

Contracts in support of companies set up by authorities to circumvent borrowing and expenditure limits   The same result has been reached in cases where an authority has itself set up a company to provide facilities and has sought to make the company financially viable by guaranteeing its debts. In *Credit Suisse v. Allerdale B.C.*[21] the Court of Appeal rejected the argument that the council's exercise of its statutory power to provide community recreational facilities was (under section 111) facilitated by the council's contract with Credit Suisse guaranteeing the company's debts in order to enable the company to raise funds untrammelled by statutory restrictions on council finance. Following the approach taken by the House of Lords in *Hazell*, the courts have treated statutory provisions as to how functions (here fund-raising functions) may be performed as, in effect, exhaustive codes. In the *Allerdale* case Peter Gibson L.J. said:

> "I cannot see that it can be within the scope of section 111 for a local authority, wishing one of its functions to be performed but unable, without contravening statutory controls on borrowing and expenditure, to borrow or expend the funds necessary for the performance of that function, to set up a company to perform that function and to guarantee the debts of that company regardless of the statutory borrowing and expenditure limits."[22]

Similarly in *Credit Suisse v. Waltham Forest L.B.C.*,[23] the Court of Appeal held that a local authority may discharge its duties to house homeless persons only by the means specified in section 69 of the Housing Act 1985, which did not include the creation and financial guarantee of a separate company.

In both cases the courts dismissed debt claims by lending banks against the guarantor councils, holding the guarantee contracts to be *ultra vires* and void. Section 1(2) of the Local Government (Contracts) Act 1997 now provides that where a financier has provided finance to a party to a section 1(1) contract other than the local authority, the local authority itself may contract with the financier in connection with the section 1(1) contract. But it appears that the act would not have saved the arrangements in the above cases for there was no section 1(1) contract between the authority and the specially-created company.[24]

Other unauthorised payments   On similar reasoning, in *Allsop v. North Tyneside Metropolitan Council*[25] voluntary severance payments to council employees in excess of those expressly provided for by statute were likewise held *ultra vires* since the express statutory provision was plainly intended to cover the field: the District Auditor (Allsop) obtained a declaration that the payments were unlawful.

Expenditure authorised by section 111   But the section does expressly authorise expenditure of money within statutory limitations. So in *R. v. DPP, ex p. Duckenfield*[26] the Divisional Court held that a police authority may fund officers' legal representation in proceedings brought by or against

---

[21] [1996] 4 All E.R. 129.
[22] *ibid.*, at 162f; see also Neill L.J. at 149c.
[23] [1996] 4 All E.R. 176.
[24] Schwehr (1998) p. 46.
[25] *The Times,* March 12, 1992.
[26] [1999] 2 All E.R. 873.

them in their professional capacity. In the case, police officers were seeking from their authority funding to support an AJR by the officers of the DPP's decision not to discontinue private prosecutions against them in respect of their role in the Hillsborough football stadium disaster — and, if the AJR failed, funding of their costs in defending those prosecutions. Such funding may be, under section 111, "conducive to the discharge of [the authority's] function" under section 6(1) of the Police Act 1996 of securing "the maintenance of an efficient and effective police force for its area". And in *R. v. Greater Manchester Police Authority, ex p. Century Motors Ltd*[27] a police authority had contracted with a commercial firm to undertake all police duties of vehicle recovery in the area. A garage involved under a previous recovery rota but now not receiving such work brought an unsuccessful AJR. The court held that a contract of the type in question was authorised by section 111 (provided that, as here, there was no delegation[28] of police statutory discretions).

Section 111 thus cannot be relied on to facilitate the discharge of statutory functions by means which are expressly or impliedly prohibited by other statutory provisions. Although contracts which breach such prohibitions are void, it may be possible, as already mentioned, for parties who have dealt in good faith and paid over money in pursuance of void contracts to recover such payments via a restitutionary remedy.[29]

(c) Contractual obligations incompatible with performance of statutory functions

Given that statutory authorities can make only such contracts as relate to functions which they are authorised expressly or impliedly to perform, it follows that they cannot make contracts which (though they may appear to relate to their statutory functions) are in fact incompatible with the performance of those functions.

(i) *Establishing incompatibility*

In *Ayr Harbour Trustees v. Oswald*,[30] Oswald sued successfully for a declaration that the Harbour Trustees could not in the exercise of their compulsory purchase powers over his waterside land require him to accept a right of way over the land as a quid pro quo for a reduction of the compensation to be paid for the "injurious affection" suffered by his neighbouring land by restriction of its harbour access. The statute empowered the Trustees to purchase the land for harbour purposes. The right of way could not lawfully be granted, for it would interfere with the use of the land for those purposes. As Lord Blackburn said, the harbour trustees' statutory powers were conferred "for the furtherance of that object which the legislature has thought sufficiently for the public good to justify it in intrusting [to] them . . .; and, consequently, . . . a contract purporting to bind them and their successors not to use those powers is void".[31]

The same approach is exemplified in *Cory (William) Ltd v. City of London Corporation*[32] — although operating here to the benefit of the public authority. The company had undertaken responsibility for municipal waste-disposal via river barges under a long-term (33-year) contract with the Corporation. The company found that it had made a poor bargain. When the Corporation made new public health byelaws greatly increasing the company's operational costs

---

[27] *The Times*, May 31, 1996.
[28] On delegation, see *section C* below.
[29] *Sub-section f*, below.
[30] (1883) 8 App. Cas. 623.
[31] *ibid.*, at 634.
[32] [1951] 2 All E.R. 85.

under the contract, the company sought a declaration that this amounted to a repudiatory breach entitling the company to withdraw at once from the contract rather than being bound to continue to perform the contract until (it was accepted by the corporation) the contract became frustrated when the byelaws took effect two years later. The company argued unsuccessfully that the Corporation had impliedly contracted not to exercise its byelaw making powers in such fashion. The claim failed on the basis that the implied term contended for would have been *ultra vires* as "an unwarrantable fetter on the corporation in the exercise of its statutory duties under the Public Health [legislation]".[33] The general contractual rule that it is an implied term that one party will not do anything to disable the other from performing the contract thus did not apply.

Ayr and *Cory* show that a contract may be void for incompatibility with statutory functions if it can be regarded as preventing or frustrating rather than as securing or facilitating their performance. In *British Transport Commission v. Westmorland C.C.*[34] the House of Lords explained that the term which the authority sought to impose in the *Ayr* case (like the term for which the company contended in *Cory*) would have been *ultra vires* because "incompatible" with the discharge of the authority's statutory functions.[35] "Incompatible" because it interfered with, rather than facilitating, the discharge of those functions.

(ii) *Incompatibility difficult to establish*

Statutory authorities have found it difficult to persuade the courts to apply the incompatibility principle to avoid contractual obligations into which they have entered. In *Birkdale District Electric Supply Co. Ltd v. Southport Corporation*[36] the House of Lords was unsympathetic to the notion that ordinary trading contracts, however restrictive, could ever be avoided as being incompatible with the due discharge of an authority's duties. (However, had the contract in *Cory* contained the term for which the company contended, that case would apparently have furnished an example.) The difficulty is that any contract validly made by a statutory authority in pursuit of a lawful statutory purpose inevitably limits the freedom of choice which the authority enjoyed immediately before it made the contract. In that sense such a contract binds the authority not to use its powers inconsistently with the contract: having accepted Smith's tender for building work, the authority must not then give the work to Jones. How then may one distinguish contracts which facilitate from those which interfere with the performance of statutory functions?

In the *Birkdale* case,[37] on taking over statutory electricity supply functions from the Birkdale local authority, the company had contracted never to charge more than the neighbouring Southport authority. Southport had succeeded to the Birkdale authority's rights and liabilities and sued the company successfully for breach of that term. The House of Lords rejected any analogy with the *Ayr* case: the price limit was to be regarded as a legitimate exercise of commercial judgment, and so of the company's statutory power to fix prices, rather than as an unlawful fetter on its future discretion to fix prices. In the *Westmorland* case,[38] the House of Lords decided that a railway company with statutory compulsory purchase powers and express powers to grant private rights of way over and under railway lines could also grant public rights of way despite the limitation which that would impose on their later activities.

Performance of the electricity supply function in the *Birkdale* case required the supply company to have the same sort of freedom as a private undertaker to secure its commercial viability: hence

---

[33] *ibid.*, at 89E.
[34] [1957] 2 All E.R. 353.
[35] *ibid.*, at 359D (Lord Simonds), 367E (Lord Radcliffe).
[36] [1926] A.C. 355 (below).
[37] *Birkdale District Electric Supply Co. Ltd v. Southport Corporation* [1926] A.C. 355.
[38] *British Transport Commission v. Westmorland C.C.* [1957] 2 All E.R. 353 (above). See also *R v. Hammersmith & Fulham L.B.C., ex p. Beddowes* [1987] 1 All E.R. 369.

the price restraint facilitated rather than frustrated the achievement of the statutory purpose. Similarly in *Stourcliff Estates Ltd v. Bournemouth Corporation*[39] the Corporation had purchased land for use as a park and later proposed to build in the park in breach of a restrictive covenant. The adjoining land-owner obtained an injunction prohibiting the proposed building. The Court of Appeal rejected the authority's attempt to shrug off its covenanted obligation by relying on Lord Blackburn's dictum in *Ayr* (above) which did not have "any application at all to the present case."[40] To allow the restrictive covenant to be avoided simply by arguing that it meant that the authority would thereafter be prevented from doing things it otherwise could do would "render it practically impossible for a municipal corporation ever to enter into a contract with a landowner for purposes of this kind".[41] Landowners would simply decline to deal with statutory authorities. Further, in *Blake v. Hendon Corporation*[42] the Court of Appeal indicated that efforts to avoid contractual undertakings of the sort in *Stourcliff* by reference to statutory functions other than those under which the contract was entered into will also be unlikely to succeed. In *Blake* the court took the view that a covenant by a public authority (in the exercise of a statutory power authorising the purchase of land for use as a park) to dedicate land as an open space would be valid. There would be no incompatibility between the covenant and the authority's general power (under the Local Government Act 1933) to sell or lease any land in the authority's possession, even though sale or lease of the land in question would be precluded by the public dedication.

(d) Statutory and contractual power to break valid contractual undertakings

In practice the incompatibility principle may only very rarely afford statutory authorities an escape route from their contractual promises. But an authority may nevertheless have an escape route quite outside the "express or implied authority" doctrine.

In the *Blake* case just mentioned, Devlin L.J. observed that "if [the selling/leasing power in] the 1933 Act had been worded in such terms that it specifically authorised the local authority to let a public park for use for some commercial purpose, the position would be different. . . . It would mean in effect that the corporation were given express statutory authority of their own motion to alter the statutory object for which they held the park."[43] Clearly, then, a specifically-directed statutory provision may in effect authorise an authority to break a binding contract. So, in *Dowty Boulton Paul Ltd v. Wolverhampton Corporation (No. 2)*[44] the local authority had in 1936 covenanted to permit the company to use the authority's airfield for 99 years. By 1970 the authority no longer wished to use the land as an airfield. Under statutory provision, any local authority land not required for an existing purpose could be appropriated for a different purpose of the authority. The Court of Appeal held that this empowered the authority to appropriate the airfield as housing land.

Under the statutory provision in question in *Dowty*, prescribed measures of compensation (but not damages for loss of profits) were available. This is commonly the position both under statutory provisions of this sort[45] and under standard form government contract "break clauses" permitting the government to terminate a contract at any time.[46] On the availability of full "loss of profit" damages, contrast the "non-commercial considerations" obligations imposed by section 17 of the

---

[39] [1908–10] All E.R. Rep. 785.
[40] *ibid.,* at 790 (Buckley L.J.).
[41] *ibid.,* at 788D (Cozens-Hardy M.R.).
[42] [1961] 3 All E.R. 601.
[43] [1961] 3 All E.R. at 609F.
[44] [1973] 2 All E.R. 491.
[45] See *e.g.* Town and Country Planning Act 1990, s.237. See also *R v. Hillingdon Health Authority, ex p. Goodwin, The Times,* December 13, 1983.
[46] See Turpin, *GPC*, pp. 243–244.

Local Government Act 1988 and discussed in Chapter 3.[47] These extend to decisions to terminate contracts,[48] and breach of the statutory obligation does entitle the wronged party to full damages.[49] This right is expressly preserved by the Local Government (Contracts) Act 1997.[50]

(e) Alleging *ultra vires* under the "express or implied authority" doctrine: public or private law?

In the *Dowty Boulton Paul Ltd* case just considered, the claimant company had brought ordinary civil proceedings against the local authority for breach of its contract to permit the claimant to use the authority's airfield. The authority's (successful) defence was that its statutory powers permitted it to appropriate the land for other uses if it no longer required it as an airfield. The case pre-dated *O'Reilly v. Mackman*,[51] but today, in similar circumstances, could the authority decline even to address the claimant company's contention that the appropriation of the land was *ultra vires* but, instead, simply invoke the rule in *O'Reilly v. Mackman*,[52] arguing that the *vires* (public law) point was one which could be determined only on AJR and that, accordingly, the claim should be struck out as an abuse of process?

In the reported cases, the contention that a particular official contract is *ultra vires* has usually been raised by or on behalf of the public authority to avoid enforcement of the contract against it. May the authority nevertheless argue that its plea of *ultra vires* in effect requires the claimant to show that the contract in question is *intra vires*; that, under the rule in *O'Reilly v. Mackman*, *vires* issues should be raised on AJR and not in civil proceedings; and that, accordingly, the claim should be struck out as an abuse of process? In *Doyle v. Northumbria Probation Committee*,[53] probation officers were suing their public authority employer for breach of contract in withdrawing a car mileage allowance. The authority's defence was that the payment of the allowance in the first place had been *ultra vires*. In order, in these circumstances, to claim the allowance, the claimants would have to show, to the contrary, that the payment would be *intra vires*. The authority argued, however, that, under the rule in *O'Reilly*, the *vires* issue (which the authority had raised some four years before the claim was commenced) could be litigated only on AJR which would now be out of time. Henry J. dismissed the authority's application for the claim to be struck out. He pointed out that the claimants were not themselves raising the *vires* point, so that their claim was purely in private law. But he grounded his decision also on the "lock-out argument"[54] that to apply *O'Reilly* in a case where claimants do have a private law cause of action might be to divest them of their right because of the very short Order 53 time limit.[55]

While applauding the decision in *Doyle*, it is difficult to accept Henry J.'s view that the claim in that case was purely in private law. Surely, wherever (as in both *Doyle* and *Dowty Boulton Paul*) the enforcement of an official contract turns upon the resolution of a *vires* issue, the case is, in *O'Reilly/Roy* terms,[56] a "mixed" public law/private law case. It is on that basis, surely, that the *O'Reilly* rule should rarely, if ever, be applied.[57]

---

[47] *Section C 2 a.*
[48] s.17(4)(c)(ii).
[49] s.19(7)(b).
[50] s.2(7).
[51] [1982] 3 All E.R. 1124.
[52] Chap. 5, *section C 1 a.*
[53] [1991] 4 All E.R. 294.
[54] Chap. 6, *section B 1.*
[55] Chap. 5, *section A 2.*
[56] *O'Reilly v. Mackman* [1982] 3 All E.R. 1124; *Roy v. Kensington and Chelsea and Westminster Family Practitioner Committee* [1992] 1 All E.R. 705: Chap. 5, *section C 1 c.*
[57] See Chap. 5, *section C 1 c; cf.* Chap. 6, *section C 1.*

(f) Balancing *ultra vires* against reasonable reliance and commercial credibility

When a public authority contract is held to be *ultra vires* under the principles discussed in *sub-sections b* or *c* above, has the other party to the contract any remedy for loss it may have suffered as a consequence?

It may be argued that in principle the right to damages for breach by a public authority of a contract which it has made should not turn on complex *vires* issues which, to a party contemplating entering into contractual relations with the authority, may be quite impenetrable. No doubt there are cases where it should have been plain that a particular contract would be *ultra vires*. But as the cases on section 111 of the Local Government Act 1972 show,[58] there are many *ultra vires* contracts where that is not the case. Here "[a]s a matter of policy, there is much to be said for the view that a citizen who contracts in good faith with a governmental body should not have to bear the risk that the contract may be beyond the legal powers of that body".[59]

Suppose that a public authority resolves to expand a public service (*e.g.* health or education) for which it is responsible. Assume that the scheme is ultimately held to be *ultra vires* but that, before any legal action is taken to challenge the validity of the scheme, the authority enters into a number of contracts in pursuance of it. It employs new staff; it enters into building contracts for the extension of existing premises; it contracts to purchase new vehicles and new office machinery and stationery. Now, if the scheme itself is *ultra vires*, all these contracts must be *ultra vires*. Surely, though, if the authority is forced to break its undertakings because the scheme is held to be *ultra vires*, the authority should be liable for the breach. It is in the public interest that public authorities should retain commercial credibility. Should they not be liable at any rate for breach of contracts which, although *ultra vires*, could not have been expected to be perceived by the other party to be so?

The obvious juridical difficulties in the notion of liability for breach of an *ultra vires* contract certainly suggest that it is for Parliament rather than the courts to find a solution here: in the company law context one may recall section 35(1) of the Companies Act 1985 which provides that "The validity of an act done by a company shall not be called into question on the ground of lack of capacity by reason of anything in the company's memorandum". Statute might protect public authorities generally from specific enforcement of *ultra vires* contracts while entitling deserving claimants to recover compensation for their breach. Such provision might apply not only to cases where the claimant could not have been expected to perceive that a contract was *ultra vires* but also to cases[60] where a valid contract is held to be subject to the later exercise by the authority of "compatible" but, to the claimant, commercially damaging public powers.[61]

In the absence of such thorough-going statutory reform, what remedies may be available under the current law?

(i) *"Certified contracts" under Local Government (Contracts) Act 1997*

The rigours of the *ultra vires* doctrine as it applies to contracts entered into by local authorities have been to some extent relaxed by sections 2–9 of the Local Government (Contracts) Act 1997. The principal effect of these provisions of the Act is:

---

[58] *Sub-section b(ii)* above.
[59] Peter Gibson L.J. in *Credit Suisse v. Allerdale B.C.* [1996] 4 All E.R. 129 at 160b.
[60] *e.g.* the *Cory* case, *sub-section c* above.
[61] Craig, *AL*, pp. 530–533, discussing the remedies available under French law.

(1) to immunise "certified contracts" from *vires* challenge except by AJR or in "audit review" proceedings.[62] Thus, in this limited context,[63] the Act excludes collateral *vires* challenge in ordinary civil proceedings; and

(2) to confer on courts in such proceedings a discretion to treat *ultra vires* certified contracts as if they had been *intra vires*.

The main provisions are as follows.

- Under section 2(2) a contract is a "certified contract" if before the expiry of the period of six weeks[64] after the contract is made, the authority has issued a certificate fulfilling requirements specified in sections 3 and 4. The requirements are complex but broadly are as follows:

- **Under section 4(3)** the certified contract (between the authority and "another person"[65]) may be for the provision for at least five years[66] of services "for the purposes of, or in connection with, the discharge by the local authority of any of its functions".[67]

  Alternatively, under section 4(4) the certified contract may be between a local authority and a person financing a section 4(3) contract and "in connection with" such contract.

  In either case, the certificate must specify the statutory provision relied on by the authority as conferring the power to make the contract.[68]

  Where the certification requirements have been met, a certificate "is not invalidated by reason that anything in the certificate is inaccurate or untrue".[69]

- Section 2(1) of the Act provides that a local authority contract "shall, if it is a certified contract, have effect . . . as if the local authority had had power to enter into it . . . " But section 2(6) provides that section 2(1) is "subject to section 5":

- Section 5(1) provides that "Section 2(1) does not apply for the purposes of determining any question arising on (a) an application for judicial review, or (b) an audit review, as to whether a local authority had power to enter into a contract . . .". However, in these contexts, as stated above, a court may determine that an *ultra vires* contract is to be treated as *intra vires*. In making such a determination the court must have regard "in particular to the likely consequences for the financial position of the local authority, and for the provision of services to the public, of a decision that the contract should not have effect".[70] How the courts will exercise this discretion remains to be seen.

- Importantly, section 6 provides in effect that a break clause[71] in a certified contract held by a court to be *ultra vires* will nevertheless be treated as *intra vires*. And in the absence of a break clause, section 7 gives similar protection to parties to *ultra vires* contracts for the period prior to the court's determination that the contract is *ultra vires*.

---

[62] Defined in, s.8.
[63] *cf. sub-section e* above for the general law on collateral *vires* challenge in cases of *ultra vires* contracts.
[64] s.2(5).
[65] s.4(3)(a).
[66] s.4(3)(b).
[67] s.4(3)(a).
[68] s.3(2)(d).
[69] s.4(1).
[70] s.5(3)(b).
[71] See generally *sub-section e* above.

As already mentioned,[72] the Local Government (Contracts) Act 1997 was designed by the government to rekindle the willingness of private financial and commercial enterprises to collaborate with local authorities in public service provision following cases such as *Hazell*,[73] *Allerdale*[74] and others described above.[75] A case such as *Hazell* itself might now fall within the certified contract provisions of the Act, as might a case such as *Rhyl U.D.C. v. Rhyl Amusements Ltd.*[76] But cases such as *Allerdale* where a local authority has created a separate company for service-provision purposes and has then contracted with a third-party financier to guarantee the company's debts would apparently not be covered. For section 4(4) (like section 1(2) already discussed[77]) presupposes a contract between the authority and the service-provider. In these cases there was no contract between the authority and the specially-created company.[78]

In terms of the general problem of the *ultra vires* contracts rule and commercial credibility, the certified contracts provisions of the 1997 Act are thus an only partially-effective response to the problems experienced in recent times in the area of local authority contracting. And, of course, the Act applies only to contracts of local authorities. The 1997 Act apart, what remedies may be available where an official contract is held to be *ultra vires* and, therefore, contract damages cannot be claimed?

(ii) *Restitution*[79]

Recourse may be had in appropriate circumstances to the "restitutionary" principle that one person should pay compensation to another if unjustly enriched at the other's expense.

A public authority will be unjustly enriched by receipt of money paid in response to an unlawful demand, *e.g.* for payment of taxes. Thus, in *Woolwich Equitable Building Society v. I.R.C. (No. 2)*[80] the revenue had assessed Woolwich to some £57 million "tax at source" liability. Woolwich paid the tax despite maintaining, and later establishing on AJR,[81] that the regulations under which the revenue had made the assessment were *ultra vires*. (Woolwich could apparently instead have refused to pay the tax and raised a collateral *vires* defence to any Revenue claim.[82]) Following Woolwich's successful AJR, the revenue repaid the tax with interest from the date of the judgment; but Woolwich successfully pursued its restitution claim for interest from the date it had paid the unlawfully demanded tax.

On the same restitutionary principle, a public authority will be regarded as having been unjustly enriched by receipt of money paid under an *ultra vires* contract. In *Westdeutsche Landesbank v. Islington B.C.*,[83] the House of Lords held that the claimant bank was entitled to restitution of a net sum (*i.e.* the amount by which payments by the bank to the authority exceeded payments in the opposite direction) of £1.15 million paid by it to the authority under an interest rate swap contract before it became obvious, following *Hazell*,[84] that the contract was void. In *Westdeutsche* the House held that the bank was entitled to restitution of the capital sum plus simple interest. But by 3:2 the House further held that under the present law the courts have no jurisdiction to award

---

[72] *Sub-section a above.*
[73] *Hazell v. Hammersmith & Fulham L.B.C.* [1991] 1 All E.R. 545.
[74] *Credit Suisse v. Allerdale B.C.* [1996] 4 All E.R. 129.
[75] *Sub-section b(ii).*
[76] [1959] 1 All E.R. 257: *sub-section b(i).*
[77] *Sub-section b(ii) above.*
[78] Schwehr (1998), p. 46.
[79] See generally LCR 227 (1994).
[80] [1992] 3 All E.R. 737, HL.
[81] *R. v. I.R.C., ex p. Woolwich Equitable Building Society* [1991] 4 All E.R. 92: Chap. 4, *section F 2.*
[82] See Laws J. in *British Steel plc v. Customs and Excise Commissioners* [1996] 1 All E.R. 1002 (Chap. 5, *section C 1 c*) at 1009b.
[83] [1996] 2 All E.R. 961, HL; on appeal from [1994] 4 All E.R. 890, CA (Hobhouse J.).
[84] *Hazell v. Hammersmith & Fulham L.B.C.* [1991] 1 All E.R. 545 (*sub-section b(ii) above*).

compound interest which, in a commercial context, justice seems plainly to demand (see the dissenting opinions of Lords Goff and Woolf).

In *Westdeutsche*, the bank's claim was commenced within six years of the payments in question, *i.e.* within the six-year limitation period for a restitution claim based (as in *Westdeutsche*) on absence or failure of contractual consideration for a payment or transfer. In *Kleinwort Benson v. Lincoln City Council*[85] Kleinwort Benson commenced restitution proceedings in respect of payments made more than six years previously but within the six years following the House of Lords' ruling in *Hazell* when the illegality of interest-rate swap transactions first became clear. This claim was necessarily founded[86] not on the time-expired cause of action based on failure of consideration but on the argument that the money had been paid by the bank under what had later (under the *Hazell* ruling) turned out to be a mistake of law. By a majority of 3:2 the House of Lords upheld Kleinwort Benson's claim, abrogating the anomalous rule precluding restitution of money paid under a mistake of law rather than of fact, and holding that payments made under a settled understanding of law which was later falsified by contrary judicial decision counted as payments made under a mistake of law which could thus be re-claimed.

Restitution provides a valuable but partial remedy in some *ultra vires* contract situations. The claimant loses the benefit of the commercial bargain which, in good faith, he has struck with the public authority. But at least he will be entitled to recover the net value of any payments made (or, presumably, goods or services provided) to the authority under the void contract. This is subject to a surviving doubt as to whether the principle applies to simple loan contracts. It may be (although in *Westdeutsche*[87] Lord Goff said that he was inclined to the contrary opinion) that the courts will refuse restitution of sums advanced on an *ultra vires* loan contract because that would be in effect indirectly to enforce the loan.

Public authorities also can sue for restitution of payments made by them in pursuance of an *ultra vires* contract, *e.g.* in the *Allsop* type of case (above).[88]

(iii) *Other possible remedies*

In the loan guarantee cases[89] no assets were transferred to the authorities. Consequently the lending banks appear to have had no claim in restitution against the authorities when the guaranteed companies failed. But might they not have claimed in tort for negligent misrepresentation? The difficulty is, of course, the reluctance of the courts to impose a duty of care on public authorities to construe their powers correctly.[90] Subject to this, reasonable reliance might in principle found either a tort claim for negligent misrepresentation or a complaint to an ombudsman for maladministration. At present, as will be seen,[91] ombudsmen in England do not have jurisdiction to order payment of compensation for maladministration. Were such jurisdiction conferred (*e.g.* on local ombudsmen[92]) maladministration would itself become a statutory tort.[93]

2 CROWN CONTRACTS

(a) Crown's unlimited contractual capacity; Crown liability

The Crown is regarded by the law as a legal person (distinct from the individual monarch who from time to time holds the office) and as possessing the same unlimited contractual capacity as a

---

[85] [1998] 4 All E.R. 513.
[86] See *ibid.* at 524g.
[87] [1996] 2 All E.R. at 972j.
[88] *Allsop v. North Tyneside Metropolitan Council, The Times,* March 12, 1992: *sub-section b(ii).*
[89] *Sub-section c(ii) above.*
[90] See Chap. 8, *section C 2 d.*
[91] Chap. 10, *sections A 1 e, A 2.*
[92] *ibid., section A 2.*
[93] *Westminster Council v. Haywood* [1996] 2 All E.R. 467 at 480, 482.

human person of full age and capacity. As explained in Chapter 3,[94] the Crown acts politically only as advised by ministers.

Many[95] contracts entered into by government departments ("Government" (or "Crown") contracts) are made by the departmental head, a minister, in his exercise, as agent, of the Crown's unlimited contractual capacity. So, *e.g.*, in *Town Investments Ltd v. Department of the Environment*[96] Lord Diplock observed that where a minister takes a lease of property for government purposes "the tenant [is] the government acting through its appropriate member or, expressed in the term of art in public law, the tenant [is] the Crown."[97]

Under section 1 of the Crown Proceedings Act 1947 the Crown may be sued in contract, the appropriate defendant being the relevant government department or (in any doubtful case) the Attorney-General.[98] Under general agency principles, the minister, department or other agent is not personally liable in respect of contracts to which the agency extends.

(b) Government contracts made in the exercise of statutory functions

If a government contract is made in the exercise of the Crown's unlimited contractual capacity, there can be no question of the contract being *ultra vires* for lack of capacity to contract. But it is often the case that a government department enters into a contract in the course of exercising statutory public functions of the department or minister. Here it may be argued that the contract will be *ultra vires* to the extent that it is incompatible with the discharge of those or other statutory functions, or breaches statutory procedural requirements, or otherwise goes outside the boundaries of statutory powers relied upon. The argument would be not that the Crown (or the minister or department as its agent) has a limited contractual capacity but that statutory provisions determine the legality of government contracting thereunder, as they do the contracting of statutory authorities generally.

In *Commissioners of Crown Lands v. Page*[99] the defendants were tenants of Crown land which had been requisitioned by the government under wartime statutory powers. They resisted the Crown's claim for rent unpaid during the requisition period, arguing that the requisition amounted to a breach of the landlord's implied covenant for quiet enjoyment which, as Devlin L.J. observed,[1] would be a defence to a claim for rent. Finding for the Crown, the Court of Appeal applied the *Ayr* and *Cory* cases[2] on unlawful fettering. If on its proper construction a covenant for quiet enjoyment purported to bind the Crown not to exercise its prerogative or statutory discretionary powers,[3] such term would be ineffective if (as would have been the case in *Page*) it were incompatible with the exercise of those powers. But, as with statutory authorities generally, "[t]hat is a different thing from saying that the Crown can never bind itself in its dealings with a subject in case it might turn out that the fulfilment of the contract was not advantageous".[4] Here again, the incompatibility test should be a difficult criterion to fulfil.

The point is unlikely to arise frequently in litigation. As shown by the cases on local authority contracts,[5] successful arguments that an official contract is *ultra vires* have usually been advanced

---

[94] *Section B 2 a.*
[95] But not all: see *sub-section b, next.*
[96] [1977] 1 All E.R. 813.
[97] *ibid.*, at 817–818.
[98] *ibid.*, s.17(3).
[99] [1960] 2 All E.R. 726.
[1] *ibid.*, at 734f.
[2] *Ayr Harbour Trustees v. Oswald* (1883) 8 App. Cas. 623; *Cory (William) Ltd v. City of London Corporation* [1951] 2 All E.R. 85: *subsection 1 c(i)* above.
[3] Devlin L.J. in *Commissioners of Crown Lands v. Page* [1960] 2 All E.R. 726 at 735D.
[4] *ibid.*, at 736H.
[5] *Sub-section 1 b and c* above.

by public authorities themselves as a means of escaping contractual liability. But, as mentioned above,[6] government contracts routinely contain "break clauses" permitting the Government to terminate the contract at any time. Since these clauses provide for payment of compensation, neither party to the contract is likely to litigate. On the other hand, with the relaxation of rules of standing for AJR,[7] a public interest challenge to the validity of a government contract involving expenditure of public funds might possibly be based on such grounds.

(c) Government contracts made in exercise of "prerogative" power

In the *Page* case (above) Devlin L.J. referred to the Crown's exercise of its *prerogative* or statutory powers. What scope is there for challenging the validity of a government contract made otherwise than in pursuit of statutory functions on the basis that the contract is outside the legal limit of the Crown's contracting powers?

In *Rederiaktiebolaget Amphitrite v. R*[8] a Swedish ship owner sued unsuccessfully for breach of contract when during the 1914–1918 war the Government reneged on its undertaking to release the claimant's ship from port. Rowlatt J. held that the claim failed outright because no contractual undertaking had been intended. But he did observe that "[the Government] cannot by contract hamper its freedom of action in matters which concern the welfare of the state".[9] In that this dictum goes far beyond the now-established "incompatibility" test it seems unlikely to be followed today. On the other hand, the case does show that the incompatibility test (difficult though it is to satisfy) may be applied as much to Crown "prerogative" as to Crown statutory contracting.

Fettering/incompatibility apart, any *vires* challenge to a "prerogative" contract prior to the *CCSU* case[10] would have seemed doomed to fail. In purely contractual terms any challenge would fail on the "unlimited capacity" point (above). In public law terms it would have been said that government contracting was an exercise of Crown contractual capacity rather than of prerogative power and that, anyway, the exercise of the prerogative (as opposed to its extent) was not a matter for the courts. As explained in Chapter 3,[11] in the light of *CCSU* and subsequent cases neither of these public law objections seems any longer insuperable. As also seen there, however, the courts have not so far been receptive to attempts to invoke judicial review in the area of government contracting. It remains to be seen whether this attitude will change, enabling a judicial review challenge, for example, to a government decision to use its contractual patronage to achieve "collateral" purposes, *i.e.* "purposes other than simply procuring required goods or services of a particular quality at the best possible price".[12]

3 CONTRACTS OF BODIES WITH "DE FACTO" OFFICIAL POWER

If government "prerogative" contracting (as well, perhaps, as official "statutory" contracting) may in time be subjected by the courts to public law principles, the same approach seems likely to be applied to the contracting activities of bodies such as SROs whose actions are reviewable under the *Datafin* doctrine.[13] Suppose, *e.g.*, that the Advertising Standards Authority were to refuse to consider tenders for its printing business from a firm which had been involved in the preparation

---

[6] *Sub-section d.*
[7] Chap. 5, *section A 3 c.*
[8] [1921] All E.R. Rep 542.
[9] *ibid.,* at 544D.
[10] *Council of Civil Service Unions v. Minister for the Civil Service* [1984] 3 All E.R. 935: Chap. 3, *section B 2 a.*
[11] *ibid.*
[12] Cane, *Intr. AL,* p. 258.
[13] *R. v. Panel on Take-overs and Mergers, ex p. Datafin plc* [1987] 1 All E.R. 564: Chap. 3, *section B 2 b.*

of advertisements of which the Authority has disapproved. Might there not be circumstances in which the blacklisted firm could mount a public law challenge? Finally, if in the future it were held that some but not all functions of a particular non-statutory body, *e.g.* the governing body of a sport or of a profession not regulated by statute, were public functions, any public law control in the contracting sphere would no doubt be confined to contracts in the exercise of its public functions.

C "CONTRACTING-OUT" — PURCHASERS, PROVIDERS AND CONSUMERS[14]

1 STATUTORY PROVISION FOR "CONTRACTING-OUT" OF PUBLIC AUTHORITY FUNCTIONS TO PRIVATE FIRMS

As mentioned in Chapter 3,[15] the "non-commercial considerations" provisions in Part II of the Local Government Act 1988 were underpinned by provisions in Part I of the Act designed to encourage "contracting-out" to private commercial firms of local authority services such as refuse collection, cleaning, schools catering, and maintenance of grounds and vehicles.[16] This policy was carried much further by Part II of the Deregulation and Contracting Out Act 1994.[17]

Under the heading "contracting out of functions",[18] sections 69(2) and 70(2) empower the government by statutory instrument to provide that specified categories of statutory functions of Ministers, "office-holders"[19] and local government may be exercised "by, or by employees of, such person as may be authorised". Thus, in effect, may be contracted-out to commercial firms run for private profit.

Judicial and rule-making and certain other constitutionally sensitive functions are excluded.[20]

Also, sections 69 and 70 apply only to official functions which under the existing law can lawfully be exercised by an officer of the statutory authority in question.[21] What are these functions?

- As a general principle an authority upon which statute has conferred discretion must exercise that discretion itself.[22] So, *e.g.*, in *Vine v. National Dock Labour Board*[23] the House of Lords held that local boards could not delegate disciplinary functions to sub-committees.

- Statute, of course, may expressly authorise delegation of discretion as, *e.g.*, in the case of local authorities which may "arrange for the discharge of any of their functions" by committees, sub-committees or officers of the authority.[24] Such provision is necessitated by the number and extent of local authority functions.

---

[14] Craig, *AL*, pp. 121–146; Freedland (1994). See generally Taggart, *Prov.*, especially Hunt (1997) and Aronson (1997).
[15] *Section C 2 a.*
[16] 1988 Act, s.2 and Sched. 1.
[17] Freedland (1995).
[18] The phrase "contracting out" appears in the Act's title and section headings but not in the sections themselves which refer to the "exercise of functions" by "authorised" persons and their employees.
[19] Defined in, s.79(1).
[20] s.71.
[21] ss.69(1)(b), 70(1)(b).
[22] See Emery and Smythe, *JR*, pp. 194–195.
[23] [1956] 3 All E.R. 939.
[24] Local Government Act 1972 ss.101, 102.

- Moreover, many other authorities have statutory powers so wide and so numerous that such delegation becomes a practical necessity.[25] Central government ministers are the most obvious example: here the courts hold that Parliament must be taken to have authorised delegation by a minister to his departmental staff at an appropriate level (the *Carltona* principle[26]). As already mentioned,[27] it has been argued[28] that the delegation of powers to Next Steps Agencies may in some cases have breached the doctrine and thus lack a legal basis.

- This authorisation is extended to other named office holders such as the companies registrar, official receivers and the Public Trustee by section 74 of the 1994 Act.

The Deregulation and Contracting Out Act 1994 thus provides for a vast delegation of official discretion to purely commercial enterprises whose interest in public service provision is necessarily entirely governed by shareholder profit-making.[29]

2 LEGAL RESPONSIBILITY UNDER CONTRACTING-OUT ARRANGEMENTS

Suppose that particular statutory functions have been contracted-out, *e.g.* refuse collection, school or hospital meals, hospital laboratory services, prison security services, school teaching services. What legal relationships arise among purchaser, contractor and consumer?

(a) Responsibility to the public

What is the legal position of members of the public, in particular the "consumers" of the services in question, *vis-à-vis* both authority and contractor?

A contracted-out function remains still in law a function of the authority. Thus, on principle, one would expect that the process of contracting-out would not affect whatever remedies (in public or private law) members of the public would have had against the authority in the absence of contracting-out. Section 72(2) of the 1994 Act appears substantially to achieve this position, providing in effect that the authority can sue and be sued in respect of its acts or omissions "in the exercise or purported exercise of" the functions in question. It would seem that, in legal proceedings by a member of the public against a contracting-out authority, both public law and private law principles will be able to be invoked in respect of acts and decisions of contractors. Section 72(2) may well rule out proceedings against the "authorised person" (*i.e.* contractor) individually, at any rate when exercising or purporting to exercise contracted-out functions. But section 72(3)(b) preserves the criminal liability of contractors and their employees.

(b) Responsibility between authority and contractor

Plainly there will be contractual arrangements between the authority and the contractor. Sections 69 and 70 refer to "exercise of functions" by authorised persons and their employees. The authorisation must be by statutory instrument,[30] but the arrangement between authority and

---

[25] Lanham (1984).

[26] *Carltona Ltd v. Commissioners of Works* [1943] 2 All E.R. 560: Chap. 3, *section B 1 b.*

[27] Chap. 3, *ibid.*

[28] Freedland (1996).

[29] See Freedland (1995), p. 23.

[30] *Sub-section 1* above.

contractor will be contractual. The enforceability of these arrangements between the parties appears to be acknowledged by section 72(3)(a) which excludes "so much of any contract made between the authorised person and the [authority] as relates to the exercise of the function" from the general principle in section 72(2) (above) that it is the authority rather than the authorised person who can sue and be sued in respect of acts or omissions of the latter.

The contract between authority and contractor may enable the authority to recoup from the contractor any loss sustained by the authority as a result of claims made against it. However, the provision in section 73 for government termination of contracting-out arrangements is significant. "It is . . . a matter of concern that section 73 has ensured that a revocation of the authority to contract-out entitles the contractor to treat the relevant contract as repudiated rather than as frustrated, thus significantly constraining the freedom of a future government to adopt a different policy with regard to contracting-out".[31]

[31] Freedland (1995), p. 23.

Chapter 10

OMBUDSMEN[1]

"Ombudsman is a Scandinavian word meaning officer or commissioner. In its special sense it means a commissioner who has the duty of investigating and reporting to Parliament on citizens' complaints against the government."[2] In the United Kingdom the Parliamentary Commissioner Act 1967 created the Parliamentary Commissioner for Administration (PCA), commonly referred to as the *Parliamentary Ombudsman* to distinguish him from *Local Government Ombudsmen* (local commissioners)[3] and other specialist ombudsmen created by later statutes.[4] As mentioned earlier,[5] there is also an increasing number of non-statutory ombudsmen created by industries and professions as part of self-regulatory regimes.

In *section A* of this chapter some account will be given of the statutory provisions governing the PCA (*sub-section 1*) and the local commissioners (*sub-section 2*). *Section B* considers both the effectiveness of complaint to an ombudsman as an avenue of legal challenge to official action and its relation to other avenues of challenge.

A STATUTORY JURISDICTIONS OF THE PARLIAMENTARY COMMISSIONER AND LOCAL COMMISSIONERS

1 THE OMBUDSMAN FOR CENTRAL GOVERNMENT: THE PARLIAMENTARY COMMISSIONER FOR ADMINISTRATION

Under section 5(1) of the Parliamentary Commissioner Act 1967 the PCA, within limits described below,[6]

> "may investigate any action taken by or on behalf of a government department or other authority to which this Act applies, being action taken in the exercise of administrative functions . . . where

---

[1] Wade and Forsyth, *AL*, pp. 79–107; 141–147; Craig, *AL*, pp. 230–243; de Smith, *JRAA*, pp. 41–58; Wheare, *Mal*, Chap. 5; Justice/A-S, Chap. 5.

[2] Wade and Forsyth, *AL*, p. 81.

[3] Created by Local Government Act 1974, Pt III.

[4] *e.g.* Health Service Commissioner (see now National Health Service Act 1977, Parliamentary and Health Service Commissioners Act 1987); Welsh Administration Ombudsman (Government of Wales Act 1998, Sched. 9).

[5] Chap. 3, *section B 2 b.*

[6] *Sub-section b.*

(a) a written complaint is duly made to [an MP] by a member of the public who claims to have sustained injustice in consequence of maladministration in connection with the action so taken; and

(b) the complaint is referred to the Commissioner . . ."

The following questions must be addressed arising from the above: to what authorities does the 1967 Act apply? What actions of such authorities may the PCA investigate? What is the meaning of "injustice in consequence of maladministration"? Who may complain, and how? What redress may be obtained? These questions are addressed in *sub-sections a–e* below.

PCA decisions subject to judicial review

It may be noted at once, however, that while the PCA has a discretion whether or not to investigate a complaint, the exercise of this discretion is subject to judicial review on the usual grounds. In *R. v. Parliamentary Commissioner for Administration, ex p Dyer*[7] D complained to the PCA about the Department of Social Security's handling of her benefit claims. She alleged both unlawful action and discourteous and inefficient handling of her case. The PCA found in favour of D and obtained from the Department an apology and a contribution of £500 towards D's expenses in conducting her complaint. But D made an AJR challenging as unreasonable or unfair (1) the PCA's decision to investigate only some of her complaints; (2) his failure to send her his draft report for comment; and (3) his refusal to re-open the investigation. The Divisional Court rejected the AJR. The court accepted that the PCA's exercises of his discretionary powers are subject to judicial review on the ordinary *Wednesbury/Padfield* basis.[8] But the court noted the broad terms in which his discretions are conferred, *e.g.* the reference in section 5(5) of the 1967 Act to the PCA deciding "in accordance with his own discretion" to initiate, continue or discontinue an investigation.[9] On this basis the court stated that it will in practice be difficult to obtain review in the absence of bad faith, improper motive or manifest absurdity.[10] Dealing with D's three allegations, the court held as to (1) that this was not *Wednesbury* unreasonable; as to (2) that fairness does not require this; and as to (3) that the PCA has no power to re-open an investigation. Once he has reported, his jurisdiction in the case is at an end.

A later case, *R. v. Parliamentary Commissioner for Administration, ex p Balchin*[11] indicates that while the PCA is unlikely to be found guilty of *Wednesbury* unreasonableness in deciding whether or not to investigate a particular complaint, his decisions on complaints which he has undertaken to investigate may be vulnerable to judicial review if a complainant can identify a specific consideration which the PCA ought to have taken, but did not take, into account in reaching his decision. In *ex p. Balchin*, B's land had been blighted by official approval of a nearby road by-pass scheme and the refusal of the local county council (Norfolk) to purchase the land. The Department of Transport (DoT) approved the scheme without pointing out to Norfolk that county councils had a new statutory discretionary power (of which Norfolk was unaware) to purchase the land. The PCA rejected B's complaint that he had suffered injustice in consequence of the DoT's maladministration in its failure to apprise Norfolk of the existence of the power. B challenged the PCA's decision by AJR. Sedley J. found for B on the basis that the decision had been reached without regard to the relevant consideration that "correct advice with the imprimatur of central government might have made a difference" to Norfolk's treatment of B.

---

[7] [1994] 1 All E.R. 375. See Marsh (1994).

[8] Chap. 4, *section C*.

[9] Local Government Act 1974, s.26(10) provides that for these purposes local commissioners shall "act at discretion".

[10] [1994] 1 All E.R. at 381h. On judicial review of broad (or "strong") statutory discretions, see further Chap. 4, *section D 1 c*.

[11] [1997] C.O.D. 146 (October 25, 1996: full report on LEXIS).

Had the PCA considered whether a difference might have been made, he might have concluded that the DoT's "maladministrative" failure caused injustice to B. For "injustice" includes "the sense of outrage aroused by unfair or incompetent administration".[12] Sedley J. said that he would quash the decision if that was necessary in order to give the PCA jurisdiction to reconsider B's complaint.

The questions identified above will now be considered.

(a) To what authorities does the 1967 Act apply?

- Under section 4,[13] the 1967 Act applies to all central government departments and to the many agencies listed in schedule 2.[14]

- "Next Steps Agencies"[15] appear to be within the PCA's jurisdiction since they act "on behalf of" their parent department within section 5(1) of the 1967 Act (above).

- Section 4[16] allows other governmental bodies ("bod[ies] whose functions are exercised on behalf of the Crown"[17]) or bodies substantially[18] funded and appointed by government to be added by Order in Council. But the section further provides — now somewhat anachronistically in the light of the development of the "contract state" — that "no entry shall be made in respect of a . . . body operating in an exclusively or predominantly commercial manner".[19] This provision is complemented by that in paragraph 9 of schedule 3[20] which excludes from the PCA's jurisdiction actions of scheduled bodies "relating to contractual or other commercial transactions [other than compulsory land purchase]".

- The PCA's jurisdiction has been extended by subsequent legislation[21] to administrative actions of the staff of courts and of some tribunals.

(b) What actions of the authorities may the PCA investigate?

(i) Action taken in the exercise of administrative functions

Section 5(1) authorises the PCA to investigate "action taken in the exercise of administrative functions" of the authority in question. It appears from *R. v. Local Commissioner for Administration, ex p. Croydon L.B.C.*[22] that "administrative" here is a broad term. (This case was an AJR by a local authority against a ruling by a local commissioner[23] but it is relevant here because it was concerned with the meaning of a statutory provision[24] in similar terms to section 5(1).) The local commissioner had upheld a parents' complaint of maladministration against a local education

[12] Quoting from the "Crossman catalogue": see *sub-section c* below.
[13] As substituted by the Parliamentary and Health Service Commissioners Act 1987, s.1(1).
[14] As substituted by *ibid.*, Sched. 1.
[15] Chap. 3, *section B 1 b.*
[16] As substituted: see subsections (2)-(5).
[17] s.4(3)(a)(ii).
[18] s.4(3)(b).
[19] s.4(6).
[20] *Sub-section b,* below.
[21] Courts and Legal Services Act 1990, s.110; Parliamentary Commissioner Act 1994.
[22] [1989] 1 All E.R. 1033.
[23] *Sub-section 2* below.
[24] Local Government Act 1974, s.26(1): *sub-section 2* below.

appeal committee in that it had failed to apply the correct tests in disposing of an appeal in respect of their child's school placement. Croydon sought judicial review of the commissioner's decision, arguing unsuccessfully that the matter was judicial rather than administrative: it appears that "administrative" includes all but legislative functions.[25] On this basis the PCA is precluded from finding maladministration in the making and content of statutory instruments but not in their application.[26]

(ii) Schedule 3 exclusions

Substantial restrictions upon what matters the PCA may investigate are however contained in Schedule 3 to the 1967 Act. Among the exclusions (in addition to the controversial "commercial transactions" exclusion mentioned above) are armed forces and civil service personnel matters[27] (also controversial[28]), various aspects of foreign affairs,[29] and of the administration of justice,[30] and the investigation of crime and protection of national security.[31]

(iii) Other remedy available

Potentially the most wide-ranging limitation upon the PCA's jurisdiction is contained in section 5(2) of the 1967 Act[32] which bars the PCA from investigating:

> "(a) any action in respect of which the person aggrieved has or had a right of appeal, reference or review to or before a [statutory or Crown 'prerogative'] tribunal;
>
> (b) any action in respect of which the person aggrieved has or had a remedy by way of proceedings in any court of law."

However, the subsection concludes with this important proviso:

> "Provided that the Commissioner may conduct an investigation notwithstanding that the person aggrieved has or had such a right or remedy if satisfied that in the particular circumstances it is not reasonable to expect him to resort or have resorted to it."

Paragraph (a) makes clear that if one has a right of administrative appeal one must use it rather than seek the help of the PCA,[33] whereas paragraph (b) excludes the Commissioner only where the complainant "has or had a [judicial] remedy". This criterion is obviously less easy to apply.

In the *Croydon* case[34] (above), Woolf L.J. said that paragraph (b)[35] contemplates "a situation where if the complaint was justified the person concerned *might be* entitled to obtain some form of remedy . . . if he had commenced proceedings within the appropriate time limits."[36] Subject to the proviso, this will rule out an ombudsman's investigation even where it is not clear that if proceedings are brought they will succeed on the merits. However it seems not to exclude investigation in a case where there is doubt as to whether, even if the complainant proves what he

---

[25] [1989] 1 All E.R. at 1043.
[26] Wade and Forsyth, *AL*, p. 91, citing PCA Select Committee Report (1968–1969 H.C. 385).
[27] Sched. 3, para. 10.
[28] See *e.g. R v. Ministry of Defence, ex p. Smith* [1996] 1 All E.R. 257: Chap. 4, *section D 2 c*.
[29] Sched. 3, paras 1–4.
[30] *ibid.*, paras 6–7.
[31] *ibid.*, para 5.
[32] Bradley (1980), pp. 331–332.
[33] *ibid.*, p. 317.
[34] *R. v. Local Commissioner for Administration, ex p. Croydon L.B.C.* [1989] 1 All E.R. 1033.
[35] Local Government Act 1974, s.26(6)(c) is in the same terms.
[36] *ibid.*, at 1044e (emphasis added).

alleges, the existing law will provide a remedy, *e.g.*, where it is not clear that the action complained of would be reviewable. A much-cited example is the PCA's investigation of the Home Office revocation of television licences which was ultimately held *ultra vires* by the Court of Appeal in *Congreve v. Home Office*.[37] The successful judicial review was at the time regarded as something of a path-breaking case in the modern expansion of judicial review jurisdiction: the PCA could not be said to be in breach of paragraph (b) in investigating such a complaint.

One may well obtain on AJR an order that an authority which has unjustifiably delayed a decision on a claim for some benefit in cash or kind (*e.g.* homeless person housing or special educational provision) should proceed promptly. But a complainant will ordinarily have no realistic hope of obtaining compensation for the delay via court proceedings.[38] However, in a case of this kind a complainant cannot, apparently, seek compensation via PCA pressure[39] where the official action in question has been held unlawful on AJR but no damages have been recovered: "Where a party has ventilated a grievance by means of judicial review it is not contemplated that they should enjoy an alternative, let alone an additive, right by way of complaint to a local government commissioner."[40] Might, though, a party seek compensation via complaint to the PCA instead of going by AJR which, he may know, will not yield a remedy of value to him?[41]

It is possible that as judicial remedies expand and become more clearly available, and now that it is established that the PCA is himself subject to judicial review if he goes outside his powers, authorities may more often successfully invoke section 5(2) to challenge the lawfulness of a PCA investigation of complaints against them. But only in an extreme case would the courts overrule an ombudsman's invocation of the proviso. This appears from the *Croydon* case (above) where the court rejected an "other remedy" challenge by the local authority only because the local commissioner invoked the proviso. (However, the court did declare the ombudsman's decision void because he had erred in law in deciding wrongly that the education appeal committee had no grounds for the decision it had made.) Moreover, in a case such as the Ministry of Agriculture's operation of the scheme to compensate poultry farmers whose flocks were slaughtered during the salmonella scare in 1989,[42] it would lie ill in the ministry's mouth to object to the PCA's exposure of "arbitrariness, lack of frankness and improper considerations"[43] on the basis that their conduct was so plainly illegal that a legal remedy would have been available and should have been pursued.

(c) What is meant by "injustice in consequence of maladministration"?

(i) *Maladministration* vis-à-vis *error of law*

"Maladministration" is not defined by the Act but is said to include "bias, neglect, inattention, delay, incompetence, ineptitude, arbitrariness and so on".[44] Quite clearly any of these vices could constitute an error of law in reaching a decision. Such error might, according to the circumstances, ground appeal, judicial review or a civil claim. As just explained, the possible availability of

[37] [1976] 1 All E.R. 697. See Chap. 5, *section C 1 c*.

[38] See *Jones v. Department of Employment* [1988] 1 All E.R. 725: Chap. 8, *section C 2 d*.

[39] On compensation via the PCA see *sub-section e* below.

[40] Turner J in *R. v. Local Commissioner for Administration, ex p. H (a minor) The Times,* January 8, 1999 (delay in providing for special educational needs).

[41] As, *e.g.,* in a case such as *R. v. Dairy Produce Quota Tribunal, ex p. Caswell* [1990] 2 All E.R. 434 (Chap. 5, *section B 2 c*).

[42] PCA's report, *Compensation to Farmers for Slaughtered Poultry*, H.C. 519 (1992–93).

[43] Wade and Forsyth, *AL*, pp. 92–93.

[44] The "Crossman catalogue" provided during the Commons debates prior to the 1967 Act; H.C. Vol. 734, col. 51 (1966). But the catalogue is not exhaustive: *R. v. Local Commissioner for Administration, ex p. Bradford M.C.C.* [1979] 2 All E.R. 881 (Lord Denning M.R.).

another remedy may or may not rule out investigation by the PCA. It is plain, in any event, that not all maladministration as above defined will ground a legal remedy to a complainant who has suffered injustice as a result of it. Many cases of delay or discourtesy may give rise to legitimate grievance but to no legal remedy. Certain levels of bias may constitute maladministration while not breaching the rule against bias for purposes of judicial review: a local authority failed in its AJR of a local commissioner's finding of maladministration in respect of councillors' pre-disposition (because of club and party loyalty) to grant planning permission for a new stand in a football stadium.[45] Moreover, the law on official tort liability shows very clearly that many official mistakes and misstatements which in ordinary parlance would be characterised as neglect or incompetence do not ground a claim in negligence. In what has been described as the PCA's "most spectacular single achievement",[46] the Barlow Clowes Affair, the PCA's investigations led to the payment by the Department of Trade and Industry (DTI) of some £150,000,000 in compensation to individual investors whose savings had been misappropriated by the Clowes investment company which had subsequently become insolvent. The PCA identified a number of respects in which the DTI's neglectful and incompetent failure properly to exercise its regulatory functions had contributed to the company's ability to misappropriate funds. Negligence actions against the DTI would have been at best highly uncertain in outcome.

(ii) *Maladministration* vis-à-vis *"merits"*

In that the PCA's remit is limited to investigating claims of maladministration, it is difficult to grasp the effect of section 12(3) of the 1967 Act which "declares" that the PCA is not authorised "to question the merits of a decision taken without maladministration". With the encouragement of the Commons Select Committee on the Parliamentary Commissioner,[47] the PCA has tended to treat this not as excluding complaints about the substance of official decisions but, rather, as emphasising that his jurisdiction is not appellate but is founded on some transgression of the framework of rules and practice within which any particular decision is taken. It is thus clear that the PCA has no jurisdiction to investigate a decision simply because he would, on balance, have decided otherwise. But "maladministration" is not confined to procedural impropriety: it can extend to errors of law which go to the merits of a decision and also to what the PCA regards as undue weight given to a particular consideration, as in the Barlow Clowes case.[48] Consider also *R. v. Local Commissioner for Administration, ex p. Eastleigh B.C.*[49] (again an AJR by a local authority against a ruling by a local commissioner, but relevant because considering the meaning of a provision[50] in the same terms as section 12(3)). It was accepted on all sides that a failure properly to carry out a properly adopted policy (here a policy on the exercise of building inspection powers) would be maladministration. Parker L.J.[51] noted that the statute does not preclude the ombudsman from questioning the merits of policy decisions where there is maladministration.

(iii) *Injustice must be "in consequence" of maladministration*

The statutory requirement that complainants must show that they have sustained "injustice in consequence of maladministration" "mean[s] that [an ombudsman] cannot report adversely on an authority unless his investigation reveals not only maladministration, but injustice . . . sustained as a consequence . . ."[52] In the *Eastleigh* case, the AJR by the authority against the local

---

[45] *R. v. Local Commissioner for Administration, ex p. Liverpool C.C.* [1999] 3 All E.R. 85.
[46] Wade and Forsyth, *AL*, p. 95.
[47] Craig, *AL*, p. 234.
[48] Wade and Forsyth, *AL*, p. 96).
[49] [1988] 3 All E.R. 151.
[50] Local Government Act 1974, s.34(3): *sub-section 2* below.
[51] *ibid.*, at 158h.
[52] Donaldson M.R., *ibid* at 156f.

commissioner succeeded on the basis that although the commissioner had correctly identified maladministration in the authority's failure to carry out its building inspection policy, his report showed that he was not satisfied that the failure had caused injustice to the claimant: even had the policy been carried out, the building defect complained of might have remained undiscovered.

(d) Who may complain to the PCA, and how?

The PCA may investigate a complaint by any individual or non-governmental body[53] claiming to have sustained injustice in consequence of maladministration.[54] The complaint must be made in writing to, and referred to the PCA by, a member of the House of Commons (*i.e.*, an M.P.).[55] Complaints must normally be made within 12 months of the action complained of.[56] The requirement for an M.P. to refer complaints to the PCA was intended not only to emphasise the role of the PCA as playing a part in parliamentary scrutiny of executive action but also to provide a mechanism for filtering out hopeless complaints. Statistics in the PCA's annual reports since 1990 suggest that this filter is becoming less ineffective than it was: up to 1992,[57] around 75 per cent of complaints referred by M.P.s were rejected by the PCA as being outside his jurisdiction. In 1998 the figure had dropped to below 50 per cent.[58]

(e) What redress may be obtained from the PCA?

The statistics show a dramatic increase over the years in the percentage of completed investigations where maladministration has been found: from around 10 per cent in the early years to 90 per cent or more in the 1990s. In 1997/98 complaints were found to be wholly or partly justified in over 93 per cent of the 371 completed full investigations undertaken by the PCA.[59] The PCA must report the results of his investigation to the referring M.P.[60] and to the authorities complained against.[61]

Where maladministration is found, a report may contain recommendations for appropriate redress after the event (the ombudsman has no power to provide interlocutory relief pending the result of an investigation).[62] Although the PCA has no power to require the provision of any redress, his recommendations are almost invariably accepted and often result in the payment of compensation to complainants — even, sometimes (as in the *Barlow Clowes* case and also in the *Sachsenhausen* case[63]) where the Government does not accept the ascription of blame. Indeed the Citizen's Charter goes so far as to state that the PCA's "recommendations on compensation cannot be ignored".[64] Successful individual complaints can precipitate a general investigation of official procedures and sometimes lead to compensation being paid in large numbers of like cases, *e.g.* cases in the late 1970s leading to rectification of deliberate underpayment of elements of some war pensions and repayments of road tax over-payments.[65] By contrast, a recent case of

---

[53] Parliamentary Commissioner Act 1967, s.6(1).
[54] s.5(1).
[55] *ibid.*
[56] s.6(3).
[57] See Table in Wade and Forsyth, *AL*, at 88.
[58] PCA Ann. Rep. (1997/98), pp. 14–16.
[59] *ibid.*, pp. 50–51.
[60] 1967 Act, s.10(1).
[61] s.10(2).
[62] Bradley (1980), p. 323.
[63] *Section B 2* below.
[64] Reid (1993), p. 224.
[65] Wade and Forsyth, *AL*, p. 100, also citing difficulties encountered by the PCA in obtaining compensation for Inland Revenue maladministration; *cf.* Bradley (1995), p. 349.

government unwillingness to accept an adverse adjudication by the PCA was that of the planning blight caused by uncertainty as to the intended route of the Channel Tunnel rail link.[66]

2 LOCAL COMMISSIONERS

Local Commissioners for Administration (LCAs) were created by the Local Government Act 1974, Pt III (subsequently amended[67]) and given a jurisdiction over specified[68] local and other authorities similar to that of the PCA over central government. Currently there is a local commissioner for each of three areas[69] into which England is divided; there are also commissioners for Wales and Scotland.

LCAs, like the PCA, may investigate complaints of injustice sustained in consequence of maladministration in connection with action taken in the exercise of administrative functions of an authority under their jurisdiction.[70] The 1974 Act contains a provision (section 34(3)) parallel to that of the 1967 Act[71] prohibiting an LCA from questioning "the merits of a decision taken without maladministration". It contains also a provision (section 26(6)) parallel to that of the 1967 Act[72] barring investigation where there is an administrative appeal or court remedy, except where the complainant could not reasonably be expected to have resorted to it. The 1974 Act (Schedule 5) also contains a list (similar to that in Schedule 3 to the 1967 Act) of matters which LCAs may not investigate, including contractual or commercial transactions. An LCA may also not investigate "any action which in his opinion affects all or most of the inhabitants of the area of the authority concerned".[73]

In contrast to the M.P. filter system for the PCA, complaints may be made by a member of the public directly to an LCA[74] or to a member of the authority concerned. As with the PCA arrangements, the mechanism of redress is via a system of reports and recommendations.[75] The LCAs, like the PCA, have no power to require redress to be made. Compensation is often recommended and often but not always paid[76] - leading to suggestions for a scheme of statutory enforcement[77] such as that which exists in Northern Ireland where the local ombudsman's findings can be enforced by the county court.[78]

B COMPLAINT TO AN OMBUDSMAN: EFFECTIVENESS IN RELATION TO OTHER AVENUES OF LEGAL CHALLENGE TO OFFICIAL ACTION

How effective is complaint to an ombudsman as an avenue of legal challenge to official action? This may be assessed by considering the extent to which such complaint, on the one hand,

---

[66] James and Longley (1996).
[67] By Local Government Act 1978, s.1, Local Government Act 1988, s.29 & Sched. 3, and Local Government and Housing Act 1989, Pt. II.
[68] 1974 Act, ss.25, 34; 1988 Act, Sched. 3, para. 4.
[69] London, the South-East and East Anglia; the North and North Midlands; the rest of England.
[70] Local Government Act 1974, s.26(1).
[71] s.12(3): *sub-section 1 c* above.
[72] s.5(2): *sub-section 1 b* above.
[73] 1974 Act, s.26(7).
[74] 1974 Act, s.26(2) as amended by 1988 Act, Sched. 3, para. 5.
[75] 1974 Act, ss.30 and 31 as amended by Local Government and Housing Act 1989, s.26.
[76] Payment is authorised by Local Government Act 1974, s.31(3) (added by Local Government Act 1978, s.1).
[77] See. *e.g.* Justice/A-S, 5.89–5.90.
[78] Commissioner for Complaints Act (NI), s.7.

overlaps and, on the other, complements or supplements other avenues of challenge. As in the previous section, the matter will be considered under five headings: Authorities; Actions subject to challenge; Grounds for challenge; Standing and procedure; Remedies.

1 AUTHORITIES

The PCA and LCAs have jurisdiction only over authorities (or categories of authority) specified by statutory provision. This is true also of authorities with jurisdiction to hear appeals against official decisions.[79] But it contrasts sharply with the judicial review jurisdiction of the High Court which is always in principle available to challenge the legality of an exercise of official power unless it has been removed or restricted by statute.[80] A former PCA has observed that conferring jurisdiction in this highly specific and piecemeal way is "an inherently inefficient process. . . . I should prefer a form of opting out of jurisdiction rather than opting into it in the light of modern circumstances".[81] Certainly it leads to anomalous exclusions from ombudsmen's jurisdiction. For example, bodies "operating in an exclusively or predominantly commercial manner" may not be added to those under the PCA's jurisdiction.[82] And although many of the agencies already within the jurisdiction under Schedule 2[83] are now required to operate in a commercial ambience,[84] all actions "relating to contractual or other commercial transactions" are excluded from the PCA's jurisdiction by Schedule 3.[85] The current approach to defining the jurisdiction of the PCA and LCAs prevents the kind of adaptation to developments in public administrative arrangements that have been possible in the context of judicial review.[86]

2 ACTIONS

As seen above, the statutory phrase "action taken in the exercise of administrative functions" excludes investigation by the PCA of the making and content of statutory instruments. Here, judicial review can provide a fruitful avenue of challenge.[87] On the other side of the coin, the PCA has shown himself willing to investigate the application and the interpretation not only of statutory instruments but also of "para-legislation" such as internal departmental rules — an area where the availability of judicial review is not firmly established.[88] For example, in the *Sachsenhausen* case, following adverse criticism by the PCA, the Foreign Office (albeit reluctantly), paid compensation to British prisoners of war whose claims to compensation had been initially rejected under the scheme adopted by the department.[89]

More generally, the "other remedy" provisions of the legislation governing the PCA[90] and LCAs[91] may appear at first sight to embody the principle that one should complain to an ombudsman only where there is no possibility of a successful AJR or civil claim to remedy the action complained of. While so strict a reading is plainly untenable when one takes account of the

---

[79] Chap. 2, *section A 2*.
[80] Chap. 1, *section B 2*.
[81] Reid (1993) pp. 224–226.
[82] *Section A 1 a* above.
[83] *ibid.*
[84] See *e.g.* Chap. 9, *section C*: Contracting-out.
[85] *Section A 1 a* above.
[86] Chap. 3, *section B 2 b*.
[87] Chap. 4, *section F*.
[88] Chap. 3, *section C 1 b*.
[89] Bradley (1980), p. 328.
[90] Above, *section A 1 b*.
[91] *Section A 2*.

proviso,[92] it remains broadly true that as the ambit of reviewable action expands,[93] so the range of official action subject to investigation by the PCA or LCAs contracts.[94] On the other hand, the boundaries of reviewable action — not to say official liability in tort and contract — are always likely to be uncertain. Moreover, where a complainant seeks compensation for injustice caused by maladministration, an ombudsman may well take the view that, in the words of the proviso, it is not reasonable to expect the complainant to resort to a judicial remedy where damages seem unlikely to be available.

Importantly in connection with the "other remedy" rule, Lord Woolf in his civil justice review has recommended that ombudsmen should "have wider scope to take on issues which could be resolved by the courts".[95] Such change (which would almost certainly require legislation) would be a highly significant step in making the ombudsman "a cheap and accessible substitute for the courts" rather than simply "provid[ing] protection for the citizen in areas lying outside the jurisdiction of the courts."[96]

3 GROUNDS

As already explained,[97] by no means all "maladministration" will ground a legal remedy via court or tribunal proceedings to a complainant who has suffered injustice as a result of it. In particular, ". . . the Ombudsman, with his ability to recommend that redress for maladministration which has led to injustice should be provided by *ex gratia* payments, is more likely [than the law of official tort liability] to benefit complainants."[98] Further, complaint to an ombudsman may provide an opportunity to scrutinise the merits of an official decision in circumstances where there is no statutory right of appeal. For he is not precluded from questioning the merits of policy decisions where maladministration is established. Recall *R. v. Local Commissioner for Administration, ex p. Eastleigh B.C.*[99] where the LCA was held entitled to criticise the council's policy of limited sewer inspection, given that in the circumstances there had been maladministration in failing to carry out even that policy. In both these respects, a complainant may have grounds for complaint which will yield the remedy he seeks only via complaint to an ombudsman.

4 STANDING AND PROCEDURE

(a) Standing

Standing to make a complaint to either the PCA[1] or an LCA[2] is conferred on persons who claim to have sustained injustice in consequence of maladministration. Under both the 1967 and 1974 Acts the phrase "a person aggrieved" is used[3] to describe such persons. This is a form of words commonly used in statutes to confer standing to appeal.[4] It includes any person whose

---

[92] *Sub-section A 1 b* above.
[93] Chap. 3, *sections B 2 b, C.*
[94] Bradley (1980), pp. 324–329.
[95] Woolf, *Interim*, Chap. 18, para. 18.
[96] Bradley (1980), p. 321; *cf.* Clothier (1986).
[97] *Section A 1 c.*
[98] Reid (1993), p. 228.
[99] [1988] 3 All E.R. 151: *section A 1 c.*
[1] *Section A 1 d* above.
[2] *Section A 2.*
[3] Parliamentary Commissioner Act 1967, s.5(2)(a) *et seq*; Local Government Act 1974, s.26(1)(b) *et seq.*
[4] See *e.g.* Chap. 2, *section B 1 c.*

legal rights have been adversely affected, but goes beyond that and may be[5] broadly coterminous with the "sufficient interest" requirement for AJR.[6] However, it is unclear whether there is the same degree of "public interest standing" under the "person aggrieved" rubric as, now, exists under Order 53.[7] LCAs, in particular, may be constrained in this respect by the provision (already quoted)[8] prohibiting them from investigating "any action which in [their] opinion affects all or most of the inhabitants of the area of the authority concerned".

In any event, *R. v. Parliamentary Commissioner for Administration, ex p. Dyer*[9] makes it clear that ombudsmen have a far broader discretion to decline to investigate a complaint from someone claiming to be a person aggrieved than the High Court asserts in considering an application for permission to AJR, where permission will be granted to anyone with a clearly arguable case.[10] Moreover, appeals, at any rate in the first instance, are invariably a matter of right for any person with standing. Civil actions too may be brought as a matter of right by a person with a cause of action. Even ignoring the MP filter for PCA complaints,[11] it is plain that in this respect access to an ombudsman is less well secured than to other avenues of legal challenge.

(b) Procedure

The private investigative procedure followed by the PCA[12] and LCAs[13] contrasts sharply with the *"party v. party,* day in court" procedure for appeals, AJRs and civil claims. Procedural reform seems likely following the Human Rights Act 1998. For misgivings are felt in Whitehall about "the operation of all the ombudsman schemes, whose procedures might breach the right to a fair trial".[14] Under current arrangements the commissioners have full access to departmental files,[15] and to obstruct a commissioner in the performance of his functions may lead to contempt proceedings.[16] Happily for complainants, commissioners charge no fees. Ombudsmen are "one of the services of the welfare state".[17]

5 REMEDIES

On the one hand, unlike courts and tribunals, neither the PCA nor LCAs have powers to require public authorities to provide remedies to successful complainants. It is thus usually the case that if one is looking to force a public authority to remedy its unlawful official action, one will be looking ultimately either to appeal or to judicial review or to the imposition by a court of civil liability and a remedy of damages and/or injunction and/or declaration.

On the other hand, (a) almost all PCA recommendations for payment of compensation[18] and many such recommendations by LCAs[19] are accepted by public authorities; and (b) the

---

[5] See LCCP 126 (1993), para. 19.11; LCR (1994), para. 12.18.
[6] Chap. 5, *section A 3.*
[7] *ibid., sub-section c.*
[8] 1974 Act, s.26(7): *section A 2* above.
[9] [1994] 1 All E.R. 375: *section A 1* above.
[10] Chap. 5, *section A 3 a.*
[11] *Section A 1 d* above.
[12] 1967 Act, ss.7–9.
[13] 1974 Act, ss.28–29.
[14] Francis Gibb writing in *The Times,* May 5, 1999.
[15] 1967 Act, s.8: see Bradley (1980) p. 322; Reid (1993) p. 224; 1974 Act, s.29.
[16] 1967 Act, s.9; 1974 Act, s.28(8), (9).
[17] Wade and Forsyth, *AL,* p. 84.
[18] *Section A 1 e* above.
[19] *Section A 2.*

ombudsmen in practice recommend the payment of compensation in respect of a far broader range of official action than is subject to civil damages.[20] It is of course true that whether and how much compensation should be recommended is very much at the ombudsman's discretion.[21] Nevertheless, for those seeking compensation, complaint to an ombudsman may be regarded as an important and salutary supplement to other avenues of challenge.

---

[20] *Section A 1 c, e* and *sub-section 3* above.
[21] Bradley (1980), p. 331.

BIBLIOGRAPHY

Allison, *Dist.*   J.W.F. Allison, *A Continental Distinction in the Common Law: A Historical and Comparative Perspective on English Public Law* (1996)

Allison (1997)   John Allison, "Theoretical and Institutional Underpinnings of a Separate Administrative Law" in Taggart, *Prov.*, Chap. 4

Anderson, *Ref.*   D. Anderson, *References to the European Court* (1995)

Aronson (1997)   Mark Aronson, "A Public Lawyer's Responses to Privatisation and Outsourcing" in Taggart, *Prov.*, Chap. 3

Arrowsmith, *Civ. Liab.*   Sue Arrowsmith, *Civil Liability and Public Authorities* (1992)

Arrowsmith (1990)   Sue Arrowsmith, "Judicial Review and the Contractual Powers of Public Authorities" (1990) 106 L.Q.R. 275

Austin (1997)   Rodney Austin, "Administrative Law's Reaction to the Changing Concepts of Public Service" in Leyland & Woods, *NH*, Chap. 1

Bailey and Gunn, *ELS*   S.H. Bailey and M. Gunn, *The Modern English Legal System* (1996, 3rd ed.)

Baldwin and McCrudden, *RPL*   R. Baldwin and C. McCrudden, *Regulation and Public Law* (1987)

Baldwin (1994)   Robert Baldwin, "Governing with Rules: the Developing Agenda" in Richardson & Genn, *ALGA*, Chap. 7

Bamforth (1995)   Nicholas Bamforth, "Protected social groups, the Refugee Convention and judicial review: the *Vraciu* case" [1995] P.L. 382

Bamforth (1998)   Nicholas Bamforth, "Parliamentary Sovereignty and the Human Rights Act 1998" [1998] P.L. 572

Barendt (1995)   Eric Barendt, "Constitutional Law and the Criminal Injuries Compensation Scheme" [1995] P.L. 357

Beatson and Matthews, *AL-Cas* J. Beatson and M.H. Matthews, *Administrative Law — Cases and Materials* (2nd ed., 1989)

Beatson (1984)   J. Beatson, "The Scope of Judicial Review for Error of Law" (1984) 4 O.J.L.S. 22

Beatson (1987)   J. Beatson, "'Public' and 'Private' in English Administrative Law" (1987) 103 L.Q.R. 34.

Beatson (1998)   Jack Beatson, "Prematurity and Ripeness for Review" in Forsyth & Hare, *Wade*, p. 221

Beloff (1994)   Michael Beloff Q.C., "Wednesbury, Padfield and All That Jazz: a Public Lawyer's View of Statute Law Reform" [1994] S.L. 147

Bingham (1991)   Sir Thomas Bingham, "Should Public Law Remedies be Discretionary?" [1991] P.L. 64

Blake and Sunkin (1998)   Charles Blake and Maurice Sunkin, "Immigration: appeals and judicial review" [1998] P.L. 583

Borrie (1989)   Sir Gordon Borrie, "The Regulation of Public and Private Power" [1989] P.L. 552

Boyron (1992)   Sophie Boyron, "Proportionality in English Administrative Law: a Faulty Translation?" [1992] O.J.L.S. 237

Bradley (1980)   A.W. Bradley, "The Role of the Ombudsman in Relation to the Protection of Citizens' Rights" [1980] C.L.J. 304

Bradley (1991)   Anthony Bradley, "The need for legislative intervention" [1991] N.L.J. 389

Bradley (1995)   A.W. Bradley, "The Parliamentary Ombudsman again — A positive report" [1995] P.L. 345

Brown and Bell, *Fr. AL*   L.N. Brown and J.S. Bell, *French Administrative Law* (4th ed., 1993)

Buckley (1984)   R.A. Buckley "Liability in Tort for Breach of Statutory Duty" (1984) 100 L.Q.R. 204

Cane, *Intr. AL*   Peter Cane, *Introduction to Administrative Law* (3rd ed., 1996)

Cane (1981)   Peter Cane "Ultra Vires Breach of Statutory Duty" [1981] P.L. 11

Cane (1994)   Peter Cane, "Mapping the Frontiers [of Judicial Review]" in P. Birks, ed., *The Frontiers of Liability, Vol. 1* (1994), p. 137

Cane (1995)   Peter Cane, "Standing up for the Public" [1995] P.L. 276

Carnwath (1996)   Sir Robert Carnwath, "The Reasonable Limits of Local Authority Powers" [1996] P.L. 244

Chitty, *Con.*   Chitty, *Contracts*, A.G. Guest and others, ed. (26th ed., 1989)

Clothier (1986)   Sir C. Clothier, "The Value of an Ombudsman" [1986] P.L. 204

Collins, *E.C.-U.K.*   L. Collins, *European Community Law in the United Kingdom* (5th ed., 1997)

Convery (1997)   Jane Convery, "Public or Private? Duty of Care in a Statutory Framework: *Stovin v. Wise* in the House of Lords" (1997) 60 M.L.R. 559

Cooke (1997)	Lord Cooke of Thorndon, "The Liberation of English Public Law" in his *Turning Points of the Common Law* (1997), p. 63
Cooke (1998)	Lord Cooke of Thorndon, "The Discretionary Heart of Administrative Law" in Forsyth & Hare, *Wade*, p. 203
C.T. Report (1980)	Council on Tribunals *Special Report 1980*, Cmnd. 7805
Craig, *AL*	P. Craig, *Administrative Law* (4th ed., 1999)
Craig (1992)	P. Craig, "Legitimate Expectations: A Conceptual Analysis" (1992) 108 L.Q.R. 79
Craig (1996)	P. Craig, "Substantive Legitimate Expectations in Domestic and Community Law" [1996] C.L.J. 289
Craig (1997)	P. Craig, "Once More Unto the Breach: the Community, the State and Damages Liability" (1997) 113 L.Q.R. 67
Craig (1998)	Paul Craig, "Ultra Vires and the Foundations of Judicial Review" [1998] C.L.J. 63
Craig and Walters (1999)	Paul Craig and Mark Walters, "The Courts, Devolution and Judicial Review" [1999] P.L. 274
Cross, *SI*	Rupert Cross, *Statutory Interpretation* (3rd ed., Bell & Engle, ed., 1995)
de la Mare (1999)	Tom de la Mare, "The Human Rights Act 1998: The Impact on Judicial Review" [1999] J.R. 32
de Smith, *JRAA*	S.A. de Smith, *Judicial Review of Administrative Action* (5th ed., 1995, Woolf & Jowell, ed.)
Dotan (1997)	Yoav Dotan, "Why Administrators should be Bound by their Policies" (1997) 17 O.J.L.S. 23
Elias (1988)	P. Elias, "Legitimate Expectations and Judicial Review" in Jowell & Oliver, *NDJR*, p. 37
Elliott (1999)	Mark Elliott, "The Ultra Vires Doctrine in a Constitutional Setting: Still the Central Principle of Administrative Law" [1999] C.L.J. 129
Emery (1987)	C.T. Emery, "Appellate Jurisdiction to Correct Errors of Law" (1987) 103 L.Q.R. 264
Emery (1992)	Carl Emery, "The Vires Defence — 'Ultra Vires' as a Defence to Criminal or Civil Proceedings" [1992] C.L.J. 308
Emery (1993)	Carl Emery, "Collateral Attack — Attacking *Ultra Vires* Action Indirectly in Courts and Tribunals" (1993) 56 M.L.R. 643
Emery (1995 Tr.)	Carl Emery, "Transfer of Cases between Public and Private Law Procedures: the English Law Commission's Proposals" [1995] C.J.Q. 163

Emery (1995 Pub.)	Carl Emery, "Public Law or Private Law? The Limits of Procedural Reform" [1995] P.L. 450
Emery (1997)	Carl Emery, "Bridging the Public-Private Divide: Putting Flesh on the Bones of the Woolf Proposals" [1997] C.J.Q. 12
Emery and Smythe, *JR*	C.T. Emery and B. Smythe, *Judicial Review* (1986)
Endicott (1998)	Timothy Endicott, "Questions of Law" (1998) 114 L.Q.R. 292
Feldman (1991)	David Feldman, "The Constitution and the Social Fund: a Novel Form of Legislation" (1991) 107 L.Q.R. 39
Fordham (1996)	Michael Fordham, "What is Anxious Scrutiny?" [1996] J.R. 81
Forsyth and Hare, *Wade*	*The Golden Metwand and the Crooked Cord — Essays in Honour of Sir William Wade Q.C.* (Christopher Forsyth and Ivan Hare (ed.), 1998)
Forsyth (1988)	C. Forsyth, "The Provenance and Protection of Legitimate Expectations" [1988] C.L.J. 238
Forsyth (1996)	Christopher Forsyth, "Of Fig Leaves and Fairy Tales: the Ultra Vires Doctrine, the Sovereignty of Parliament and Judicial Review" [1996] C.L.J. 122
Forsyth (1998)	Christopher Forsyth, "'The Metaphysic of Nullity' — Invalidity, Conceptual Reasoning and the Rule of Law" in Forsyth & Hare, *Wade*, p. 141
Franks	Franks Committee Report on *Administrative Tribunals and Enquiries*, Cmnd. 218 (1957)
Fredman and Morris (1991)	Sandra Fredman and Gillian Morris, "Public or Private? State Employees and Judicial Review" [1991] L.Q.R. 298
Fredman and Morris (1994)	Sandra Fredman and Gillian Morris, "The Costs of Exclusivity: Private and Public Re-examined" [1994] P.L. 69
Freedland (1994)	M. Freedland, "Government by Contract & Public Law" [1994] P.L. 86
Freedland (1995)	M. Freedland, "Privatising *Carltona*: Part II of the Deregulation and Contracting Out Act 1994" [1995] P.L. 21
Freedland (1996)	M. Freedland, "The rule against delegation and the *Carltona* doctrine in an agency context" [1996] P.L. 19
Galligan, *Discr. Pwr*	D.J. Galligan, *Discretionary Powers* (1986)
Ganz (1997)	Gabriele Ganz, "Delegated Legislation: A Necessary Evil or a Constitutional Outrage?" in Leyland & Woods, *NH*, Chap. 3
Garner, *AL*	J. Garner, *Administrative Law* (8th ed., B.L. Jones & K. Thompson, ed., 1996)

Genn (1994)

Hazel Genn, "Tribunal Review of Administrative Decision-Making" in Richardson & Genn, *ALGA*, Chap. 11

Gordon, *JRLP*

R. Gordon, *Judicial Review, Law & Procedure* (2nd ed., 1995)

Gordon and Barlow (1992)

Richard Gordon and Craig Barlow, "When is a defence not a defence?" [1992] N.L.J. 1765

Hadfield, *JRTA*

Judicial Review, a Thematic Approach (Brigid Hadfield, ed., 1995)

Hadfield (1995)

Brigid Hadfield, "Judge-proofing Reviewable Decisions — Should the Judges be Trusted with Review?" in Hadfield, *JRTA*, Chap. 9

Harden, *CS*

Ian Harden, *The Contracting State* (1992)

Hare (1998)

Ivan Hare, "The Separation of Powers and Judicial Review for Error of Law" in Forsyth & Hare, *Wade*, p. 113

Harlow, *CGT*

Carol Harlow, *Compensation and Government Torts* (1982)

Harlow (1995)

Carol Harlow, "Why Public Law is Private Law" in *Reform of Civil Procedure* (Zuckerman & Cranston, ed., 1995), Chap. 11

Harlow (1997)

Carol Harlow, "Back to Basics: Reinventing Administrative Law" [1997] P.L. 245

Harlow and Rawlings, *L&A*

Carol Harlow and Richard Rawlings, *Law and Administration* (2nd ed., 1997)

Harris (1992)

B.V. Harris, "The 'Third Source' of Authority for Government Action" [1992] L.Q.R. 626

Harris, O'Boyle and Warbrick, *ECHR*

Law of the European Convention on Human Rights (1995)

Hartley, *Foundns*

T.C. Hartley, *The Foundations of European Community Law* (4th ed., 1998)

Hunt (1997)

Murray Hunt, "Constitutionalism and the Contractualisation of Government" in Taggart, *Prov.*, Chap. 2

Irvine (1996 *Wed.*)

Lord Irvine, "Judges and Decision-Makers: the Theory and Practice of *Wednesbury* Review" [1996] P.L. 59

Irvine (1996 Resp.)

Lord Irvine, "Response to Sir John Laws" [1996] P.L. 636

James and Longley (1996)

Rhoda James and Diane Longley, "The Channel tunnel rail link, the Ombudsman and the Select Committee" [1996] P.L. 38

Jowell and Oliver, *NDJR*

New Directions in Judicial Review (J. Jowell and D. Oliver, ed., 1988)

Jowell and Lester (1987)

Jeffrey Jowell and Anthony Lester, "Beyond *Wednesbury*: Substantive Principles of Administrative Law" [1987] P.L. 368

Jowell and Lester (1988)

Jeffrey Jowell and Anthony Lester, "Proportionality: Neither Novel nor Dangerous" in Jowell & Oliver, *NDJR*, p. 51

Justice/A-S

JUSTICE/All Souls Committee Report, *Administrative Justice: Some Necessary Reforms* (1988)

Justice/PLP, *PI*

Justice/Public Law Project, *A Matter of Public Interest* (1996)

Kolinsky (1997)

Daniel Kolinsky, "Standing (at the Leave Stage): ex p. Dixon" [1997] J.R. 213

LCCP 126 (1993)

Law Commission Consultation Paper No. 126, *Administrative Law: Judicial Review and Statutory Appeals* (1993)

LCR 73 (1976)

Law Commission Report No. 73, *Remedies in Administrative Law* (1976)

LCR 226 (1994)

Law Commission Report No. 226, *Administrative Law: Judicial Review and Statutory Appeals* (1994)

LCR 227 (1994)

Law Commission Report No. 227, *Restitution of Payments Made Under a Mistake of Law* (1994)

Lanham (1984)

David Lanham, "Delegation and the Alter Ego Principle" (1984) 100 L.Q.R. 587

Laws (1993)

Sir John Laws, "Is the High Court the Guardian of Fundamental Constitutional Rights?" [1993] P.L. 59

Laws (1995)

Sir John Laws, "Law and Democracy" [1995] P.L. 72

Laws (1996)

Sir John Laws, "The Constitution: Morals and Rights" [1996] P.L. 622

Le Sueur (1995)

"Justifying Judicial Caution: Jurisdiction, Justiciability and Policy" in Hadfield, *JRTA*, Chap. 8

Le Sueur and Sunkin (1992)

A.P. Le Sueur and Maurice Sunkin, "Applications for Judicial Review: the Requirement of Leave" [1992] P.L. 102

Lester (1994)

Lord Lester, "*Pepper v. Hart* Revisited" [1994] S.L. 10

Lester (1996)

Lord Lester, "Government compliance with international human rights law: a new year's legitimate expectation" [1996] P.L. 187

Leyland and Woods, *NH*

Administrative Law Facing the Future: Old Constraints and New Horizons (Peter Leyland and Terry Woods, ed., 1997)

Lewis, *JRPL*

C. Lewis, *Judicial Remedies in Public Law* (1992)

Lewis (1992)

Clive Lewis, "The Exhaustion of Alternative Remedies in Administrative Law" [1992] C.L.J. 138

Lindsay (1995)

Alistair Lindsay, "Delay in Judicial Review Cases: a Conundrum Solved?" [1995] P.L. 417

Lyell (1994)

Sir Nicholas Lyell, "*Pepper v. Hart*: the Government Perspective" [1994] S.L. 1

Marsh (1994) — Norman S. Marsh, "Judicial review of the decisions of the Parliamentary Commissioner for Administration" [1994] P.L. 347

Mureinik (1982) — E. Mureinik, "The Application of Rules: Law or Fact?" (1982) 98 L.Q.R. 587

N S Report (1998) — *Next Steps Report 1998*, Cm. 4273

Neill (1998) — Sir Patrick Neill Q.C., "The Duty to Give Reasons: the Openness of Decision-making" in Forsyth & Hare, *Wade*, p. 161

Oliver (1987) — Dawn Oliver, "Is the *Ultra Vires* Rule the Basis of Judicial Review?" [1987] P.L. 543

Oliver (1993) — Dawn Oliver, "Judicial review and the shorthandwriters" [1993] P.L. 214

Pannick (1988) — "What is a Public Authority for the Purposes of Judicial Review?" Jowell & Oliver, *NDJR*, p. 23

Pannick (1992) — D. Pannick, "Who is Subject to Judicial Review and in Respect of What?" [1992] P.L. 1

Pannick (1998) — David Pannick, "Principles of interpretation of Convention rights under the Human Rights Act and the discretionary area of judgment" [1998] P.L. 545

Pitt (1985) — G. Pitt, "Law, Fact and Casual Workers" (1985) 101 L.Q.R. 217

PCA Ann. Rep. (1997/98) — Parliamentary Commissioner's *Annual Report 1997–98*, H.C. No. 845

PLP (1994) — Public Law Project *Annual Report 1994–95*

Rawlings (1994) — Richard Rawlings, "Legal Politics: The UK and Ratification of the Treaty on European Union" [1994] P.L. 367

Reid (1993) — W.K. Reid, "What's the good of law in a case o' the kind?" [1993] P.L. 221

Richardson & Genn, *ALGA* — *Administrative Law and Government Action: the Courts and Alternative Mechanisms of Review* (Genevra Richardson and Hazel Genn, ed., 1994)

Rights Brought Home — Government White Paper *Rights Brought Home: the Human Rights Bill*, Cm. 3782 (1997)

Rubinstein, *JI* — A. Rubinstein, *Jurisdiction and Illegality* (1965)

Rudden and Wyatt, *BCL* — *Basic Community Laws* (6th ed., Bernard Rudden and Derrick Wyatt, ed., 1996)

Schiemann (1990) — Sir Konrad Schiemann, "Locus Standi" [1990] P.L. 342

Schiemann (1996) — Lord Justice Schiemann, "Interventions in Public Interest Cases" [1996] P.L. 240

Sedley (1994)   Sir Stephen Sedley, "The Sound of Silence: Constitutional Law Without a Constitution" 110 (1994) L.Q.R. 270

Sedley (1995)   Sir Stephen Sedley, "Human Rights: a Twenty-First Century Agenda" [1995] P.L. 386

Sedley (1998)   Sir Stephen Sedley, "The Crown in its Own Courts" in Forsyth & Hare, *Wade*, p. 253

Schwarze, *EAL*   J. Schwarze, *European Administrative Law* (1992)

Schwehr (1998)   Belinda Schwehr, "Local Government (Contracts) Act 1997" [1998] J.R. 45

Supperstone and Goudie, *JR*   M. Supperstone and J. Goudie, *Judicial Review* (1991)

Taggart, *Prov.*   *The Province of Administrative Law* (M. Taggart, ed., 1997)

Taggart (1997)   M. Taggart, "The Province of Administrative Law Determined?" in Taggart, *Prov.*, Chap. 1

Tanney (1994)   Anthony Tanney, "Procedural Exclusivity in Administrative Law" [1994] P.L. 51

Turpin, *GPC*   Colin Turpin, *Government Procurement and Contracts* (1989)

Wade and Forsyth, *AL*   Sir W. Wade and C. Forsyth, *Administrative Law* (7th ed., 1994)

Wade, *CF*   H.W.R. Wade, *Constitutional Fundamentals* (revised ed., 1989)

Wade (1985)   H.W.R. Wade, "Procedure and Prerogative in Public Law" (1985) 101 L.Q.R. 180

Wade (1986)   H.W.R. Wade, "Judicial Review of Ministerial Guidance" (1986) 102 L.Q.R. 173

Wade (1987)   H.W.R. Wade, "New Vistas of Judicial Review" (1987) 103 L.Q.R. 323

Wade (1996)   H.W.R. Wade, "Sovereignty — Revolution or Evolution?" (1996) 112 L.Q.R. 568

Weir (1989)   T. Weir "Governmental Liability" [1989] P.L. 40

Wheare, *Mal*   K.C. Wheare, *Maladministration and its Remedies* (1973)

Winfield and Jolowicz, *Tort*   Winfield and Jolowicz, *Tort* (14th ed., W.V.H. Rogers, ed., 1994)

Woolf, *Access*   Lord Woolf, *Access to Justice — Final Report*, July 1996

Woolf, *Interim*   Lord Woolf, *Access to Justice — Interim Report*, June 1995

Woolf, *PPNC*   Sir Harry Woolf, *Protection of The Public — A New Challenge* (1990)

Woolf (1986)   Sir Harry Woolf, "Public Law — Private Law: Why the Divide?" [1986] P.L. 220

Woolf (1992)   Sir Harry Woolf, "Judicial Review: a Possible Programme for Reform" [1992] P.L. 221

Woolf (1995)   Lord Woolf, "Droit Public — English Style" [1995] P.L. 57

Woolf (1998)   Lord Woolf, "Judicial Review — the Tensions Between the Executive and the Judiciary" (1998) 114 L.Q.R. 579

Yeats (1994)   Ian Yeats, "Findings of Fact: the Role of the Courts" in Richardson & Genn, *ALGA*, Chap. 6

Zamir, *Dec*   Lord Woolf and J. Woolf, *Zamir & Woolf on the Declaratory Judgment* (2nd ed., 1993)

INDEX

All references are to page numbers